*France's Arab Policy*

# France's Arab Policy

## FROM DE GAULLE TO MACRON

### Hichem Karoui

Global East-West (London)

Copyright © 2024 by Hichem Karoui
The Voice of the Mediterranean /Global East-West

All rights reserved. No part of this book may be reproduced in any manner whatsoever without written permission except in the case of brief quotations embodied in critical articles and reviews.

First Printing, 2024

# Contents

| | | |
|---|---|---:|
| I | Introduction: Overview of Franco-Arab Relations | 1 |
| II | Colonial Legacy and Early Diplomacy (Pre-1958) | 15 |
| | References For Further Reading | 31 |
| III | De Gaulle's Vision: Redefining Franco-Arab Relations (1958-1969) | 34 |
| | References For Further Reading | 54 |
| IV | Navigating the Cold War (1950s-1980s) | 58 |
| | References For Further Reading | 75 |
| V | Decolonization and Independence (1960s-1970s) | 77 |
| | References For Further Reading | 95 |
| VI | Economic Partnerships and Energy Interests (1970s-1990s) | 97 |
| | References For Further Reading | 114 |
| VII | Cultural Diplomacy and Exchange Programs | 116 |
| | References For Further Reading | 133 |
| VIII | France and the Gulf States | 136 |
| | References For Further Reading | 155 |
| IX | Franco-Arab Cooperation in Education and Research | 158 |

## Contents

References For Further Reading    175

X   Challenges of Terrorism and Security Cooperation    177

References For Further Reading    197

XI   Human Rights and Democracy Promotion    200

References For Further Reading    218

XII   Peacekeeping and Conflict Resolution Efforts    220

References For Further Reading    238

XIII   Environmental Cooperation and Sustainable Development    241

References For Further Reading    259

XIV   France's Role in Arab Spring Revolutions    262

References For Further Reading    285

XV   Macron's Presidency: A New Era in Franco-Arab Relations    288

References For Further Reading    306

XVI   Economic Reforms and Investment Opportunities    309

References For Further Reading    331

XVII   Immigration Policies and Integration Challenges    334

References For Further Reading    350

XVIII   France's Role in the Middle East Conflicts    353

References For Further Reading    372

XIX   Security Threats and Regional Stability    374

References For Further Reading    390

XX   France's Influence in North Africa    392

References For Further Reading    408

## Contents

| | | |
|---|---|---|
| XXI | Soft Power and Public Diplomacy | 410 |
| | References For Further Reading | 427 |
| XXII | Gender Equality and Women's Rights | 429 |
| | References For Further Reading | 446 |
| XXIII | France's Role in Refugee Crises | 449 |
| | References For Further Reading | 466 |
| XXIV | Cybersecurity and Digital Diplomacy | 469 |
| | References For Further Reading | 486 |
| XXV | Future of Franco-Arab Relations | 489 |
| | References For Further Reading | 507 |
| XXVI | Conclusion | 510 |

# Introduction: Overview of Franco-Arab Relations

The relationship between France and the Arab world is deeply rooted in history, marked by a complex tapestry of interactions that have shaped contemporary diplomatic, cultural, and economic ties. The enduring nature of these Franco-Arab relations can be traced back to historical bonds that have transcended geopolitical shifts and regional transformations. Throughout the centuries, French engagement with the Arab world has been characterized by a multifaceted exchange of knowledge, ideas, and trade, which has left an indelible mark on both societies.

Dating back to the medieval period and the Crusades era, there has been a notable interplay of influence and interaction between the French and the Arab countries. The cultural exchanges during this period gave rise to enduring artistic, architectural, and intellectual legacies that continue to define the collective heritage of both regions. As Europe transitioned into the modern age, the colonial expansion of France into North Africa further solidified its engagement with the

Arab world, setting the stage for a dynamic intercontinental relationship that continues to evolve today.

In the present day, Franco-Arab relations encompass a broad spectrum of engagements, including political alliances, economic collaborations, and cultural partnerships. The strategic significance of the Arab world, particularly in light of its energy resources, geopolitical relevance, and cultural diversity, underscores the continued importance of French diplomatic overtures in the region. Furthermore, a substantial Arab diaspora within France and the broader European context has contributed to a complex web of societal and cultural interactions that transcend national boundaries.

Notably, the enduring nature of France and the Arab world interactions also underscores the challenges and opportunities inherent in navigating a diverse set of historical narratives, religious beliefs, and political aspirations. This convergence of complexities has engendered intricate patterns of cooperation and occasional discord, reflecting the multi-layered nature of contemporary Franco-Arab relations. Moreover, as globalization redefines diplomatic paradigms, the dynamics of power, influence, and cooperation between France and the Arab world continuously evolve, requiring a nuanced understanding of historical underpinnings and present realities.

In examining the overview of Franco-Arab relations, it is imperative to acknowledge the interconnectedness of past legacies with contemporary geopolitical frameworks. Understanding the endurance of these interactions necessitates a comprehensive appraisal of historical bonds and present-day complexities that define the multifaceted partnership between France and the Arab world.

## *Purpose and Scope of the Book*

This book aims to provide a comprehensive and insightful analysis of Franco-Arab relations' historical, political, economic, and cultural dimensions. By examining the intricate dynamics between France and the Arab world, this work sheds light on the complexities and nuances that have shaped this relationship. Through an interdisciplinary approach, the book offers a balanced and nuanced portrayal of the multifaceted interactions between these actors, encompassing both collaborative endeavors and contentious issues. The scope of this book extends beyond traditional diplomatic narratives, delving into pivotal themes such as colonial legacy, decolonization, energy partnerships, cultural exchanges, security cooperation, and contemporary challenges. By engaging with diverse topics, the book seeks to provide readers with a holistic understanding of Franco-Arab relations, transcending narrow perspectives and shallow analyses. Furthermore, this book endeavors to fill existing gaps in the literature by offering fresh insights and perspectives on the evolving nature of this vital geopolitical partnership. The overarching goal is to equip readers with a comprehensive and detailed resource that informs and stimulates critical thinking and informed discourse on the subject matter. We hope this book will be an essential reference for scholars, policymakers, students, and all interested in gaining a deeper insight into Franco-Arab relations. By scrutinizing this relationship's historical trajectory and contemporary dynamics, the book seeks to contribute to a more profound comprehension of Franco-Arab relations' past, present, and future, fostering greater awareness and strategic reasoning in navigating this critical interface of international affairs.

## *Methodology and Research Approach*

A comprehensive and rigorous methodology is essential to analyzing Franco-Arab relations, ensuring the accuracy and reliability of the research findings. This book adopts a multidisciplinary approach that draws upon historical analysis, political science, international relations, and cultural studies. By integrating these various disciplines, we aim to provide a holistic understanding of the complexities inherent in the diplomatic interactions between France and the Arab world.

The research approach undertaken for this endeavor is primarily qualitative, encompassing extensive literature review, archival research, and interviews with key stakeholders, including diplomats, policy-makers, scholars, and representatives from civil society organizations. By delving into primary sources such as diplomatic correspondence, official documents, and speeches, we strive to unearth the underlying motivations and strategies shaping Franco-Arab relations over time.

Furthermore, this book incorporates a comparative analysis of Franco-Arab relations with other diplomatic relationships, enabling a nuanced assessment of the distinct features and challenges involved. The case study method illustrates specific instances and events that have been pivotal in shaping the trajectory of Franco-Arab relations, offering valuable insights into the dynamics of this enduring partnership.

The utilization of theoretical frameworks is integral to our research approach. They provide a conceptual lens to interpret the complex interplay of historical, geopolitical, and cultural factors. Blending theoretical perspectives with empirical evidence allows a deeper comprehension of the underlying power dynamics, identities, and interests underpinning Franco-Arab relations.

Moreover, a thematic analysis framework is utilized to categorize and analyze the multifaceted dimensions of Franco-Arab relations, allowing for the identification of recurring themes, divergences, and convergences within this diplomatic landscape. This thematic approach enables the exploration of diverse aspects such as economic cooperation, security partnerships, cultural exchange, and human rights diplomacy, thus enriching the breadth of analysis.

Lastly, an inclusive and reflexive research approach is adopted, recognizing the agency and perspectives of diverse stakeholders within the Franco-Arab context. This inclusive stance aims to encapsulate the voices and experiences of various actors, acknowledging the nuances and complexities embedded within this multifaceted relationship. It ultimately contributes to a more nuanced and comprehensive understanding of Franco-Arab relations.

## *Historical Context and Rationale*

The historical context of Franco-Arab relations is rooted in a complex interplay of colonial legacies, geopolitical interests, and cultural exchanges that have shaped the dynamics between France and the Arab world. Dating back to European colonialism, particularly in North Africa and the Middle East, France established a significant presence in the region, lasting and impacting these territories' social, political, and economic structures. This colonial legacy continues to influence diplomatic relations and partnerships in the contemporary era, providing the foundation for understanding the deep ties and occasional tensions between France and Arab countries.

Understanding the historical rationale behind the development of Franco-Arab relations is essential for discerning the motivations, challenges, and opportunities that have characterized this bilateral engagement. The historical context encompasses pivotal moments such as the decolonization process, the emergence of independent Arab states, and the reconfiguration of power dynamics in the post-World War II era. These historical shifts have contributed to the evolution of diplomatic strategies, mutual dependencies, and areas of cooperation between France and the Arab world.

Furthermore, the rationale for exploring the historical context lies in its capacity to offer insights into the enduring impact of historical events on contemporary diplomatic engagements. By delving into the history of Franco-Arab relations, we gain a deeper appreciation for the complexities, sensitivities, and cultural nuances that inform diplomatic interactions and policy decisions today. Additionally, examining the historical rationale provides a framework for analyzing the continuity and transformation of Franco-Arab relations amidst shifting global paradigms, regional conflicts, and socioeconomic developments.

Moreover, pursuing historical context and rationale bridges past experiences and prospects in Franco-Arab relations. It enables a comprehensive assessment of the legacies, lessons, and unresolved issues that bear significance for policymakers, diplomats, scholars, and stakeholders invested in expanding and diversifying bilateral ties. Ultimately, situating Franco-Arab relations within their historical context illuminates the layered narratives, identities, and interests that converge in shaping the multifaceted partnership between France and the Arab world.

## *Significance of Colonial Legacy in Modern Diplomacy*

The colonial legacy has undeniably left an indelible mark on modern diplomacy, particularly in Franco-Arab relations. The historical remnants of colonialism continue to shape the dynamics of diplomatic interactions between France and the Arab world, influencing policies, perceptions, and power structures. Understanding the significance of this colonial legacy is crucial in comprehending the complexities and nuances of contemporary Franco-Arab relations, as it provides crucial insights into the historical grievances, power differentials, and enduring narratives that underpin diplomatic engagements. This section delves into the multifaceted significance of colonial legacies in shaping the landscape of modern diplomacy between France and the Arab countries. Firstly, the imposition of colonial rule by European powers in the Middle East and North Africa reshaped the socio-political and economic structures of the region, engendering lasting consequences that continue to reverberate in present-day diplomatic relations. The extraction of resources, imposition of boundaries, and imposition of governance systems during the colonial era heavily influenced the trajectory of development, statehood, and national identities within the Arab world. These factors have directly impacted diplomatic discourse and negotiations between France and the Arab states, contributing to ongoing conflicts, economic dependencies, and identity politics. Additionally, the colonial legacy has also left a deep imprint on the psyche of both the colonizer and the colonized, shaping mutual perceptions, biases, and lingering sentiments of resentment or entitlement. The legacy of cultural assimilation, linguistic impositions, and erasure of indigenous identities during the colonial era continues to influence diplomatic encounters, with echoes of past oppressions still resonating in contemporary negotiations. Furthermore, examining the colonial legacy through the lens of diplomacy unveils the persisting power differentials and hierarchies embedded within international relations. France's historical role as a colonial power and its subsequent influence over former colonies inherently shape the power dynamics and asymmetrical relationships that define modern diplomatic engagements. This unequal distribution of power and privileges stemming from the colonial past informs the negotiation strategies, policy formulations, and structural inequalities that characterize Franco-Arab diplomacy. Ultimately, comprehending the significance of the colonial legacy in modern diplomacy serves as a vital prerequisite for discerning the intricacies, challenges, and potential pathways for recalibrating Franco-Arab relations in the 21st century.

## *The Evolution of Diplomatic Policies*

Throughout history, the relationship between France and the Arab world has been shaped by a complex interplay of diplomatic policies. From the colonial era to the present day, both regions have undergone significant transformations, influencing the nature and priorities of their diplomatic engagements. At the onset, colonial expansion and imperialism defined French relations with Arab countries, establishing power dynamics that continued to influence modern diplomacy. This historical context paved the way for the evolution of diplomatic policies as both France and the Arab world sought to redefine their roles on the global stage.

The decolonization period marked a pivotal juncture in the evolution of diplomatic policies as former colonies gained independence and embarked on nation-building efforts. This era witnessed a shift in diplomatic priorities, necessitating a nuanced approach to bilateral and multilateral relations. France's engagement with newly independent Arab countries required a delicate balance between acknowledging historical ties and adapting to the principles of sovereignty and self-determination.

The following decades saw new geopolitical realities emerge, including the Cold War and its impact on Franco-Arab relations. France navigated this tumultuous period by recalibrating its diplomatic policies to accommodate the competing interests of superpowers while simultaneously fostering partnerships with Arab states. Economic cooperation, military alliances, and cultural exchanges became integral components of France's diplomatic strategy, illustrating the multifaceted nature of diplomatic engagement.

As the global landscape continued to evolve, so did the diplomatic policies of France and the Arab world. Changing economic dynamics, technological advancements, and security challenges prompted a re-evaluation of strategic priorities and collaborative initiatives. The 21st century has witnessed an increasing emphasis on issues such as counterterrorism, energy security, environmental sustainability, and human rights, shaping the contours of contemporary diplomatic policies.

Furthermore, the digital era has revolutionized diplomatic practices, enabling real-time communication, public diplomacy, and international advocacy through digital platforms. France and Arab countries have embraced these technological advancements to amplify their diplomatic outreach and foster greater understanding and cooperation among diverse populations.

In light of these transformative trends, the evolution of diplomatic policies reflects a dynamic interplay of historical legacies, geopolitical shifts, and contemporary imperatives. Understanding this evolution is crucial for comprehending the complexities and possibilities that characterize Franco-Arab relations today, laying the foundation for substantive analysis in this comprehensive exploration of diplomatic history and contemporary interactions.

## *Major Themes Addressed in This Book*

The major themes addressed in this book encompass a wide array of critical issues and pivotal events that have shaped the complex tapestry of Franco-Arab relations throughout history. At the heart of this examination lies an exploration of the intricate interplay between colonial legacies, geopolitical forces, economic dynamics, cultural exchanges, security concerns, and the evolving nature of diplomatic ties. The narrative delves into the multifaceted dimensions of France's engagement with the Arab world, shedding light on the historical contexts, nuanced power dynamics, and the contemporary challenges and opportunities that define this relationship. Key themes include the legacy of colonialism and its enduring impact on diplomatic initiatives and regional dynamics, the role of cultural diplomacy in fostering mutual understanding and collaboration, the significance of economic partnerships and energy interests, the complexities of security cooperation in an era marked by terrorism and geopolitical tensions, the promotion of human rights and democratic values, as well as the role of France in peacekeeping efforts and conflict resolution within the region. Additionally, the book addresses the imperatives of sustainable development and environmental cooperation, France's influence in North Africa, its engagement in the Middle East conflicts, the interplay of soft power and public diplomacy, gender equality and women's rights, migration challenges and integration policies, and the emerging domains of cybersecurity and digital diplomacy. This book aims to comprehensively understand the essential themes underpinning Franco-Arab relations through an in-depth analysis, offering insights into the broader implications for global politics, security, and socio-economic development. Ultimately, it seeks to illuminate the interconnectedness of these themes and their relevance in shaping the future trajectory of this vital international partnership.

## Structure of the Book

The book is organized into a comprehensive analysis of Franco-Arab relations, from historical perspectives to contemporary diplomatic dilemmas. Each chapter delves into specific facets of this complex relationship, thoroughly examining key events, policies, and interactions that have shaped Franco-Arab relations over time. The book's structure aims to provide a multidimensional understanding of the nuances and intricacies inherent in this dynamic diplomatic engagement. The chapters are meticulously crafted to offer a cohesive narrative, guiding readers through the evolution of Franco-Arab relations and shedding light on the factors driving this bilateral interaction. Moreover, the chronological arrangement of chapters enables readers to grasp the progressive transformations and pivotal milestones that have influenced the course of these relations. Special emphasis is given to the contextual depth of each chapter, drawing on historical, political, cultural, and socio-economic dimensions to present a holistic portrayal of Franco-Arab relations. Furthermore, the chapters are interlinked, creating a coherent flow that aids in comprehending the continuity and shifts within this diplomatic paradigm. This interconnectedness allows a nuanced understanding of the intersecting themes and developments shaping Franco-Arab relations. In addition, the book incorporates diverse perspectives and analytical frameworks, incorporating insights from renowned scholars, diplomats, and experts in the field of international relations. This inclusive approach enriches the discourse with multifaceted views and interpretations, fostering a more comprehensive and insightful examination of the intricate dynamics at play. The book's structure encourages readers to deeply understand the complexities, challenges, and opportunities inherent in Franco-Arab relations, thereby equipping them with a nuanced lens to analyze and comprehend this vital aspect of global diplomacy.

## Importance for Contemporary Policy Makers

In the contemporary geopolitical landscape, Franco-Arab relations hold immense significance for policymakers at both regional and international levels. These relations have historical roots and present ongoing complexities and opportunities directly impacting global peace, security, and socioeconomic cooperation. Understanding and navigating these dynamics is crucial for contemporary policymakers for several reasons.

Firstly, the proximity of the Arab world to Europe and its strategic importance in various global affairs make Franco-Arab relations a focal point for decision-makers. The interconnectedness of economic, energy, and security interests necessitates a nuanced understanding of the diplomatic ties between France and the Arab countries. Policymakers need to acknowledge the impact of these relations on a wide range of issues, including trade flows, energy security, and counterterrorism efforts.

Secondly, with ongoing conflicts and crises in the Middle East and North Africa, the role of France in mediating and contributing to regional stability is paramount. Contemporary policymakers must assess the implications of French engagement in conflict resolution, peacekeeping missions, and humanitarian interventions within the Arab world. This involves evaluating the effectiveness of France's diplomatic initiatives and its alignment with broader regional and international strategies for sustainable peace and security.

Moreover, as the global community grapples with challenges such as migration, refugee crises, and the impact of extremism, policymakers need to recognize the implications of Franco-Arab relations on these interconnected issues. France's policies regarding immigration, multiculturalism, and integration of diverse communities directly intersect with its relations with Arab countries, thereby shaping its domestic and foreign policy agendas. Recognizing the influence of these dynamics is essential for formulating comprehensive policies that address societal cohesion, human rights, and global migration patterns.

Additionally, contemporary policymakers must consider the evolving cultural, educational, and scientific exchanges between France and the Arab world. These exchanges promote mutual understanding, foster academic partnerships, and address shared challenges such as climate change and technological innovation. As such, policymakers need to assess the role of these cooperative endeavors in advancing shared goals and bridging societal divides across borders.

Lastly, the context of Franco-Arab relations intersects with broader international frameworks, including the European Union, the United Nations, and regional organizations. Contemporary policymakers are tasked with navigating the alignment of France's engagements with Arab countries within these multilateral frameworks and examining the implications for global governance structures and collective action on transnational issues.

In conclusion, grasping the multifaceted nature of Franco-Arab relations is indispensable for contemporary policymakers seeking to formulate informed, effective, and inclusive strategies. By recognizing these relations' historical, geopolitical, and socio-economic dimensions, policymakers can cultivate diplomatic approaches that promote stability, cooperation, and prosperity in an increasingly interdependent world.

## *Preview of Subsequent Chapters*

The subsequent chapters of this book will delve deeper into the multifaceted and dynamic relationship between France and Arab countries, exploring a wide range of historical, political, economic, and social aspects influencing their interactions.

Chapter 1, 'Colonial Legacy and Early Diplomacy (Pre-1958),' will set the historical context by examining colonialism's impact on Franco-Arab relations and early diplomatic engagements before the Algerian War of Independence.

In Chapter 2, 'De Gaulle's Vision: Redefining Franco-Arab Relations

(1958-1969),' we will explore Charles de Gaulle's visionary approach and its pivotal role in reshaping the diplomatic landscape between France and Arab countries.

Navigating through the complexities of the Cold War era, Chapter 3, 'Navigating the Cold War (1950s-1980s),' will unravel the intricate dynamics of Franco-Arab relations amidst global power struggles and regional conflicts.

The subsequent chapter, 'Decolonization and Independence (1960s-1970s),' will illuminate the processes of decolonization and the emergence of independent Arab states, alongside the challenges and opportunities they presented for Franco-Arab relations.

As we progress, Chapter 5, 'Economic Partnerships and Energy Interests (1970s-1990s),' will illuminate the evolution of economic collaboration and the growing significance of energy resources in shaping bilateral ties.

Moreover, a dedicated section will probe 'Cultural Diplomacy and Exchange Programs', reflecting on the cultural initiatives and exchange programs that have enriched the mutual understanding between France and Arab countries.

Additionally, ' France and the Gulf States will dissect France's engagement with the Gulf States, emphasizing the strategic partnerships and unique dynamics defining their interactions.

In' Franco-Arab Cooperation in Education and Research, ' we will also examine the role of education and research in fostering cooperation.

Furthermore, the book will address contemporary challenges such as terrorism, security cooperation, human rights, and peacekeeping efforts in subsequent chapters to provide a comprehensive understanding of the complexities facing Franco-Arab relations.

The final chapters of this book will discuss the future of Franco-Arab relations, analyze potential trajectories, explore the role of soft power and digital diplomacy, and address pressing issues like gender equality, refugee crises, and cybersecurity.

Throughout these chapters, readers will gain valuable insights into the historical progression, current dynamics, and prospects of the enduring relationship between France and the Arab world, offering a nuanced portrayal that transcends conventional narratives.

# Colonial Legacy and Early Diplomacy (Pre-1958)

## Historical Context of French Colonization in the Arab World

The onset of French colonial interests in the Arab world can be traced back to the seventeenth century when France established a significant presence in the region. Motivated by pursuing lucrative trade routes and religious missions, French expeditions entered the Arab world, marking the beginning of a complex and enduring relationship between France and the Arab states. The allure of potential commerce and strategic advantages prompted French explorers and traders to navigate the diverse landscapes and cultures of the Arab world, laying the groundwork for future colonial endeavors. Concurrently, religious motivations also influenced French involvement in the region, as missionaries sought to propagate Christianity and establish a lasting spiritual footprint. This convergence of economic and religious imperatives shaped the early phases of French colonization in the Arab world, setting the stage for subsequent historical developments and diplomatic challenges.

## Initial French Expeditions and Establishments

The period of initial French expeditions and establishments in the Arab world marks a crucial juncture in the history of Franco-Arab relations. During the 19th century, France embarked on numerous expeditions to establish its presence in various regions of the Arab world, motivated by economic, political, and strategic interests. These endeavors established French colonies, protectorates, and spheres of influence across North Africa and the Middle East, shaping the trajectory of future diplomatic engagements and setting the stage for complex interactions between the French and Arab societies. The French conquest of Algeria in 1830 signaled the beginning of an era of expansion into the Maghreb region, leading to the annexation of Tunisia in 1881 and Morocco in 1912. Through military campaigns and strategic alliances with local leaders, the French colonial empire expanded across present-day Algeria, Tunisia, and Morocco, bringing about profound transformations in governance, administration, and social structures. France extended its influence in the Levant by establishing Lebanon as a mandate territory after World War I, cementing its foothold in the eastern Mediterranean. Furthermore, French expeditions in Egypt and the Arabian Peninsula, though not resulting in direct colonial rule, demonstrated France's ambitions to assert its power and interests in the broader Arab world. Establishing trade outposts, consulates, and military garrisons facilitated the projection of French influence and paved the way for subsequent diplomatic deployments. These initial expeditions and fortified establishments established the groundwork for diplomatic relations, cultural exchanges, and economic activities that would unfold in the coming decades. Moreover, they engendered intricate interaction, coexistence, and conflict dynamics that continue to shape the contemporary landscape of Franco-Arab relations.

Understanding the nuanced intricacies of the initial French expeditions and establishments is imperative for comprehending the historical context underpinning the intricate tapestry of Franco-Arab diplomacy and cooperation.

## *Impact of French Colonial Policy on Arab Societies*

French colonial policy had a profound and enduring impact on the social, economic, and political fabric of Arab societies during the period preceding 1958. The imposition of French administration and governance in the Arab territories brought about transformative changes that would reverberate for generations. The colonizers implemented policies aimed at consolidating their control over the region, leading to far-reaching consequences for the indigenous populations. French rule disrupted longstanding socio-economic structures, often exploiting local resources for the benefit of the colonial power. This exploitation resulted in significant socio-economic disparities, as wealth and resources were channeled to France while Arab communities faced hardship and marginalization. Furthermore, the imposition of French cultural norms and values, alongside widespread conversion to Christianity, created a schism within Arab societies, altering traditional belief systems and societal dynamics. The introduction of Western education and language further contributed to a cultural shift, impacting the Arab identity and fostering a sense of alienation and loss of heritage. Additionally, the French policy of divide and rule exacerbated inter-tribal conflicts and religious tensions, sowing seeds of discord that would resonate through the post-colonial era. Moreover, establishing arbitrary borders and administrative divisions by the colonial authorities disregarded historical and ethnic affiliations, resulting in lasting geopolitical challenges and animosities. A key consequence of French colonial policy was the undermining of Arab self-determination and governance, restricting the development of indigenous institutions and stifling the emergence of independent leadership. This legacy of subjugation and dependence perpetuated a struggle for autonomy and sovereignty that would define the early diplomatic engagements between France and the newly formed Arab states. Ultimately, the impact of French colonial policy on Arab societies was multifaceted, leaving an indelible imprint on the regional landscape and shaping the trajectory of Franco-Arab relations.

## *Economic Exploitations and Resource Management*

Economic exploitation and resource management during the colonial period in the Arab world played a significant role in shaping the relationship between France and the Arab countries. French colonial policy was driven by extracting valuable resources from the region, including natural reserves such as oil, gas, and minerals. The exploitation of these resources not only contributed to France's economic growth and development but also profoundly affected the socio-economic landscape of the Arab countries. The extraction and management of resources were often carried out with minimal consideration for the environmental impact or the welfare of local populations. This approach led to the depletion of natural resources and, in some cases, irreversible damage to the ecosystems. Additionally, the economic exploitation resulted in a significant disparity in wealth distribution, with the profits largely benefiting French businesses and government coffers. At the same time, the local communities faced economic marginalization and limited access to the benefits derived from their resources. Moreover, the management of resources was intricately linked to establishing trade routes and transportation infrastructure, which further facilitated the extraction and exportation of resources to France. This process reinforced the economic dependence of the Arab colonies on France, perpetuating a relationship characterized by unequal economic power dynamics. The exploitation of resources also had lasting implications on the post-colonial economies of the Arab states, as it influenced their industrial and economic structures, resource ownership, and foreign investment patterns. In contemporary Franco-Arab relations, the legacy of economic exploitation continues to influence diplomatic and economic interactions, as issues related to resource ownership, fair trade, and investment practices remain contentious. Understanding the historical context of economic exploitations and resource management is crucial to comprehensively assess the complexities that underpin the modern-day diplomatic and economic relations between France and the Arab world.

## *Cultural and Educational Influences*

The cultural and educational influences of French colonialism in the Arab world played a significant role in shaping the socio-political landscape of the region. As France expanded its colonial empire into the Middle East and North Africa, it sought to propagate French culture, language, and educational systems. This led to establishing French-language schools and cultural institutions and disseminating French literature, arts, and sciences throughout the Arab territories under its control. French cultural hegemony became deeply rooted in the fabric of Arab societies, influencing social norms, intellectual discourse, and artistic expressions. Promoting French culture was a means of exerting dominance and a tool for cultural assimilation and social engineering.

Furthermore, the educational system introduced by the French colonial administration profoundly impacted the intellectual development of the local population. While the primary objective was to educate the local elite in Western knowledge and values, it inadvertently fostered an intellectual awakening and awareness among the Arab youth. The exposure to French literature, philosophy, and scientific advancements sparked a new wave of critical thinking and ideological ferment in the Arab intelligentsia. This, in turn, laid the foundation for a burgeoning nationalist and anti-colonial sentiment as young Arab intellectuals began questioning the legitimacy of French rule and advocating for self-determination and independence.

Moreover, the French cultural and educational institutions provided a platform for intercultural exchanges and hybridization of ideas. Arab scholars, writers, and artists engaged with French intellectuals, contributing to a cross-pollination of literary, artistic, and philosophical movements. This interaction enriched the cultural tapestry of the Arab world and France, fostering a mutual exchange of ideas that transcended national boundaries.

In conclusion, French colonialism's cultural and educational influences in the Arab world had a multifaceted impact, from promoting French cultural hegemony and shaping societal norms to inadvertently nurturing a spirit of resistance and intellectual awakening among the Arab populace. Understanding these influences is crucial in comprehending the complexities of Franco-Arab relations and the historical roots of cultural dynamics in the region.

## *Resistance and Nationalist Movements in the Arab Region*

Resistance and nationalist movements in the Arab region during the colonial era were pivotal in shaping the trajectory of Franco-Arab relations. The imposition of French colonial rule ignited a wave of resistance and fervent nationalism among Arab populations as they sought to reclaim their sovereignty and cultural autonomy. These movements were often characterized by diverse strategies, including armed uprisings, civil disobedience, and intellectual opposition, all aimed at challenging and ultimately overthrowing the colonial yoke.

The emergence of prominent leaders such as Sheikh Izz ad-Din al-Qassam in Palestine, Abd el-Krim in Morocco, and Habib Bourguiba in Tunisia symbolized the defiance and determination of the Arab people in their struggle for independence. Their revolutionary fervor inspired widespread grassroots mobilization and galvanized support for the nationalist cause, transcending geographical boundaries and ethnic differences. These movements encapsulated the spirit of resistance and unity, giving voice to the aspirations of Arab communities to break free from foreign domination.

In addition to armed resistance, nationalist movements also leveraged cultural and literary platforms to express discontent and rally support for their cause. Poets, writers, and intellectuals played a pivotal role in articulating the collective grievances of the Arab populace, illuminating the injustices perpetuated under colonial rule and advocating for self-determination. Their writings and impassioned speeches served as potent instruments of propaganda, disseminating the spirit of nationalism and resilience throughout the Arab diaspora.

Moreover, women's involvement in these movements was instrumental in challenging traditional gender roles and empowering female activists to actively participate in the struggle for liberation. Women played multifaceted roles as educators, caregivers, and even combatants, defying societal norms and contributing significantly to the fabric of resistance and nationalism.

The legacy of these movements reverberates in the contemporary socio-political landscape, underscoring the enduring impact of resistance and nationalist fervor in shaping the Arab world's quest for autonomy and self-governance. It laid the groundwork for subsequent diplomatic engagements and bilateral treaties, influencing the discourse of mutual respect, recognition, and cooperation between France and the Arab countries.

## *Diplomatic Relations and Early Treaties*

The period preceding 1958 marked a pivotal era in the evolution of Franco-Arab relations, characterized by establishing diplomatic ties and negotiating crucial treaties. At the heart of this historical juncture was the intricate web of alliances and engagements that sought to navigate the complexities of colonial governance, indigenous resistance, and shifting power dynamics. As France solidified its presence across the Arab world, diplomatic relations became instrumental in shaping history and influencing the trajectory of cooperation and conflict resolution. The early treaties forged during this period laid the groundwork for future engagements, delineating spheres of influence and trade agreements and facilitating cultural exchange. These treaties also established the parameters of territorial control and resource exploitation, laying bare the intricacies of power dynamics and strategic interests. Diplomatic maneuvers played a pivotal role in consolidating French authority and engaging with local leaders to navigate the complex terrain of governance, economic collaboration, and regional stability. Furthermore, these early treaties set the stage for enduring partnerships and alliances, fostering the convergence of strategic interests and leveraging soft power through cultural, educational, and economic exchanges. The negotiation and implementation of these treaties were challenging, as they often encountered resistance from nationalist movements and indigenous populations striving for autonomy and self-determination. Thus, the landscape of early diplomacy was characterized by a delicate balance of coercion, collaboration, and compromise. The careful calibration of diplomatic relations and the equitable negotiations of treaties became indispensable tools for France to sustain its influence and assert its geopolitical agenda across the Arab world. As such, the study of early treaties and diplomatic engagements unravels the underlying nuances of power dynamics, cultural entanglements, and the interplay of political interests that continue to shape contemporary Franco-Arab relations.

## *Role of Religion in Colonial Governance*

Religion played a significant role in shaping the dynamics of colonial governance in the Arab world during the pre-1958 period. French colonial rule intersected with various religious traditions and practices, often influencing and being influenced by them in a complex and multi-faceted manner. The impact of religion on colonial governance can be observed across several dimensions, including political, social, and cultural aspects.

One notable aspect of the role of religion in colonial governance was the use of religious institutions and leaders as intermediaries between the colonial administration and the local population. The French authorities frequently engaged with religious figures to gain influence and control over the Arab communities. This practice allowed the colonial powers to leverage existing religious structures to maintain order and assert authority while legitimizing their rule in the eyes of the native population.

At the same time, the colonial governance of the Arab world often sparked tensions with local religious authorities and movements. The imposition of French laws, policies, and secular ideologies clashed with traditional religious practices and belief systems, leading to resistance and anti-colonial sentiment fueled by religious fervor. Religious leaders and organizations became central figures in the resistance against colonial rule, mobilizing communities and providing ideological justification for the struggle for independence.

Furthermore, religion operated as a crucial tool for the French colonial administration to navigate and understand the diverse social and cultural landscapes of the Arab world. By recognizing and engaging with various religious traditions, the colonial powers could implement governance strategies that accounted for the nuances and intricacies of local customs and beliefs. This approach, however, also led to instances of manipulation and exploitation of religious differences for political gains, further complicating the dynamics of colonial governance.

The role of religion in colonial governance extended beyond domestic matters to influence diplomatic relations and international politics. France's interactions with Arab countries were often mediated through religious contexts, with issues such as missionary activities, religious freedoms, and protection of holy sites becoming pivotal points of negotiation and contention. The interplay between religion and diplomacy added complexity to Franco-Arab relations and shaped the trajectory of early diplomatic engagements.

In summary, the role of religion in colonial governance during the pre-1958 period was multifaceted, encompassing both cooperative and adversarial dynamics. Its impact reverberated through the political, social, and cultural spheres, shaping the complexities of colonial rule and laying the groundwork for subsequent developments in Franco-Arab relations.

## *Decolonization Processes Pre-1958*

The period of decolonization in the Arab world before 1958 was a complex and transformative era that reshaped the region's political, social, and economic landscapes. The aftermath of World War II and the declining imperial power of European countries, including France, set the stage for a series of movements to gain independence from colonial rule. This struggle for freedom and sovereignty marked a critical juncture in the history of Franco-Arab relations and had far-reaching implications for diplomatic practices and international relations. Decolonization processes were not uniform across the Arab world and were influenced by many factors, including local resistance, global geopolitics, and the evolving strategies of colonial powers. Each case of decolonization presented unique challenges and opportunities for both the colonizer and the colonized. In some instances, negotiations and peaceful transitions paved the way for independence, while in others, protracted conflicts and armed struggles characterized the decolonization process. The impact of decolonization extended beyond mere political autonomy, with profound implications for economic systems, cultural identity, and social structures. It sparked debates on national identity, governance models, and the role of external players in shaping the future of the newly independent states. French decolonization in the Arab world involved intricate diplomatic maneuvers and negotiations, as well as resistance movements that sought to assert the rights of Arab populations. Furthermore, the experiences of decolonization fundamentally shaped the subsequent diplomatic engagements between France and the newly independent Arab states, laying the groundwork for a new phase of bilateral relations. Understanding the nuances and complexities of decolonization processes is crucial in comprehending the dynamics of contemporary Franco-Arab diplomacy and the enduring legacy of colonialism on the region's socio-political landscape.

## *Transition to Post-Colonial Diplomacy*

The transition from colonial rule to post-colonial diplomacy in the Arab world marked a significant turning point in the historical narrative of Franco-Arab relations. This pivotal period, characterized by evolving power dynamics and shifting global alliances, necessitated reconfiguring diplomatic strategies and foreign policy objectives for France and the newly independent Arab countries.

Following the tumultuous process of decolonization, France was compelled to recalibrate its approach to diplomatic engagement with the Arab world. A determining factor in this transition was the imperative to forge a new, mutually beneficial relationship founded on cooperation and respect. The legacy of colonialism cast a long shadow over the initial years of post-colonial diplomacy, as disparities in economic development, cultural ties, and political influence continued to shape the dynamics of Franco-Arab relations.

Central to the transition to post-colonial diplomacy was recognizing the Arab countries as sovereign entities, each with distinct national interests and aspirations. France sought to position itself as a partner committed to supporting the development and prosperity of these emerging nations while safeguarding its strategic interests in the region. This required a delicate balance between acknowledging historical grievances and laying the foundation for a renewed partnership based on equality and mutual benefit.

As part of the transitional phase, France undertook a multifaceted diplomatic effort to nurture bilateral and multilateral ties with Arab countries. This involved negotiating new treaties and agreements that delineated the parameters of cooperation in various domains, such as trade, security, culture, and development. Simultaneously, France endeavored to leverage its extensive cultural and educational resources to foster greater understanding and collaboration between French and Arab societies.

Amidst the geopolitical realignments of the post-colonial era, France also confronted complex geopolitical challenges, including navigating the Cold War rivalries and addressing the ramifications of regional conflicts. The intricate interplay of international politics and the emergence of pan-Arab movements further shaped the trajectory of Franco-Arab diplomacy during this period.

The transition to post-colonial diplomacy represented a critical juncture for France to reaffirm its commitment to engaging with the Arab world as an equal and respectful partner.

## IN A NUTSHELL

> To understand France's colonial legacy and early diplomacy in the Arab world before 1958, we need to examine several key aspects: initial French expeditions and establishments, the impact of French colonial policy on Arab societies, economic exploitation and resource management, cultural and educational influences, resistance and nationalist movements, diplomatic relations and early treaties, the role of religion in colonial governance, and the decolonization processes leading to post-colonial diplomacy.

## Initial French Expeditions and Establishments

### Algeria

France's colonial involvement in the Arab world began with the invasion of Algeria in 1830. The initial phase saw the appropriation of vast tracts of land, which were transferred to European settlers. This marked a shift from a policy of limited occupation to one of active settlement, necessitating greater military intervention and the development of administrative systems to manage the land and its people.

### Tunisia and Morocco

In Tunisia, the French established a protectorate in 1881, while in Morocco, the protectorate was established in 1912. These protectorates allowed France to exert control while maintaining the appearance of local sovereignty. The French administration in these regions focused on consolidating power through treaties and agreements with local rulers.

## Impact of French Colonial Policy on Arab Societies

### Economic Exploitation and Resource Management

French colonial policy was heavily geared towards economic exploitation. In Algeria, for instance, the French appropriated fertile lands for European settlers, disrupting local agricultural practices and economies. The colonies were used primarily as sources of raw materials and markets for French manufactured goods. This created an imbalanced trade relationship that favored France and left the colonies economically dependent and underdeveloped.

**Cultural and Educational Influences**

The French colonial administration implemented policies aimed at cultural assimilation. In Algeria, Tunisia, and Morocco, French became the language of administration and education. The French educational system was introduced to inculcate French values and culture, often at the expense of local traditions and languages. This policy of assimilation was met with resistance and had long-term impacts on the cultural identity of the colonized societies.

## Resistance and Nationalist Movements in the Arab Region

### Algeria

Resistance to French rule in Algeria was persistent and often violent. The National Liberation Front (FLN) led a brutal war of independence from 1954 to 1962, which resulted in significant loss of life and ultimately led to Algeria's independence.

### Morocco and Tunisia

In Morocco, the nationalist movement was spearheaded by the Istiqlal Party, which sought independence through both political and armed struggle. Similarly, in Tunisia, the Neo Destour party played a crucial role in mobilizing the population against French rule, leading to independence in 1956.

## *Diplomatic Relations and Early Treaties*

France's early diplomatic efforts in the Arab world involved negotiating treaties that established protectorates while ostensibly respecting local sovereignty. These treaties often included clauses that allowed France to control foreign policy and defense, effectively reducing the autonomy of the local rulers.

**Role of Religion in Colonial Governance**

Religion played a complex role in French colonial governance. In predominantly Muslim regions like Algeria, Tunisia, and Morocco, the French administration sought to control religious institutions and practices. This included the regulation of Islamic education and the appointment of religious leaders who were sympathetic to French interests. The French also used religious differences to their advantage, promoting divisions between different ethnic and religious groups to maintain control.

**Decolonization Processes Pre-1958**

The decolonization process in the Arab world was marked by a combination of political negotiations and violent uprisings. In Tunisia and Morocco, the process was relatively peaceful, with France granting independence in 1956 after negotiations with nationalist leaders. In Algeria, however, the decolonization process was marked by a protracted and bloody war of independence that only ended in 1962.

## Transition to Post-Colonial Diplomacy

Post-colonial diplomacy in the Arab world involved France attempting to maintain influence through economic and military means. This included the establishment of bilateral agreements that allowed France to retain a degree of control over the newly independent states' economies and military affairs. However, the legacy of colonialism continued to strain relations, as former colonies sought to assert their sovereignty and reduce French influence.

In summary, France's colonial legacy in the Arab world before 1958 was characterized by economic exploitation, cultural assimilation, and significant resistance from local populations. The decolonization process varied across the region, with some countries achieving independence through negotiation and others through violent struggle. The transition to post-colonial diplomacy saw France attempting to maintain its influence, albeit with limited success.

# References For Further Reading

Al Sakbani, Nisreen, and Juline Beaujouan. "Education in Syria: Hidden Victim of the Conflict of Weapon of War?" Journal of Peace Education, (2024), 1–21. doi:10.1080/17400201.2024.2325493.

Alvaredo, Facundo, Denis Cogneau, and Thomas Piketty. "Income Inequality under Colonial Rule. Evidence from French Algeria, Cameroon, Tunisia, and Vietnam and Comparisons with British Colonies 1920–1960." Journal of Development Economics 152, no. 152 (September 2021): 102680. https://doi.org/10.1016/j.jdeveco.2021.102680.

Brown, L. Carl. "The Many Faces of Colonial Rule in French North Africa." Revue de l'Occident Musulman et de La Méditerranée 13, no. 1 (1973): 171–91. https://doi.org/10.3406/remmm.1973.1201.

Burke, Edmund. "Pan-Islam and Moroccan Resistance to French Colonial Penetration, 1900–1912." The Journal of African History 13, no. 1 (January 1972): 97–118. https://doi.org/10.1017/s0021853700000281.

Cowen, Robert, and Terri Kim. "Comparative Education and Intercultural Education: Relations and Revisions." Comparative Education 59, no. 3 (2023): 379–97. doi:10.1080/03050068.2023.2234690.

Diouf, Mamadou." The French Colonial Policy of Assimilation and the Civility of the Originaires of the Four Communes (Senegal): A Nineteenth Century Globalization Project". Development and Change Vol. 29 (1998), 671-696. Institute of Social Studies 1998. Published by Blackwell Publishers Ltd, 108 Cowley Rd, Oxford OX4 1JF, UK.

El Kallab, Tania. "French colonial trade patterns: facts and impacts". African Journal of Agricultural and Resource Economics Volume 13 Number 1 pages 15-30.

FERWERDA, JEREMY, and NICHOLAS L. MILLER. "Political Devolution and Resistance to Foreign Rule: A Natural Experiment." American Political Science Review 108, no. 3 (August 2014): 642–60. https://doi.org/10.1017/s0003055414000240.

Heggoy, Alf Andrew. "Education in French Algeria: An Essay on Cultural Conflict." Comparative Education Review 17, no. 2 (1973): 180–97. http://www.jstor.org/stable/1186812.

Joffé, E. G. H. "The Moroccan Nationalist Movement: Istiqlal, the Sultan, and the Country." The Journal of African History 26, no. 4 (1985): 289–307. https://doi.org/10.1017/S0021853700028759.

Launay, Robert, and Benjamin F. Soares. "The Formation of an 'Islamic Sphere' in French Colonial West Africa." Economy and Society 28, no. 4 (1999): 497. https://www.academia.edu/608674/The_formation_of_an_Islamic_sphere_in_French_colonial_West_Africa.

Lizotte, Christopher. "Rethinking Laïcité as a Geopolitical Concept." Modern & Contemporary France 31, no. 3 (2023): 305–21. doi:10.1080/09639489.2023.2167964.

MARIELLE, DEBOS . "Colonial Violence and Resistance in Chad (1900-1960) | Sciences Po Mass Violence and Resistance - Research Network." colonial-violence-and-resistance-chad-1900-1960.html, January 25, 2016. https://www.sciencespo.fr/mass-violence-war-massacre-resistance/en/document/colonial-violence-and-resistance-chad-1900-1960.html.

Ozcan, Yusuf . "ANALYSIS - French Colonialism More than Just 'Grave Mistake.'" www.aa.com.tr, December 24, 2019. https://www.aa.com.tr/en/europe/analysis-french-colonialism-more-than-just-grave-mistake-/1682250.

Saharso, Sawitri, and Veit Bader. "Colonial and Post-Colonial Governance of Islam: Continuities and Ruptures." Www.academia.edu 1 (2011). https://www.academia.edu/21111612/Colonial_and_post_colonial_governance_of_Islam_continuities_and_ruptures.

Sylla, Ndongo Samba, Fanny Pigeaud, and Chris Dite. "Africa: How France Continues to Dominate Its Former Colonies in Africa." Cadtm.org, April

26, 2021. https://www.cadtm.org/Africa-How-France-Continues-to-Dominate-Its-Former-Colonies-in-Africa.

Tilmatine, Mohand. "French and Spanish Colonial Policy in North Africa: Revisiting the Kabyle and Berber Myth." Www.academia.edu, 2018. https://www.academia.edu/48250003/French_and_Spanish_colonial_policy_in_North_Africa_revisiting_the_Kabyle_and_Berber_myth.

Waite, Sean. "History and Identity: Tracing the Legacy of Colonial History in Modern French Identity." British Online Archives, October 23, 2020. https://microform.digital/boa/posts/category/articles/381/history-and-identity-tracing-the-legacy-of-colonial-history-in-modern-french-identity.

Watanabe, Shoko. "Making an Arab-Muslim Elite in Paris: The Pan-Maghrib Student Movement of the 1930s." International Journal of Middle East Studies 53, no. 3 (August 2021): 439–54. https://doi.org/10.1017/s0020743821000337.

Wyrtzen, Jonathan D. "Middle Eastern and North African Nationalisms." Edited by Aviel Roshwald, Cathie Carmichael, and Matthew D'Auria. Cambridge University Press. Cambridge: Cambridge University Press, 2023. https://www.cambridge.org/core/books/abs/cambridge-history-of-nationhood-and-nationalism/middle-eastern-and-north-african-nationalisms/439B18B8CAC2FB67CBF7A82CF2388F1F.

# De Gaulle's Vision: Redefining Franco-Arab Relations (1958-1969)

## Introduction to de Gaulle's Foreign Policy Ideas

Charles de Gaulle's impact on French foreign policy was rooted in philosophical and ideological underpinnings that propelled France onto the global stage during transformative international dynamics. At the core of de Gaulle's approach lay a commitment to reasserting France's status as a significant world power while navigating the complexities of post-World War II geopolitics. With a keen focus on safeguarding French sovereignty and national interests, de Gaulle sought to carve out a distinct position for France within the international community that balanced pragmatism with an unwavering sense of grandeur. Central to his vision was the idea of preserving France's independence, both politically and militarily, while actively shaping global affairs. This involved embracing a form of 'grandeur' that harkened back to France's historical role as a dominant player in international relations. This concept intertwined national pride, strategic autonomy, and diplomatic prowess. De Gaulle's foresight extended beyond mere realpolitik; it encapsulated a broader narrative of Franco-centric leadership within a rapidly shifting global order. Furthermore, de Gaulle emphasized the importance of maintaining strong and dignified relationships with former colonial territories, particularly the Arab world, understanding the need to reconcile past disparities and foster a new era of cooperation based on mutual respect and shared interests. By doing so, de Gaulle envisioned France as a guardian of its destiny and a beacon of stability, influence, and moral authority in an increasingly multifaceted international arena. This quest for France's rightful place in the world arena was imbued with de Gaulle's belief in the enduring relevance of French cultural and intellectual heritage. This ethos shaped his diplomatic aspirations and France's role in the Franco-Arab sphere. Embodying a distinctive blend of realism, nationalism, and charisma, de Gaulle's foreign policy ideals laid the groundwork for redefining France's global identity and its role in Franco-Arab relations during a pivotal historical period.

## Contextual Framework: Post-War Realities and Franco-Arab Relations

Significant transformations in global geopolitical dynamics marked the period following World War II. As the dust settled after the devastation of war, nations sought to redefine relationships and establish new alliances. Against this backdrop, Franco-Arab relations experienced a pivotal shift, shaped by the emerging realities of a post-war world.

The decolonization movement, which gathered momentum during this era, played a crucial role in redefining the relationship between France and Arab countries. Former French colonies in North Africa and the Middle East clamored for independence, triggering a seismic shift in the region's power dynamics. France's response to these aspirations is a defining factor in the evolution of Franco-Arab relations, reflecting both the complexities of historical entanglements and the aspirations for renewed cooperation.

Furthermore, the rise of pan-Arabism and the quest for regional unity after colonialism added complexity to the Franco-Arab dynamic. Leaders such as Gamal Abdel Nasser of Egypt and Habib Bourguiba of Tunisia advocated for solidarity among Arab countries, influencing France's strategic calculations in the region. This ideological and political landscape set the stage for reevaluating diplomatic relations, underlining the enduring impact of historical legacies on the contemporary Franco-Arab discourse.

Economic considerations also underscored the evolving Franco-Arab relations, as newly independent Arab countries sought to assert their sovereignty in shaping trade and investment partnerships. The abundance of natural resources in the Arab world presented opportunities for economic collaboration, compelling France to recalibrate its approach to regional engagement. Energy security and trade dynamics became pivotal factors in reshaping the bilateral ties, highlighting the intricate intersections of political, economic, and strategic interests in the Franco-Arab equation.

In navigating the post-war realities, France found itself at a crossroads, compelled to reconcile its historical legacy as a colonial power with the imperatives of a rapidly changing global order, and the period leading up to de Gaulle's ascendancy witnessed the forging of these new trajectories, setting the stage for a transformative era in Franco-Arab relations. Understanding the complex contextual framework of post-war realities is essential for unraveling the nuances defining this critical historical juncture.

## De Gaulle's Ascendancy and Initial Stance Towards Arab Countries

Charles de Gaulle's rise to power amid a tumultuous post-war period marked a significant turning point for French foreign policy, particularly concerning its relations with the Arab world. As he assumed office in 1958, de Gaulle brought with him a vision of reinvigorating France's presence on the global stage, and this included an intentional recalibration of policies towards Arab countries. De Gaulle's initial stance towards the Arab world was characterized by a departure from traditional colonial frameworks, as he sought to assert France's independent foreign policy, distinct from the influences of the United States and the former colonial powers. Recognizing the shifting dynamics in the Middle East and North Africa, de Gaulle aimed to position France as a key player in regional affairs, guided by a combination of pragmatism and historical understanding. By acknowledging the aspirations of Arab countries for self-determination and independence, de Gaulle's early overtures aimed at establishing a new foundation for Franco-Arab relations. This approach involved a delicate balancing act, navigating the complexities of post-colonial sentiments while safeguarding France's regional strategic interests. Through diplomatic initiatives and engagement with Arab leaders, de Gaulle sought to forge partnerships based on mutual respect and equal footing, setting the stage for a pivotal shift in French foreign policy. His efforts to cultivate ties with Arab countries laid the groundwork for future diplomatic endeavors, shaping the trajectory of Franco-Arab relations for years to come. De Gaulle's astute navigation of this critical juncture in history reflected his diplomatic acumen and underscored the evolving nature of global geopolitics in an era of decolonization and redefined alliances.

## Strategic Shifts: Nuclear Policy and Military Presence in the Mediterranean

In the wake of shifting global dynamics and evolving Franco-Arab relations, Charles de Gaulle initiated a series of strategic shifts that significantly shaped France's foreign policy in the Mediterranean region during the late 1950s and 1960s. At the core of these shifts lay de Gaulle's vision of asserting France as an independent power capable of influencing geopolitical affairs on its own terms. This approach was underpinned by developing a robust nuclear policy and establishing a formidable military presence in the Mediterranean. De Gaulle's pursuit of nuclear capability, culminating in France's successful testing of its first atomic bomb in 1960, marked a pivotal moment in the nation's defense strategy. This move bolstered France's position as a nuclear power and sent a clear message regarding its autonomy and determination to safeguard its interests. Concurrently, de Gaulle sought to consolidate French military presence in the Mediterranean, viewing the region as a critical nexus for advancing France's political and security objectives. Establishing military bases in strategic locations such as Corsica and North Africa underscored France's commitment to exerting influence and projecting power across the Mediterranean basin. Furthermore, this heightened military presence supported France's broader diplomatic initiatives and engagement with Arab countries, signaling its readiness to play a pivotal role in regional stability and security. These strategic shifts prompted the reevaluation of traditional alliances and dependencies, positioning France as a proactive and assertive actor in the Mediterranean theater. By emphasizing the significance of nuclear deterrence and reinforcing its military posture, France, under de Gaulle, it has demonstrated a willingness to chart an independent course while actively shaping the dynamics of Franco-Arab relations. The implications of these strategic choices reverberated beyond the immediate geopolitical landscape, significantly impacting the trajectory of French foreign policy and setting the stage for multifaceted engagements with the Arab world. As such, de Gaulle's calculated maneuvers in refining France's nuclear policy and expanding its military footprint represent a defining chapter in the historical evolution of Franco-Arab relations, reflecting the complexities and intricacies of navigating global power dynamics in an era of transformation.

## The Suez Crisis and its Aftermath

The Suez Crisis of 1956 represented a pivotal historical event in Franco-Arab relations, significantly impacting the region's political landscape and strategic alliances. Against the backdrop of decolonization and Cold War hostilities, the crisis underscored the complexities of global power dynamics and tested de Gaulle's diplomatic acumen. The conflict, triggered by President Gamal Abdel Nasser's nationalization of the Suez Canal and subsequent Anglo-French-Israeli military intervention, revealed the fragility of colonial legacies and the growing assertiveness of Arab nationalism. France's participation in the ill-fated military campaign alongside traditional adversary Britain strained its relationship with not only the Arab world but also the United States, which viewed the intervention as infringing upon its strategic interests. Despite the military setbacks and international censure, de Gaulle astutely recalibrated French policy, recognizing the need to cultivate ties with independent Arab countries and promote a balanced approach to regional conflicts. The aftermath of the Suez Crisis saw France reassessing its role, acknowledging the shifting power dynamics in the Middle East and North Africa. This transformative period prompted a strategic realignment as France sought to engage with emerging post-colonial states on terms that respected their sovereignty and aspirations for self-determination. Moreover, the crisis catalyzed redefining France's role as a mediator and peacemaker in the Arab world, laying the foundation for future diplomatic initiatives and cooperation. In the broader context, the Suez Crisis and its aftermath heralded a new chapter in Franco-Arab relations, underscoring the imperative of adaptability and nuance in navigating geopolitical challenges and fostering enduring partnerships.

---

## Charles de Gaulle's foreign policy significantly redefined France's relations with the Arab countries in several key ways:

### 1. Shift from Colonial Power to Partner

De Gaulle recognized the inevitability of decolonization and sought to transform France's relationship with the Arab world from that of a colonial power to a partner and mediator. This was exemplified by his decision to grant independence to Algeria in 1962 after years of conflict, ending over a century of French rule in the country.

### 2. Support for Arab Causes

In a major break from previous French policies, de Gaulle adopted a pro-Arab stance, particularly after the Six-Day War in 1967. He criticized Israel's occupation of Palestinian territories and imposed an arms embargo on Israel, aligning France with Arab countries. This move significantly improved France's standing in the Arab world.

### 3. Pursuit of Independence and Non-Alignment

De Gaulle sought to assert France's independence from the superpowers and position it as a non-aligned mediator in the Middle East. This included reducing military cooperation with Israel and developing closer ties with Arab states, distancing France from its traditional allies like the US and UK.

## 4. Economic and Cultural Engagement

De Gaulle pursued economic cooperation and cultural diplomacy with Arab countries. France sought to secure trade agreements, particularly in the energy sector, and promoted French language and culture in the region, enhancing its soft power and influence.

## 5. Balancing East-West Politics

While supporting Arab causes, de Gaulle also aimed to balance France's relations between the East and West. This delicate balancing act, exemplified by his stance during the Six-Day War, allowed France to maintain a degree of cooperation with Israel while improving ties with Arab states. De Gaulle's policies laid the foundation for France's continued engagement with the Arab world and its role as a mediator in the region. His emphasis on independence, cultural diplomacy, and balanced relations has influenced subsequent French leaders, shaping France's approach to the Middle East

## *Bilateral Engagements: Key Diplomatic Missions and Agreements*

Following the tumultuous period of the Suez Crisis and its aftermath, Charles de Gaulle's diplomatic endeavors in redefining Franco-Arab relations were characterized by a series of significant bilateral engagements marked by strategic agreements and nuanced negotiations. De

Gaulle's vision of an independent and assertive France on the world stage led to a proactive approach to fostering alliances with vital Arab countries to establish a more balanced and autonomous foreign policy. One of the pivotal missions during this period was strengthening ties between France and Algeria, culminating in the Évian Accords of 1962. This landmark agreement paved the way for Algerian independence and laid the groundwork for a new chapter in Franco-Arab relations. Furthermore, de Gaulle's diplomatic efforts extended to forging partnerships with Egypt, Iraq, and Syria, emphasizing mutual economic cooperation, cultural exchange, and military collaboration. These initiatives aimed to position France as a trusted ally in the Arab world while ensuring strategic interests were safeguarded. The Quai d'Orsay, France's Ministry of Foreign Affairs, was central in coordinating and executing these diplomatic missions, orchestrating high-level dialogues and mediating complex negotiations. Notably, the Algiers Agreement 1964, which delineated the borders between Tunisia and Algeria, showcased France's commitment to facilitating peaceful resolutions to regional disputes and promoting stability in North Africa. In addition to state-level engagements, de Gaulle's administration actively pursued cultural diplomacy to enhance mutual understanding and foster goodwill. Cultural exchange programs, academic collaborations, and arts initiatives fueled the cultural dialogue between France and Arab countries, imprinting a lasting legacy on interpersonal relationships and societal perceptions. These bilateral engagements were underpinned by respect, reciprocity, and recognition of each nation's sovereignty, contributing to developing enduring partnerships. As such, the period spanning 1958 to 1969 witnessed a paradigm shift in Franco-Arab relations, characterized by dynamic diplomatic missions and far-reaching agreements that continue to shape international politics and global interactions.

## Cultural Influence and Media Representation

In the complex tapestry of Franco-Arab relations during 1958-1969, cultural influence and media representation were pivotal elements shaping the perceptions and narratives between France and the Arab world. Cultural exchange initiatives, including establishing cultural centers, art exhibitions, and scholarly forums, aimed to foster mutual understanding and appreciation of each other's heritage. French literature, music, and cinema found an increasingly receptive audience in the Arab world, while Arabic literature, traditions, and artistic expressions gained visibility in France. This intercultural dialogue enhanced bilateral ties and contributed to a more nuanced portrayal of the respective societies in media representations. French and Arab media outlets played a crucial role in shaping the public discourse on diplomatic developments and societal progress. The portrayal of cultural events, diplomatic visits, and economic collaborations significantly influenced public opinion and policy perceptions. However, this exchange was not without challenges, as cultural misunderstandings and misrepresentations occasionally led to tensions, highlighting the sensitivity and complexity of cultural diplomacy. As the era witnessed significant geopolitical transformations and sociocultural evolutions, media representation became a contested terrain where diverse voices sought to assert their interpretations and narratives. This chapter delves into the multifaceted nature of cultural influence and media representation in Franco-Arab relations, shedding light on the intricate dynamics that shaped perceptions, fostered empathy, and sometimes fueled controversies. By examining the impact of cultural initiatives and media portrayals, we gain deeper insights into the evolving relationship between France and the Arab world during this transformative period, illuminating the enduring significance of cultural engagement in international diplomacy.

## Challenges Faced in Balancing East-West Politics

Balancing East-West politics posed a significant challenge for France during the era of de Gaulle's redefined Franco-Arab relations. Amidst the backdrop of the Cold War, France encountered intricate diplomatic dilemmas as it sought to navigate the complex web of alliances and rivalries between the Western bloc led by the United States and the Eastern bloc dominated by the Soviet Union. The interplay of ideologies, economic interests, and geopolitical dynamics further complicated France's efforts to maintain equilibrium in its foreign policy approach. Additionally, the burgeoning influence of pan-Arabism and the non-aligned movement necessitated astute maneuvering to avoid alienating key partners on either side of the ideological divide. Concurrently, France's historical ties with former colonies in North Africa and the Middle East added layers of complexity to this geopolitical juggling act. Furthermore, France's aspirations for maintaining its status as a major global power while upholding its commitment to Arab countries demanded delicate diplomatic finesse. The quest to assert French influence while avoiding overt dependence on either the Western or Eastern camp called for nuanced strategies and adroit diplomacy. Bilateral relationships with key Arab states needed to be cultivated while ensuring that these engagements did not provoke antagonism from Western allies. Nonetheless, the exigencies of geopolitical pragmatism often dictated the need to make calculated concessions to safeguard French interests within the broader panorama of East-West politics. These challenges heightened the imperative for France to deftly tread the fine line between collaboration and autonomy in its international relations. Navigating the intricate geopolitics of the era demanded adept negotiation skills, shrewd assessment of global dynamics, and an acute understanding of the divergent interests at play within the East-West dichotomy. In this complex milieu, France grappled with the formidable task of harmonizing its engagements with the Eastern and Western spheres while pursuing its goals of redefining its relations with the Arab world.

> *Charles de Gaulle's stance on the Israeli-Palestinian conflict marked a significant shift in France's foreign policy toward the Arab world. Here are the key elements of his approach:*

1. Support for Arab Causes after 1967 Six-Day War Prior to 1967, France under de Gaulle maintained relatively good relations with Israel. However, after the Six-Day War in June 1967, de Gaulle adopted a pro-Arab stance and criticized Israel's occupation of Palestinian territories. He imposed an arms embargo on Israel, while continuing to supply weapons to Arab states.
2. Condemnation of Israeli Occupation In a press conference in November 1967, de Gaulle strongly condemned Israel's occupation of Arab lands, stating that Israel was establishing "an occupation that inevitably involves oppression, repression and expulsions." He accused Israel of expansionist ambitions and warned against the consequences of such policies.
3. Support for Palestinian Rights De Gaulle expressed support for Palestinian rights and self-determination. He criticized Israel's treatment of Palestinian refugees and its refusal to allow their return, stating, "It is the Israeli refusal to allow the refugees to return to their homes that is the chief cause of this conflict."
4. Shift Towards Arab World De Gaulle's stance was part of a

broader strategy to reorient France's foreign policy towards the Arab world, distancing itself from its traditional allies like the US and UK. He sought to position France as a mediator in the region and improve relations with Arab countries, particularly after the end of the Algerian War in 1962.

5. Balancing East-West Politics While supporting Arab causes, de Gaulle also aimed to balance France's relations between the East and West. He sought to assert France's independence from the superpowers and establish it as a non-aligned mediator in the Middle East.

De Gaulle's policies marked a significant departure from France's previous close ties with Israel and laid the foundation for France's continued engagement with the Arab world and its role as a mediator in the Israeli-Palestinian conflict. His stance, though controversial at the time, influenced subsequent French leaders and shaped France's approach to the Middle East peace process.

## *Impact Assessment: Franco-Arab Relations at the End of de Gaulle Era*

The end of de Gaulle's era significantly impacted Franco-Arab relations, marked by a complex interplay of diplomatic achievements and enduring challenges. De Gaulle's vision for redefining Franco-Arab relations from 1958 to 1969 ushered in a nuanced engagement era that continues reverberating in modern-day foreign policy discourse. At the time of de Gaulle's departure from office, France had established itself as a key player in the Arab world with lasting implications. The legacy of de Gaulle's policies has left an indelible mark on French diplomatic engagements in the Middle East and North Africa. It is essential to evaluate the outcomes of this transformative period to comprehend the trajectory of Franco-Arab relations. One of the primary impacts can be attributed to France's autonomy and strengthened position on the global stage. Through his assertive approach, de Gaulle bolstered France's independent stance, notably by withdrawing from the integrated military command of NATO and developing closer ties with Arab countries. This shift in strategy reshaped the dynamics within the Western bloc and paved the way for a more diversified and autonomous French foreign policy. Furthermore, de Gaulle's overtures towards the Arab world contributed to recalibrating the geopolitical balance in the region. By cultivating strategic partnerships with countries such as Algeria, Egypt, and Syria, France expanded its influence and diversified its network of allies. This strategic diversification offered France a pivotal role in mediating international conflicts and interventions in the Arab world. However, amidst these successes, challenges arose in maintaining equilibrium between Western and Arab alliances. The complexities of balancing these relationships became evident as conflicting interests emerged, particularly during the Suez Crisis and the subsequent aftermath. These challenges underscored the intricacies of navigating Franco-Arab relations, as divergent geopolitical agendas often collided. Additionally, the enduring legacy of de Gaulle's policies influenced France's subsequent foreign policy initiatives. The principles of sovereignty and non-alignment, championed during de Gaulle's tenure, continue to inform France's diplomatic engagements in the Arab world. The precedent set by de Gaulle has perpetuated a legacy of nuanced and independent foreign policy, positioning France as an influential mediator in regional affairs. In hindsight, the impact assessment of Franco-Arab relations at the end of de Gaulle's era underscores the enduring significance of this transformative period. By discerning the consequences of de Gaulle's visionary diplomacy, one can glean valuable insights into the evolution of French foreign policy and its enduring impact on the Arab world.

## Legacy and Continuing Influence on French Foreign Policy

Following Charles de Gaulle's tenure, the legacy of his foreign policy decisions continued to exert a profound influence on France's approach to Franco-Arab relations. De Gaulle's bold and independent stance in reshaping diplomatic ties with Arab countries significantly contributed to the enduring influence of his policies on contemporary French foreign affairs. This section explores the long-term implications of de Gaulle's vision and diplomatic initiatives, shedding light on their sustained impact on the nation's policies and international standing. De Gaulle's commitment to pursuing an assertive and sovereign foreign policy and his emphasis on fostering strategic autonomy for France laid the groundwork for the continued prominence of Franco-Arab relations in French diplomatic strategy. His unwavering dedication to this relationship cleaved a path for subsequent leaders to navigate the complexities of Franco-Arab dynamics with a nuanced understanding of historical context and geopolitical considerations. The enduring influence of de Gaulle's legacy is evidenced in France's ongoing engagement with the Arab world and its proactive role in mediating regional conflicts and promoting cultural exchange. Furthermore, de Gaulle's visionary approach to diversifying diplomatic partners beyond traditional alliances has engendered a multifaceted and adaptive foreign policy framework that still endures. This enduring legacy has fostered strong economic, cultural, and defense ties between France and Arab countries, positioning the relationship as a pivotal component of France's broader international agenda. Moreover, the imprint of de Gaulle's principled pursuit of an autonomous and balanced foreign policy has permeated successive administrations, shaping the continuity and adaptability of France's strategic engagements in the Arab world.

By consolidating a legacy rooted in pragmatic diplomacy and mutual respect, de Gaulle set a standard for future leaders to uphold when navigating the complex landscape of Franco-Arab relations. The enduring influence of de Gaulle's vision continues to guide France's diplomatic endeavors, reinforcing the significance of sustained dialogue, cooperation, and mutual understanding in shaping the trajectory of Franco-Arab relations within the broader scope of French foreign policy.

# IN A NUTSHELL

> ## De Gaulle's Foreign Policy and Franco-Arab Relations
>
> ### 1. Contextual Framework: Post-War Realities and Franco-Arab Relations
>
> After World War II, France's foreign policy was heavily influenced by its colonial legacy and the emerging Cold War dynamics. The Middle East, particularly the Arab world, was a region of significant interest due to historical ties, economic interests, and geopolitical considerations. France had established strong cultural and political connections with countries like Syria and Lebanon, which were former French mandates, and maintained a complex relationship with North African countries, especially Algeria, which was a French colony until 1962.
>
> ### 2. De Gaulle's Ascendancy and Initial Stance Towards Arab Countries

When Charles de Gaulle came to power in 1958, he sought to redefine France's foreign policy to restore its grandeur and independence. Initially, France's relations with the Arab world were strained due to its colonial policies and its close military cooperation with Israel. However, de Gaulle's approach marked a significant shift. He recognized the importance of the Arab world and aimed to establish France as a mediator and a major player in the region, independent of the superpowers.

### 3. Strategic Shifts: Nuclear Policy and Military Presence in the Mediterranean

De Gaulle's nuclear policy was a cornerstone of his strategy to assert France's independence. By developing an independent nuclear arsenal, de Gaulle aimed to ensure France's security and enhance its international standing. This policy also influenced France's military presence in the Mediterranean, where it sought to balance the influence of the United States and the Soviet Union. De Gaulle's vision included maintaining a strong naval presence and establishing military bases, which were crucial for projecting power and securing French interests in the region.

### 4. The Suez Crisis and its Aftermath

The Suez Crisis of 1956 was a turning point in Franco-Arab relations. The crisis highlighted the limitations of Franco-British power and the need for a new approach. De Gaulle, who came to power shortly after the crisis, drew lessons from the event, realizing that France could not rely on its traditional allies, the UK and the US. This led to a reassessment of France's foreign policy, emphasizing independence and a more balanced approach towards the Arab world. De Gaulle's decision to support Arab countries during the Six-Day War in 1967, including imposing an arms embargo on Israel, was a significant move that improved France's standing in the Arab world.

## 5. Bilateral Engagements: Key Diplomatic Missions and Agreements

De Gaulle's era saw several key diplomatic missions and agreements that strengthened Franco-Arab relations. Notably, the Évian Accords in 1962 ended the Algerian War and granted Algeria independence, which was a major step in mending relations with the Arab world. De Gaulle also pursued diplomatic engagements with other Arab countries, fostering economic, cultural, and military cooperation. These efforts were aimed at positioning France as a key partner and mediator in the region.

## 6. Cultural Influence and Media Representation

France's cultural diplomacy played a significant role in its relations with the Arab world. The promotion of French language and culture, along with educational and cultural exchanges, helped build strong ties. French media and intellectuals often highlighted the shared history and cultural connections between France and the Arab world, which contributed to a positive image of France in the region. This cultural influence was a vital component of de Gaulle's broader strategy to enhance France's soft power.

## 7. Challenges Faced in Balancing East-West Politics

Balancing relations between the East and the West was a

significant challenge for de Gaulle. His policy of non-alignment and independence often put France at odds with both the US and the USSR. In the Middle East, this meant navigating complex political landscapes and maintaining relations with both Arab countries and Israel. De Gaulle's stance during the Six-Day War, where he criticized Israel and supported Arab countries, exemplified this delicate balancing act. Despite these challenges, de Gaulle's policies generally succeeded in enhancing France's influence in the region.

## 8. Impact Assessment: Franco-Arab Relations at the End of de Gaulle Era

By the end of de Gaulle's era, France had significantly improved its relations with the Arab world. De Gaulle's policies had established France as a key player in the Middle East, respected for its independent stance and support for Arab causes. The shift from a colonial power to a partner and mediator was a major achievement, and France's cultural and economic ties with the region were stronger than ever. However, the legacy of colonialism and ongoing geopolitical tensions continued to pose challenges.

## 9. Legacy and Continuing Influence on French Foreign Policy

De Gaulle's foreign policy laid the foundation for France's continued engagement with the Arab world. His emphasis on independence, cultural diplomacy, and balanced relations has influenced subsequent French leaders. The Gaullist approach of supporting Arab causes while maintaining a degree of cooperation with Israel has persisted, shaping France's role as a mediator in the region. De Gaulle's legacy is evident in France's ongoing efforts to balance its relations with the West and the Arab world, and its active involvement in Middle Eastern affairs.

In conclusion, Charles de Gaulle's foreign policy significantly redefined France's relations with the Arab countries, establishing a framework that has continued to influence French diplomacy in the region. His strategic shifts, diplomatic engagements, and cultural initiatives helped transform France from a colonial power to a respected partner in the Arab world.

# References For Further Reading

Bbc.co.uk. "BBC NEWS | Europe | France's Own Lesson from Suez," November 1, 2006. http://news.bbc.co.uk/2/hi/europe/6102536.stm.

Ben-Gurion, David . "Ben-Gurion Letter to French General Charles de Gaulle (December 1967)." www.jewishvirtuallibrary.org, December 6, 1967. https://www.jewishvirtuallibrary.org/ben-gurion-letter-to-french-general-charles-de-gaulle-december-1967.

Blanchard, Pascal . "The Paradox of Arab France." The Cairo Review of Global Affairs, June 27, 2016. https://www.thecairoreview.com/essays/the-paradox-of-arab-france/.

Boniface , Pascal . "Beyond Islamophobia: France's Policies toward the Arab World." IRIS, December 22, 2020. https://www.iris-france.org/153125-beyond-islamophobia-frances-policies-toward-the-arab-world/.

Bréville, Benoît. "When France Was a Friend to the Palestinians." Le Monde diplomatique, November 1, 2023. https://mondediplo.com/2023/11/08france.

Charillon, Frédéric . "In Pursuit of a Grand Strategy." The Cairo Review of Global Affairs, October 31, 2018. https://www.thecairoreview.com/essays/in-pursuit-of-a-grand-strategy/.

Cohen, Samy. "De Gaulle et Israël. Le Sens d'Une Rupture." Edited by Élie Barnavi and Saul Friedländer. OpenEdition Books. Genève: Graduate Institute Publications, 1985. https://books.openedition.org/iheid/2009?lang=en.

Elmusa, Sharif . "A Palestinian Gandhi or an Israeli de Gaulle? Why the Context of Violence Matters." The Cairo Review of Global Affairs, February 1, 2024. https://www.thecairoreview.com/essays/a-palestinian-gandhi-or-an-israeli-de-gaulle-why-the-context-of-violence-matters/.

fcc.uchicago.edu. "The Franco-Arab Thing: Exploring Centuries of Franco-Arab Relations | France Chicago Center." Accessed May 18, 2024. https://fcc.uchicago.edu/the-franco-arab-thing-exploring-centuries-of-franco-arab-relations/.

Filiu, Jean-Pierre. "France and the June 1967 War." Chapter. In The 1967 Arab-Israeli War: Origins and Consequences, edited by Wm Roger Louis and Avi Shlaim, 247–63. Cambridge Middle East Studies. Cambridge: Cambridge University Press, 2012.

Filiu, Jean-Pierre. "De Gaulle's France and the June 1967 War." sciencespo.hal.science. Cambridge University Press, 2012. https://sciencespo.hal.science/hal-03415392.

Gordon, Philip H., 'Charles De Gaulle and the Nuclear Revolution', in John Gaddis, and others (eds), Cold War Statesmen Confront the Bomb: Nuclear Diplomacy Since 1945 (Oxford, 1999; online edn, Oxford Academic, 16 Nov. 2004), https://doi.org/10.1093/0198294689.003.0010, accessed 18 May 2024.

———. "France and the June 1967 War." Edited by Avi Shlaim and Wm Roger Louis. Cambridge University Press. Cambridge: Cambridge University Press, 2012. https://www.cambridge.org/core/books/abs/1967-arabisraeli-war/france-and-the-june-1967-war/D058FF7760B60EF04038E4F441ADACF9.

Foreign affairs committee, SENAT. "Going Nuclear in the Middle East." www.senat.fr, n.d. https://www.senat.fr/rap/rapport_en_moyen_orient/rapport_en_moyen_orient16.html.

Franceinfo. "VRAI OU FAUX. Quelles Étaient Les Relations Entre de Gaulle et Israël ?," October 16, 2023. https://www.francetvinfo.fr/monde/proche-orient/israel-palestine/vrai-ou-faux-quelles-etaient-les-relations-entre-de-gaulle-et-israel_6126009.html.

Gresh, Alain. "Orient XXI - Le Journal En Ligne de Référence Du Monde Arabe et Musulman." orientxxi.info, September 5, 2017. https://orientxxi.info/magazine/de-gaulle-the-jews-a-people-sure-of-itself-and-domineering.

Hamza, Assiya . "October 17, 1961: A Massacre of Algerians in the Heart of Paris." FRANCE 24, October 12, 2021. https://webdoc.france24.com/october-17-1961-massacre-algerians-paris-france-police-history/chapter-1.html.

Howell, Mark. "Looking Back: De Gaulle Tells American Forces to Leave France." Royal Air Force Mildenhall, March 23, 2010. https://www.mildenhall.af.mil/News/Article-Display/Article/272283/looking-back-de-gaulle-tells-american-forces-to-leave-france/.

Jewish Telegraphic Agency. "See French Embargo on War Materiel as Move to Weaken Israel, Win Arab Favor," January 8, 1969. https://www.jta.org/archive/see-french-embargo-on-war-materiel-as-move-to-weaken-israel-win-arab-favor.

KATZ, YAAKOV . "How Charles de Gaulle Fathered Israel's Tech Revolution 50 Years Ago." The Jerusalem Post | JPost.com, June 2, 2017. https://www.jpost.com/opinion/editors-notes-de-gaulle-and-israels-technological-revolution-494578.

Keohane, Daniel . "NATO, the EU, and the Curse of Suez." Carnegie Europe, October 14, 2016. https://carnegieeurope.eu/strategiceurope/64859.

Lakomy, Miron. "THE 'ARAB SPRING' in FRENCH FOREIGN POLICY," n.d. https://www.cejiss.org/images/issue_articles/2012-volume-6-issue-3-4/article-04-0.pdf.

Perrier, Guy . "1962: The End of the War in Algeria | Chemins de Mémoire." www.cheminsdememoire.gouv.fr, n.d. https://www.cheminsdememoire.gouv.fr/en/revue/1962-end-war-algeria-0.

Shahwan, Najla M. "De Gaulle's Presidency and Israeli–French Relations." Daily Sabah, January 23, 2020. https://www.dailysabah.com/op-ed/2020/01/22/de-gaulles-presidency-and-israeli-french-relations.

The Six-Day War. "France," n.d. https://www.sixdaywar.org/players/france/.

Uysal, Selin . "France's Diplomatic Role in the Middle East Post-October 7 | the Washington Institute." www.washingtoninstitute.org, February 2, 2024. https://www.washingtoninstitute.org/policy-analysis/frances-diplomatic-role-middle-east-post-october-7.

Vaïsse, Maurice . "De Gaulle and Algeria | Chemins de Mémoire." www.cheminsdememoire.gouv.fr, May 2012. https://www.cheminsdememoire.gouv.fr/en/de-gaulle-and-algeria.

Van Der Made, Jan. "Why France and the Middle East Have Such a Deep and Lingering Past." RFI, December 3, 2021. https://www.rfi.fr/en/international/20211203-why-france-and-the-middle-east-have-such-a-deep-and-lingering-past. Washington Report on Middle East Affairs, October/November 1999, pages 81-82. https://www.wrmea.org/1999-october-november/de-gaulle-calls-jews-domineering-israel-an-expansionist-state.html

Watson, Adam, 'The Aftermath of Suez: Consequences for French Decolonization:', in Wm. Roger Louis, and Roger Owen (eds), Suez 1956: The Crisis and its Consequences, Clarendon Paperbacks (Oxford, 1991; online edn, Oxford Academic, 3 Oct. 2011), https://doi.org/10.1093/acprof:oso/9780198202417.003.0019, accessed 18 May 2024.

# IV

# Navigating the Cold War (1950s-1980s)

## Overview of the Global Political Climate

The 1950s and 1980s witnessed a complex geopolitical landscape dominated by the intense rivalry between the two superpowers, the United States and the Soviet Union. This rivalry, known as the Cold War, had far-reaching implications for global politics and international relations, significantly shaping the dynamics of alliances and conflicts worldwide. The profound ideological and strategic differences between the USSR-led communist bloc and the USA-led capitalist bloc led to heightened tension and competition, often characterized by proxy wars, arms races, and diplomatic maneuvering.

The division of the world into these two opposing blocs created a bipolar international system, with countries aligning themselves with either the Western or Eastern camps based on their political ideologies, economic systems, and strategic interests. This bipolarity not only defined the power dynamics in global affairs but also influenced the domestic politics of many nations, including those in the Arab world. The superpower rivalry permeated various aspects of foreign policy, economics, military strategy, and cultural exchange.

The Cold War's overarching influence on global politics extended to regions beyond the immediate sphere of major power competition, including the Middle East and North Africa. For France, a key player in this period, the interplay between superpower dynamics and regional considerations shaped its strategic approach towards the Arab world. Understanding the broader context of the global political climate is essential for comprehending France's pursuit of its strategic interests in the Arab world and its diplomatic engagements amid the complexities of the Cold War era.

## France's Strategic Interests in the Arab World

From the 1950s to the 1980s, France was keenly interested in fostering strategic partnerships within the Arab world. The overarching objective was to advance French influence in the region while navigating the complexities of the Cold War dynamics. France identified the Arab world as a crucial area for geopolitical and economic interests due to its significant energy resources, proximity to vital trading routes, and historical ties dating back to colonial times. This strategic interest was further amplified by France's desire to maintain a foothold in the Middle East and counterbalance the influence of the United States and the Soviet Union.

A key aspect of France's strategic interests lay its desire to secure reliable access to oil and natural gas reserves in several Arab countries. Recognizing the geopolitical importance of the Middle East's energy resources, France sought to cultivate strong relationships with key Arab states to ensure a steady energy supply for its domestic consumption and industrial growth. Additionally, France aimed to leverage these partnerships to bolster its position as a major player in the global energy market, cementing its status as an influential actor in shaping the international energy landscape.

Beyond energy considerations, France strategically positioned itself to capitalize on the economic potential offered by the Arab world.

France aimed to enhance its economic standing by promoting trade and investment ties by engaging in mutually beneficial partnerships with Arab states. Furthermore, the Arab world presented lucrative opportunities for French businesses across various sectors, from infrastructure development to defense contracts, creating a symbiotic economic relationship that enhanced France's economic prowess.

The strategic significance of the Arab world to France extended beyond economic and energy interests. Viewing the region as a gateway to Africa and Asia, France recognized the value of maintaining a solid presence in the Arab world to reinforce its broader geopolitical influence and security posture. Additionally, France aimed to showcase its diplomatic finesse and leadership ability by actively participating in key regional affairs and mediating disputes, ultimately positioning itself as a pivotal player in shaping the political trajectory of the Arab world.

In this context, France's strategic interests in the Arab world during the Cold War era constituted a multifaceted and deliberate pursuit of economic, geopolitical, and security imperatives, underscoring the depth of France's engagement with the Arab states and its enduring impact on Franco-Arab relations.

## *Bilateral Relations Amid US-Soviet Rivalries*

During the Cold War, France navigated a complex web of diplomatic challenges as it sought to maintain and advance its relations with Arab states amidst the intensifying rivalry between the United States and the Soviet Union. As the global superpowers vied for influence and control, France faced the delicate task of balancing its strategic interests in the Arab world while aligning with its Western allies. This intricate dance of diplomacy required astute finesse and nuanced decision-making by French leaders.

The United States, as the leader of the Western bloc, exerted considerable pressure on France to support its policies and initiatives in the region. At the same time, the Soviet Union sought to leverage its relationships with Arab states to expand its sphere of influence. Amid this geopolitical maneuvering, France had to carefully calibrate its foreign policy to prevent being overshadowed by the dominant power struggles between the superpowers. This often meant treading a fine line between cooperation and autonomy while navigating the shifting sands of international politics.

France's bilateral relations with Arab states were shaped not only by the overarching dynamics of the Cold War but also by the specific historical, cultural, and economic ties that bound them together. The intricate tapestry of these relations demanded constant attention and skillful negotiation. France sought to engage Arab states as partners in mutually beneficial endeavors while simultaneously fostering its distinct identity and interests within the broader geopolitical landscape.

Moreover, the localized conflicts and ideological confrontations within the Arab world added an extra layer of complexity to France's bilateral engagements. The rise of pan-Arabism and the enduring legacies of colonialism contributed to a multifaceted landscape where France had to navigate various competing narratives and interests deftly. This necessitated a deep understanding of local grievances and aspirations and a strategic approach that balanced pragmatism with principled diplomacy.

Amidst these challenges, French leaders skillfully crafted a sophisticated approach to bilateral relations that reflected both the exigencies of the Cold War and the enduring significance of the Franco-Arab bond. This period witnessed a delicate interplay of strategic alignments, economic partnerships, and cultural exchange, all of which left an indelible mark on the subsequent trajectory of Franco-Arab relations.

## *The Suez Crisis and Its Aftermath*

Amid the intensifying Cold War dynamics, the Suez Crisis of 1956 represented a pivotal juncture in Franco-Arab relations and global geopolitics. The crisis was triggered by President Gamal Abdel Nasser's nationalization of the Suez Canal, challenging Western powers and marking the decline of traditional colonial dominance in the Middle East. France, alongside the United Kingdom, sought to regain control of the strategically vital waterway, leading to a controversial military intervention. However, the intervention faced significant opposition from the United States and the Soviet Union, highlighting the complex and shifting alliances of the era. The Suez Crisis strained Franco-Arab relations as it exposed conflicting interests between France and several Arab states while also illuminating broader regional tensions and aspirations for independence. The aftermath of the Suez Crisis saw France recalibrating its approach to the Arab world, acknowledging the need for a more nuanced and balanced strategy that considered Arab aspirations for sovereignty and autonomy. This period of reassessment and adjustment significantly shaped the trajectory of Franco-Arab relations in the subsequent decades, influencing policy decisions and diplomatic engagements. Furthermore, the Suez Crisis contributed to the evolving power dynamics within the Arab world, fostering a greater sense of unity and solidarity against external interference and neo-colonial ambitions. The repercussions of the Suez Crisis reverberated across the global political landscape, redefining alliances, triggering ideological shifts, and reinforcing the importance of diplomacy and multilateral cooperation in addressing contentious geopolitical disputes. Ultimately, the Suez Crisis and its aftermath serve as a defining chapter in the history of Franco-Arab relations, offering valuable insights into the intricate interplay of interests, ideologies, and aspirations that continue to shape international affairs today.

## French Military and Economic Aid to Arab States

Throughout the Cold War, France played a significant role in providing military and economic assistance to various Arab states, strategically positioning itself as a key ally. The provision of military aid was driven by France's desire to counterbalance the influence of other global powers, such as the United States and the Soviet Union, in the Arab world. The supply of advanced weaponry, including fighter aircraft, tanks, and naval vessels, strengthened the defense capabilities of Arab states and consolidated bilateral ties with France.

Moreover, France also extended economic aid to support the development and modernization of infrastructure, industries, and educational institutions in Arab countries. This assistance aimed to foster economic growth, stability, and self-sufficiency while deepening Franco-Arab relations. Economic aid often took the form of grants, concessional loans, and technical expertise, enhancing key sectors such as agriculture, energy, and telecommunications.

In addition to bolstering military and economic aid, France engaged in extensive training programs for Arab military and civilian personnel, further solidifying collaborative partnerships. This exchange of knowledge and skills facilitated the effective utilization of the provided resources and cultivated enduring relationships between France and Arab states. The training initiatives covered areas ranging from military tactics and logistics to administrative governance and technological advancements, reinforcing the capacity of Arab states to address internal and external challenges.

Furthermore, French assistance played a pivotal role in shaping the geopolitical landscape of the Arab world, influencing regional power dynamics and fostering mutual interests. By aligning its aid with the strategic objectives of Arab states, France positioned itself as a trusted partner, promoting stability and influence amid Cold War rivalries. The reciprocation of this partnership was evident in the alignment of policy positions, joint military exercises, and coordinated diplomatic endeavors that underpinned the collaborative efforts between France and its Arab counterparts.

Overall, France's comprehensive military and economic aid to Arab states during the Cold War period had a lasting impact on the region's socio-political and security landscape. This chapter on Franco-Arab relations underscored the complexities and nuances of international alliances, highlighting the interplay of strategic imperatives, historical legacies, and shared aspirations for peace and prosperity.

## The Role of Intelligence and Espionage

During the Cold War era, intelligence and espionage played a crucial and often clandestine role in shaping Franco-Arab relations. As France sought to assert its influence in the Arab world while navigating the global power dynamics, intelligence gathering and covert operations became instrumental in understanding the political landscape and advancing French interests. The intelligence agencies of France and various Arab states were actively involved in collecting information, conducting surveillance, and influencing decision-making processes, often operating in the shadows of diplomacy.

French intelligence agencies, notably the Direction Générale de la Sécurité Extérieure (DGSE), engaged in intricate espionage activities across the Arab world, aiming to gain insights into the policies and strategies of regional actors, monitor potential threats, and secure vital information about the activities of rival powers such as the United States and the Soviet Union. These efforts were aimed at safeguarding French economic and military interests and maintaining strategic alliances with key Arab partners. Simultaneously, Arab states employed their intelligence apparatus to safeguard their sovereignty, counter foreign influence, and gather strategic intelligence to advance their national agendas.

The clandestine nature of intelligence operations during this period often led to diplomatic sensitivities and international incidents. Espionage activities, including covert operations, counterintelligence, and propaganda efforts, heightened the distrust between nations and complicated bilateral relationships. The revelation of espionage activities could lead to public outrage, diplomatic crises, and strained relations between France and Arab states.

Furthermore, the impact of intelligence and espionage extended beyond traditional state-to-state interactions, influencing the dynamics of regional conflicts, internal power struggles, and insurgent movements. From covert support for independence movements to clandestine assistance in suppressing dissent, intelligence agencies on both sides sought to shape the political landscape in ways that furthered their respective national interests. The blurred lines between intelligence, diplomacy, and military interventions underline the complex interplay of covert operations in the context of Franco-Arab relations during the Cold War.

As the tensions of the Cold War permeated international relations, the role of intelligence and espionage in Franco-Arab connections underscored the intricacies and covert maneuvers that underpinned the pursuit of strategic advantage. These clandestine efforts not only reflected the high-stakes competition of the era but also left a lasting imprint on the subsequent evolution of Franco-Arab relations, shaping the dynamics of trust, suspicion, and rivalry that continue to influence diplomatic interactions to this day.

## *Diplomatic Challenges and Triumphs*

The period spanning the 1950s to the 1980s marked a tumultuous time for Franco-Arab relations, as both diplomatic challenges and triumphs significantly shaped the course of history. Amid the backdrop of the Cold War, France encountered numerous diplomatic hurdles in its efforts to navigate the complex web of alliances and conflicts within the Arab world. The overarching challenge lay in balancing its strategic interests with its commitment to upholding regional stability and security.

One of the paramount diplomatic challenges was the delicate balancing act required to maintain relations with various Arab states while navigating its ties with other global powers. As the United States and the Soviet Union vied for influence, France confronted safeguarding its position without alienating its Arab partners. This intricate diplomatic dance often called for deft negotiations and nuanced diplomacy, as any misstep could significantly affect the geopolitical landscape.

However, amongst these challenges, notable triumphs also underscored France's adeptness in diplomacy. The successful navigation of politically sensitive issues such as the Algerian Crisis and the aftermath of the Suez Crisis demonstrated France's ability to effectively engage in dialogue and mediation, fostering positive outcomes that bolstered its standing in the Arab world.

Moreover, the skillful execution of multilateral diplomacy and the forging of strategic alliances in the face of regional tensions showcased France's capacity to broker agreements and facilitate cooperation, thereby contributing to maintaining peace and stability in the Middle East and North Africa.

Furthermore, the artful deployment of cultural diplomacy and soft power initiatives enabled France to deepen its cultural and intellectual connections with Arab states, transcending political boundaries and laying the groundwork for enduring partnerships.

Ultimately, the era was defined by a delicate interplay of challenges and triumphs, with France navigating a complex diplomatic terrain marked by shifting power dynamics and competing interests. The lessons and experiences from this period continue to resonate in contemporary Franco-Arab relations, serving as a testament to the enduring significance of skillful diplomacy in shaping international affairs.

## *France's Nuclear Policy and Arab Reactions*

France's development of nuclear weapons during the Cold War significantly influenced its relations with Arab states and the broader Middle East region. The decision to pursue a nuclear arsenal had far-reaching implications and elicited diverse reactions from Arab states, shaping the geopolitical landscape in profound ways.

Amid global power struggles and heightened tensions, France's nuclear policy evoked apprehension and strategic calculations among

Arab leaders. The perceived threat of nuclear proliferation in the region led to concerns about maintaining regional stability and security. Arab states, already grappling with their dynamics and conflicts, viewed France's nuclear ambitions as a factor that could intensify existing challenges and exacerbate the balance of power in the region.

Furthermore, France's nuclear program intersected with the Arab-Israeli conflict, adding another layer of complexity to the geopolitical dynamics. France's acquisition of nuclear capabilities inevitably impacted the strategic calculus of Arab states, shaping their diplomatic maneuvers and military strategies. The specter of potential nuclear escalation catalyzed the reevaluation of alliances and defense postures, contributing to uncertainty and strategic repositioning across the region.

The news of France testing its first nuclear weapon in the Sahara Desert in 1960 triggered widespread alarm and condemnation among Arab countries, raising questions about the implications for regional security and the broader international non-proliferation efforts. These developments prompted Arab leaders to voice their concerns on various global platforms while advocating for multilateral efforts to prevent the further spread of nuclear arms.

As French nuclear capabilities continued to evolve, Arab reactions encompassed a spectrum of responses, ranging from diplomatic negotiations and appeals for disarmament to strategic recalibrations and defensive measures. The intricate interplay between France's nuclear policy and Arab reactions underscored the intricate web of geopolitical considerations, mutual suspicions, and attempts at mitigating the risks of nuclear escalation in the region.

In hindsight, the ramifications of France's nuclear policy and the resulting Arab reactions serve as a compelling chapter in the history of Franco-Arab relations, leaving a lasting imprint on regional security, power dynamics, and diplomatic discourse.

## Cultural Exchanges and Propaganda

During the Cold War era, cultural exchanges and propaganda played a significant role in shaping Franco-Arab relations. France, with its rich cultural heritage and tradition, actively engaged in cultural exchanges with Arab countries to promote mutual understanding, foster goodwill, and exert influence. These exchanges encompassed various forms of cultural expression, including art, literature, music, cinema, and education. Through institutions such as the Institut Français and cultural centers established in Arab capitals, France sought to showcase its culture and language while promoting dialogue and collaboration between French and Arab artists, scholars, and intellectuals. Such initiatives aimed to create lasting bonds and positive perceptions that would transcend political tensions and ideological differences, fostering long-term partnerships and alliances. At the same time, both overt and covert propaganda was employed by both French and Arab governments to shape public opinion and influence attitudes towards one another. This often involved state-sponsored media campaigns, cultural events, and educational initiatives emphasizing shared values, historical ties, and common aspirations. While cultural exchanges sought to build bridges and promote mutual respect, propaganda was used to persuade and influence, often serving geopolitical objectives and interests. It is important to assess the impact of these cultural exchanges and propaganda efforts on shaping the narratives and perceptions that continue to influence Franco-Arab relations today. By examining these endeavors' strategies, messages, and repercussions, we gain insight into the intricate dynamics of soft power, public diplomacy, and the enduring legacy of cultural engagement in international affairs.

## Assessing the Impact on Subsequent Franco-Arab Relations

The intricate web of cultural exchanges and propaganda during the

Cold War period profoundly impacted the subsequent Franco-Arab relations, leaving a lasting legacy that continues to shape diplomatic, economic, and social interactions. The strategic deployment of cultural diplomacy and propaganda by France and Arab countries during this era resounded across multiple spheres, influencing perceptions, policies, and mutual understanding. Considering the multifaceted nature of these impacts, evaluating them comprehensively and with nuance is essential to gain a holistic understanding of their effects on the current state of Franco-Arab relations. During the Cold War, cultural exchanges were a potent tool for fostering bilateral ties and shaping public opinion in France and the Arab world. French cultural institutions actively promoted the dissemination of French language, arts, literature, and academic exchange programs in Arab countries, aiming to cultivate favorable perceptions of France and its values. Simultaneously, Arab states utilized cultural exchanges to showcase their rich heritage, traditions, and contributions to humanity, seeking to bolster their global standing and foster alliances with France amid geopolitical rivalries. Propaganda, on the other hand, was wielded as a means of advancing political agendas, promoting ideologies, and shaping public narratives. Both France and Arab countries engaged in propagandistic efforts to garner support, vilify adversaries, and sway public opinion in their favor. Such campaigns unfolded through various mediums, including media, literature, films, and educational curricula, influencing how each side was perceived by the other and their respective populations. The enduring legacies of these Cold War dynamics are discernible in contemporary Franco-Arab relations. The cultural imprints left by decades of exchange programs endure through shared educational and linguistic connections, cultural appreciation, and collaborative initiatives in the arts and academia. Furthermore, the echoes of propagandistic efforts resonate in persistent stereotypes, biases, and historical grievances that periodically infuse diplomatic discourse and public perceptions. Despite the complexities and enduring influences of Cold War-era cultural exchanges and propaganda, it is imperative to recognize that subsequent Franco-Arab relations have also evolved in response to shifting geopolitical realities, demographic changes, and socioeconomic dynamics. While the past continues to inform the present, contemporary interactions reflect a dynamic interplay of interests, aspirations, and mutual dependencies, transcending the shadow of Cold War legacies. Hence, a nuanced assessment of these impacts is crucial for attaining a comprehensive understanding of the dynamics that continue to shape Franco-Arab relations in the present day.

# IN A NUTSHELL

France's diplomacy in the Arab world during the Cold War era was a complex interplay of strategic interests, bilateral relations amid global rivalries, and a series of diplomatic, military, and cultural maneuvers. This period, spanning from the 1950s to the 1980s, saw France navigating the tumultuous waters of international politics, marked by its efforts to maintain a distinct stance from the superpowers, the United States and the Soviet Union, while pursuing its interests in the Arab world.

## *France's Strategic Interests in the Arab World*

France's strategic interests in the Arab world were multifaceted, encompassing political, economic, and cultural dimensions. Historically, France had established strong ties with the Arab world, dating back to its colonial presence in North Africa. During the Cold War, France sought to maintain and expand its influence in the region, driven by the desire for access to oil resources, markets for its exports, including arms, and the need to manage the complex relationship with its former colonies.

## Bilateral Relations Amid US-Soviet Rivalries

France's approach to bilateral relations in the Arab world was significantly influenced by the overarching US-Soviet rivalries. France aimed to position itself as an alternative power, offering support to Arab states without the political conditions often attached by the superpowers. This stance was exemplified by Charles de Gaulle's "Arab policy," which sought to provide a third way for non-aligned countries, balancing between the capitalist West and the communist East.

## The Suez Crisis and Its Aftermath

The Suez Crisis of 1956 was a pivotal moment in Franco-Arab relations and a significant event in the Cold War context. France, alongside Britain and Israel, launched a military intervention in Egypt following President Nasser's nationalization of the Suez Canal. The crisis highlighted France's strategic interests in the region but also exposed the limitations of its power. The intervention was met with strong international opposition, including from the United States, leading to a withdrawal and a reevaluation of France's strategy in the region.

## French Military and Economic Aid to Arab States

Following the Suez Crisis, France continued to provide military and economic aid to Arab states, partly as a means to maintain its influence and counterbalance the growing presence of the US and the Soviet Union. This included arms sales and support for infrastructure projects. France's relationship with Iraq and Libya, in particular, showcased its willingness to engage with regimes that were often at odds with Western interests, in pursuit of economic and strategic benefits.

## The Role of Intelligence and Espionage

Intelligence and espionage played crucial roles in France's diplomatic strategy in the Arab world. While specific operations remain largely classified, it is known that France actively gathered intelligence to inform its foreign policy decisions and to navigate the complex political landscape of the Middle East. This included efforts to monitor the activities of rival powers and to influence outcomes in line with French interests.

## Diplomatic Challenges and Triumphs

France faced numerous diplomatic challenges in the Arab world, from managing the fallout of the Suez Crisis to navigating the intricacies of the Arab-Israeli conflict. Despite these challenges, France achieved several diplomatic triumphs, including its role in mediating conflicts and its successful maintenance of strong relationships with key Arab states, even as regional dynamics shifted.

## France's Nuclear Policy and Arab Reactions

France's development of a nuclear arsenal in the 1960s was a significant aspect of its foreign policy, aimed at asserting its independence and enhancing its status as a global power. The Arab world's reaction to France's nuclear policy was mixed, with some states expressing concern over nuclear proliferation while others viewed it as a counterbalance to Israel's nuclear capabilities.

## Cultural Exchanges and Propaganda

Cultural exchanges and propaganda were important tools for France in promoting its interests and values in the Arab world. This included educational initiatives, cultural missions, and media broadcasts aimed at strengthening Franco-Arab ties and countering Soviet and American influence.

## Assessing the Impact on Subsequent Franco-Arab Relations

The Cold War era laid the groundwork for subsequent Franco-Arab relations, with France's policies during this period having a lasting impact. France's efforts to maintain a distinct and independent foreign policy, coupled with its strategic and economic interests in the region, have continued to shape its interactions with Arab states. The legacy of the Suez Crisis, in particular, serves as a reminder of the complexities of Franco-Arab relations and the challenges of navigating global rivalries.

In conclusion, France's diplomacy in the Arab world during the Cold War was characterized by a delicate balancing act, as it sought to pursue its strategic interests while navigating the geopolitical tensions of the era. The outcomes of these efforts have had enduring implications for Franco-Arab relations, reflecting the intricate interplay of local, regional, and global dynamics.

# References For Further Reading

CIA Directorate of Intelligence. "France's Policy Toward the Middle East. Secret Report (declassified). 7 March 1969.<br> https://www.cia.gov/readingroom/docs/CIA-RDP79-00927A006900060003-0.pdf

"20th-Century International Relations - Arab States, Nasser, Suez Canal, and Soviet Satellites | Britannica." Www.britannica.com, www.britannica.com/topic/20th-century-international-relations-2085155/The-Suez-Crisis.

Boniface , Pascal . "Is France Cooling toward Its Arab Friends? | YaleGlobal Online." Archive-Yaleglobal.yale.edu, 18 Apr. 2007, archive-yaleglobal.yale.edu/content/france-cooling-toward-its-arab-friends. Accessed 19 May 2024.

Boniface, Pascal . "Beyond Islamophobia: France's Policies toward the Arab World." IRIS, 22 Dec. 2020, www.iris-france.org/153125-beyond-islamophobia-frances-policies-toward-the-arab-world/.

Dagres, Holly. "Under Macron's Leadership, France Is Leading a Middle Power Strategy in the Gulf. Here's How." Atlantic Council, 16 Aug. 2022, www.atlanticcouncil.org/blogs/menasource/under-macrons-leadership-france-is-leading-a-middle-power-strategy-in-the-gulf-heres-how/.

El Karoui, Hakim . "A New Strategy for France in a New Arab World." Institut Montaigne, Aug. 2017, www.institutmontaigne.org/en/publications/new-strategy-france-new-arab-world.

Fayet, Héloïse. "What Strategic Posture Should France Adopt in the Middle East?" The French Institute of International Relations , Nov. 2022.

Lakomy, Miron. "The Arab Spring in French Foreign Policy." Central European Journal of International and Security Studies, vol. 6, no. 3, 22 Nov. 2022, www.cejiss.org/the-arab-spring-in-french-foreign-policy. Accessed 21 Nov. 2022.

Rapnouil, Manuel Lafont. "Alone in the Desert? How France Can Lead Europe in the Middle East." ECFR, 10 Apr. 2018, ecfr.eu/publication/alone_in_the_desert_how_france_can_lead_europe_in_the_middle_east/.

The Editors of Encyclopedia Britannica. "Suez Crisis | Summary, Location, Dates, Significance, & Facts." Encyclopædia Britannica, 25 Jan. 2019, www.britannica.com/event/Suez-Crisis.

Webster, Richard A. "Western Colonialism - the Sinai-Suez Campaign (October–November 1956) | Britannica." Www.britannica.com, www.britannica.com/topic/Western-colonialism/The-Sinai-Suez-campaign-October-November-1956.

# V

# Decolonization and Independence (1960s-1970s)

## Overview of Decolonization and Independence Movements

The twentieth century witnessed a monumental shift in the global political landscape, marked by the decolonization and independence movements that swept across various African and Asian territories. This transformative era, characterized by the dismantling of colonial empires and the assertion of national identities, significantly impacted French policy and its position on the world stage. As numerous regions emerged from the shadow of colonial rule, their struggles for self-determination reverberated far beyond their borders, driving discussions on sovereignty, human rights, and international diplomacy. Within this backdrop of historical change, the decolonization process posed profound challenges to both the colonized nations and the former colonial powers, fundamentally reshaping the dynamics of global relations.

## The Impact of the Algerian War on French Policy

The Algerian War, also known as the Algerian War of Independence, deeply impacted French domestic and international policy. The conflict lasted from 1954 to 1962, marking a significant turning point in France's colonial history and had far-reaching implications for its geopolitical standing. The brutal and protracted nature of the war forced France to confront the unsustainable nature of its colonial rule and compelled a reevaluation of its approach to overseas territories.

At the outset, the Algerian War exposed deep internal divisions within French society and government. The conflict stirred passionate debates about the moral and ethical justification for maintaining colonial dominance. The atrocities committed by both French forces and Algerian factions drew international condemnation and placed France in an increasingly isolated position on the world stage. This led to a reassessment of France's global image and its role as a colonial power, prompting a reconsideration of its broader foreign policy objectives.

The Algerian War also profoundly impacted French military strategy and capabilities. The guerilla warfare tactics employed by the Algerian National Liberation Front (FLN) posed significant challenges for the French military, exposing vulnerabilities in conventional warfare methods. This prompted a rethinking of military doctrine and a shift towards more nuanced approaches to asymmetric conflicts. Furthermore, the strain imposed on French resources by the prolonged conflict highlighted the potential risks and diminishing returns associated with maintaining extensive colonial holdings.

Internationally, the Algerian War reconfigured France's relationships with other global powers and regional actors. The conflict's protracted nature diverted attention and resources away from other pressing geopolitical issues, exacerbating tensions and frictions with key allies and partners. Additionally, the war underscored the limits of French influence in shaping events in its former colonies and eroded France's prestige as a global arbiter.

Ultimately, the Algerian War fundamentally altered France's

approach to decolonization and independence across its territories, serving as a crucial catalyst for reshaping its post-colonial policies. The lessons learned from the conflict resonated far beyond Algeria and reverberated throughout the French Empire, laying the groundwork for a new era of diplomatic priorities and strategic imperatives.

## Shifts in French Political Ideology and Colonial Administration

The decolonization process of the 1960s and 1970s brought about significant shifts in French political ideology and colonial administration. The Algerian War marked a turning point in France's approach to its overseas territories, prompting a reevaluation of colonial policies and reconfiguring its national identity. This period witnessed the emergence of new political ideologies that sought to reconcile the ideals of Republicanism with the realities of empire and decolonization. Changes in colonial administration accompanied the shift in political ideology as France grappled with the complexities of granting independence while maintaining influence in the region. Additionally, decolonization led to a reexamination of the legal and institutional frameworks governing colonial governance. Establishing new diplomatic relationships and redrawing boundaries raised questions about sovereignty and territorial integrity, forcing France to adapt its administrative structures to accommodate the aspirations of newly independent nations. Furthermore, the decolonization era saw a transformation in French society's cultural and social fabric, as the country navigated the challenges of post-colonial identity and intercultural exchange. This period also posed economic challenges for France, as it had to recalibrate its trade and investment policies in light of the changing geopolitical landscape. Ultimately, the shifts in French political ideology and colonial administration during this period had far-reaching implications for Franco-Arab relations and the broader dynamics of global diplomacy. These changes not only shaped the future of France's engagement with the Arab world but also reverberated across the international stage, contributing to the reconfiguration of power dynamics and the emergence of new alliances and partnerships.

## Case Studies: Morocco and Tunisia Gain Independence

Morocco and Tunisia serve as compelling case studies in the decolonization process, providing valuable insights into the complexities and challenges faced by both nations as they achieved independence from French colonial rule. Their experiences offer a nuanced understanding of the socio-economic, cultural, and political dynamics that unfolded during their transition to sovereignty.

In the case of Morocco, the country's journey towards independence was characterized by a complex interplay of internal resistance, international pressures, and strategic negotiations with the French colonial authorities. The Rif War and subsequent pro-independence movements, led by figures such as Allal al-Fassi and Mohammed V, demonstrated the tenacity and resilience of Moroccans in their pursuit of self-determination. Moreover, the involvement of international organizations, such as the United Nations, played a pivotal role in advocating for Morocco's sovereignty and highlighting the imperative of decolonization in the post-World War II era.

Similarly, Tunisia's quest for independence was marked by persistent struggles against colonial oppression and exploitation. The emergence of influential leaders like Habib Bourguiba, whose pro-independence efforts galvanized the Tunisian populace, exemplified the depth of national sentiment and aspirations for autonomy. The Tunisian Nationalist Movement, alongside diplomatic initiatives and international support, contributed to the gradual unraveling of French hegemony and the eventual attainment of independence for Tunisia.

Both Morocco and Tunisia navigated an intricate path toward

independence, encountering formidable obstacles and enduring sacrifices along the way. Their successful liberation from colonial dominance not only reshaped the geopolitical landscape of North Africa but also inspired other colonized territories worldwide. The legacies of independence movements in these nations continue to resonate, cementing the significance of their historical trajectories and the enduring spirit of sovereignty.

## *Economic Implications of Independence for France*

The decolonization process in North Africa and the Middle East during the 1960s was a pivotal juncture with far-reaching economic ramifications for France. The transition of former colonies to independent states had significant implications for France's economy, trade relations, and geopolitical influence. As these territories gained sovereignty, France experienced shifts in its access to natural resources, labor markets, and export destinations, triggering a reassessment of its economic strategies and policies.

One of the immediate economic consequences of decolonization was the loss of preferential access to raw materials and markets that French colonial rule had previously guaranteed. This change disrupted established trade patterns and forced French industries to adapt to new procurement channels. Furthermore, the withdrawal from overseas territories meant relocating or closing businesses reliant on colonial resources and labor, leading to internal restructuring and realignment within the French economy.

Another key aspect of decolonization's economic impact was the reconfiguration of investment patterns. With newly independent countries establishing their own economic systems and regulatory frameworks, French businesses faced challenges in maintaining their dominant positions in sectors ranging from agriculture and mining to manufacturing and finance. Migrating capital and expertise from former colonies also presented hurdles, necessitating navigating legal barriers and negotiating terms with post-colonial governments.

Additionally, the repositioning of former colonies within the global economic landscape compelled France to recalibrate its international trade and development policies. The emergence of independent states created opportunities for diversification and expansion, prompting France to engage in bilateral and multilateral partnerships to secure new markets, promote technological transfers, and foster cooperative ventures. Conversely, managing the economic repercussions of decolonization also demanded careful navigation of geopolitical tensions and rivalries as different global powers sought to influence the trajectories of newly liberated nations.

France's response to the economic transformations wrought by decolonization also encompassed initiatives in aid provision, technical assistance, and investment incentives to maintain its influence and pursue its interests in strategic domains. This era witnessed the formulation of new economic aid programs, trade agreements, and cultural exchanges designed to foster mutually beneficial ties and ensure a continued presence in areas vital to France's economic well-being and geopolitical standing.

In conclusion, the era of decolonization ushered in complex economic challenges and opportunities for France, compelling a re-evaluation of its economic priorities, international engagements, and developmental objectives. The economic implications of independence reverberated profoundly across various sectors and dimensions, shaping France's economic trajectory and its enduring relationships with former colonies in an evolving global order.

## Legal and Diplomatic Frameworks Established Post-Independence

Following the attainment of independence by various Arab states from their former colonial powers, including France, establishing legal and diplomatic frameworks became paramount in shaping their governance structures and international relations. This pivotal phase marked the transition from colonial rule to nationhood, requiring the formation of new legal systems and diplomatic protocols to govern internal affairs and interact with the global community.

At the core of this transition was the development of constitutions that defined the fundamental laws of the newly independent states. These foundational documents were instrumental in establishing the rights and responsibilities of citizens, delineating the structure of governance, and outlining the balance of power between branches of government. Moreover, they often reflected the aspirations and values of the respective nations, laying the groundwork for legal and administrative frameworks that would endure the test of time.

Simultaneously, the newly independent states engaged in the delicate process of crafting diplomatic strategies and engaging with the international community. Developing diplomatic ties with former colonial powers such as France while forging relationships with other nations required a nuanced approach that balanced national interests, historical alliances, and geopolitical dynamics. Bilateral and multilateral agreements were pivotal in solidifying these diplomatic ties and addressing trade, security, and cultural exchange issues.

The establishment of embassies and consulates abroad signified the formal entry of these sovereign entities onto the world stage, enabling them to participate in global forums, cultivate international partnerships, and advocate for their interests. Furthermore, membership in international organizations and institutions allowed these newly independent states to assert their presence and contribute to shaping the direction of global politics and socio-economic development. The United Nations and its various agencies emerged as key platforms for these nations to amplify their voices on critical issues affecting the international community.

Amidst these developments, challenges inevitably arose, ranging from border and refugee crises to complex trade negotiations and human rights concerns. Navigating these complexities required astute diplomatic acumen and a commitment to upholding principles of sovereignty, territorial integrity, and non-interference in internal affairs. The legal and diplomatic frameworks established post-independence played a pivotal role in addressing these challenges, providing a basis for dialogue, conflict resolution, and collective action within the global arena.

As these legal and diplomatic structures evolved over time, they became integral components of the national identity and reinforced the autonomy and agency of these newly independent states. They continue to shape international relations and serve as enduring symbols of sovereignty, resilience, and diplomacy in the post-colonial era.

## *Cultural Transition and Identity Formation in Newly Independent States*

Decolonization and achieving independence marked a significant turning point in the history of many Arab states, as it ushered in a period of intense cultural transition and identity formation. The newfound freedom from colonial rule brought about a resurgence of national pride and a collective reclamation of cultural heritage. This section will delve into the multifaceted aspects of this cultural rebirth, examining the impact on language, art, literature, religion, and traditional practices.

Language played a pivotal role in shaping the post-independence cultural landscape. Many newly independent Arab states sought to elevate their native languages to a central position, aiming to revive and promote linguistic traditions that had been marginalized during the colonial era. In some cases, efforts were made to purge remnants of colonial languages from official use, signifying a decisive break from the colonial past and consolidating the indigenous identity.

Art and literature became powerful expressions of the evolving cultural ethos. Artists and writers seized the opportunity to reinterpret, celebrate, and preserve their national narratives, drawing inspiration from historical epics, folklore, and societal upheavals. These creative endeavors served not only as a testament to the spirit of resistance against colonial subjugation but also as a means to articulate the aspirations and struggles of the newly sovereign nations.

Religion, deeply intertwined with the fabric of Arab societies, assumed renewed significance in the post-independence era. Revitalizing religious values and practices often played a vital role in reinforcing national identity and unifying in diverse, multi-ethnic societies. Furthermore, the resurgence of religious discourse and reclaiming religious institutions from colonial influence became integral elements in the cultural rejuvenation process.

Traditional practices and customs underwent a phase of reevaluation and reinvention, seeking to strike a balance between preserving cultural authenticity and adapting to the demands of modernity. Communities engaged in introspective dialogues regarding preserving indigenous traditions while embracing progressive socio-cultural changes. This phase of identity formation was characterized by a conscious effort to navigate the complexities of globalization without compromising the essence of the nation's cultural ethos.

The cultural transition and identity formation in newly independent Arab states embody a rich tapestry of revival, adaption, and innovation. It is a narrative of resilience, creativity, and determination that continues to shape the contemporary cultural landscape of the Arab world.

## *Franco-Arab Relations Post-Decolonization*

The decolonization of Arab states in the 1960s and 1970s marked a significant turning point in Franco-Arab relations. With the end of colonial rule, France sought to redefine its relationship with the newly independent Arab countries, acknowledging their sovereignty and engaging in diplomatic dialogue to build mutually beneficial partnerships. The post-decolonization era witnessed a complex interplay of political, economic, and cultural dynamics that continue to shape Franco-Arab relations today. From a professional standpoint, it is crucial to analyze the evolution of this relationship within the broader context of international politics and regional cooperation. Following decolonization, France faced the challenge of recalibrating its foreign policy to accommodate the aspirations of Arab countries for self-determination and autonomy. This period saw the emergence of new diplomatic frameworks and treaty agreements to foster collaboration in various sectors, such as trade, education, and defense. Moreover, France recognized the significance of building cultural bridges and promoting dialogue between the French and Arab communities, leading to initiatives in language exchange programs, academic partnerships, and artistic collaborations. As part of its diplomatic efforts, France navigated the Middle East's complex geopolitical landscape, balancing its relationships with Arab states alongside its commitments to other global alliances. The oil crisis of the 1970s further underscored the strategic importance of maintaining stable and amicable ties with Arab oil-producing countries, influencing the direction of bilateral relations. Throughout this period, the Franco-Arab dialogue encompassed political and economic domains and extended to security, human rights, and regional stability. Discussions on conflict resolution and peacekeeping initiatives in the Arab world became recurring themes in Franco-Arab relations, reflecting France's commitment to contributing to the region's peaceful development. In conclusion, the post-decolonization era marked a crucial phase in the evolution of Franco-Arab relations, characterized by a multifaceted exchange of ideas, interests, and challenges. Understanding the historical trajectory of this relationship provides valuable insights into the current state of affairs. It offers a foundation for shaping the future trajectory of Franco-Arab relations from a professional perspective.

## *Influence of Global Powers on Arab Sovereignty*

As Arab countries embarked on the strategic path towards

sovereignty post-colonization, they found themselves navigating a complex geopolitical landscape influenced by global powers. The dynamics of the Cold War era played a pivotal role in shaping the trajectory of Arab sovereignty as superpowers vied for influence and control within the region. The United States and the Soviet Union engaged in a high-stakes competition to extend their spheres of influence, often leveraging their political, military, and economic capabilities to shape the internal and external affairs of newly independent Arab states. This interference from external powers had profound implications for the sovereignty and self-determination of Arab countries as they sought to carve out their paths free from external coercion or manipulation.

The influence of global powers extended beyond political maneuvering, encompassing economic and developmental aid packages that, while ostensibly aimed at fostering stability and progress, often came with strings attached. Nations faced the dilemma of weighing the advantages of economic support against the potential loss of autonomy and decision-making power. Furthermore, the influx of arms sales and military engagements from foreign entities added another layer of complexity to nation-building and state consolidation. The repercussions of these strategic alliances and dependencies continue to reverberate through the socio-political fabric of Arab countries.

Moreover, the impact of global powers on Arab sovereignty transcended traditional diplomatic channels, permeating cultural, ideological, and social domains. Media, educational curricula, and cultural exchanges became battlegrounds for competing narratives and ideologies propagated by external actors, influencing the collective consciousness and sense of identity within Arab societies. This underscored the multifaceted nature of global influence, which was not limited to overt political interventions but encompassed a comprehensive spectrum of soft power tactics.

It is imperative to critically examine the lasting ramifications of this intense external involvement in Arab sovereignty as it shapes contemporary geopolitics and regional dynamics. Arab countries' experience is a testament to the enduring struggle for genuine autonomy in the face of formidable international pressures. By scrutinizing the historical context of global powers' influence, we gain valuable insights into the complexities of sovereignty, agency, and resilience within the ever-evolving tapestry of international relations.

## Assessment of Long-Term Outcomes of Decolonization

Decolonization was a pivotal turning point in history, marking the end of centuries of colonial rule and the emergence of independent nations. As we assess the long-term outcomes of decolonization, we must consider the multifaceted impacts on both the former colonizers and the newly liberated states. The process of decolonization had profound geopolitical, economic, social, and cultural ramifications that continue to shape international relations and regional dynamics to this day.

One key aspect of assessing the long-term outcomes of decolonization is the legacy of power structures left by former colonial rulers. While independence granted self-governance to many nations, the legacies of colonial borders, economic dependencies, and political systems have had lasting repercussions. These factors have often led to internal conflicts, ethnic tensions, and struggles for national identity, posing significant challenges to the stability and governance of newly independent states.

Economically, the impact of decolonization on the former colonial powers has been notable. Many colonial powers experienced shifts in trade patterns, resource access, and geopolitical influence due to losing their colonies. The need to adapt to a new global economic landscape and redefine their role in international affairs has propelled several former colonial powers, including France, to reassess their economic strategies and engagement with post-colonial states.

Furthermore, the long-term outcomes of decolonization have had enduring cultural and societal implications. The newfound independence brought with it a resurgence of national pride, efforts to reclaim cultural heritage, and the promotion of local languages and traditions. Simultaneously, it also prompted complex processes of nation-building, state formation, and the establishment of governing institutions, laying the groundwork for the evolving socio-political landscapes witnessed in the post-colonial era.

In Franco-Arab relations and the broader international community, the long-term outcomes of decolonization have contributed to reshaping diplomatic alliances, development partnerships, and cultural exchanges. This reconfiguration has resulted in an ever-evolving Franco-Arab relationship that continues to be influenced by the historical legacies and contemporary realities arising from the decolonization era.

As we critically assess the long-term outcomes of decolonization, it becomes evident that the process was not just a historical event but a transformative phenomenon with far-reaching and enduring effects. Recognizing the complexities and intricacies of these outcomes is essential for comprehensively understanding the evolution of global affairs and advancing mutually beneficial relationships between erstwhile colonizers and formerly colonized nations.

## IN A NUTSHELL

> The decolonization of Arab states from French rule in the 1960s and 1970s was a pivotal period that reshaped France's policies, ideologies, and relations with the Arab world. Here is an analysis of the key elements you requested:

## 1- The Impact of the Algerian War on French Policy

The Algerian War of Independence (1954-1962) was a watershed moment that profoundly impacted French policy and precipitated the decolonization process. The protracted and bloody conflict exposed the limitations of France's colonial ambitions and the unsustainability of its assimilation policies. The war's aftermath led to a reevaluation of France's strategic interests, with President Charles de Gaulle recognizing the need to grant Algeria independence through the Évian Accords of 1962. This marked a significant shift from France's previous stance of maintaining its colonial empire at all costs.

## 2- Shifts in French Political Ideology and Colonial Administration

The Algerian War and the broader decolonization movement catalyzed shifts in French political ideology and colonial administration. The conflict challenged the traditional Gaullist vision of a unified French empire and exposed the contradictions of the "civilizing mission" rhetoric. Intellectuals and policymakers grappled with the legacy of colonialism, leading to a fragmentation of the previously dominant Marxist consensus. This ideological shift paved the way for a more nuanced understanding of the complexities of colonial rule and the need for self-determination.

## 3- Case Studies: Morocco and Tunisia Gain Independence

Morocco and Tunisia were among the first Arab states to gain independence from France in the late 1950s. In Morocco, the nationalist Istiqlal party's sustained resistance and international pressure led to the restoration of Sultan Mohammed V and the signing of the La Celle-St-Cloud agreements in 1956, granting independence. Similarly, in Tunisia, the Neo Destour party's campaign, led by Habib Bourguiba, culminated in negotiations with France and full independence in 1956. These cases exemplified the growing momentum of Arab nationalism and the shifting power dynamics in the region.

## 4- Economic Implications of Independence for France

The loss of colonial territories had significant economic implications for France. The French economy had benefited from access to raw materials, markets, and labor from its colonies. Independence disrupted these economic ties, leading to challenges in sectors like agriculture, mining, and manufacturing. However, France also sought to maintain economic influence in the newly independent states through trade agreements, investment, and technical cooperation.

## 5- Legal and Diplomatic Frameworks Established Post-Independence

The transition to independence necessitated the establishment of new legal and diplomatic frameworks between France and the Arab states. Agreements like the Évian Accords with Algeria and the Franco-Tunisian Cooperation Treaty aimed to regulate issues such as citizenship, property rights, and economic relations. Diplomatic ties were also recalibrated, with France seeking to maintain influence in the region while respecting the sovereignty of the newly independent nations.

## 6- Cultural Transition and Identity Formation in Newly Independent States

Decolonization triggered a process of cultural transition and identity formation in the newly independent Arab states. These states grappled with the legacies of French cultural influence, language, and education systems. Efforts were made to assert national identities, promote Arab culture, and reconcile the colonial past with aspirations for modernity and development.

## 7- Franco-Arab Relations Post-Decolonization

In the post-decolonization era, France sought to cultivate a distinct policy towards the Arab world, positioning itself as a non-aligned power and an alternative to the superpowers. This approach, exemplified by de Gaulle's "Arab policy," aimed to maintain French influence and foster cooperation with Arab states on economic, cultural, and strategic fronts. However, tensions and challenges persisted, such as France's stance during the Arab-Israeli conflicts.

## 8- Influence of Global Powers on Arab Sovereignty

The decolonization process occurred within the broader context of the Cold War and the rivalry between the United States and the Soviet Union. The newly independent Arab states navigated these global power dynamics, seeking to assert their sovereignty while also aligning with one or the other superpower for economic and strategic reasons. This external influence shaped the political trajectories and alliances of the Arab states in the post-colonial era.

## 9- Assessment of Long-Term Outcomes of Decolonization

The long-term outcomes of decolonization in the Arab world were complex and multifaceted. While independence marked the end of direct colonial rule, the legacies of colonialism persisted in various forms, including economic dependencies, cultural influences, and unresolved territorial disputes. The process of nation-building and identity formation in the post-colonial states was often fraught with challenges, including internal conflicts, authoritarian tendencies, and the resurgence of religious and ethnic tensions. Nevertheless, decolonization also paved the way for greater self-determination, the assertion of Arab nationalism, and the pursuit of economic and social development agendas tailored to the needs of the newly independent states. In conclusion, the decolonization of Arab states from French rule was a transformative period that reshaped policies, ideologies, and relations between France and the Arab world. While the process was marked by challenges and complexities, it ultimately led to the emergence of independent Arab nations and a recalibration of France's role in the region

# References For Further Reading

Barrett, Roby. Tunisia, Algeria, and Morocco: Change, Instability, and Continuity in the Maghreb. JSOU Report 17-3. The JSOU Press. MacDill Air Force Base, Florida. 2017.https://www.jsou.edu/Home/OpenFile?path=https%3A%2F%2Fjsouapplicationstorage.blob.core.windows.net%2Fpress%2F114%2F17-3.pdf

"AP ® European History COURSE and EXAM DESCRIPTION Effective Fall 2017 INCLUDING: Course Framework with Contextual Information Instructional Section a Practice Exam," 2017. https://secure-media.collegeboard.org/digitalServices/pdf/ap/ap-european-history-course-and-exam-description.pdf.

Boniface, Pascal . "Beyond Islamophobia: France's Policies toward the Arab World." IRIS, December 22, 2020. https://www.iris-france.org/153125-beyond-islamophobia-frances-policies-toward-the-arab-world/.

Boughton, James M. "The IMF and the Silent Revolution." Imf.org, 2019. https://www.imf.org/external/pubs/ft/silent/index.htm.

Chabal, Emile. "French Political Culture in the 1970s." Geschichte Und Gesellschaft 42, no. 2 (June 1, 2016): 243–65. https://doi.org/10.13109/gege.2016.42.2.243.

———. "French Political Culture in the 1970s Liberalism, Identity Politics and the Modest State," 2016. https://emilechabal.com/files/frenchpolcult70s.pdf.

cvce.eu. "Independence for Morocco and Tunisia - Decolonisation: Geopolitical Issues and Impact on the European Integration Process - CVCE Website." Cvce.eu, 2019. https://www.cvce.eu/en/education/unit-content/-/unit/dd10d6bf-e14d-40b5-9ee6-37f978c87a01/2796f581-3e5a-4dff-9fbe-fd3d48966b38.

House, Jim. "The Colonial and Post-Colonial Dimensions of Algerian Migration to France, an Article from History in Focus." History.ac.uk, 2019. https://archives.history.ac.uk/history-in-focus/Migration/articles/house.html.

Johnson, Timothy Scott. "The Age of Fracture." Books & Ideas, December 7, 2015. https://booksandideas.net/The-Age-of-Fracture.

reviews.history.ac.uk. "Decolonization and the French of Algeria: Bringing the Settler Colony Home | Reviews in History," January 2017. https://reviews.history.ac.uk/review/2052.

Waine, Pierre Gilbert & Charlotte Vorms & translated by Oliver. "How the Algerian War Shaped French Cities." Metropolitics, March 21, 2012. https://metropolitics.org/How-the-Algerian-War-shaped-French.html.

# VI

# Economic Partnerships and Energy Interests (1970s-1990s)

## Introduction to Economic Partnerships

Economic partnerships between France and the states during the 1970s-1990s stemmed from a complex interplay of political, economic, and strategic motives. As the global dynamics were shifting post-decolonization, both France and the Arab states recognized the mutual benefits that could be derived from fostering solid economic ties. For France, seeking economic partnerships with Arab states was a means to offset its declining influence in its former colonies and a strategic move to gain access to vital energy resources, particularly oil and gas. Additionally, France aimed to position itself as a key player in the geopolitics of the Middle East and North Africa, leveraging economic cooperation to enhance diplomatic influence. On the other hand, Arab countries saw economic partnerships with France as an opportunity to diversify their trading relationships and accelerate economic development through access to French technology, expertise, and investment. The oil boom in the Arab world presented a lucrative opportunity for

France to engage in extensive trade and investment activities while simultaneously providing Arab states an avenue to invest their new-found wealth in the developed French economy. These economic partnerships were underpinned by the shared goal of fostering economic growth, stability, and prosperity, solidifying Franco-Arab relations during this crucial period.

## *The Evolution of Energy Dependencies*

As Franco-Arab relations evolved from the 1970s to the 1990s, a critical aspect of this transformation was the evolution of energy dependencies. This period marked a significant shift in global energy dynamics, with the Middle East and North Africa emerging as key players in the international energy landscape. In order to secure its energy needs, France entered into strategic partnerships with Arab countries to ensure a stable oil and natural gas supply. The rise in energy demand and geopolitical shifts propelled these partnerships to the forefront of Franco-Arab relations. These energy dependencies were crucial for powering the French economy and played a pivotal role in shaping diplomatic ties between France and the Arab world. The diversification of energy sources and the emergence of new regional energy players further complicated the dynamics of these dependencies. Amid these developments, France navigated intricate political landscapes, balancing its energy interests with broader geopolitical considerations. The complex interplay between energy, economics, and diplomacy during this period underscores the layered nature of Franco-Arab relations. Moreover, as global energy markets continued to evolve, technological advancements and shifting alliances added another dimension to this evolving narrative of energy dependencies. The 1970s and 1980s witnessed the impact of multiple oil crises on global energy markets, altering the calculus of energy cooperation between France and the Arab world. Furthermore, France's pursuit of nuclear energy collaborations with Arab states signified a strategic diversification of its energy portfolio, laying the groundwork for long-term partnerships in the nuclear sector. Concurrently, environmental concerns and sustainable energy initiatives began to influence the discourse on energy dependencies, prompting collaborative efforts to address the challenges of climate change and energy sustainability. Amidst the challenges and opportunities presented by evolving energy dependencies, the intricate tapestry of Franco-Arab relations continued to be shaped by the quest for energy security, economic interests, and geopolitical realities. Understanding the nuances of this evolution is fundamental to comprehending the multifaceted nature of Franco-Arab relations during this pivotal period.

## *Key Bilateral Trade Agreements*

Throughout the 1970s and 1980s, France actively pursued key bilateral trade agreements with numerous Arab countries to bolster economic cooperation and diversify its commercial ties. These agreements were essential in laying down the framework for mutually beneficial trade relationships, encompassing a wide array of industries such as energy, technology, infrastructure, and consumer goods. The primary focus was fostering long-term partnerships transcending mere buyer-seller dynamics, emphasizing sustainable development, investment growth, and knowledge exchange.

These agreements facilitated the flow of goods and services and paved the way for collaborative ventures in research and development, education, and cultural exchanges. They played a pivotal role in solidifying France's presence in the regional markets by setting up mechanisms for fair trade practices, tariff reductions, and investment protections. Furthermore, these pacts laid the groundwork for aligning regulatory standards and policies, thus streamlining the business environment and minimizing trade barriers.

The implementation of these bilateral trade agreements resonated far beyond economic spheres, contributing to the overall diplomatic relations between France and its Arab counterparts. By fostering interdependence and mutual benefit, they created an atmosphere of trust and cooperation that transcended geopolitical challenges and short-term economic fluctuations. They served as strategic tools for consolidating Franco-Arab ties and reinforcing a shared vision of prosperity and stability.

From a macroeconomic perspective, these agreements catalyzed a surge in cross-border investments, technology transfers, and knowledge sharing. They propelled the growth of traditional sectors like energy and infrastructure and laid the foundation for various nascent industries. France's commitment to nurturing these partnerships was underscored by its diplomacy-driven approach, which focused on engaging with Arab states as equal partners in progress rather than mere commodities in the global marketplace.

As the decade progressed, the growing importance of these bilateral trade agreements would significantly influence the course of Franco-Arab economic relations, setting the stage for the next phase of collaboration and co-development. The cumulative impact of these initiatives would redefine the economic landscape and lay the groundwork for enduring partnerships rooted in shared values, aspirations, and prosperity.

## *French Investments in Arab Oil and Gas Industries*

France, historically possessing a robust energy sector, sought to solidify its position as a key player in the Arab oil and gas industries during the 1970s to 1990s. The country's engagements centered on securing access to vital energy resources, fostering economic growth, and strengthening diplomatic ties with Arab states. French companies, supported by the government, embarked on strategic investments in the lucrative oil and gas sectors across the Arab world. These endeavors were characterized by joint ventures and partnerships with prominent state-owned entities, enabling France to secure stakes in major oil and gas fields and infrastructure projects. Notably, numerous French multinational corporations, leveraging their expertise in the energy domain, capitalized on opportunities to participate in exploration, production, refining, and distribution activities in Arab countries. Furthermore, the collaborations encompassed technological transfers, knowledge sharing, and capacity building, contributing to the modernization and optimization of the Arab energy sector. The investments made by France paved the way for substantial advancements in infrastructure development, technological innovation, and operational efficiency in the Arab oil and gas industries. Additionally, these ventures facilitated the exchange of best practices, regulatory frameworks, and industry standards, thereby fostering mutual growth and sustainability. It is imperative to acknowledge that the relationships forged through these investments transcended mere economic interests, laying the foundation for enduring Franco-Arab partnerships. Moreover, the synergies not only bolstered France's energy security but also facilitated the socioeconomic development of the host nations, aligning with the overarching goal of fostering mutual prosperity. While the French investments in Arab oil and gas industries reaped significant benefits, they also encountered challenges, ranging from geopolitical complexities and market fluctuations to environmental concerns and cultural nuances. Therefore, managing these investments necessitated astute navigation of multifaceted socio-political landscapes and dynamic market conditions. Looking ahead, the evolution of French investments in Arab oil and gas industries during this period is a testament to the enduring significance of energy partnerships in shaping bilateral relations and global energy dynamics.

## Development of Nuclear Energy Collaborations

The development of nuclear energy collaborations between France and Arab countries marked a pivotal shift in their economic partnerships during the 1970s and 1990s. As a global leader in nuclear technology, France sought to establish cooperative ventures with Arab countries to facilitate the development of nuclear energy programs. This collaborative effort aimed at addressing the growing energy demands in the region and diversifying the energy mix beyond reliance on fossil fuels. The establishment of nuclear energy collaborations paved the way for knowledge transfer, technical expertise exchange, and joint research and development initiatives. Additionally, it fostered diplomatic ties and served as a cornerstone for long-term economic cooperation. French expertise in nuclear technology contributed significantly to advancing peaceful nuclear programs in several Arab countries, promoting energy independence and sustainability. These collaborations also facilitated the training and education of local personnel, empowering them with the necessary skills to manage and operate nuclear facilities, thereby bolstering human capital in the energy sector. Furthermore, the proliferation of nuclear energy collaborations reinforced mutual trust and solidarity between France and Arab states, transcending traditional economic alliances and enriching the bilateral relationship. The strategic nature of these collaborations bore testament to the shared vision of harnessing technological advancements for the collective benefit of both parties. Despite geopolitical challenges and global uncertainties, the joint pursuit of nuclear energy initiatives demonstrated resilience and steadfast commitment to innovation and progress. As such, the development of nuclear energy collaborations stands as a testament to the enduring synergy between France and Arab countries in pioneering sustainable solutions for meeting the energy needs of the present and future generations.

## Impact of Global Oil Crises on Franco-Arab Relations

The global oil crises of the 1970s profoundly impacted the dynamics of Franco-Arab relations. The series of oil shocks, including the Arab oil embargo in 1973 and the Iranian Revolution in 1979, reshaped the economic and geopolitical landscape of the Middle East and beyond, profoundly affecting the relationship between France and the Arab world. These crises exposed the vulnerability of Western economies to disruptions in the oil supply and highlighted the strategic significance of the Arab oil-producing countries. This period witnessed a significant shift in power dynamics as the Arab states gained leverage and asserted influence over energy policies and international relations. In particular, the Organization of Arab Petroleum Exporting Countries (OAPEC) played a pivotal role in coordinating oil policies and exerting pressure on Western nations, including France. The oil crises led to a reevaluation of France's energy security and diversification strategies, prompting efforts to reduce dependence on Arab oil and explore alternative energy sources. Furthermore, the economic repercussions of the oil crises reverberated globally, fueling inflation, recession, and energy shortages in France and other Western countries. This economic turmoil strained diplomatic ties and trade relations between France and Arab oil-producing nations, underscoring the interconnectedness of energy and international politics. Despite the challenges the oil crises posed, they also renewed a renewed focus on dialogue and cooperation between France and the Arab world. Recognizing the mutual interdependence in the energy sector, both sides sought to mitigate potential disruptions and enhance stability through long-term partnerships and joint ventures. The experiences of navigating the oil crises fostered a deeper understanding of shared interests and the imperative of fostering sustainable energy initiatives. In sum, the global oil crises of the 1970s and 1980s left an indelible mark on Franco-Arab relations, prompting a reconfiguration of economic and energy strategies while highlighting the complex intersection of geopolitics, economics, and energy security.

## Diversification of Energy Sources and Sustainable Energy Initiatives

In the wake of the global oil crises and the growing concerns about environmental sustainability, France and Arab countries embarked on a journey towards diversifying their energy sources and embracing sustainable energy initiatives. The shift towards diversification was driven by the realization that overdependence on traditional fossil fuels posed significant economic and environmental risks. This marked a pivotal moment in Franco-Arab relations as both parties acknowledged the need to embrace cleaner and renewable energy sources. The collaborative efforts focused on exploring alternative energy solutions to reduce reliance on conventional oil and gas resources.

One of the central pillars of the diversification strategy was the emphasis on renewable energy technologies such as solar, wind, and hydroelectric power. France and Arab countries recognized the immense potential of these sustainable energy sources and initiated joint research and development projects to harness their benefits. This collaborative approach fostered technological innovation and strengthened bilateral ties through shared expertise and knowledge exchange.

Furthermore, sustainable energy initiatives were integrated into policy frameworks and strategic planning at both national and regional levels. This involved implementing regulatory measures, incentives for renewable energy investments, and establishing sustainable energy infrastructure. Adopting sustainable energy initiatives was underpinned by the mutual commitment to mitigating climate change effects and achieving energy security.

The collaboration between France and Arab countries in diversifying energy sources also extended to promoting energy efficiency and conservation measures. Both parties implemented comprehensive energy efficiency programs targeting various sectors, including transportation, industry, and residential areas. These initiatives aimed to optimize energy consumption, reduce carbon emissions, and enhance energy productivity, contributing to environmental sustainability and economic resilience.

As the 1970s progressed into the 1990s, the collective efforts in pursuing sustainable energy initiatives yielded tangible outcomes. Several successful pilot projects and commercial ventures in renewable energy were realized, signaling a shift towards a more diversified and environmentally conscious energy landscape. The Franco-Arab collaboration in this arena serves as a testament to the significance of sustainable energy as a catalyst for fostering long-term economic growth, environmental preservation, and international cooperation. Looking ahead, the commitment to diversifying energy sources and sustainable energy initiatives continues to be integral to the ongoing evolution of Franco-Arab relations, laying the groundwork for a more resilient and sustainable energy future.

## Economic Impact Assessment from the 1970s to the 1990s

During the 1970s and 1980s, Franco-Arab economic relations underwent significant transformations, primarily influenced by the global energy landscape and geopolitical shifts. This period saw an unprecedented increase in energy demands, particularly for oil and gas, which had profound implications for France and the Arab world. The two decades were marked by fluctuating oil prices and subsequent energy crises, shaping the dynamics of their economic partnerships. The Arab oil embargo of 1973, in response to Western support for Israel during the Yom Kippur War, caused a seismic shock in global energy markets. As a result, France, heavily reliant on Middle Eastern oil, faced economic repercussions and energy insecurities, prompting intensified diplomatic measures to stabilize energy supplies. Furthermore, the Iran-Iraq War in the 1980s led to further disruptions in oil markets, posing challenges for sustained economic growth and energy security across Franco-Arab relations. French engagement with Arab countries expanded beyond energy to encompass infrastructure development, arms exports, and diverse investments. Diversifying economic ties aimed to reduce dependency on volatile energy markets and foster mutually beneficial economic growth. These developments not only impacted France's economic landscape but also played a crucial role in shaping the political and social stability of Arab countries. Moreover, the 1970s and 1980s witnessed the evolution of sustainable energy initiatives, as both France and Arab countries recognized the imperative of mitigating environmental impacts and promoting renewable energy sources. The intensifying focus on sustainable energy marked a pivotal shift in the economic cooperation between France and the Arab world, laying the groundwork for long-term collaboration in environmental sustainability and technological innovation. In hindsight, the economic impact assessment from the 1970s to the 1990s showcases the intricate interplay of geopolitical, economic, and environmental factors that continue to shape the enduring Franco-Arab relations, setting the stage for future strategic partnerships and collaborations.

## *Challenges and Controversies*

The period spanning the 1970s to the 1990s was marked by a multitude of challenges and controversies within the scope of Franco-Arab economic partnerships and energy interests. One of the primary struggles stemmed from the fluctuating global oil market, with OPEC embarking on several oil crises that significantly impacted the economic landscape. The resulting price volatility and supply disruptions posed substantial challenges for both French and Arab economies, leading to strained diplomatic relations at times. Additionally, the era saw mounting concerns about environmental sustainability and the carbon footprint associated with traditional energy sources. This sparked debates surrounding the necessity of transitioning towards cleaner and renewable energy alternatives. Another pivotal controversy emerged from geopolitical tensions, especially within regional conflicts, which posed obstacles to seamless economic collaborations. Political instability in certain Arab countries created uncertainties for long-term investment and bilateral trade agreements, prompting discussions around risk mitigation strategies. Furthermore, the differing economic agendas and policy priorities between France and various Arab states often led to complex negotiations and disagreements. These divergences encompassed import-export regulations, investment incentives, and intellectual property rights, presenting hurdles in fostering harmonious economic partnerships. Moreover, cultural differences and varying business practices sometimes give rise to misunderstandings and friction in commercial dealings. Lastly, the contentious issue of energy security loomed large as both French and Arab stakeholders grappled with ensuring a stable and dependable energy supply amidst evolving geopolitical dynamics. The need to balance national interests with broader international commitments further complicated the landscape, leading to deliberations on energy diversification and strategic reserve management. As the global economic and political arenas underwent profound transformations, these challenges and controversies demanded astute navigation and proactive measures to safeguard the vitality of Franco-Arab economic partnerships and energy interests.

## *Future Outlook on Economic and Energy Partnerships*

The future outlook on economic and energy partnerships between France and the Arab world is influenced by a complex interplay of geopolitical, economic, and environmental factors. As we progress into the 21st century, several key trends are expected to shape the nature of these partnerships. Firstly, diversification of energy sources will be a pivotal focus for both France and Arab countries. With the increasing global emphasis on sustainable energy and the imperative to mitigate climate change, there is an evident shift towards renewable energy investments and technological collaborations. French expertise in nuclear energy and renewable technologies can significantly contribute to this transition, fostering a new era of cooperation. Secondly, as digitalization and innovation redefine industries, strategic alliances in technology and the digital economy are poised to emerge as a cornerstone of future economic partnerships. French leadership in sectors like aerospace, automotive, and digital infrastructure presents opportunities for collaboration with Arab counterparts to drive technological advancements and enhance competitiveness on a global scale. Additionally, the socio-economic dynamics, especially the aspirations of the youth population in Arab countries, will play a crucial role in shaping the nature of economic engagements. Initiatives focusing on education, entrepreneurship, and skills development can foster greater socio-economic integration, bolstering bilateral trade and investment. Moreover, France and Arab countries must address the evolving challenges related to geopolitical instability, migration flows, and security concerns. A forward-looking approach to addressing these complexities will enhance mutual trust and foster an environment conducive to sustainable economic and energy partnerships. Furthermore, aligning economic policies, regulatory frameworks, and institutional structures will play a vital role in creating an enabling environment for cross-border investments and business collaborations. Harmonizing standards and leveraging financial mechanisms that promote long-term sustainable development will be central to nurturing resilient economic ties. Lastly, the future outlook underscores the significance of fostering people-to-people contacts and cultural exchanges to strengthen the foundation of economic partnerships. Promoting intercultural dialogue, language training, and research collaborations will facilitate better understanding and create avenues for innovative cross-border initiatives. In essence, the future of economic and energy partnerships between France and the Arab world holds immense potential, provided that both parties are proactive in navigating emerging challenges and seizing opportunities underpinned by shared values and mutual respect.

## IN A NUTSHELL

> ***1970s energy crisis** Significant period of fuel shortages and economic stagnation*
>
> **Cause:** Triggered by the Yom Kippur War and Iranian Revolution, along with peak oil production in late 1960s to early 1970s.
> **Consequence:** Led to the first major shift towards energy-saving technologies and enduring economic stagnation.
> **Economic impact:** Induced economic recessions and compelled adjustments in local economies to boost efficiency in petroleum usage.
> **Resolution:** By the 1980s, recessions and efficiency improvements helped stabilize and then lower petroleum prices. **Beneficiaries** Petroleum-rich countries and oil-producing regions, like Texas and Alaska, saw economic booms.

The period from the 1970s to the 1990s witnessed a significant evolution in the economic and energy partnerships between France and the Arab countries, shaped by global events, strategic interests, and shifting dynamics. Here's a summary of the previous analysis:

### 1 - The Evolution of Energy Dependencies

During this period, France's energy dependency on Arab oil-producing nations grew substantially. In the aftermath of the 1973 oil crisis, France recognized the need to diversify its energy sources and reduce reliance on a single supplier. This led to increased imports of oil and gas from Arab countries, particularly Algeria, Saudi Arabia, and the Gulf states. By the 1990s, France had become a major importer of Arab energy resources, with the Arab world accounting for a significant portion of its energy supply.

## 2- Key Bilateral Trade Agreements

To facilitate economic cooperation and secure energy supplies, France pursued bilateral trade agreements with several Arab countries. Notable examples include the Franco-Algerian Cooperation Agreement (1983), which aimed to strengthen economic ties and energy partnerships, and the Franco-Saudi Al-Khafji Agreement (1989), which granted France a stake in the Al-Khafji oil field in Saudi Arabia.

## 3- French Investments in Arab Oil and Gas Industries

French energy companies, such as Total and Elf Aquitaine (later merged into TotalEnergies), actively invested in the Arab oil and gas industries during this period. Total, in particular, established a significant presence in the United Arab Emirates, Qatar, and Yemen, participating in exploration, production, and refining activities. These investments not only secured energy supplies for France but also generated substantial revenues and economic opportunities.

## 4- Development of Nuclear Energy Collaborations

France's expertise in nuclear energy technology led to

collaborations with several Arab countries interested in developing peaceful nuclear programs. In the 1970s, France signed nuclear cooperation agreements with Egypt, Iraq, and Libya, providing training, technical assistance, and the construction of research reactors. However, some of these partnerships faced challenges due to political instability and concerns over nuclear proliferation.

## 5- Impact of Global Oil Crises on Franco-Arab Relations

The 1973 and 1979 oil crises had a profound impact on Franco-Arab relations. While France initially maintained a neutral stance during the 1973 crisis, it later shifted towards a more pro-Arab position, seeking to strengthen ties with oil-producing nations. The crises highlighted France's vulnerability to energy disruptions and the need for diversification and cooperation with Arab partners.

## 6- Diversification of Energy Sources and Sustainable Energy Initiatives

In response to the oil crises and growing environmental concerns, France began exploring alternative energy sources and promoting sustainable energy initiatives. This included investments in nuclear power, which became a significant component of France's energy mix, as well as early efforts in renewable energy sources like solar and wind.

## 7- Economic Impact Assessment from the 1970s to the 1990s

The economic impact of Franco-Arab energy partnerships during this period was substantial. France benefited from secure energy supplies, which supported its industrial and economic growth. Arab countries, in turn, gained access to French technology, expertise, and investment opportunities. However, the oil crises and fluctuating energy prices also posed economic challenges, leading to periods of trade deficits and economic adjustments for France.

## 8- Challenges and Controversies

While the economic and energy partnerships between France and the Arab world yielded mutual benefits, they were not without challenges and controversies. Political instability in some Arab countries, concerns over nuclear proliferation, and human rights issues occasionally strained relations. Additionally, environmental and sustainability concerns surrounding fossil fuel exploitation emerged as growing issues towards the end of the 20th century.

## 9- Future Outlook on Economic and Energy Partnerships

Looking ahead, the future of Franco-Arab economic and energy partnerships will likely be shaped by the global transition towards renewable and sustainable energy sources. France's commitment to reducing its carbon footprint and promoting clean energy technologies may lead to a shift in its energy partnerships, with a greater emphasis on collaborations in areas such as solar, wind, and hydrogen. However, the long-standing economic ties and energy interdependencies between France and the Arab world suggest that these partnerships will continue to evolve and adapt to changing global dynamics and priorities. In conclusion, the period from the 1970s to the 1990s witnessed a deepening of economic and energy ties between France and the Arab world, driven by strategic interests, energy dependencies, and global events. While challenges and controversies arose, these partnerships played a significant role in shaping the economic and energy landscapes of both regions. As the world transitions towards a more sustainable energy future, the nature of these partnerships is likely to evolve, presenting both opportunities and challenges for continued cooperation and mutual benefit.

# References For Further Reading

France – National Pathway Toward Sustainable Food Systems.https://www.unfoodsystemshub.org/docs/unfoodsystemslibraries/national-pathways/france/2023-07-21--national-pathway-france--en.pdf?sfvrsn=6af74cd4_1

" France Report on Sustainable Development Goal Implementation".https://sustainabledevelopment.un.org/content/documents/10726Report%20SDGs%20France.pdf

Energy.Gov. "At COP28, U.S., Canada, France, Japan, and UK Announce Plans to Mobilize $4.2 Billion for Reliable Global Nuclear Energy Supply Chain". December 7, 2023. https://www.energy.gov/articles/cop28-us-canada-france-japan-and-uk-announce-plans-mobilize-42-billion-reliable-global

Arab News. "Saudi Arabia, France Sign MoU on Energy Cooperation," July 9, 2023. https://www.arabnews.com/node/2334546/business-economy

El-Naggar, Saíd. "2 Foreign and Intratrade Policies of the Arab Countries: The Basic Issues1." www.elibrary.imf.org. International Monetary Fund, December 15, 1992. https://www.elibrary.imf.org/display/book/9781557753052/C2.xml

Tommaso Cavina, ET. Al. "Five Key Action Areas to Put Europe's Energy Transition on a More Orderly Path | McKinsey." www.mckinsey.com, n.d. https://www.mckinsey.com/capabilities/sustainability/our-insights/five-key-action-areas-to-put-europes-energy-transition-on-a-more-orderly-path

European Parliamentary Research Service. "BRIEFING Energy Cooperation with Non-EU Countries," September 2023. https://www.europarl.europa.eu/RegData/etudes/BRIE/2023/753942/EPRS_BRI%282023%29753942_EN.pdf

IEA. "Energy Policy Review," 2021. https://iea.blob.core.windows.net/assets/7b3b4b9d-6db3-4dcf-a0a5-a9993d7dd1d6/France2021.pdf

International Trade Administration. "France - Energy (ENG)." www.trade.gov, October 12, 2021. https://www.trade.gov/country-commercial-guides/france-energy-eng

Schramm, Lucas. "The Neglected Integration Crisis: France, Germany and Lacking European Co-Operation during the 1973/1974 Oil Shock." Journal of Common Market Studies 62, no. 2 (July 9, 2023). https://doi.org/10.1111/jcms.13518

The French Ministry for the Armed Forces. "CLIMATE & DEFENCE STRATEGY," April 2022. https://www.defense.gouv.fr/sites/default/files/ministere-armees/Presentation%20Climate%20ans%20defence%20strategy.pdf

Valeria Jana Schwanitz, A. Wierling, Heather Jean, Constantin von Beck, Simon Dufner, Ingrid Knutsdotter Koren, Tobias Kraudzun, Timothy Marcroft, Lukas A Mueller, and Jan Pedro Zeiss. "Statistical Evidence for the Contribution of Citizen-Led Initiatives and Projects to the Energy Transition in Europe." Scientific Reports 13, no. 1 (March 2, 2023). https://doi.org/10.1038/s41598-023-28504-4

World Energy Council. "History of the World Energy Congress." Accessed May 19, 2024. https://www.worldenergy.org/experiences-events/world-energy-congress/history-of-the-world-energy-congress.world-nuclear.org

"Nuclear Power in France - World Nuclear Association," April 25, 2024. https://world-nuclear.org/information-library/country-profiles/countries-a-f/france.world-nuclear.org

"Nuclear Power in the United Arab Emirates - World Nuclear Association," April 2, 2024. https://world-nuclear.org/information-library/country-profiles/countries-t-z/united-arab-emirates

ENI. "Our Growth in Renewable Energy Production," n.d. https://www.eni.com/en-IT/actions/energy-sources/renewables.html.

# VII

# Cultural Diplomacy and Exchange Programs

## Introduction to Franco-Arab Cultural Exchange

Cultural interactions have long played a pivotal role in shaping the complex tapestry of Franco-Arab relations. These exchanges encompass a rich and diverse array of art, literature, language, history, cuisine, and traditions, connecting two civilizations with deep-rooted historical and contemporary ties. The significance of cultural diplomacy lies in its ability to foster mutual understanding, tolerance, and appreciation for each other's heritage, thus transcending political and geographical boundaries. The Franco-Arab cultural exchange serves as a vehicle for promoting intercultural dialogue, challenging stereotypes, and building enduring connections. It enables the exploration and celebration of shared values alongside acknowledging differences, leading to enriched perspectives and nuanced understandings between the French and Arab worlds. Moreover, it offers a platform for individuals to engage in meaningful cross-cultural experiences, nurturing empathy and goodwill at the heart of sustained bilateral relationships. This dynamic interplay of ideas and expressions has the power to transcend language barriers, nurturing bonds based on mutual respect and admiration. As France and the Arab world seek to navigate contemporary global challenges, cultural exchanges provide a fertile ground for cooperation and collaboration toward shared prosperity and peace. The historical resonance of cultural diplomacy initiatives underscores their transformative potential in contributing to a positive and enduring relationship between France and the Arab countries, setting the stage for exploring and harnessing the full spectrum of human creativity and expression.

## *Historical Overview of Cultural Diplomacy Initiatives*

The historical foundation of Franco-Arab cultural diplomacy initiatives can be traced back to the early interactions between France and Arab countries. From the medieval period, when Arabic scholars made significant contributions to various fields such as mathematics, astronomy, and medicine, to the Renaissance era, which witnessed a resurgence of interest in Islamic art and philosophy, cultural exchanges have played a crucial role in shaping the relationship between the two regions. In the modern context, the 19th and 20th centuries saw the formalization of cultural diplomacy efforts, with France establishing cultural centers, institutes, and alliances across the Arab world. These initiatives aimed to foster mutual understanding, celebrate diversity, and promote intellectual dialogue. Furthermore, historical events such as the French Protectorate in Morocco and Tunisia and the colonial rule in Algeria influenced the development of cultural ties and exchanges. Post-independence, efforts were made to redefine cultural relations more equal and respectful, leading to mutual collaborations in literature, arts, music, and education. The evolving landscape of Franco-Arab cultural diplomacy reflects a complex interplay of historical, political, and socio-economic factors, highlighting the enduring significance of cultural exchange in international relations. As both regions navigate shifting geopolitical dynamics, the historical overview serves as a valuable foundation for understanding the nuances and complexities of cultural diplomacy initiatives and their impact on fostering enduring ties between France and the Arab world.

## *Major Cultural Exchange Programs and Their Impact*

Cultural exchange programs between France and the Arab world have played a significant role in fostering mutual understanding, bridging cultural gaps, and promoting cross-cultural dialogue. These programs encompass various activities to deepen cultural ties and facilitate meaningful exchanges between artists, scholars, students, and professionals from both regions. One of the most impactful initiatives is the exchange of artistic performances and exhibitions, which provide a platform for showcasing the diversity and richness of French and Arab cultural heritage. These events celebrate artistic expression and serve as avenues for intercultural dialogue and collaboration. Furthermore, language exchange programs and cultural festivals have been instrumental in promoting linguistic proficiency and enhancing appreciation for each other's traditions. The impact of these initiatives goes beyond mere cultural appreciation; they contribute to the creation of people-to-people solid connections and foster lasting friendships. Educational exchange programs have also been pivotal in nurturing future leaders and building a global network of young professionals committed to bilateral cooperation and understanding. Through student exchange programs, scholarships, and joint research initiatives, French and Arab institutions have empowered countless individuals to immerse themselves in each other's academic environments, harnessing knowledge and expertise to address common challenges. Such intellectual exchange has yielded innovations in various fields, from science and technology to the humanities and social sciences. By leveraging cultural diplomacy, France and the Arab world have succeeded in building enduring relationships that transcend geographical boundaries, political differences, and historical complexities. As these programs continue to evolve, it is imperative to evaluate their impacts rigorously, identifying areas for improvement and ensuring that they remain relevant and responsive to the ever-changing dynamics of global cultural interaction.

## *Role of French Institutes in the Arab World*

French Institutes are pivotal in shaping cultural diplomacy and fostering mutual understanding between France and the Arab world. These institutes are bastions of French language education, academic collaboration, and cultural immersion, enriching the ties between the two regions. These institutions facilitate communication and encourage cross-cultural dialogue and knowledge sharing by promoting linguistic exchange through comprehensive language courses, translation workshops, and proficiency exams. Moreover, they provide a platform for Arab students to pursue higher education in France, creating a dynamic flow of intellectual capital and nurturing future leaders with a deep appreciation for Franco-Arab relations. The establishment of cultural centers and libraries by these institutes further signifies the commitment to preserving and promoting the rich heritage of both regions, fostering an environment conducive to scholarly exchange, research collaborations, and creative endeavors. In addition to academic pursuits, the institutes organize art exhibitions, film screenings, and performing arts events, showcasing the diversity and creativity of French and Arab cultures. This serves as a testament to the profound impact of artistic expressions in transcending societal boundaries and fostering intercultural understanding. Furthermore, the institutes often collaborate with local educational and cultural institutions, thus promoting a sense of shared heritage and collective cultural identity. Through their diverse programs and initiatives, the French Institutes in the Arab world actively contribute to cultivating a more interconnected and harmonious global community, where individuals from both realms can engage in meaningful dialogue, celebrate mutual respect, and work towards a more prosperous future.

## *Cinema and Arts as Tools for Cultural Dialogue*

Cinema and the arts are powerful mediums for fostering cultural understanding and dialogue between France and the Arab world. Film and art's visual and emotional impact transcends linguistic and cultural barriers, allowing for a deep exchange of ideas, values, and experiences. French and Arab filmmakers have collaborated on numerous projects that entertain audiences and provoke thoughtful discussions and reflections on shared human experiences. From thought-provoking documentaries to captivating feature films, the cinematic collaborations between France and the Arab world have opened windows into each other's cultures, histories, and societal intricacies. These films often catalyze meaningful conversations and enhance appreciation of cross-cultural diversity. Likewise, the world of visual arts has offered a platform for artists from both regions to express their unique perspectives, traditions, and contemporary realities through exhibitions, installations, and joint artistic endeavors. Using visual imagery, symbolism, and storytelling in art has enabled impactful connections between individuals from different backgrounds. French and Arab artists have utilized their creativity to dismantle stereotypes, challenge misconceptions, and celebrate the richness of their respective cultures. This artistic exchange serves as a bridge that connects people on a profound level, nurturing an environment of mutual respect and admiration. Furthermore, the collaborative production of theatrical performances, dance recitals, and musical compositions has provided opportunities for shared creative expression, promoting artistic unity and cooperation. These cultural manifestations are not merely forms of entertainment but also instrumental in promoting cross-cultural empathy, harmony, and cooperation. Through such collective artistic endeavors, both regions have enriched their social fabric, engendered mutual understanding, and cultivated enduring bonds built on mutual respect and creativity. As such, the convergence of cinema and the arts has significantly contributed to the multifaceted tapestry of Franco-Arab cultural diplomacy, playing a pivotal role in fostering enduring partnerships and nurturing a climate of meaningful intercultural exchange.

## *Literary Exchanges and Translation Projects*

Literary exchanges and translation projects are pivotal in fostering mutual understanding and appreciation between France and the Arab world. These endeavors serve as dynamic channels for transcultural dialogue, enhancing awareness of diverse literary traditions and enriching the cultural tapestry of both regions. The exchange of literary works and their translation amplifies authors' voices across borders and transcends language barriers to convey universal human experiences. Through meticulous translation projects, French and Arab literature is accessible to broader audiences, facilitating cross-cultural empathy and intercultural communication.

French-Arab literary exchange initiatives encompass various genres, including fiction, poetry, philosophy, and historical writings. Initiatives such as literary festivals, book fairs, and author residencies provide platforms for writers and intellectuals from both regions to engage in meaningful conversations, share perspectives, and immerse themselves in each other's literary landscapes. This encourages a deeper appreciation of cultural nuances and fosters collaborative creativity and the exploration of common themes that transcend geographical boundaries.

Translation projects form the cornerstone of literary diplomacy, enabling works of renowned French and Arab authors to reach audiences beyond their native languages. Translation grants and fellowships promote the transmutation of literary masterpieces, nurturing a global readership that can savor the distinct flavors of French and Arab literature. Whether it's an evocative Arabic poem reaching French readers or a compelling French novel captivating Arab audiences, the power of translated literature lies in its ability to bridge divergent cultural contexts and offer a panoramic view of the shared human experience.

Moreover, literary exchanges and translation projects contribute to dispelling cultural stereotypes and misconceptions, creating mutual platforms for intellectual exchange and introspection. By translating literary works, linguistic and cultural barriers are overcome, thus fostering an environment of inclusivity and mutual respect. As translators meticulously navigate the intricate nuances of language and culture, they enable audiences to embrace the richness and diversity of literary expressions from both realms, promoting cross-cultural harmony and appreciation.

In conclusion, literary exchanges and translation projects are enduring testaments to the profound connection between France and the Arab world. By facilitating the dissemination of literary treasures across linguistic and cultural boundaries, these initiatives ignite a symphony of cross-cultural dialogues and lay the foundation for enduring bonds of friendship and understanding.

## *Educational Initiatives and Scholarships*

Promoting educational initiatives and scholarships is a cornerstone in fostering enduring Franco-Arab relations. These programs catalyze cross-cultural understanding, academic collaboration, and human resource development. French institutions have actively engaged in the provision of scholarships to Arab students, thereby facilitating academic exchanges and nurturing future leaders in various fields. The scholarships offered by renowned French universities and academic institutions provide opportunities for Arab students to pursue higher education in France, gaining exposure to diverse academic disciplines and cultural experiences. These initiatives also extend to French language learning programs, enabling individuals from the Arab world to enhance their linguistic capabilities, thus further facilitating effective communication and mutual understanding. Furthermore, educational partnerships between France and Arab countries have resulted in joint research projects, academic conferences, and collaborative degree programs, enriching the intellectual landscape and promoting knowledge sharing. Such initiatives are pivotal in cultivating a cadre of professionals with a deep appreciation for French and Arab cultures, fostering a network of alumni who serve as ambassadors of goodwill and cooperation. Moreover, establishing cultural centers and exchange platforms has been vital in promoting academic dialogue and facilitating intellectual discourse between scholars, researchers, and students from France and the Arab world. These platforms have served as hubs for hosting academic events and spaces for cultural integration, encouraging intercultural dialogue and the exploration of shared values. Despite the success of these educational initiatives, challenges such as linguistic barriers, bureaucratic hurdles, and financial constraints pose obstacles to the optimal realization of these endeavors. Addressing these challenges requires sustained commitment from both French and Arab stakeholders to streamline administrative procedures, provide adequate support systems, and ensure equitable access to educational opportunities. These challenges can be mitigated through strategic collaboration and innovative approaches, paving the way for a more inclusive and dynamic educational landscape that fosters more robust ties between France and the Arab world. Educational initiatives and scholarships are potent tools for nurturing a generation of global citizens with the skills, knowledge, and cultural empathy needed to navigate an interconnected world.

## Challenges and Barriers to Cultural Engagement

Cultural engagement between France and the Arab world, while enriching and mutually beneficial, is not without its set of challenges and barriers. These obstacles often arise from differences in language, values, traditions, and societal norms, which can create misunderstandings and impediments to effective cultural exchange. Additionally, political tensions and historical conflicts may cast shadows over cultural initiatives, leading to reluctance or sensitivity in certain areas. One significant challenge is the need for a nuanced understanding of cultural sensitivities, as well-received actions or messages in one context may be misinterpreted in another. This calls for careful navigation and diplomacy to ensure that cultural engagements remain respectful and inclusive.

Moreover, logistical hurdles such as visa restrictions, bureaucratic complexities, and funding shortages can hinder the smooth implementation of cultural exchange programs. Finding the right balance between preserving cultural authenticity and introducing innovative elements poses another dilemma. While cultural exchange aims to promote appreciation and understanding, avoiding unintentional commodification or appropriation of cultural assets is essential.

Cultural engagement also faces barriers to reaching diverse audiences and ensuring equal participation across different social strata and regions. Differences in access to resources and infrastructure may result in unequal opportunities for individuals to benefit from cultural exchange, thus reinforcing existing disparities. The fast-evolving digital landscape and globalized media further complicate the landscape of cultural engagement, presenting both opportunities and challenges in shaping public perceptions and narratives. Moreover, resistance to change and sentiment toward preserving traditional values could impede the embrace of contemporary cultural expressions in some circles.

In addition to these intrinsic challenges, external factors, including geopolitical shifts, security threats, and economic instability, can significantly impact cultural engagement efforts. These multifaceted challenges require adept approaches, strategic collaborations, and continuous dialogue to foster an environment where cultural engagement can thrive despite obstacles. By addressing these challenges and breaking down barriers, meaningful and long-lasting cultural connections can be forged, ultimately reinforcing the foundations of Franco-Arab relations.

## Case Studies: Successful Bilateral Cultural Projects

In exploring successful bilateral cultural projects between France and the Arab world, it is imperative to delve into specific case studies that exemplify the positive impact of cultural diplomacy. One noteworthy endeavor is the Alliance Française network, which has been pivotal in promoting the French language and culture across various Arab countries. With its diverse language courses, cultural events, and resource centers, the Alliance Française has fostered cross-cultural understanding and dialogue, paving the way for fruitful arts, literature, and education exchanges.

Another compelling case study is the renowned Institut du Monde Arabe in Paris, a pioneering institution dedicated to showcasing the richness and diversity of Arab cultures. Through its exhibitions, symposiums, and educational programs, the institute has contributed significantly to the appreciation and recognition of Arab heritage in France, thus strengthening Franco-Arab cultural ties.

Furthermore, the success of collaborative artistic ventures cannot be overlooked. Establishing co-productions and cultural festivals such as the Franco-Arab Film Festival has proven instrumental in creating a platform for filmmakers and artists from both regions to collaborate and showcase their creative endeavors to diverse audiences. This fosters artistic exchange and enhances mutual understanding and appreciation of each other's cultural narratives.

Additionally, educational partnerships have yielded significant results in promoting cultural exchange. The establishment of joint academic initiatives and scholarship programs, such as the Erasmus+ program, has facilitated the mobility of students and professionals between

France and Arab countries, nurturing a generation of individuals with deep-rooted cross-cultural competencies.

Finally, heritage preservation and restoration projects are a testament to the enduring collaboration in cultural diplomacy. Joint efforts in preserving historical sites, artifacts, and traditions have bolstered cultural conservation and served as tangible expressions of mutual respect and appreciation for each other's heritage.

These case studies provide compelling evidence of the positive outcomes of bilateral cultural projects between France and the Arab world. They underscore the profound impact of cultural diplomacy in fostering enduring relationships, mutual respect, and intercultural dialogue while laying the groundwork for further collaborative endeavors that will continue to enrich the cultural landscape of both regions.

## *Looking Forward: Future Directions in Cultural Diplomacy*

In contemplating the future of Franco-Arab cultural diplomacy, it becomes imperative to envision the evolving landscape of cultural exchange and its potential impact on bilateral relations. With the advancement of technology and communication, a remarkable opportunity arises to leverage digital platforms for enhancing cross-cultural dialogues and promoting mutual understanding. Embracing innovative strategies in virtual art exhibitions, virtual reality experiences, and online educational collaborations can significantly broaden the scope of cultural diplomacy. Moreover, harnessing the power of social media and digital storytelling can amplify the reach and resonance of shared cultural narratives, fostering a sense of interconnectedness among diverse communities. Amidst the shifting geopolitical dynamics and socio-cultural transformations, there is a burgeoning need for culturally sensitive initiatives that transcend boundaries and resonate with contemporary audiences. Furthermore, the nascent field of environmental and sustainable cultural practices presents a promising avenue for future cultural diplomacy endeavors. By advocating for eco-friendly cultural exchange programs, such as sustainable art installations and green cultural events, France and Arab countries can forge enduring partnerships rooted in shared commitments to environmental stewardship. Collaborative efforts in preserving tangible and intangible cultural heritage also hold immense promise for consolidating cultural ties and nurturing cross-border solidarity. Emphasizing the preservation of archaeological sites, traditional crafts, and indigenous knowledge systems can engender a renewed appreciation for the richness of Franco-Arab cultural heritage, underscoring the intrinsic value of cultural diversity in an increasingly globalized world. Adopting an interdisciplinary approach by integrating cultural diplomacy into broader policy frameworks can enhance its efficacy and relevance in the contemporary era. By aligning cultural exchange initiatives with diplomatic priorities, development agendas, and peace-building strategies, France and Arab countries can synergize their efforts toward fostering inclusive and sustainable cultural dialogue. As the horizons of cultural diplomacy continue to expand, it is crucial to underscore the significance of youth engagement and intercultural education in shaping the future trajectory of Franco-Arab relations. Investing in youth-centered cultural exchange programs, cross-cultural mentorship opportunities, and collaborative research endeavors can nurture a new generation of global citizens equipped with the cultural competencies necessary to navigate complex global challenges. In essence, the future of cultural diplomacy between France and the Arab world hinges on cultivating a dynamic, inclusive, and forward-looking approach that transcends traditional paradigms and embraces the transformative potential of cultural interconnectedness.

## IN A NUTSHELL

> ### *Higher education in the Arab world*
> Non-compulsory, post-secondary education across 22 Arab states
>
> **Historical roots**
> Originating from ancient centers like Al-Azhar University in the 10th century, it reflects a rich history of intellectual exchange and cultural diffusion.
>
> **Geographical span**
> Covers countries across the Middle East and North Africa.
>
> **Early beginnings**
> Modern higher education traces back to colonial and missionary establishments in the early 19th century, initially catering to the upper class in major cities.
>
> **Challenges and opportunities**
> Faces issues such as quality assurance, accessibility, and brain drain while also seizing opportunities from globalization and technological advances.
>
> **Contemporary evaluation**
> Despite significant evolution and efforts to enhance access and gender equality, Arab universities often receive low rankings in global comparison.
>
> French cultural diplomacy and exchange programs with

Arab countries have played a significant role in fostering mutual understanding, promoting cultural dialogue, and strengthening bilateral relations. Here is an in-depth look at the various aspects of these initiatives:

## Historical Overview of Cultural Diplomacy Initiatives

French cultural diplomacy in the Arab world has a long history, dating back to the colonial era when France established cultural and educational institutions in its colonies. Post-independence, France continued to leverage cultural diplomacy to maintain influence and foster goodwill. The establishment of the Institut du Monde Arabe in Paris in 1980 is a notable example, serving as a hub for promoting Arab culture in France and facilitating cultural exchanges.

## Major Cultural Exchange Programs and Their Impact

Several cultural exchange programs have been instrumental in promoting cross-cultural understanding between France and Arab countries. Programs like the Arab Youth Volunteering for a Better Future and the Arab American National Museum's Global Fridays have brought together young people and artists from different Arab countries to work on community service projects and cultural events. These programs have helped to build networks, foster mutual respect, and enhance cultural appreciation.

## Role of French Institutes in the Arab World

French cultural institutes, such as the Institut Français, have been pivotal in promoting French culture and language in the Arab world. These institutes organize a wide range of activities, including language courses, cultural events, and academic exchanges. They serve as platforms for dialogue and collaboration, helping to bridge cultural gaps and promote French-Arab relations.

## Cinema and Arts as Tools for Cultural Dialogue

Cinema and the arts have been powerful tools for cultural dialogue between France and the Arab world. French film festivals often feature Arab films, and vice versa, providing a platform for showcasing diverse narratives and fostering understanding. Initiatives like the Louvre Abu Dhabi, a result of a diplomatic agreement between France and the UAE, exemplify how art can serve as a conduit for cultural exchange and dialogue.

## Literary Exchanges and Translation Projects

Literary exchanges and translation projects have been crucial in promoting Arab literature in France and vice versa. Programs like LEILA – Promoting Arabic Literature in Europe aim to enhance the visibility of contemporary Arab literature through translation and publication. UNESCO's translation programs have also played a significant role in facilitating the exchange of literary works between the Arab world and other regions.

## Educational Initiatives and Scholarships

Educational initiatives and scholarships have been key components of French cultural diplomacy. France offers numerous scholarships to Arab students, enabling them to pursue higher education in French institutions. These programs not only provide educational opportunities but also foster long-term cultural and academic ties. The shift towards English medium instruction (EMI) in some Arab countries, while maintaining French as a significant language of instruction, reflects the evolving dynamics of educational exchanges.

## Challenges and Barriers to Cultural Engagement

Despite the successes, there are challenges and barriers to cultural engagement between France and the Arab world. Political instability, cultural differences, and historical legacies of colonialism can sometimes hinder effective cultural diplomacy. Additionally, the lack of representation and inclusion of diverse voices from the Arab world in cultural exchanges remains a significant issue.

## Future Directions in Cultural Diplomacy

Looking ahead, the future of French cultural diplomacy in the Arab world will likely focus on enhancing mutual understanding and addressing contemporary global challenges. This includes promoting sustainable development through cultural initiatives, leveraging digital technologies for virtual cultural exchanges, and fostering inclusive and equitable cultural dialogues. Strengthening partnerships with local cultural institutions and supporting grassroots cultural initiatives will also be crucial for the continued success of cultural diplomacy efforts. In conclusion, French cultural diplomacy and exchange programs with the Arab world have made significant contributions to fostering mutual understanding and cultural dialogue. While challenges remain, the continued commitment to cultural engagement and the exploration of new avenues for collaboration hold promise for the future of Franco-Arab relations.

# *References For Further Reading*

Abbad, Kouider. "Cultural Manifestations in Literary Translation from Arabic into English and French the Case of the English and French Translations of Ahlem Mostaghanemi's Novel Thakirat Al-Jassad." Thesis (MA), 2016. https://spectrum.library.concordia.ca/id/eprint/982183/1/Kouider_MA%20_S2017.pdf.

Abdel Latif, Muhammad M. M., and Majed M. Alhamad. "Arabicization or Englishization of Higher Education in the Arab World? Controversies, Policies and Realities." Frontiers in Psychology 14 (February 15, 2023). https://doi.org/10.3389/fpsyg.2023.1093488.

Abozaid, Ahmed M. "The Politics of Teaching International Relations in the Arab World: A Critique." E-International Relations, May 20, 2021. https://www.e-ir.info/2021/05/20/the-politics-of-teaching-international-relations-in-the-arab-world-a-critique/.

ATLAS. "LEILA – Promoting Arabic Literature in Europe – ATLAS – Association Pour La Promotion de La Traduction Littéraire." Accessed May 19, 2024. https://www.atlas-citl.org/leila/.

Clarke, David. "Cultural Diplomacy." Oxford Research Encyclopedia of International Studies, November 19, 2020. https://doi.org/10.1093/acrefore/9780190846626.013.543.

Darraj, Faisal . "The Peculiar Destinies of Arab Modernity | Darat al Funun." daratalfunun.org, 2013. https://daratalfunun.org/?page_id=298.

FasterCapital. "Challenges Faced in Cultural Exchange Programs and How to Overcome Them," n.d. https://fastercapital.com/topics/challenges-faced-in-cultural-exchange-programs-and-how-to-overcome-them.html.

Fekri, Editors, Hassan -Aloisia De Trafford -Mohsen, and Youssef Foreword. "Cultural Heritage and Development in the Arab World," n.d. https://www.bibalex.org/arf/en/gra1106_df_20081102_book.pdf.

Hallaq, Dounya . "Double Interview with Sonja Hegasy and Jowe Harfouche." @GI_weltweit. Accessed May 19, 2024. https://www.goethe.de/ins/be/en/kul/eur/ela/23473233.html.

"OPEN METHOD of COORDINATION (OMC) WORKING GROUP of EU MEMBER STATES EXPERTS on the ROLE of PUBLIC ARTS and CULTURAL INSTITUTIONS in the PROMOTION of CULTURAL DIVERSITY and INTERCULTURAL DIALOGUE REPORT on the ROLE of PUBLIC ARTS and CULTURAL INSTITUTIONS in the PROMOTION of CULTURAL DIVERSITY and INTERCULTURAL DIALOGUE," 2014. https://ec.europa.eu/assets/eac/culture/library/reports/201405-omc-diversity-dialogue_en.pdf.

Roig-Sanz, Diana, and Reine Meylaerts. "General Introduction. Literary Translation and Cultural Mediators. Toward an Agent and Process-Oriented Approach." Springer EBooks, January 1, 2018, 1–37. https://doi.org/10.1007/978-3-319-78114-3_1.

Sapiro, Gisèle. "The Transnational Literary Field between (Inter)-Nationalism and Cosmopolitanism." Journal of World Literature 5, no. 4 (November 4, 2020): 481–504. https://doi.org/10.1163/24056480-00504002.

Sekinat Adejoke Kola-Aderoju. "The Muslim World and the Development of Science and Technology: Phase in History." South Florida Journal of Development 4, no. 2 (April 20, 2023): 737–54. https://doi.org/10.46932/sfjdv4n2-009.

UNESCO. "Cutting Edge | from Standing out to Reaching Out: Cultural Diplomacy for Sustainable Development | UNESCO." www.unesco.org, January 27, 2022. https://www.unesco.org/en/articles/cutting-edge-standing-out-reaching-out-cultural-diplomacy-sustainable-development.

Unesco.org. "The Arabic Language in UNESCO Translation Programs," 2023. https://www.unesco.org/en/articles/arabic-language-unesco-translation-programs.

Van De Peer, Stefanie. "Seascapes of Solidarity." Edited by Stephanie Hemelryk

Donald, Kaya Davies Hayon, and Lucia Sorbera. Alphaville: Journal of Film and Screen Media, no. 18 (December 1, 2019): 38–53. https://doi.org/10.33178/alpha.18.04.

# VIII

# France and the Gulf States

## Historical Overview of Franco-Gulf Relations

The diplomatic relations between France and the Gulf States have evolved significantly since the aftermath of World War II. Initially, France sought to establish trade partnerships and political ties with the Gulf region as it emerged as a critical player in the global energy market. In the 1950s and 1960s, France actively engaged with the Gulf monarchies, mainly focusing on energy cooperation and strategic alliances. Significant milestones in these early years included the establishment of diplomatic missions, trade agreements, and discussions on regional security. The oil embargo of 1973 further underscored the importance of Gulf countries for France's energy security, leading to intensified diplomatic efforts and increased economic collaboration. Notable high-level visits from French officials to the Gulf States during this period strengthened bilateral relations and laid the groundwork for future cooperation. Over the years, the relationship expanded beyond economic interests to encompass broader strategic goals, including defense cooperation and cultural exchanges.

The late 20th century saw a significant intensification of diplomatic engagements characterized by enhanced military partnerships and technological collaborations. France became a key supplier of defense equipment and technology to Gulf countries, reflecting the deepening strategic alignment between the two sides. As the Gulf States diversified their economies beyond oil, France also extended its support in areas such as infrastructure development, renewable energy, and education. These developments further cemented the multidimensional nature of Franco-Gulf relations.

In recent decades, France has continued to prioritize its ties with the Gulf amid evolving geopolitical dynamics. The establishment of strategic dialogues and mutual defense agreements has underscored the parties' shared strategic interests and concerns. High-profile visits by French leaders and members of the Gulf royal families have played a crucial role in nurturing these relationships and exploring avenues for enhanced collaboration. Through these exchanges and dialogue mechanisms, both parties have worked towards achieving common objectives related to security, counterterrorism, and regional stability.

The historical overview demonstrates the evolution of Franco-Gulf relations from an initial focus on energy cooperation to a comprehensive partnership encompassing political, economic, and strategic dimensions. It underscores the strategic significance of the Gulf region for France and the depth of the multifaceted engagement between the two.

## *Political Alliances and Strategic Interests*

France has historically maintained strong political alliances with the Gulf States, leveraging its diplomatic prowess to navigate complex regional dynamics. These alliances' strategic interests are multifaceted, reflecting a confluence of geopolitical, security, and economic considerations. The Gulf region is strategically vital for France due to its vast energy resources, maritime trade routes, and pivotal role in global affairs. This has led to enduring partnerships built on mutual respect, shared values, and common strategic objectives. From a geopolitical perspective, France's commitment to ensuring stability and security in the Gulf aligns with its broader foreign policy agenda. The volatile nature of the Middle East underscores the imperative of cultivating political alliances that can serve as pillars of stability in the region. As such, France has actively engaged in diplomatic dialogues, mediations, and peace efforts to foster cooperation and mitigate conflicts. Additionally, the Gulf States' geopolitical positioning has facilitated collaborative endeavors aimed at curtailing transnational security threats, including terrorism, extremism, and arms proliferation. This convergence of strategic interests has culminated in joint military exercises, intelligence sharing, and defense agreements to bolster the collective security architecture. On an economic front, political alliances have unlocked opportunities for Franco-Gulf cooperation in diverse sectors, including infrastructure development, technological innovation, and investment ventures. Furthermore, France's alignment with the Gulf States on matters of international significance, such as climate change, sustainable development goals, and human rights advocacy, speaks to the depth of its political commitments. As the geopolitical landscape continues to evolve, France remains steadfast in nurturing its political alliances and advancing its strategic interests in the Gulf, cognizant of the ever-changing dynamics and the imperative of adaptability in diplomacy.

## *Economic Ties and Trade Agreements*

France has a longstanding and multifaceted economic relationship with the Gulf States, characterized by trade agreements, investment flows, and collaborative ventures. The economic ties between France and the Gulf States have evolved significantly, particularly in energy, infrastructure, finance, and technology. This chapter delves into the intricate web of economic interactions, shedding light on the key elements that have shaped the economic landscape between these partners.

The Gulf States, endowed with vast oil and natural gas reserves, have driven economic collaboration with France. The strategic significance of the Gulf region as an energy powerhouse has led to extensive trade agreements, enabling France to secure a consistent supply of energy resources while contributing to the development of Gulf economies. Furthermore, French companies have played instrumental roles in the diversification efforts of Gulf economies, engaging in large-scale infrastructure projects, including transportation, urban development, and sustainable energy initiatives. These partnerships have bolstered economic growth in the Gulf and provided lucrative opportunities for French businesses, propelling innovation and knowledge exchange. On the trade front, France has been a key trading partner for the Gulf States, with bilateral trade volumes witnessing steady growth. Trade agreements have facilitated the exchange of goods and services, fostering economic interdependence and collaboration. France's expertise in aerospace, defense, and luxury goods has also resulted in fruitful trade relations, further strengthening the economic bonds between the two parties. Moreover, developing free and special economic zones in the Gulf has encouraged French businesses to establish a robust presence, promoting commerce and investment. As the Gulf States strive to diversify their economies, France has emerged as a strategic partner in critical sectors, providing the necessary expertise and technological advancements. The economic ties between France and the Gulf States underscore a mutually beneficial partnership that continues to thrive, contributing to both entities' economic prosperity and resilience.

## *Military Cooperation and Arms Deals*

France's engagement with the Gulf States in military cooperation and arms deals has been a crucial component of their bilateral relations. The strategic alignment between France and the Gulf countries has led to significant defense partnerships characterized by the sale of advanced weapons systems, joint military exercises, and security cooperation initiatives. The region's geopolitical dynamics have played a pivotal role in shaping the nature of these military collaborations, with both France and the Gulf States recognizing the importance of enhancing their defense capabilities and addressing regional security challenges. The French government has actively sought to bolster its ties with Gulf nations by providing cutting-edge defense technologies, including fighter jets, naval vessels, and missile defense systems. In return, the Gulf States have demonstrated a keen interest in acquiring French military equipment to modernize their armed forces and reinforce their defense posture. Moreover, the mutual commitment to counterterrorism efforts and maritime security has facilitated extensive collaboration in intelligence sharing, training programs, and defense infrastructure development. Beyond arms sales, joint military exercises and training missions have served as instrumental platforms for enhancing interoperability and strengthening military-to-military relationships. The exchange of expertise in cybersecurity, reconnaissance, and asymmetrical warfare has further deepened the levels of cooperation between France and its Gulf counterparts. However, it is essential to acknowledge that the military cooperation and arms deals between France and the Gulf States have not been without controversy. Criticisms surrounding human rights issues, the potential impact on regional stability, and concerns about the escalation of conflicts have raised ethical and geopolitical considerations. As such, the intricate balance between defense collaboration and broader diplomatic objectives remains an ongoing debate. The trajectory of military cooperation and arms deals will continue to shape the strategic landscape of Franco-Gulf relations, influencing both regional security dynamics and global defense industries.

## *Energy Partnerships and Nuclear Developments*

France has established significant energy partnerships with the Gulf States, leveraging its nuclear technology and renewable energy expertise to foster bilateral cooperation. The Gulf States, endowed with vast hydrocarbon resources, have sought diversification of their energy mix and have turned to France for collaboration in nuclear power development. The United Arab Emirates (UAE) is a key partner, initiating the Barakah nuclear power plant project in cooperation with French companies such as EDF and Areva. This landmark venture reflects the mutual commitment of France and the UAE to sustainable energy solutions and underscores the significance of their strategic partnership. Additionally, France has provided expertise and technological support for developing nuclear power infrastructure in other Gulf nations, contributing to the region's energy security and economic development. Moreover, exchanging knowledge and best practices in renewable energy has been a focal point of cooperation between France and the Gulf States. As part of a broader effort to promote sustainable energy sources, France has facilitated cross-country dialogues and joint initiatives to harness the region's solar and wind power potential. This collaborative approach not only addresses the growing energy demands of the Gulf States but also aligns with global efforts to mitigate climate change and reduce carbon emissions. Furthermore, the emphasis on energy partnerships has led to establishing research and development collaborations, paving the way for innovation in clean energy technologies and enhancing the overall resilience of the Gulf States' energy infrastructure. In light of these developments, it is evident that France's involvement in energy partnerships and nuclear developments with the Gulf States has contributed to long-term sustainable growth and strengthened the strategic ties between the parties.

## *Cultural Exchanges and Influence*

The cultural exchanges between France and the Gulf States have significantly contributed to both societies' mutual understanding and enrichment. French art, literature, cinema, and cuisine have profoundly impacted the Gulf's cultural landscape, while Gulf culture has also found its way into contemporary French society. Cultural diplomacy has played a pivotal role in fostering these exchanges, with initiatives such as art exhibitions, film festivals, and music performances facilitating the interaction between the two regions.

French educational and cultural institutions have been instrumental in promoting the French language and culture in the Gulf. Alliance Française branches, French schools, and universities have provided platforms for cross-cultural dialogue, language learning, and artistic collaborations. These institutions serve as hubs for knowledge exchange and foster intellectual and artistic connections that transcend geographical boundaries.

The influence of Gulf patronage on France's arts and cultural heritage sector cannot be overlooked. Investments from Gulf patrons have supported the restoration of historical monuments, the establishment of museums, and the promotion of traditional arts and crafts in France. This cultural philanthropy has not only preserved cultural heritage but has also facilitated intercultural dialogue and understanding.

Moreover, the growing tourism between France and the Gulf States has contributed to the exchange of cultural experiences. French tourists exploring the modern architecture and vibrant urban life of cities like Dubai and Doha are exposed to the rich traditions and hospitality of the Gulf. Conversely, the picturesque landscapes of France, its renowned museums and art galleries, and its rich history offer Gulf visitors a glimpse into the diverse cultural tapestry of France.

Additionally, the media and the digital sphere have become influential channels for cultural exchange. Collaboration between French and Gulf media outlets and the proliferation of digital content has enabled the dissemination of cultural productions, artistic expressions, and intellectual discourses across borders, fostering an ongoing conversation between the two regions.

The impact of these cultural exchanges extends beyond mere appreciation of art and traditions. They have nurtured an environment where mutual respect, curiosity, and creativity flourish, laying the foundation for enduring partnerships and greater global harmony. As

France and the Gulf States engage in cultural dialogue, the potential for deeper understanding and collaboration across various domains continues to evolve, promising a more interconnected and culturally enriched future.

## French Expatriates and Community Dynamics

The French expatriate community in the Gulf States represents a diverse and influential group that has contributed significantly to the region's cultural, economic, and social fabric. Comprising professionals from various industries, including finance, education, healthcare, and hospitality, the French expatriates have established thriving communities across the Gulf countries. These communities serve as hubs for cultural exchange, knowledge sharing, and networking opportunities, fostering a dynamic personal and professional growth environment. The French expatriates play an instrumental role in promoting cross-cultural understanding and enhancing bilateral relations between France and the Gulf States.

One notable aspect of the French expatriate community is its active involvement in promoting educational and cultural initiatives. French schools, cultural centers, and language institutes have been established in the Gulf States, offering quality education and enriching programs that promote the French language, arts, and traditions. This provides valuable educational opportunities for expatriates and their families and contributes to the host countries' overall cultural landscape. The French expatriates actively engage with local communities through these institutions, creating bridges of understanding and mutual respect.

Moreover, the French expatriate community serves as a platform for fostering business connections and economic partnerships between France and the Gulf States. Many French expatriates hold critical positions in multinational corporations, financial institutions, and entrepreneurial ventures, contributing to the growth and diversification of the Gulf economies. Their expertise, innovation, and international perspective add value to the business environment while facilitating trade and investment opportunities between France and the Gulf region. French expatriates often participate in industry-specific forums, networking events, and collaborative projects, further strengthening the economic ties between the two regions.

In addition to their professional endeavors, the French expatriates actively engage in philanthropic and community development initiatives, demonstrating a commitment to corporate social responsibility and sustainable development. Whether through charitable organizations, environmental conservation efforts, or volunteering activities, the French expatriate community continuously seeks to positively impact the local society, contributing to the overall well-being and prosperity of the Gulf States.

Despite the myriad contributions of the French expatriate community, challenges and adjustments are inherent to expatriate life, including navigating cultural differences, adapting to local regulations, and addressing the needs of a diverse community. This necessitates ongoing dialogue and collaboration between the expatriate community, local authorities, and diplomatic representatives to address concerns and enhance the expatriate experience. By fostering a spirit of inclusivity, mutual respect, and cooperation, the French expatriates play a pivotal role in shaping the dynamic tapestry of Franco-Gulf relations, embodying the enduring partnership between France and the Gulf States.

## *Human Rights Discussions and Controversies*

In Franco-Gulf relations, human rights discourse has been a complex and multifaceted issue. The Gulf States have faced criticism and scrutiny from various international organizations and advocacy groups regarding their human rights records. This has posed challenges for France in navigating its diplomatic ties with these nations while upholding its principles on human rights. From concerns over restrictions on freedom of speech and expression to issues related to labor rights and the treatment of migrant workers, the Gulf region has been under the global spotlight for its human rights practices. French expatriates living in the Gulf States have also raised concerns about their rights and protections, sometimes leading to diplomatic tensions. Moreover, as the Gulf economies have grown, there have been debates about the impact of economic development on human rights standards. France's stance on human rights in the Gulf States has been a delicate balancing act, aiming to address these concerns while maintaining constructive dialogue and cooperation. However, this approach has also faced its share of criticisms, with some arguing that commercial interests have overridden human rights considerations. The controversies surrounding the sale of arms and military equipment to Gulf countries have intensified the debate on France's ethical responsibilities in its trade relationships. The intricate interplay between geopolitical interests, economic partnerships, and human rights advocacy continues to shape the discourse on Franco-Gulf relations. As France and the Gulf States seek to strengthen their strategic alliances and mutual benefits, reconciling human rights discussions and controversies remains an ongoing challenge. Addressing these complex issues requires a nuanced understanding of the region's cultural, political, and economic dynamics, along with a commitment to fostering constructive dialogues and promoting universal human rights standards.

## *Challenges and Criticisms of Bilateral Relations*

In examining the bilateral relations between France and the Gulf States, it is essential to acknowledge the numerous challenges and criticisms that have emerged over the years. One of the primary areas of contention revolves around human rights issues. France's cooperation with the Gulf States has come under scrutiny due to concerns regarding political freedoms, the treatment of migrant workers, and the status of women in these societies. These contentious issues have generated debates within French society and the international community, leading to criticisms of France's approach to diplomacy with the Gulf region. Additionally, the perceived lack of transparency in specific arms deals and military cooperation agreements between France and the Gulf States has raised questions about such partnerships' ethical considerations and potential consequences. Furthermore, economic dependencies and trade imbalances have been a point of contention, with critics pointing to the potential impact on France's autonomy in foreign policy and the risk of being overly influenced by the economic power of the Gulf States. The challenges also extend to cultural exchanges and the influence of Gulf-based organizations and individuals, with concerns about attempts to shape French narratives and policies through soft power initiatives. Moreover, environmental and sustainability issues have been a source of criticism, particularly concerning energy partnerships and the ecological impact of joint ventures. These challenges pose significant dilemmas for policymakers and diplomats, requiring careful navigation to foster constructive relationships while addressing valid criticisms and concerns. Despite these hurdles, it is imperative to recognize that bilateral relations are dynamic and subject to continuous evolution. As such, the prospects for Franco-Gulf cooperation offer opportunities to address these challenges and criticisms through strategic dialogue, mutual understanding, and the pursuit of common goals. By engaging in transparent discussions, fostering respect for human rights, promoting sustainable practices, and seeking to achieve a balanced and mutually beneficial partnership, France and the Gulf States can work towards mitigating the criticisms and overcoming the challenges that have arisen in their bilateral relations.

## *Future Prospects in Franco-Gulf Cooperation*

As Franco-Gulf cooperation enters a new era, its future prospects are marked by both opportunities and challenges. The evolving geopolitical landscape, changing economic dynamics, and shifting global priorities will likely shape the nature of engagement between France and the Gulf states in the coming years.

One key aspect of future cooperation is security and defense. With the rising threats of regional instability and non-state actors, there is a growing imperative for enhanced security collaboration between France and the Gulf states. This could involve joint military exercises, intelligence sharing, and strategic dialogues to address common security concerns and counter emerging threats in the region.

Moreover, as technological advancements continue to reshape the global economy, there is immense potential for deeper collaboration in innovation and technology between France and the Gulf states. From renewable energy initiatives to digital infrastructure development, leveraging each other's strengths in research and development can pave the way for a mutually beneficial partnership that drives sustainable growth and progress in diverse sectors.

In addition, economic diversification efforts in the Gulf states present an opportune arena for increased trade and investment ties with France. As these countries seek to reduce their reliance on oil revenue and expand their economic horizons, France's expertise in various industries, such as aerospace, healthcare, and luxury goods, can contribute significantly to the diversification goals of the Gulf economies. Strengthening economic cooperation will foster prosperity and reinforce the interconnectedness of both regions' markets.

Cultural exchange and people-to-people ties are another promising avenue for strengthening Franco-Gulf cooperation in the future. Facilitating student exchanges, promoting cultural festivals, and encouraging tourism can foster greater mutual understanding and appreciation between the societies, laying the groundwork for enduring partnerships across multiple domains.

However, despite the promising outlook, some challenges must be navigated as part of the prospects. Geopolitical complexities, regional rivalries, and differing policy priorities may obstruct seamless cooperation. Moreover, navigating human rights considerations and addressing social issues will require delicate diplomacy and a commitment to shared values.

In conclusion, the future of Franco-Gulf cooperation holds immense promise, provided both sides demonstrate a shared willingness to innovate, adapt, and collaborate in addressing emerging opportunities and challenges. By leveraging their strengths and synergizing their efforts, France and the Gulf states can forge a resilient and forward-looking partnership that contributes to regional stability, economic prosperity, and mutual advancement.

# IN A NUTSHELL

## 1. Historical Overview of Franco-Gulf Relations

France has maintained longstanding relations with the Gulf states, dating back to the 19th century when it sought to expand its influence in the region. However, ties strengthened significantly after the Gulf nations gained independence in the 1960s and 1970s. Key milestones include:

- 1995: France signed a defense agreement with the UAE, allowing for military intervention if the UAE is threatened.
- 2009: France established its first permanent military base in the Gulf region, the French Naval Base in Abu Dhabi, UAE.
- 2007: France announced a strategic partnership with the UAE.

France has traditionally viewed the Gulf as a region of strategic importance due to its energy resources, trade routes, and geopolitical position. It has aimed to project influence and secure economic and security interests in the area.

## 2. Political Alliances and Strategic Interests

France and the Gulf Cooperation Council (GCC) states share common concerns over regional security issues like terrorism, political Islam, and Iranian influence. This has driven closer political coordination and strategic partnerships, especially with the UAE and Saudi Arabia.

France sees the UAE as a key partner in confronting regional threats and has backed the UAE's interventions in Libya and Yemen. It has also supported the Saudi-led coalition's operations in Yemen despite human rights criticisms.

Both sides view their partnership as a way to counterbalance other powers like Turkey, Iran, and political Islam movements in the region. France aims to maintain its influence amid a perceived US disengagement from the Middle East.

## 3. Economic Ties and Trade Agreements

Economic cooperation is a cornerstone of Franco-Gulf relations. Key aspects include:

- Trade: France is a major trade partner, with non-oil trade with the UAE reaching $7.5 billion in 2019. Saudi Arabia is also an important trade partner for France.
- Investment: The UAE and France have signed agreements to boost bilateral investment, including a $19

billion investment partnership in 2021. Major UAE sovereign wealth funds have invested substantially in French companies and sectors like technology and renewable energy.
- Business: Over 600 French companies operate in the UAE, while around 50 Emirati firms have invested in France. The two countries launched a joint business council in 2023 to facilitate economic cooperation.

## 4. Military Cooperation and Arms Deals

Defense cooperation is extensive, with France being a major arms supplier to Gulf states like the UAE and Saudi Arabia. Notable deals include:

- 2021: UAE signed contracts worth €16 billion for 80 Rafale jets, 12 helicopters and armaments from France.
- 2015: Egypt purchased 24 Rafale jets, a frigate and missiles from France in deals worth billions.
- 2014: Saudi Arabia purchased 4 corvettes from France.

France argues these arms sales support its strategic partnerships and influence in the region. However, human rights groups have criticized weapons transfers given the Gulf states' involvement in conflicts like Yemen.

## 5. Energy Partnerships and Nuclear Developments

Energy cooperation is a major focus given France's interests in securing supplies and the Gulf's role as an energy hub. Key areas include:

- 2022: France and UAE established a Comprehensive Strategic Energy Partnership to cooperate across sectors like oil/gas, renewables and nuclear energy.
- Nuclear: France has supported the UAE's nuclear energy program, including providing technology, fuel and training. It has praised the UAE's Barakah nuclear plant.
- Renewables: French firms like EDF are involved in major renewable energy projects in the Gulf, such as the Mohammed bin Rashid Al Maktoum Solar Park in Dubai.

The two sides aim to develop partnerships in emerging areas like hydrogen, carbon capture and marine energy research.

## 6. Cultural Exchanges and Influence

Cultural ties are an important aspect, with France aiming to promote its language, education and cultural influence in the Gulf through initiatives like:

- The Louvre Abu Dhabi Museum, a major cultural project opened in 2017 with French expertise and content.
- The Paris-Sorbonne University in Abu Dhabi was established in 2006.
- Archaeological missions, French schools and language institutes across the Gulf states.
- Restoration projects like the Chateau de Fontainebleau are funded by the UAE.

France sees cultural outreach as a way to build long-term partnerships and project its soft power in the region.

## 7. French Expatriates and Community Dynamics

There are sizable French expatriate communities in the Gulf, especially in the UAE where over 30,000 French nationals reside. Their presence is linked to the economic, educational and cultural cooperation between France and the Gulf states.

However, community dynamics and rights issues have occasionally caused friction, such as controversies over French opposition figures operating in the Gulf or French concerns over expatriate security amid regional tensions.

## 8. Human Rights Discussions and Controversies

France's close defense and economic ties with Gulf monarchies have faced criticism from human rights groups over the lack of scrutiny on human rights issues in those countries. Key concerns include:

- Involvement of Gulf states like Saudi Arabia and UAE in the Yemen conflict and associated civilian casualties.
- Lack of political freedoms, rights issues concerning women, use of the death penalty, and treatment of migrant workers in the Gulf states.

France has generally prioritized its strategic interests over vocal human rights criticism of its Gulf partners. But it claims to raise rights issues through diplomatic channels.

## 9. Challenges and Criticisms of Bilateral Relations

While France touts its strategic partnerships in the Gulf, critics point to several challenges:

- Accusations that France overlooks human rights for commercial interests and regional influence.
- Perceptions that France is getting caught between US and Chinese spheres of influence amid great power rivalry in the Gulf.
- Questions over the long-term reliability of Gulf partners given their transactional foreign policies and shifting alliances.
- Concerns that deepening defense ties could embroil France in regional conflicts like Yemen.

There are also debates around France's approach being too unilateral and not aligned with EU policies towards the Gulf.

## 10. Future Prospects in Franco-Gulf Cooperation

Despite the challenges, France and Gulf states are likely to maintain close strategic ties given their mutual interests:

- France aims to preserve its economic, political and cultural influence in a region it views as strategically vital.
- Gulf states value France as a partner that can provide security, arms, nuclear/energy cooperation and political support distinct from the US.
- Both sides seek to counterbalance threats like Iran,

Turkey and political Islam in the region through their partnership.

However, France may face growing pressure to address human rights more substantively. Navigating great power rivalries involving the US, China and Russia in the Gulf could also test this partnership's future trajectory. In summary, while deep-rooted and multi-faceted, Franco-Gulf ties will likely remain an avenue for pragmatic cooperation underpinned by strategic interests, but with inherent complexities to manage.

# References For Further Reading

Abdel Ghafar, Adel . "France and the UAE: A Deepening Partnership in Uncertain Times." Brookings, October 28, 2021. https://www.brookings.edu/articles/france-and-the-uae-a-deepening-partnership-in-uncertain-times/.

Bianco, Cinzia. "Renewable Relations: A Strategic Approach to European Energy Cooperation with the Gulf States." ECFR, June 16, 2023. https://ecfr.eu/publication/renewable-relations-a-strategic-approach-to-european-energy-cooperation-with-the-gulf-states/.

Catherine Delano Smith. "Spain - Franco's Spain, 1939–75." In Encyclopædia Britannica, February 24, 2019. https://www.britannica.com/place/Spain/Francos-Spain-1939-75.

Dagres, Holly. "Under Macron's Leadership, France Is Leading a Middle Power Strategy in the Gulf. Here's How." Atlantic Council, August 16, 2022. https://www.atlanticcouncil.org/blogs/menasource/under-macrons-leadership-france-is-leading-a-middle-power-strategy-in-the-gulf-heres-how/.

elysee.fr. "France-United Arab Emirates Joint Statement on the Occasion of the State Visit to France of Sheikh Mohamed Bin Zayed al Nahyan, President of the UAE 18-19 July 2022," July 20, 2022. https://www.elysee.fr/en/emmanuel-macron/2022/07/20/france-united-arab-emirates-joint-statement-on-the-occasion-of-the-state-visit-to-france-of-sheikh-mohamed-bin-zayed-al-nahyan-president-of-the-uae-18-19-july-2022.

étrangères, Ministère de l'Europe et des Affaires. "France and Saudi Arabia." France

Diplomacy - Ministry for Europe and Foreign Affairs, n.d. https://www.diplomatie.gouv.fr/en/country-files/saudi-arabia/france-and-saudi-arabia-65100/.

Fayet, Héloïse. "What Strategic Posture Should France Adopt in the Middle East?," November 2022. https://www.ifri.org/sites/default/files/atoms/files/fayet_focus112_pmo_us_2023.pdf.

France Diplomacy - Ministry for Europe and Foreign Affairs. "15th Session of the UAE-France Strategic Dialogue Discusses Growing Cooperation between UAE & France (19.06.23)." France Diplomacy, 2019. https://www.diplomatie.gouv.fr/en/country-files/united-arab-emirates/events/article/15th-session-of-the-uae-france-strategic-dialogue-discusses-growing-cooperation.

France in the UK. "France and UAE Extend Their Strategic Partnership," July 20, 2022. https://uk.ambafrance.org/France-and-UAE-extend-their-strategic-partnership.

International Federation for Human Rights , FIDH : "Arms Sales: France and the United Arab Emirates, Partners in the Crimes Committed in Yemen?" International Federation for Human Rights, December 14, 2021. https://www.fidh.org/en/region/europe-central-asia/france/arms-sales-france-and-the-united-arab-emirates-partners-in-the-crimes.

Lester, Stephanie. "A History of Franco-Iranian Relations." American Iranian Council, October 1, 2017. http://www.us-iran.org/news/2017/10/19/a-history-of-franco-iranian-relations.

Ministère de l'Europe et des Affaires étrangères. "France and Egypt." France Diplomacy - Ministry for Europe and Foreign Affairs, n.d. https://www.diplomatie.gouv.fr/en/country-files/egypt/france-and-egypt-64940/.

Ministère des armées . "Report to Parliament," 2022. https://www.defense.gouv.fr/sites/default/files/ministere-armees/Report%20to%20Parliament%20on%20France%20s%20Arms%20Exports.pdf.

SGDSN. "National Strategic Review 2022," December 2, 2022. https://www.sgdsn.gouv.fr/files/files/rns-uk-20221202.pdf.

Thiebaud, Eva. "Orient XXI." Orient XXI, May 20, 2024. https://orientxxi.info/magazine/unworthy-agreement-between-france-and-the-united-arab-emirates.

Vitrand, Louis. "UAE and France: A Key, and Challenging, Relationship - Foreign Policy Research Institute." www.fpri.org, September 7, 2023. https://www.fpri.org/article/2023/09/uae-and-france-a-key-and-challenging-relationship/.

www.mofa.gov.ae. "UAE Embassy in Paris-Bilateral Relationship," n.d. https://www.mofa.gov.ae/en/Missions/Paris/UAE-Relationships/Bilateral-Relationship.

www.mofa.gov.ae. "UAE Embassy in Paris-Economic Cooperation." Accessed May 20, 2024. https://www.mofa.gov.ae/en/Missions/Paris/UAE-Relationships/Economic-Cooperation.

# IX

# Franco-Arab Cooperation in Education and Research

## Historical Overview of Franco-Arab Educational Ties

The historical overview of Franco-Arab educational ties delves into the roots and evolution of educational relations between France and Arab countries, spanning back to the colonial era and encompassing significant milestones that have shaped the bilateral educational landscape. The colonial legacy profoundly impacted the education systems in many Arab countries, as French educational institutions and curricula were often established and implemented during this period. This laid the foundation for the subsequent development of educational ties between France and the Arab world. The post-colonial era witnessed a concerted effort to redefine these relations, with both sides recognizing the value of fostering educational cooperation to strengthen diplomatic, cultural, and economic bonds. Notable developments include establishing formal agreements and initiatives to promote academic collaboration, exchange programs, and mutual recognition of qualifications. Moreover, the historical overview explores key educational reforms and strategies implemented in France and Arab countries to enhance educational ties, such as promoting language learning, cultural exchanges, and joint research partnerships. It also examines the pivotal role of educational ties in facilitating people-to-people connections, knowledge transfer, and the nurturing of future leaders and professionals. By tracing the historical trajectory of Franco-Arab educational relations, we gain insights into the enduring significance of education as a cornerstone of bilateral cooperation and its transformative impact on the broader Franco-Arab partnership.

## *Key Bilateral Agreements and Initiatives*

Bilateral agreements and initiatives are pivotal in shaping the landscape of Franco-Arab cooperation in education and research. These agreements are the foundation for fostering enduring partnerships between France and Arab countries, facilitating the exchange of knowledge, expertise, and resources in the academic realm. It is imperative to delve into the specifics of these agreements to grasp their significance and impact comprehensively. At the core of these agreements are carefully crafted frameworks that outline the parties' mutual commitments, rights, and obligations. By establishing formal structures for cooperation, these agreements provide a roadmap for collaborative endeavors, addressing areas such as student exchanges, joint research projects, faculty mobility, and curriculum development. They often encompass diverse educational sectors, including primary and secondary education, higher education, vocational training, and scientific research, reflecting the comprehensive nature of the collaboration. Furthermore, the initiatives arising from these agreements span a broad spectrum, promoting cultural understanding, linguistic diversity, and academic excellence. One prominent example is the establishment of dual-degree programs between French and Arab universities, enabling students to earn qualifications from both systems and gain enriching cross-cultural experiences. Additionally, collaborative research initiatives have driven innovations in renewable energy and sustainable development to healthcare and information technology, resulting in tangible benefits for both regions. Moreover, these bilateral agreements emphasize the facilitation of language learning, emphasizing the importance of linguistic proficiency in fostering meaningful academic and cultural exchanges. They support promoting the French language in Arab educational institutions and, conversely, facilitate the teaching of Arabic in French schools, contributing to a more interconnected and linguistically diverse educational environment. The significance of these agreements extends beyond academia, influencing public policy and diplomatic relations between France and Arab countries. They serve as catalysts for broader cooperation in areas such as trade, technology transfer, and people-to-people exchanges, amplifying the impact of educational collaboration on the socio-economic fabric of both regions. These key bilateral agreements and initiatives form the cornerstone of Franco-Arab cooperation in education and research, manifesting a commitment to harmonious co-development and mutual growth.

## *French Language Promotion and Academic Exchanges*

France has long been committed to promoting the French language as an international tool for communication and dialogue, especially within the Arab world. This commitment is evident through various programs and initiatives to disseminate the French language and enhance academic exchanges between French and Arab-speaking nations. The establishment of French cultural institutes, alliances, and linguistic centers across the Arab world is a testament to this dedication. These institutions play a pivotal role in fostering linguistic and cultural understanding while serving as hubs for educational collaboration.

Through these platforms, the French government and academic institutions actively promote the teaching and learning of the French language, enabling individuals in Arab countries to access educational resources, scholarship opportunities, and cultural insights. Moreover, academic exchanges facilitate the mobility of students, researchers, and educators, substantiating bilateral ties and facilitating knowledge transfer. Notably, partnerships between universities in France and the Arab world have led to joint degree programs, collaborative research projects, and sharing educational best practices. Such collaborations enrich academic curricula, generating an environment conducive to cross-cultural understanding and innovation. Furthermore, the emphasis on French language promotion and academic exchanges bridges deeper Franco-Arab relations, influencing multifaceted cooperation in various fields beyond education and research. Ultimately, these efforts aim to cultivate a diverse, interconnected community of scholars, fostering mutual respect and appreciation for linguistic, cultural, and intellectual diversity across borders.

## *Joint Research Programs and Innovation Collaborations*

Joint research programs and innovation collaborations have fostered strong ties between France and Arab countries. This section delves into the multifaceted landscape of collaborative research initiatives and their profound impact on mutual development and progress. The joint research endeavors encompass various disciplines, from advanced technology and environmental sustainability to healthcare and social sciences. These initiatives serve as a bridge for knowledge exchange, leveraging the collective expertise of scholars and scientists from both regions. Leveraging the complementary strengths and resources, research partnerships have yielded groundbreaking innovations that address complex global challenges. Moreover, these collaborations enhance scientific knowledge and contribute to economic growth and societal well-being. French and Arab institutions have established numerous joint research centers, fostering an environment conducive to cross-cultural understanding and impactful discoveries. These hubs act as incubators for interdisciplinary research, promoting the exchange of ideas and best practices. Furthermore, innovation collaborations extend beyond academic institutions, engaging industry leaders and governmental agencies in driving technological advancement and sustainable development. Through joint funding and resource mobilization, these initiatives harness the potential of diverse talent pools to tackle pressing issues such as climate change, renewable energy, and public health. The success stories resulting from such collaborations underscore the transformative power of collaborative innovation. They testify to the tangible outcomes achievable when nations unite for the greater good. However, challenges such as linguistic barriers, administrative complexities, and varying regulatory frameworks pose significant hurdles to seamless collaboration. Therefore, streamlining administrative processes and establishing platforms for effective communication are essential steps toward maximizing the impact of joint research programs. As we explore the future trajectory of Franco-Arab collaboration in research and innovation, identifying emerging fields and aligning research priorities will be pivotal. Embracing emerging technologies, nurturing entrepreneurial ecosystems, and addressing societal needs through innovative solutions will form the cornerstone of future joint endeavors. The trajectory of Franco-Arab cooperation in research and innovation is poised to shape the global knowledge economy, steering advancements that transcend geographical boundaries and contribute to the collective prosperity of both regions.

## *Higher Education Opportunities for Arab Students in France*

France has long been recognized as a global leader in higher education, with its prestigious universities and institutions attracting students worldwide. Arab students, particularly, have sought educational opportunities in France, drawn by its rich history, cultural diversity, and academic excellence. The appeal of studying in France extends beyond its renowned educational institutions to encompass its vibrant arts and culture, dynamic social environment, and the opportunity to immerse oneself in the French language. Arab students pursuing higher education in France benefit not only from the academic rigor and innovative research opportunities but also from the invaluable cross-cultural experiences that contribute to their personal and professional development. France's commitment to fostering a welcoming and inclusive environment for international students is evident through its extensive support services, including language assistance, intercultural programs, and guidance for navigating the higher education landscape. With a wide range of disciplines and specializations available, Arab students can pursue their academic interests and career aspirations while gaining a global perspective. Additionally, numerous scholarship programs and financial aid options facilitate access to higher education for Arab students, further strengthening the ties between France and the Arab world. As part of France's broader efforts to enhance Franco-Arab cooperation in education, initiatives such as joint degree programs, collaborative research projects, and strategic partnerships with Arab institutions continue to expand the horizons for Arab students seeking to study in France. The exchange of knowledge, ideas, and perspectives within the higher education framework further enriches the bilateral relations between France and the Arab countries, fostering mutual understanding and paving the way for future collaboration in various fields. By embracing diversity and nurturing academic excellence, France remains an inviting destination for Arab students who aspire to excel in their educational pursuits and contribute meaningfully to the global community.

## Role of Cultural Institutes and Alliances

Cultural institutes and alliances play a pivotal role in shaping the landscape of Franco-Arab cooperation in education and research. These institutions serve as an instrumental bridge to foster mutual understanding, promote cultural exchange, and strengthen academic collaboration between France and the Arab world. French cultural institutions abroad, such as Institut Français and Alliance Française, have promoted the French language, arts, and culture in the Arab world. Through a network of branches across various Arab countries, these institutes organize language courses, cultural events, and educational programs that enhance mutual appreciation and cultural dialogue. Additionally, collaborations between French universities and Arab cultural organizations have led to establishing cultural centers and academic partnerships to facilitate academic exchanges and joint research initiatives. These alliances provide a platform for scholars, artists, and intellectuals from both regions to engage in intellectual discourse, share knowledge, and foster enduring ties. By nurturing an environment where cultural diversity is celebrated, and intercultural dialogue is encouraged, these institutions play a crucial role in strengthening people-to-people connections and fostering a sense of shared heritage and common identity. Furthermore, cultural institutes and alliances serve as ambassadors of soft power, projecting favorable images of their respective countries and promoting educational opportunities and academic excellence. Their efforts in organizing cultural exhibitions, film festivals, and artistic performances enrich both regions' cultural tapestry and contribute to breaking down stereotypes and building bridges between diverse communities. The role of these institutions extends beyond the realm of cultural diplomacy, as they actively support academic exchanges, student mobility, and collaborative research projects, thereby nurturing a fertile ground for long-term partnerships in education and research. Looking ahead, the continued investment in cultural institutes and alliances will be integral in furthering the objectives of Franco-Arab cooperation, creating avenues for sustained academic engagement, and fostering a spirit of intellectual curiosity and exchange across borders.

## *Impact Analysis: Educational Exchanges on Bilateral Relations*

Educational exchanges between France and Arab countries have played a pivotal role in shaping bilateral relations, fostering mutual understanding, and strengthening diplomatic ties. These exchanges have facilitated academic collaboration and contributed significantly to the cultural, social, and economic dimensions of the Franco-Arab relationship. The impact of such educational interactions transcends traditional diplomacy, serving as a cornerstone for long-term partnership and cooperation.

One key impact of educational exchanges is the promotion of intercultural dialogue and mutual respect. By facilitating student and faculty mobility, these exchanges provide opportunities for individuals from diverse backgrounds to engage in meaningful cross-cultural experiences. This fosters greater empathy, tolerance, and appreciation of each other's cultures, ultimately developing enduring personal and professional relationships between the two regions.

Furthermore, educational collaborations have transferred knowledge, expertise, and best practices in various academic disciplines. French universities and research institutions have shared their wealth of knowledge with their counterparts in Arab countries, contributing to capacity building and skill development. Similarly, Arab scholars and students studying in France have brought fresh perspectives and innovative ideas, enriching the academic environment and promoting intellectual exchange.

Educational exchanges have had a significant economic impact in addition to cultural and intellectual enrichment. They have facilitated the creation of networks and partnerships between academic institutions, fostering collaborative research projects, joint publications, and technology transfer. These partnerships have also generated commercial linkages, entrepreneurship, and innovation opportunities, thereby stimulating economic growth and knowledge-based competitiveness in both regions.

Moreover, educational collaborations have promoted cross-border mobility and enhanced global citizenship. By nurturing a cohort of globally-minded graduates, these exchanges have contributed to a more interconnected world, where individuals are equipped to address transnational challenges and contribute to global solutions. This interconnectedness has bolstered people-to-people ties, bridged divides, and created a shared responsibility for addressing common societal issues.

As the dynamics of international relations continue to evolve, the impact of educational exchanges on Franco-Arab bilateral relations is poised to remain profound. By nurturing a new generation of leaders, professionals, and change-makers, such exchanges ensure the sustainability of the Franco-Arab partnership, fostering a climate of collaboration, trust, and solidarity. Recognizing the transformative power of educational collaborations, it is imperative for both France and Arab countries to further invest in such initiatives, thereby paving the way for a future characterized by mutual respect, prosperity, and shared progress.

## *Case Studies: Successful Franco-Arab Educational Projects*

In examining successful Franco-Arab educational projects, it is imperative to consider the comprehensive range of initiatives that have significantly contributed to strengthening bilateral ties and fostering mutual understanding. One noteworthy case study is the establishment of joint degree programs between prestigious French and Arab universities to nurture a new generation of leaders equipped with cross-cultural competencies. These programs have enriched academic environments and produced graduates who actively contribute to advancing cooperation between France and Arab countries in various fields. Another compelling example is the collaborative research endeavors in renewable energy, sustainable development, and public health. By leveraging shared expertise and resources, these projects have yielded impactful outcomes that address critical societal challenges while fortifying the bond between France and Arab countries. Furthermore, the implementation of cultural exchange initiatives, including immersive language programs, artistic collaborations, and heritage preservation efforts, has played a pivotal role in deepening mutual respect and appreciation for each other's rich heritage. These projects have effectively promoted intercultural dialogue and facilitated the interchange of knowledge, thus laying a solid foundation for enduring the Franco-Arab partnership in education and culture. Additionally, the establishment of scholarship schemes and faculty exchange programs has facilitated the mobility of students and academics between France and Arab states, thereby nurturing long-term connections and fostering a spirit of collaboration. These initiatives have enabled individuals to gain exposure to diverse educational systems and perspectives, broadening their intellectual horizons and contributing to the pool of talent that drives innovation and progress. Lastly, prestigious research hubs and academic institutions in both regions have paved the way for strategic collaborations in cutting-edge scientific disciplines, leading to groundbreaking discoveries and technological advancements. These joint efforts have elevated the status of academic institutions and positioned Franco-Arab cooperation as a driving force in tackling global challenges through knowledge sharing and innovation. These case studies exemplify the substantial impact of successful Franco-Arab educational projects in shaping a more interconnected, informed, and prosperous future for both regions.

## *Current Challenges and Barriers to Cooperation*

Franco-Arab cooperation in education and research has challenges and barriers, which warrant careful consideration and strategic interventions. One prominent challenge lies in the differing educational systems and standards between France and Arab countries. These disparities can lead to the non-recognition of academic qualifications, hindering the smooth transfer of students and researchers between the two regions. Language barriers and cultural differences impede effective communication and collaboration, affecting the potential for meaningful partnerships in educational ventures. critical barrier pertains to the political and socio-economic instabilities that have plagued certain Arab countries, leading to disruptions in academic exchange programs, research partnerships, and educational initiatives. Some regions' lack of stable governance and security concerns hampers establishing long-term, sustainable educational collaborations. Moreover, limited resources and investment in education, particularly in conflict-affected areas, pose significant obstacles to fostering robust Franco-Arab educational ties., bureaucratic hurdles, visa regulations, and immigration policies present practical challenges for students, scholars, and educators seeking to engage in cross-border educational activities. The complex administrative procedures and visa restrictions can impede the mobility of individuals, inhibiting the flow of knowledge and expertise between France and Arab countries. Additionally, funding constraints and financial disparities can constrain the scalability and impact of joint research projects and academic partnerships. The absence of a unified framework for mutual recognition of qualifications, credit transfers, and degree equivalence perpetuates ambiguities and obstacles for students and professionals looking to navigate the educational landscapes across these regions. These discrepancies require inclusive dialogues and streamlined mechanisms to enhance coherence and transparency in educational systems. Lastly, ensuring the protection of academic freedom, intellectual property rights, and ethical scientific conduct in collaborative projects remains a pertinent concern in fostering trusted Franco-Arab education and research affiliations. Addressing these multifaceted challenges demands concerted efforts, innovative solutions, and sustained commitment from stakeholders to nurture enduring and mutually beneficial educational partnerships.

## *Future Prospects and Strategic Recommendations*

In light of the challenges and barriers to Franco-Arab cooperation in education and research, it is crucial to outline a path forward that leverages opportunities and addresses existing limitations. The prospects for educational and research collaboration between France and Arab countries are promising, given the mutual benefits of knowledge exchange and intellectual synergies. To navigate the complexities ahead, strategic recommendations can be formulated to guide policymakers, academic institutions, and stakeholders toward a more effective and sustainable partnership. Firstly, there is a need to enhance institutional linkages and create a framework for long-term collaboration. This involves establishing joint research centers, fostering twinning programs between universities, and providing sustained funding mechanisms for collaborative projects. Moreover, strategic recommendations must address language barriers by expanding French language teaching initiatives in Arab countries and providing language support for Arab students in France. This linguistic bridge will facilitate greater academic mobility and cultural understanding. Investing in science, technology, engineering, and mathematics (STEM) education is essential for driving innovation and addressing societal challenges in both regions. This could involve joint funding for research in priority areas such as renewable energy, healthcare, and environmental sustainability. Furthermore, diversifying scholarship opportunities and increasing access to higher education for Arab students in France can contribute to human capital development and build a network of future leaders with cross-cultural competence. An emphasis on intercultural competence and global citizenship within curricula will prepare students to navigate interconnected global challenges. Looking ahead, it is imperative to integrate digital technologies and e-learning platforms into cooperative educational programs to overcome geographic constraints and enhance accessibility. Embracing online learning can help strengthen research collaboration and facilitate virtual academic exchanges. As part of strategic recommendations, fostering people-to-people ties through cultural events, student forums, and joint academic conferences should be prioritized. These activities can foster lasting partnerships, mutual understanding, and the exchange of best practices. Finally, engaging in ongoing dialogue and sharing best practices in educational policy, quality assurance, and accreditation systems is essential to align standards and promote academic integrity. By implementing these strategic recommendations, Franco-Arab cooperation in education and research can realize its full potential, contributing to a unified pursuit of knowledge and fostering a robust intellectual ecosystem.

## IN A NUTSHELL

Franco-Arab cooperation in education and research has a long history and continues to be an important aspect of the bilateral relations between France and Arab countries. Wec summarize it as follows:

### *Historical Educational Ties*

France has maintained educational and cultural ties with the Arab world for centuries, dating back to the colonial era. After many Arab nations gained independence in the 1950s and 1960s, France sought to preserve its linguistic and cultural influence through educational cooperation. Some key historical milestones include:

- Establishment of French schools, universities and cultural centers across North Africa and the Levant in the 19th/early 20th centuries.
- Post-independence agreements to continue French language teaching and exchange programs with newly independent Arab states.
- Creation of institutions like the French University of Egypt (1908) and the French Institute of Damascus (1923) to promote French culture.

## *Bilateral Agreements and Initiatives*

Over the decades, France has signed numerous bilateral agreements with Arab countries to facilitate educational and research cooperation:

- Cultural cooperation agreements covering areas like exchange of students/researchers, establishment of educational institutions, teaching of French language etc.
- Creation of joint institutions like the Sorbonne University Abu Dhabi (2006) through government partnerships.
- Initiatives like the Arabic Language Centre in Abu Dhabi (2021) to promote Arabic language and cultural exchanges.

## Academic Exchanges and Mobility

One of the cornerstones of Franco-Arab educational ties has been the exchange of students, faculty and researchers between institutions:

- Over 700 Arab students study at Sciences Po annually through university partnerships across 11 Arab countries.
- France hosts over 100,000 Arab students, the largest foreign student community. Arab students are attracted by French universities' reputation.
- Mobility programs like Erasmus facilitate exchanges of European and Arab students/faculty between partner institutions.

## Higher Education Cooperation

Cooperation in higher education has been extensive, with French universities establishing branch campuses, joint degrees and research collaborations with Arab counterparts:

- Examples: Sorbonne University Abu Dhabi, French University in Egypt, Louvre Abu Dhabi museum project.
- Joint research projects, visiting faculty programs between French and Arab universities in fields like science, medicine, engineering etc.
- Partnerships to develop expertise in emerging areas like artificial intelligence, renewable energy, space exploration.

## Challenges and Barriers

While the cooperation has been multi-faceted, it has also faced some challenges and criticisms:

- Concerns over lack of research quality, funding gaps and inadequate training/mentorship for Arab researchers.
- Accusations that France prioritizes economic/strategic interests over addressing issues like academic freedom in Arab partners.
- Language barriers, difficulties in navigating publishing processes for Arab scholars in international journals.
- Debates around increasing Arab representation in French/Western editorial boards and research governance.

## Future Prospects

Despite the challenges, the educational and research ties between France and the Arab world are expected to continue given their mutual interests:

- France aims to maintain its linguistic, cultural and economic influence in a region of strategic importance.
- Arab countries value France's expertise in higher education, research and seek cooperation in emerging fields like AI, energy etc.
- Initiatives to enhance research quality, training and mobility are underway to bridge gaps.
- However, addressing concerns over academic freedom,

research integrity and inclusivity will likely remain works in progress.

In summary, while deep-rooted historically, Franco-Arab cooperation in education and research will need to continually evolve to tackle emerging challenges and maximize shared benefits in a changing global knowledge landscape.

# References For Further Reading

Elgamri, A., Mohammed, Z., El-Rhazi, K., Shahrouri, M., Ahram, M., Al-Abbas, A.-M., & Silverman, H. (2024). Challenges facing Arab researchers in conducting and publishing scientific research: a qualitative interview study. Research Ethics, 20(2), 331-362. https://doi.org/10.1177/17470161231214636

Al Khaldi, Salem. "Education Policies in the GCC States" first published January 2007 in Dubai, United Arab Emirates, by the Gulf Research Center, as part of the GRC Research Papers Series. https://www.files.ethz.ch/isn/97639/2007-01_Education_Policies_in_GCC_States_Digital_5830.pdf

Almuhaidib, Shadan, Rawan Alqahtani, Haifa F. Alotaibi, Asma Saeed, Sahar Alnasrallah, Fayez Alshamsi, Saleh A. Alqahtani, and Waleed Alhazzani. "Mapping the Landscape of Medical Research in the Arab World Countries: A Comprehensive Bibliometric Analysis." Saudi Medical Journal 45, no. 4 (April 1, 2024): 387–96. https://doi.org/10.15537/smj.2024.45.4.20230968.

Anderson, Porter. "Abu Dhabi Arabic Language Centre Partners with France's Institut Du Monde Arabe." Publishing Perspectives, November 17, 2021. https://publishingperspectives.com/2021/11/abu-dhabi-arabic-language-centre-partners-with-frances-institut-du-monde-arabe/.

Campus France. "EU European Universities Initiative: 16 French Institutions Selected." Accessed May 22, 2024. https://www.campusfrance.org/en/universites-europeennes-16-etablissements-francais-17-projets-selectionnes.

Elgamri A, Mohammed Z, El-Rhazi K, Shahrouri M, Ahram M, Al-Abbas AM, Silverman H. Challenges Facing Arab Researchers in Publishing Scientific Research: A Qualitative Interview Study. Res Sq [Preprint]. 2023 Jul 14:rs.3.rs-3129329. doi: 10.21203/rs.3.rs-3129329/v1. PMID: 37503191; PMCID: PMC10371160.

El Karoui, Hakim. "A New Strategy for France in a New Arab World." Institut Montaigne, August 2017. https://www.institutmontaigne.org/en/publications/new-strategy-france-new-arab-world.

Ministère de l'Europe et des Affaires étrangères. "French Schooling Abroad."

France Diplomacy - Ministry for Europe and Foreign Affairs. Accessed May 22, 2024. https://www.diplomatie.gouv.fr/en/french-foreign-policy/francophony-and-the-french-language/french-schooling-abroad/.

France in the UK. "France and UAE Extend Their Strategic Partnership," July 20, 2022. https://uk.ambafrance.org/France-and-UAE-extend-their-strategic-partnership.

international.univ-rennes2.fr. "Global Partnerships Map | Rennes 2 University." Accessed May 22, 2024. https://international.univ-rennes2.fr/our-international-partners.

Isit. "Coming to ISIT from Abroad." Accessed May 22, 2024. https://www.isit-paris.fr/en/mobility-at-isit/.

La France aux Émirats arabes unis. "The Measures for Developing French Education Abroad," October 7, 2019. https://ae.ambafrance.org/The-measures-for-developing-French-education-abroad.

Ministère de l'Europe et des Affaires étrangères . "15th Session of the UAE-France Strategic Dialogue Discusses Growing Cooperation between UAE & France (19.06.23)." France Diplomacy - Ministry for Europe and Foreign Affairs. France Diplomacy, 2019. https://www.diplomatie.gouv.fr/en/country-files/united-arab-emirates/events/article/15th-session-of-the-uae-france-strategic-dialogue-discusses-growing-cooperation.

Sciences Po. "Sciences Po and the Middle East & North Africa." Accessed May 22, 2024. https://www.sciencespo.fr/en/international/sciencespo-world/middle-east-north-africa/.

Vitrand, Louis . "UAE and France: A Key, and Challenging, Relationship - Foreign Policy Research Institute." www.fpri.org, September 7, 2023. https://www.fpri.org/article/2023/09/uae-and-france-a-key-and-challenging-relationship/.

www.aefe.fr. "AEFE | Les Établissements d'Enseignement Français En Réseau." Accessed May 22, 2024. https://www.aefe.fr/reseau-scolaire-mondial/les-etablissements-denseignement-francais-en-reseau.

www.gcc-sg.org. "Cooperation in Education." Accessed May 22, 2024. https://www.gcc-sg.org/en-us/CooperationAndAchievements/Achievements/CooperationinthefieldofHumanandEnvironmentAffairs/Pages/Cooperationineducation.aspx.

www.unige.ch. "Agreements by Country - International - Partenariats - UNIGE," April 2, 2020. https://www.unige.ch/internationalrelations/en/agreements/agreements/agreements-country/.

www.unistra.fr. "International Partnerships - Université de Strasbourg." Accessed May 22, 2024. https://www.unistra.fr/international/partenariats-internationaux/international-partnerships.

# X

# Challenges of Terrorism and Security Cooperation

## Overview of Terrorism Trends in Franco-Arab Relations

Terrorism trends have significantly influenced the dynamics of Franco-Arab relations over the years, shaping policies and strategies aimed at addressing security challenges. The rise of extremist groups, coupled with key incidents, has left a lasting impact on the relationship between France and Arab states. The emergence of organizations such as al-Qaeda and later ISIS has not only posed direct security threats but has also affected diplomatic engagements, leading to increased tension and stringent security measures. France has faced numerous attacks, including those carried out by individuals with ties to radicalized networks operating in parts of the Arab world. These incidents have not only resulted in tragic loss of lives but have also had far-reaching implications on bilateral ties, often straining cooperation in various domains. Furthermore, the complex nature of terrorism trends within the region has demanded concerted efforts to tackle the root causes and prevent the spread of extremist ideologies. The evolving nature of terrorist threats has necessitated continuous adaptation of counter-terrorism strategies, highlighting the need for enhanced vigilance and collaboration between France and Arab states. Additionally, incidents such as the Paris and Nice attacks have underscored the transnational nature of terrorism and the interconnectedness of security concerns between France and Arab states. As such, understanding these trends is crucial in formulating comprehensive approaches to address security challenges and foster sustainable Franco-Arab relations. Moreover, geopolitical shifts and conflicts in the Middle East have further contributed to the dynamic landscape of terrorism, impacting mutual perceptions and fostering a climate of uncertainty. This overview of terrorism trends aims to provide a nuanced understanding of how these factors have shaped the intricacies of Franco-Arab relations, shedding light on the multifaceted nature of security cooperation and the ongoing efforts to mitigate the impact of terrorism on diplomatic engagements.

## *Historical Incidents and Their Impact on Bilateral Ties*

Throughout the history of Franco-Arab relations, several significant historical incidents have profoundly influenced the bilateral ties between France and Arab states. These incidents have shaped diplomatic relationships and left a lasting impact on cultural perceptions, security cooperation, and economic partnerships. One such pivotal event was the Algerian War of Independence from 1954 to 1962, which marked a tumultuous period in Franco-Arab relations, leading to deep-seated mistrust and strained ties. The aftermath of this conflict had a profound impact on the region's political landscape and significantly influenced France's approach to its former colonies. Additionally, the ongoing Israeli-Palestinian conflict has been a constant source of tension and divergence in Franco-Arab relations, with France often seeking to play a mediating role. Moreover, historical incidents like the Gulf War, the

Lebanon Civil War, and various terrorist attacks in both France and Arab countries have led to shifts in security policies and counterterrorism strategies. These events have prompted intensive dialogues and collaborations between France and Arab states to address shared security concerns. Furthermore, the repercussions of colonization and decolonization have continued reverberating through the socio-political fabric of Franco-Arab relations, necessitating a delicate balance between acknowledging past injustices and forging constructive paths forward. Understanding the historical context of these incidents is essential to comprehend the complexities and sensitivities underpinning contemporary Franco-Arab relations. While these historical episodes have sometimes created rifts and challenges, they have also catalyzed resilient efforts to build cooperative frameworks and foster mutual understanding. As we navigate the nuanced terrain of historical incidents, it becomes evident that addressing the legacy of these events is pivotal in shaping the future trajectory of Franco-Arab relations, paving the way for comprehensive cooperation and sustainable partnerships.

## *Key Anti-Terrorism Policies and Strategies*

In response to the complex and evolving threat of terrorism, both France and Arab states have implemented a range of policies and strategies aimed at combating this menace. The key anti-terrorism policies and strategies include legislative measures, law enforcement tactics, intelligence operations, international cooperation, and counter-radicalization initiatives. France has enacted strict counterterrorism laws and measures to enhance its domestic security posture, including surveillance capabilities, border controls, and preventive detention for individuals suspected of involvement in terrorist activities. Additionally, the country has prioritized community engagement and outreach programs to address radicalization and prevent the spread of extremist ideologies.

Similarly, Arab states have adopted anti-terrorism policies and strategies tailored to their unique security challenges. These efforts often involve bolstering law enforcement capacities, enhancing border security, and implementing measures to track and disrupt terrorist financing networks. Furthermore, Arab countries have prioritized regional cooperation and information sharing to effectively combat transnational terror threats that pose a significant risk to their stability and prosperity.

An essential component of these policies and strategies is integrating advanced technology and intelligence capabilities to identify and neutralize terrorist networks. France and Arab states have invested in sophisticated surveillance technologies, cyber defense capabilities, and data analytics to enhance their ability to anticipate and thwart potential terrorist plots. Moreover, they have strengthened their collaboration with international partners and organizations to address the global nature of terrorism, recognizing that a coordinated effort is essential to confront this multifaceted challenge.

Additionally, addressing the root causes of terrorism through comprehensive counter-radicalization strategies has become increasingly pivotal in the overall anti-terrorism framework. This approach promotes social inclusion, empowers local communities, and fosters dialogue to counter extremist narratives. By investing in education, employment opportunities, and religious moderation, France and Arab states aim to dissuade individuals from embracing radical ideologies and prevent the recruitment of new adherents to violent extremism.

As the threat landscape evolves, the adaptability of anti-terrorism policies and strategies remains paramount. Constant review and refinement are necessary to respond effectively to emerging trends, such as the proliferation of online radicalization and the intersection of terrorism with other illicit activities. Furthermore, counterterrorism measures' ethical and legal dimensions require ongoing scrutiny to ensure that human rights and civil liberties are safeguarded while addressing security imperatives.

Ultimately, the comprehensive and nuanced approach taken by France and Arab states in formulating and implementing anti-terrorism policies and strategies underscores their shared commitment to preserving peace, stability, and security within the Franco-Arab context.

## Security Collaborations Between France and Arab states

The security collaborations between France and Arab states have been shaped by a complex interplay of historical, geopolitical, and socioeconomic factors. Dating back to the colonial era, France's influence in the Middle East and North Africa has laid the foundation for multifaceted security partnerships with Arab states. These collaborations extend across various domains, including military cooperation, intelligence sharing, law enforcement coordination, and joint counterterrorism operations. France's historical ties with countries such as Algeria, Tunisia, Morocco, Lebanon, and Egypt have significantly influenced its security engagements within the region. Furthermore, France's strategic interests in combating terrorism and ensuring regional stability have led to extensive security collaborations with Arab states. The exchange of expertise, training programs, and technology transfer forms essential components of these collaborations, enhancing the capacity of both France and Arab countries to address shared security concerns. Additionally, diplomatic dialogues and high-level summits have served as platforms for aligning security objectives, fostering trust, and developing joint frameworks for tackling transnational security threats. The evolving nature of security challenges, including terrorism, cyber threats, and illicit arms trafficking, has necessitated adaptive and dynamic security collaborations between France and Arab states. This has resulted in the implementation of comprehensive security initiatives, including border control measures, information-sharing mechanisms, and capacity-building projects. Moreover, the emergence of non-traditional security threats, such as climate change-induced vulnerabilities and hybrid warfare tactics, has urged France and Arab states to engage in strategic foresight and holistic security planning. Despite the complexities inherent in Franco-Arab security collaborations, concerted efforts have been made to promote mutual understanding, respect sovereignty, and align legal frameworks to ensure effective security cooperation. While historical legacies and contemporary geopolitical shifts influence these collaborations, both parties recognize the imperative of collective action and solidarity in addressing multifaceted security challenges. As these partnerships continue to evolve, fostering trust, transparency, and inclusivity will be pivotal in building resilient and responsive security architectures. The convergence of interests, values, and aspirations underpins the enduring nature of security collaborations between France and Arab states, serving as a cornerstone for regional peace and stability.

## Challenges Faced by Joint Counterterrorism Efforts

A myriad of complex challenges confront the collaborative efforts between France and the Arab states in countering terrorism. One of the foremost hurdles is the multiplicity of terrorist organizations operating in the region, each with its unique goals, tactics, and alliances. These groups often exploit transnational borders and regional instabilities to establish safe havens, making it challenging for security forces to combat their operations effectively.

Furthermore, differing legal and judicial systems across participating countries pose significant obstacles to seamless cooperation. Variations in laws concerning extradition, information sharing, and prosecution procedures can hinder the swift and unified response essential to combating terrorist networks' agility.

Another impediment stems from the intricate geopolitical landscape of the Middle East and North Africa, marked by historical conflicts, sectarian tensions, and proxy warfare. These complexities create divergent priorities and strategic interests among the Arab states and

France, thereby impacting the alignment of their counterterrorism objectives.

In addition, radicalization and recruitment pose a critical challenge to joint efforts. Extremist ideologies continue to spread through various channels, including social media and religious institutions, fostering the growth of homegrown terrorists and foreign fighters. Addressing the root causes of radicalization while respecting individual freedoms and privacy rights remains an ongoing dilemma in devising effective counterterrorism strategies.

Moreover, the financing of terrorism represents a persistent challenge to security cooperation. Illicit financial flows, money laundering, and the exploitation of informal economies provide the necessary resources for terrorist activities, necessitating enhanced financial intelligence and regulatory measures across national and international levels.

Finally, balancing robust security measures and upholding fundamental civil liberties is the overarching challenge. Implementing stringent surveillance, border controls, and counter-radicalization initiatives must be accompanied by safeguards to prevent the infringement of human rights, potential ethnic profiling, and the alienation of marginalized communities. Striking this delicate equilibrium is crucial to preserving trust and cooperation within Franco-Arab counterterrorism endeavors.

Addressing these multifaceted challenges demands commitment, flexibility, and openness to innovative approaches. Overcoming these barriers is imperative for successfully mitigating terrorism threats and cultivating enduring security partnerships between France and the Arab states.

## *Role of Intelligence Sharing in Enhancing Security Measures*

Intelligence sharing is pivotal in bolstering security measures and thwarting terrorist activities within the framework of Franco-Arab relations. As threats continue to evolve with the changing dynamics of terrorism, intelligence gathering, analysis, and dissemination collaboration become indispensable for staying ahead of adversaries. By leveraging the expertise and resources of both French and Arab states, intelligence sharing facilitates the early detection of potential threats and enhances the efficacy of preemptive and preventive actions. This strategic partnership enables the pooling of diverse intelligence capabilities, including human intelligence, signal intelligence, and imagery intelligence, thereby creating a comprehensive and multi-faceted approach to addressing security challenges.

Effective intelligence sharing relies on establishing robust communication channels and protocols for exchanging sensitive information. It involves building mutual trust and understanding between various intelligence agencies, law enforcement entities, and security apparatuses across borders. Furthermore, it demands harmonizing legal frameworks and data protection regulations to ensure seamless and lawful transmission of intelligence while safeguarding individual rights and privacy concerns. Integrating advanced technologies and analytical tools is also paramount in processing and interpreting shared intelligence, enabling timely and actionable insights derived from the gathered data.

Moreover, intelligence sharing fosters a collective response to combating transnational terrorism, creating a unified front against common threats. The alignment of strategic objectives and the coordination of intelligence operations enable swift and coordinated responses to emerging risks, effectively disrupting terrorist networks and activities. Additionally, shared intelligence empowers the formulation of evidence-based policies and the implementation of targeted interventions, thereby mitigating vulnerabilities and enhancing overall resilience.

However, the efficacy of intelligence sharing hinges on addressing inherent challenges, including cultural differences, language barriers, and political sensitivities. Building a collaborative intelligence-sharing framework necessitates overcoming historical distrust and geopolitical complexities while prioritizing the common goal of ensuring regional and global security. Moreover, the need for continuous evaluation and adaptation of intelligence-sharing mechanisms to counter emerging threats cannot be overstated. Embracing innovation and evolving strategies is imperative in addressing the ever-changing tactics employed by terrorist organizations.

In essence, the role of intelligence sharing in Franco-Arab security cooperation epitomizes the synergy of efforts aimed at curbing terrorism and fortifying national and regional stability. By harnessing shared knowledge, expertise, and resources, stakeholders can proactively address security threats, uphold the rule of law, and preserve the safety and well-being of communities. This collaborative intelligence ecosystem serves as a beacon of resilience and unwavering determination in countering the complex, multifaceted challenges posed by terrorism.

## *Impact of Globalization on Terrorism Dynamics*

Globalization has significantly transformed the landscape in which terrorism operates, presenting both challenges and opportunities for counterterrorism efforts within the Franco-Arab context. The interconnected nature of the modern world has facilitated the spread of extremist ideologies, funding sources, and the movement of terrorist operatives transcending national boundaries, posing a complex set of challenges for security agencies and policymakers. Advances in technology and communication have amplified the reach and impact of terrorist propaganda, enabling recruitment and radicalization on a global scale. Additionally, the ease of international travel and trade has created new channels for the illicit movement of arms, funds, and individuals, further complicating security measures. Furthermore, the emergence of digital platforms and social media has provided terrorists with unprecedented tools for coordinating attacks, disseminating propaganda, and evading traditional law enforcement efforts. In this context, the globalization of terrorism has necessitated a paradigm shift in the approach to security cooperation between France and Arab states. A comprehensive understanding of transnational networks and threat vectors is crucial for effectively countering the evolving dynamics of terrorism within and beyond regional borders. Moreover, the intersection of globalization and terrorism underscores the importance of fostering multilateral partnerships, information sharing, and intelligence cooperation at an international level. Beyond addressing the immediate manifestations of terrorism, it is essential for stakeholders to collectively address the underlying socio-economic and political grievances that are exploited by extremist groups, thus requiring a holistic and long-term approach to countering radicalization and violence. Efforts to combat terrorism must be rooted in respect for human rights and fundamental freedoms, guarding against the erosion of civil liberties in the pursuit of security. Furthermore, the complexity of addressing transnational threats demands the continual adaptation of legal frameworks and international conventions to prosecute and extradite perpetrators while upholding due process effectively. In conclusion, the impact of globalization on terrorism dynamics highlights the imperative of adaptive, integrated, and ethical approaches to security cooperation, emphasizing collaboration, innovation, and the protection of universal values and rights.

## *Legal and Ethical Considerations in Counterterrorism*

The fight against terrorism raises complex legal and ethical considerations for both France and the Arab states involved in bilateral cooperation. As counterterrorism measures are implemented, ensuring that these actions adhere to international law, human rights standards, and ethical principles is imperative. One of the central challenges lies in striking a balance between safeguarding national security and respecting individual liberties. This necessitates carefully examining legal frameworks governing surveillance, detention, and interrogation practices. Additionally, there is a critical need to uphold due process and fair trial rights for suspected terrorists. The use of intelligence gathered through surveillance or informants must also align with principles of proportionality and necessity to avoid infringing on privacy rights. Furthermore, issues related to extraterritorial operations, drone strikes, and targeted killings demand clear legal guidelines and accountability mechanisms to prevent unlawful actions. In the context of transnational terrorism, legal complexities arise from overlapping jurisdictions, extradition processes, and the handling of foreign fighters. Moreover, questions surrounding the engagement of private military contractors and the conduct of proxy warfare underscore the multidimensional nature of legal challenges in counterterrorism efforts. Ethically, there is an inherent tension between employing force to combat terrorist threats and upholding humanitarian values. The collateral impact on civilian populations, risk of wrongful targeting, and potential for abuse of power pose severe ethical dilemmas. Furthermore, efforts to counter extremist narratives and radicalization bring forth questions of censorship, freedom of expression, and cultural sensitivity. Addressing these ethical concerns necessitates a comprehensive approach integrating moral reflections into policy decision-making and operational practices. Overall, navigating counterterrorism's legal and ethical dimensions requires a nuanced understanding of the evolving threat landscape and a steadfast commitment to upholding fundamental rights and ethical principles while ensuring collective security.

## Evaluating the Effectiveness of Current Security Cooperation

Evaluating the effectiveness of current security cooperation between France and Arab states is critical in assessing the progress and impact of collaborative counterterrorism efforts. This assessment necessitates a comprehensive analysis of various facets of security cooperation, including intelligence sharing, joint operational activities, policy alignment, and the overall outcomes achieved in countering terrorism and ensuring stability in the region. Firstly, it is imperative to thoroughly review the existing mechanisms for intelligence sharing and coordination between the respective security agencies of France and the Arab countries. This involves scrutinizing the efficiency of information exchange, the timeliness of intelligence dissemination, and the extent to which shared intelligence has contributed to thwarting terrorist activities. Moreover, the evaluation process should investigate the effectiveness of joint operational activities conducted in security cooperation. This entails examining the success of conducting coordinated counter-terrorism operations, addressing transnational threats, and promoting regional security without compromising sovereignty. Additionally, the assessment should consider the degree of alignment in policy frameworks and legal measures both parties adopt to combat terrorism. It is crucial to evaluate the harmonization of laws, extradition procedures, and judicial cooperation to ensure that perpetrators of terrorism are brought to justice swiftly and effectively. Furthermore, a comprehensive analysis of Franco-Arab security partnerships' overall outcomes and impact is essential in this evaluation. This involves studying the tangible results achieved in disrupting terrorist networks, preventing radicalization, and providing a secure environment for communities in both France and Arab states. Moreover, the assessment should take into account the adaptability of security cooperation to evolving threats such as cyber terrorism, biological warfare, and unconventional tactics employed by extremist groups. The evaluation process must also consider the socio-political implications and public perceptions of security cooperation, aiming to understand how the collaborative efforts have influenced relationships between the involved nations and their citizens. Lastly, the assessment should anticipate and address potential areas of improvement, highlighting the need for enhanced collaboration, technological advancements, capacity building, and strengthening legal frameworks to further fortify Franco-Arab security partnerships. By critically evaluating the effectiveness of current security cooperation, pertinent insights can be gleaned to refine strategies, consolidate strengths, and reinforce the commitment towards combatting terrorism while fostering peace and stability in the region.

## Future Prospects for Franco-Arab Security Partnerships

The prospects for Franco-Arab security partnerships are shaped by a complex and rapidly evolving global security landscape. In the coming years, France and Arab states must recalibrate their security cooperation frameworks in response to emerging threats and geopolitical shifts. One of the key aspects that will influence the future trajectory of Franco-Arab security partnerships is the changing nature of terrorism and extremism. As extremist groups continue to adapt and exploit technological advancements, it becomes essential for both parties to devise innovative strategies to counter these evolving threats. Additionally, the proliferation of non-traditional security challenges such as cyber threats, hybrid warfare, and transnational crime demands a comprehensive and adaptable approach to security cooperation. The future of Franco-Arab security partnerships also hinges on enhancing intelligence-sharing mechanisms and joint operational capabilities. Strengthening information exchange and collaborative action will be pivotal in effectively preempting and responding to security threats. Furthermore, addressing underlying socio-economic factors that contribute to radicalization and instability will be critical in shaping the long-term success of security partnerships. This involves investing in sustainable development, education, and social cohesion programs that can help mitigate the drivers of insecurity. Geopolitically, the shifting power dynamics and regional realignments underscore the need for agile and pragmatic security alliances between France and Arab states. Navigating geopolitical uncertainties while upholding shared security objectives will demand foresight, astute diplomacy, and sustained dialogue. Moreover, fostering trust and mutual respect through cultural exchanges and people-to-people contacts will be instrumental in consolidating long-term security partnerships. Lastly, adapting to environmental and climate-related security challenges and exploring collaborative initiatives in this domain will be imperative for shaping resilient and sustainable security partnerships. By envisioning security cooperation through a holistic and forward-looking lens, France and Arab states can forge enduring alliances that transcend immediate threats and yield lasting stability. Embracing adaptability, innovation, and inclusivity in security strategies will be essential for navigating the nuanced security landscape of tomorrow.

# IN A NUTSHELL

## Terrorism and Security Cooperation between France and the Arab States

The cooperation between France and Arab states in combating terrorism and enhancing security has evolved significantly over the years. This relationship is characterized by historical incidents, strategic policies, intelligence sharing, and various challenges. Here is a detailed analysis of the different aspects of this cooperation:

## Historical Incidents and Their Impact on Bilateral Ties

- **Suez Crisis (1956)**: The Franco-British-Israeli intervention in Egypt strained relations with Arab states but also highlighted the need for strategic cooperation in the region.
- **Algerian War of Independence (1954-1962)**: This conflict had a profound impact on Franco-Arab relations, particularly with Algeria, shaping future security and counterterrorism policies.

## Impact on Bilateral Ties

These historical incidents have often led to periods of tension but also underscored the necessity for cooperation in addressing mutual security concerns. The legacy of colonialism and subsequent independence movements have influenced the dynamics of Franco-Arab relations, necessitating a careful balance between historical grievances and contemporary security needs

## Key Anti-Terrorism Policies and Strategies

### France's Approach

**Military Action**: France has taken determined military action against terrorist groups, notably through operations like Barkhane in the Sahel and Chammal in Iraq and Syria.

**International Cooperation**: France works closely with international partners, including the Arab League and the United Nations, to combat terrorism and stabilize conflict regions.

**Counter-Radicalization**: France has implemented programs to prevent radicalization and curb terrorist propaganda, including high-level dialogues and cooperation with digital companies to remove terrorist content online.

### Arab States' Approach

- **Regional Cooperation**: Arab states, through the Arab League, have engaged in various initiatives to combat terrorism, including mediation efforts in conflict zones like Libya and Yemen.
- **Capacity Building**: Many Arab states have focused

on building their counterterrorism capacities through training programs and international partnerships.

## Challenges Faced by Joint Counterterrorism Efforts

### Political and Diplomatic Challenges

- **Divergent Interests**: Differences in political priorities and strategic interests can complicate joint counterterrorism efforts. For example, varying stances on conflicts in Syria and Yemen can create friction.
- **Human Rights Concerns**: Balancing security measures with respect for human rights remains a significant challenge, with criticisms often directed at both France and Arab states for their counterterrorism practices.

### Operational Challenges

- **Coordination and Communication**: Effective coordination and communication between different national agencies and international partners are crucial but often difficult to achieve.
- **Resource Allocation**: Ensuring adequate resources and funding for counterterrorism initiatives is a persistent challenge, particularly in regions with limited financial capabilities.

## Role of Intelligence Sharing in Enhancing Security Measures

### Importance of Intelligence Sharing

- **Enhanced Security**: Intelligence sharing is critical for identifying and neutralizing terrorist threats. It allows for better coordination and timely responses to emerging threats.
- **Frameworks for Cooperation**: Various frameworks, such as regular meetings, standardized communication, and joint training, have been established to facilitate intelligence sharing between France and Arab states.

### Examples of Cooperation

- **NATO and EU Initiatives**: France participates in NATO and EU initiatives that include intelligence sharing with Mediterranean and Arab partners, enhancing collective security measures.

## Impact of Globalization on Terrorism Dynamics

### Increased Connectivity

- **Global Networks**: Globalization has facilitated the spread of terrorist ideologies and the formation of transnational terrorist networks, making it more challenging to combat terrorism on a national level.
- **Cyber Threats**: The rise of cyber terrorism and the

use of the internet for radicalization and recruitment have added new dimensions to the threat landscape.

## Response Strategies

- **International Collaboration**: Addressing the global nature of terrorism requires robust international collaboration, including joint operations, intelligence sharing, and coordinated policy responses.

## Legal and Ethical Considerations in Counterterrorism

### Legal Frameworks

- **International Law**: Counterterrorism efforts must comply with international law, including human rights and humanitarian law, to ensure legitimacy and effectiveness.
- **National Legislation**: Both France and Arab states have enacted laws to strengthen their counterterrorism capabilities, but these laws must balance security needs with civil liberties.

### Ethical Challenges

- **Human Rights**: Ensuring that counterterrorism measures do not violate human rights is a significant ethical challenge. Practices such as surveillance, detention, and interrogation must be conducted within legal and ethical boundaries.

## Effectiveness of Current Security Cooperation

### Successes

- **Operational Achievements**: Joint operations and intelligence sharing have led to the disruption of several terrorist plots and the weakening of terrorist networks in regions like the Sahel and the Middle East.
- **Capacity Building**: Training programs and capacity-building initiatives have enhanced the counterterrorism capabilities of Arab states, contributing to regional stability.

### Areas for Improvement

- **Coordination**: There is a need for better coordination and integration of efforts across different agencies and countries to maximize the effectiveness of counterterrorism measures.
- **Resource Allocation**: Ensuring sustained funding and resources for counterterrorism initiatives remains a challenge, particularly in conflict-affected regions.

## Future Prospects for Franco-Arab Security Partnerships

### Strengthening Cooperation

- **Enhanced Frameworks**: Developing more robust and flexible frameworks for cooperation, including

regular dialogues, joint training, and shared resources, can strengthen Franco-Arab security partnerships.
- **Focus on Emerging Threats**: Addressing emerging threats such as cyber terrorism and the use of new technologies by terrorist groups will be crucial for future cooperation.

## Addressing Challenges

- **Balancing Security and Rights**: Future efforts must balance the need for effective security measures with the protection of human rights and civil liberties.
- **Sustainable Development**: Integrating counterterrorism efforts with broader development and governance initiatives can address the root causes of terrorism and promote long-term stability.

In summary, Franco-Arab cooperation in counterterrorism and security has made significant strides but continues to face challenges. By enhancing intelligence sharing, addressing legal and ethical considerations, and focusing on emerging threats, this partnership can be further strengthened to effectively combat terrorism and promote regional stability.

# References For Further Reading

"ACTION PLAN AGAINST TERRORISM". Le Premier ministre Edouard Philippe, 13 July 2018. https://www.sgdsn.gouv.fr/files/files/Publications/20181004-plan-d-action-contre-le-terrorisme-anglais.pdf

"A MORE CONTESTED WORLD. Global Trends 2040." National Intelligence Council, March 2021. https://www.dni.gov/files/ODNI/documents/assessments/GlobalTrends_2040.pdf.

Amb. DE RIVIERE, NICOLAS . "France Is Very Concerned by the Current Escalation in the Middle East." France ONU, February 5, 2024. https://onu.delegfrance.org/france-is-very-concerned-by-the-current-escalation-in-the-middle-east.

Amb. DE RIVIÈRE, NICOLAS. "Strengthening Cooperation between the Arab League and the UN Remains Essential." France ONU, June 8, 2023. https://onu.delegfrance.org/strengthening-cooperation-between-the-arab-league-and-the-un-remains-essential.

European Council. "EU Fight against Terrorism - Consilium." Europa.eu. European Council, 2017. https://www.consilium.europa.eu/en/policies/fight-against-terrorism/.

France Diplomacy. "Terrorism: France's International Action." France Diplomatie :: Ministry for Europe and Foreign Affairs. France Diplomatie - Ministry for Europe and Foreign Affairs, 2018. https://www.diplomatie.gouv.fr/en/french-foreign-policy/security-disarmament-and-non-proliferation/terrorism-france-s-international-action/.

history.state.gov. "Foreign Relations of the United States, 1955–1957, Suez

Crisis, July 26–December 31, 1956, Volume XVI - Office of the Historian," 1990. https://history.state.gov/historicaldocuments/frus1955-57v16/d637.

history.state.gov. "Foreign Relations of the United States, 1958–1960, Western Europe, Volume VII, Part 2 - Office of the Historian," 1993. https://history.state.gov/historicaldocuments/frus1958-60v07p2/d309.

Ministère de l'Europe et des Affaires étrangères. "France and Cyber Security." France Diplomatie - Ministry for Europe and Foreign Affairs. France Diplomatie, 2015. https://www.diplomatie.gouv.fr/en/french-foreign-policy/digital-diplomacy/france-and-cyber-security/.

press.un.org. "Strategic Partnership between United Nations, Arab League Vital for Transformation of Region, Senior Official Tells Security Council | UN Press," June 8, 2023. https://press.un.org/en/2023/sc15315.doc.htm.

Ragazzi, Francesco. "Les Études Du Ceri Centre d'Études et de Recherches Internationales towards 'Policed Multiculturalism'? Counter-Radicalization in France, the Netherlands and the United Kingdom," December 2014. https://www.sciencespo.fr/ceri/sites/sciencespo.fr.ceri/files/Etude_206_anglais.pdf.

Shpiro, Shlomo. "The Communication of Mutual Security: Frameworks for European-Mediterranean Intelligence Sharing," n.d. https://www.nato.int/acad/fellow/99-01/shpiro.pdf.

Triandafyllidou, Anna. "Addressing Cultural, Ethnic & Religious Diversity Challenges in Europe a Comparative Overview of 15 European Countries," 2011. https://migrant-integration.ec.europa.eu/sites/default/files/2011-06/docl_21233_187704397.pdf.

United Nations. "Office of Counter-Terrorism |." www.un.org, 2023. https://www.un.org/counterterrorism/.

———. "Without Adequate Guardrails, Artificial Intelligence Threatens Global Security in Evolution from Algorithms to Armaments, Speaker Tells First Committee | UN Press." press.un.org, October 24, 2023. https://press.un.org/en/2023/gadis3725.doc.htm.

www.eeas.europa.eu. "League of Arab States (LAS) and the EU | EEAS," August 3, 2021. https://www.eeas.europa.eu/eeas/league-arab-states-las-and-eu_en.

Yakoubi, Myriam. "The French, the British and Their Middle Eastern Mandates

(1918-1939): Two Political Strategies." Revue Française de Civilisation Britannique. French Journal of British Studies XXVII, no. 1 (January 4, 2022). https://journals.openedition.org/rfcb/8787.

# XI

# Human Rights and Democracy Promotion

### Setting the Context

Exploring human rights and democracy within the Franco-Arab relations context is pertinent and multifaceted. Understanding the historical evolution of these themes in the Arab world and examining the principles that guide France's approach to promoting them is essential for assessing the current landscape and charting a course for the future. Complex dynamics, including colonial legacies, regional power struggles, and waves of social change have marked the socio-political history of the Arab countries. Against this backdrop, the recognition and protection of fundamental human rights have been subject to fluctuating interpretations and applications. From the early movements for decolonization to the modern-day challenges of state-building and governance, the struggle for human rights has been intrinsic to the region's narrative. Furthermore, as a cornerstone of democratic governance, the advocacy for human rights aligns with the principles underlying the vision of peaceful coexistence and sustainable development. These goals are aspirational and pragmatic, as they are inherently tied to the Franco-Arab partnership's stability, progress, and prosperity. In light of this, delving into the nuances of human rights and democracy promotion serves various objectives. Firstly, it offers an opportunity to comprehend the intricacies and nuances of the historical evolution of these concepts, acknowledging the contextual specificities and the diverse trajectories of the Arab countries. Secondly, it enables an examination of the philosophical underpinnings that guide France's commitment to upholding universal human rights and nurturing democratic values, highlighting the interconnectedness of these principles on the global stage. Thirdly, it allows for assessing the efficacy and challenges of bilateral and multilateral initiatives to advance human rights and democracy in the Arab world. Lastly, it provides a platform to discuss the evolving trends and emerging issues concerning human rights and democracy within Franco-Arab relations, projecting potential pathways for future collaboration and mutual understanding. By addressing these dimensions, this section aims to lay a comprehensive foundation for understanding the relevance, complexities, and implications of promoting human rights and democracy in Franco-Arab relations.

## Historical Overview of Human Rights in Arab Countries

The historical backdrop of human rights in Arab countries is intricately woven with societal, political, and cultural dynamics that have shaped the region's development. As we delve into this historical overview, it is crucial to acknowledge the rich and diverse heritage of Arab countries, encompassing a wide array of civilizations, religions, and traditions. It is within this multifaceted context that the evolution of human rights can be examined. From the ancient codes of Hammurabi to the Islamic legal tradition and the subsequent colonial era, the trajectory of human rights in Arab countries has been marked by periods of progress, adaptation, and transformation. The foundational principles of justice, equality, and dignity are deeply embedded in the historical narratives of these nations, resonating in pre-Islamic poetry, Islamic jurisprudence, and customary practices. However, the colonial legacy, independence movements, and modern nation-state formations have also significantly influenced the region's articulation and protection of human rights. The struggle for self-determination, sovereignty, and civil liberties has been ongoing as Arab countries have sought to navigate the complexities of internal governance and external interventions. Moreover, juxtaposing traditional values, religious precepts, and contemporary demands has engendered diverse perspectives on interpreting and implementing human rights. It is imperative to recognize the agency and aspirations of Arab societies in shaping their visions of rights and freedoms amid complex geopolitical realities. This historical overview provides a critical foundation for understanding the contextual nuances and challenges in promoting human rights in Arab countries, underscoring the need for nuanced approaches that respect local histories and aspirations while advancing universal principles of human dignity and freedom.

## *France's Philosophical Foundations of Liberty and Equality*

France's commitment to the philosophical foundations of liberty and equality has played a pivotal role in shaping its approach towards promoting human rights and democracy in the Arab world. Rooted in the Enlightenment ideals of the 18th century, France's national identity is deeply intertwined with the principles of liberty, equality, and fraternity, which have influenced its foreign policy and diplomatic efforts. The philosophical underpinnings of these values can be traced back to influential thinkers such as Jean-Jacques Rousseau, Montesquieu, and Voltaire, whose ideas continue to inspire contemporary discussions on human rights and democratic governance. The French Revolution of 1789 was a watershed moment that solidified these principles within the nation's conscience, leading to the adoption of the Declaration of the Rights of Man and the Citizen. This foundational document espoused universal principles of human rights. Moreover, the French legal tradition, emphasizing individual rights and the rule of law, has further reinforced the country's dedication to upholding fundamental freedoms domestically and internationally. This historical context provides the framework through which France engages with Arab countries on human rights and democratization matters. France's philosophical foundations of liberty and equality serve as a cornerstone of advocating for the protection of civil liberties, freedom of expression, and advancing democratic governance across the Arab world. These principles guide France's diplomatic engagements and partnerships with Arab governments and civil society organizations as it seeks to promote pluralism, tolerance, and civic participation. Furthermore, France views promoting women's rights, minority rights, and the rule of law as essential components of the broader human rights framework and democracy. By integrating these values into its foreign policy initiatives, France aims to foster sustainable political development and social progress while respecting the diverse cultural and religious landscapes of the Arab region. This commitment is reflected in France's support for civil society initiatives, independent media organizations, and human rights defenders working to advance democratic reforms and protect fundamental freedoms in Arab countries. Through dialogues, capacity-building programs, and financial assistance, France strives to empower local actors to strengthen democratic institutions, judicial independence, and participatory governance structures in the Arab world. France's philosophical approach, grounded in the principles of liberty and equality, underscores its enduring commitment to advancing human rights and democratization in the Arab world. By leveraging its historical legacy and contemporary experiences, France endeavors to foster inclusive societies, responsive governments, and accountable institutions in collaboration with Arab partners. This principled engagement exemplifies France's unwavering dedication to upholding the universal values of human rights and democracy while respecting the cultural specificities and aspirations of the diverse communities within the Arab region.

## Bilateral Initiatives for Democracy Support

France's commitment to democracy support in Arab countries goes beyond rhetoric, underscored by tangible bilateral initiatives to foster democratic governance and respect for human rights. Through diplomatic channels and strategic partnerships, France has continually engaged with Arab states to bolster institutional capacity, promote civic participation, and uphold the principles of a free and fair electoral process. Key to this endeavor is the provision of technical assistance and training programs tailored to the specific needs of each partner country. Such initiatives focus on strengthening the judiciary, enhancing electoral frameworks, and empowering civil society organizations to play a more active role in shaping public policies. Moreover, France's emphasis on promoting media pluralism and freedom of expression is fundamental in advancing democratic values and ensuring transparency within governance structures. The exchange of best practices and expertise further enriches these initiatives as France collaborates closely with its Arab counterparts to share knowledge and build sustainable mechanisms for democratic governance. These bilateral efforts are emblematic of France's unwavering dedication to supporting the emergence of robust and inclusive democratic systems in the Arab world. By forging enduring partnerships and fostering mutual understanding, France continues to play a pivotal role in laying the groundwork for democratic advancement across the region.

## Case Studies: Successful Interventions and Challenges

In examining Franco-Arab relations within the context of human rights and democracy promotion, it becomes essential to delve into specific case studies that highlight both successful interventions and the challenges faced by France and Arab countries. One such case study is the transition in Tunisia following the Arab Spring. France played a crucial role in supporting the establishment of democratic processes and institutions, providing financial aid and technical assistance to facilitate the country's progress towards greater political openness and respect for human rights. The successful democratic transition in Tunisia is a notable achievement resulting from bilateral cooperation between France and the Tunisian government, showcasing the positive impact of targeted interventions in promoting democratic values. Conversely, the situation in other Arab countries, such as Syria and Libya, presents significant challenges for democracy promotion. The complex conflicts and geopolitical dynamics in these countries have posed formidable obstacles to efforts aimed at fostering democratic governance and upholding human rights. France's involvement in addressing these challenges has been met with mixed results, underscoring the intricate nature of democratization processes in conflict-ridden environments. The case study of Algeria also offers insights into the delicate balance between advocating for human rights and maintaining diplomatic relations. France has navigated the complexities of engaging with the Algerian government while simultaneously promoting fundamental rights and democratic reforms, epitomizing the nuanced approach required in such circumstances. By critically analyzing these case studies, it is evident that successful interventions in human rights and democracy are contingent upon tailored strategies, sustained commitment, and an acute awareness of local contexts and sensitivities. Moreover, the challenges encountered underscore the need for adaptable and context-specific approaches to effectively advance democratic principles in the diverse landscape of Arab countries. Through a comprehensive examination of such case studies, a deeper understanding of the opportunities and obstacles inherent in promoting human rights and democracy in Franco-Arab relations emerges, providing valuable insights for future initiatives and policy frameworks.

## Multilateral Efforts and International Cooperation

In human rights and democracy promotion, France has consistently emphasized the significance of multilateral efforts and international cooperation to address challenges and advance common objectives. With a deep-rooted commitment to upholding universal human rights standards, France actively engages in collaborative initiatives with regional and global partners, recognizing that collective action is essential for effecting meaningful change.

France's involvement in multilateral human rights advocacy is manifested through its active participation in international organizations such as the United Nations, the European Union, and the Council of Europe. These platforms serve as critical arenas for dialogue, consensus-building, and the formulation of shared strategies to promote democratic governance, the rule of law, and fundamental freedoms in Arab countries and beyond. Through these forums, France leverages its diplomatic influence to advocate for protecting human rights defenders, reinforcing democratic institutions, and eradicating systemic injustices.

Furthermore, France strongly emphasizes fostering cooperation and coordination with other like-minded states, non-governmental organizations, and civil society actors committed to championing human rights causes. By facilitating exchanges of best practices, expertise, and resources, France aims to strengthen the capacities of local advocates and institutions, tailoring interventions to the specific needs and contexts of individual countries. This approach underscores France's recognition of the intrinsic value of inclusive partnerships and the necessity of recognizing and respecting the agency of local communities in pursuing human rights goals.

The engagement in multilateral efforts also extends to supporting transitional justice mechanisms, conflict resolution, and peacebuilding initiatives in regions grappling with protracted conflicts and political instability. France seeks to contribute to establishing mechanisms that address past injustices, promote reconciliation, and lay the foundations for sustainable peace, underlining the interdependence between human rights, stability, and development.

Acknowledging the complexities and nuanced dynamics inherent in multilateral endeavors related to human rights and democracy promotion is imperative. The diverse cultural, historical, and political contexts within Arab countries necessitate comprehensive approaches that recognize the individuality of each nation's journey toward realizing human rights aspirations. As such, France remains dedicated to engaging in meaningful dialogues, fostering mutual understanding, and patiently building consensus to navigate differing perspectives and priorities.

France views multilateral efforts and international cooperation as indispensable for advancing a shared vision of a world where dignity, equality, and justice prevail. While acknowledging the inherent challenges and constraints of such collaborative endeavors, France remains unwavering in working alongside the international community to cultivate a global environment conducive to fulfilling human rights and flourishing democratic values.

## *Criticism and Controversies*

Criticism and controversies surrounding France's promotion of human rights and democracy in the Arab world have been subject to intense debate and scrutiny. One central point of contention revolves around the perceived alignment of France's approach with its own geopolitical and economic interests. Critics argue that France has, at times, prioritized strategic alliances and trade partnerships over holding Arab countries accountable for human rights abuses, potentially undermining the credibility of its advocacy efforts. Additionally, some voices within the international community have raised concerns about the potential imposition of Western democratic models on Arab societies, citing cultural insensitivity and the risk of exacerbating internal tensions and opposition. These concerns reflect a broader skepticism regarding the universal applicability of Western principles in non-Western contexts and necessitate a thoughtful reassessment of France's methodologies. Furthermore, there have been criticisms of selective interventionism, with claims that France has been inconsistent in its responses to human rights violations based on political expediency, thereby compromising the integrity and impact of its advocacy. The degree of reliance on diplomatic channels and soft-power measures, as opposed to more assertive actions, has also elicited divergent opinions within both French and Arab societies. This critique highlights the need for a delicate balance between fostering constructive dialogue and leveraging diplomatic leverage to effect meaningful change. Another contentious area is the perceived lack of consultative and participatory approaches in crafting and implementing democratization initiatives, with stakeholders questioning the inclusivity and transparency of decision-making processes. This absence of genuine engagement with local actors and communities raises valid concerns about imposed reforms' long-term efficacy and sustainability. Lastly, debates have arisen regarding the role of historical colonial legacies and their potential influence on contemporary policies, stirring complex reflections on postcolonial power dynamics and underlying motivations. Addressing these criticisms and controversies requires a deep reflection on France's strategies and an open dialogue with all relevant parties to recalibrate approaches that respect the autonomy and diversity of Arab societies while upholding universal values.

## *Current Trends and Emerging Issues*

The landscape of human rights and democracy promotion in the Franco-Arab context constantly evolves, shaped by emerging trends and issues that demand attention and strategic responses. One notable trend is the growing digital activism in Arab countries, where social media and online platforms have become powerful tools for advocating human rights, exposing injustices, and mobilizing citizens for democratic change. This presents both opportunities and challenges for diplomatic engagement as governments navigate the impact of digital activism on domestic politics and international relations. Additionally, the issue of migration and displacement has significant implications for human rights, with France and Arab countries facing complex humanitarian and legal considerations in addressing the needs of refugees and asylum seekers while upholding their rights. Furthermore, the rise of populism and nationalist sentiments in some regions threatens universal human rights values and may require nuanced approaches to foster dialogue and understanding. The role of civil society organizations and non-governmental entities in promoting human rights cannot be overlooked, as these actors often drive grassroots movements and advocate for policy reforms. Fostering partnerships and collaboration with civil society groups becomes essential for advancing democratic principles. Moreover, the intersection of technology and human rights introduces new ethical and legal dilemmas, from cybersecurity concerns to the ethical use of artificial intelligence in surveillance and control. France's commitment to human rights and democracy promotion requires an informed approach to address these challenges while seizing opportunities presented by technological advancements. In the realm of gender equality and women's rights, ongoing efforts to empower women politically, economically, and socially intersect with broader human rights agendas. Encouraging women's participation in decision-making processes and addressing gender-based violence are critical components of a comprehensive human rights framework—finally, environmental degradation and climate change present interconnected human rights challenges, particularly in vulnerable communities. Recognizing the inherent link between environmental sustainability and human rights underscores the necessity for holistic approaches to address these intertwined issues. Effective diplomacy in navigating current trends and emerging issues demands adaptability, empathy, and a deep understanding of the evolving dynamics within Franco-Arab relations.

## Future Directions for Franco-Arab Relations in Human Rights

The future of Franco-Arab relations in the context of human rights holds significant implications for both regions and the global community. As we move forward, France and Arab countries must recalibrate their approach towards a more inclusive, effective, and coordinated strategy that advances fundamental human rights principles while respecting cultural nuances and sovereignty. This chapter delves into the potential pathways and considerations crucial for shaping the future trajectories of human rights in Franco-Arab relations.

1. Strengthening Educational and Exchange Programs: Enhancing mutual understanding and collaboration through educational partnerships, cultural exchange programs, and academic initiatives can foster greater awareness and respect for human rights values. By investing in youth empowerment and educational opportunities, both regions can cultivate a future generation of leaders committed to upholding human rights and democratic principles.
2. Promoting Dialogue and Multilateral Diplomacy: It is essential to emphasize the importance of constructive dialogue and multilateral diplomacy in addressing human rights challenges. France and Arab countries should engage in sustained, respectful dialogues within international forums and organizations to foster consensus-building and collective action on human rights issues. It is paramount to work collaboratively towards creating norms, standards, and mechanisms that uphold human rights accountability and transparency.
3. Leveraging Technology and Digital Initiatives: Harnessing the potential of technology and digital diplomacy can provide innovative solutions for promoting human rights and democracy. Utilizing digital platforms for advocacy, information dissemination, and civil society engagement can amplify voices, facilitate

access to information, and nurture a vibrant public sphere. However, this approach requires careful consideration and safeguards to mitigate risks such as censorship and privacy rights infringement.
4. Empowering Civil Society and Grassroots Movements: Empowering civil society organizations and grassroots movements is pivotal in advancing human rights and democratic values. France and Arab countries should prioritize support for civil society initiatives, ensuring an enabling environment for independent voices, activism, and civic participation. Strengthening legal frameworks and protections for human rights defenders, journalists, and marginalized communities is essential to fostering inclusive and resilient societies.
5. Navigating Complex Geopolitical Realities: Understanding the complex geopolitical dynamics that shape Franco-Arab relations and human rights is vital. Striking a balance between pragmatic engagement and principled advocacy amidst geopolitical challenges necessitates astute diplomatic maneuvering. France and Arab countries must navigate regional power dynamics, conflicts, and security concerns while upholding human rights at the forefront of their collaborations and policy decisions.

In conclusion, the future of Franco-Arab relations in human rights hinges upon fostering a common commitment to universal human rights values while embracing diversity and cultural distinctiveness. By prioritizing inclusive and sustainable strategies, both regions can fortify their partnership and contribute meaningfully to the global promotion of human rights and democratic governance.

## *Summary and Concluding Remarks*

In summary, the complex and evolving nature of Franco-Arab relations in the domain of human rights underscores the significance of continued dialogue, cooperation, and introspection. As France and Arab countries navigate the intricate landscape of human rights and democracy promotion, it is imperative to acknowledge the historical contexts and cultural nuances that shape these relationships. While progress has been made through bilateral and multilateral initiatives, addressing the criticisms and controversies surrounding intervention and recalibrating strategies for a more significant impact is essential.

Moreover, the convergence of geopolitical shifts, technological advancements, and social movements demands a proactive approach toward safeguarding and advancing human rights. France's commitment to its philosophical foundations of liberty and equality, along with the diverse experiences and aspirations of Arab societies, serves as a focal point for future engagement. Both regions can nurture a more inclusive and rights-respecting landscape by leveraging soft power and public diplomacy, fostering intercultural exchange, and aligning economic partnerships with human rights considerations.

Concluding this discourse, the path forward for Franco-Arab relations in human rights rests on a foundation of mutual respect, constructive dialogue, and transparent collaboration. This involves acknowledging past shortcomings, learning from successful endeavors, and embracing innovation to address current and emerging challenges. Through sustained efforts to build trust, share best practices, and amplify marginalized communities' voices, France and Arab countries can collectively chart a more equitable and dignified future. The journey towards upholding human rights and promoting democracy is dynamic and nuanced, requiring adaptability, empathy, and unwavering dedication. As this book concludes, the pursuit of a harmonious and rights-centric partnership between France and Arab countries stands as an enduring imperative, contributing not only to regional stability but also to the global advancement of fundamental freedoms and democratic principles.

## IN A NUTSHELL

> ### *Human rights in the Middle East*
> Shaped by the legal and political development of international human rights law
> **Universal Declaration of Human Rights**
> Egypt, Iran, and Pakistan signed in 1948, while Saudi Arabia did not, citing cultural and religious context
> **Cairo Declaration of Human Rights in Islam**
> Adopted by 45 member states of the OIC in 1990, based on Shari'a law
> **Arab Charter on Human Rights**
> Entered into force in March 2017, with several Arab states ratifying it
> **Arab Human Rights Committee**
> Established in 2009 to oversee compliance with the Arab Charter on Human Rights
>
> France has had a complex relationship with human rights and democracy in the Arab world, shaped by its historical ties, strategic interests, and philosophical foundations. Here is an analysis of various aspects of this dynamic:

## Historical Overview of Human Rights in Arab Countries

Many Arab nations have struggled with upholding human rights and democratic principles since gaining independence in the 20th century. Some key issues include:

- Authoritarian regimes, lack of free elections, and restrictions on civil liberties like freedom of speech, assembly etc.
- Women's rights issues, discrimination against minorities and migrants.
- Use of torture, arbitrary detentions, lack of due process under security laws.
- Conflicts, civil wars exacerbating human rights violations like civilian casualties, displacement etc.

However, there have also been pro-democracy movements demanding reform, notably the Arab Spring protests starting in 2011 across several countries.

## France's Philosophical Foundations

France's approach is rooted in the ideals of "liberté, égalité, fraternité" (liberty, equality, fraternity) from the French Revolution. Key aspects include:

- Emphasis on individual freedoms, human rights as universal values.
- Secularism and separation of religion from state.
- Promoting democratic governance, rule of law.

However, France has also faced criticism over issues like religious intolerance, ethnic/racial discrimination, and colonial legacies that contradict these principles.

## Bilateral Initiatives and Case Studies

France has pursued a mix of bilateral initiatives to support human rights and democracy in Arab nations:

- Development aid for governance, civil society, women's empowerment projects.
- Military interventions against authoritarian regimes, e.g. in Mali (2013), Libya (2011).
- Support for pro-democracy protests during the Arab Spring, e.g. in Tunisia.

However, France has also faced criticism for prioritizing strategic/economic interests over human rights at times:

- Arms sales to Gulf monarchies involved in Yemen conflict despite civilian casualties.
- Reluctance to criticize human rights violations by close partners like Algeria, Morocco.

## Multilateral Efforts and Cooperation

France cooperates with multilateral bodies on human rights in the Arab world:

- Support for UN peacekeeping, mediation efforts to resolve conflicts.

- Promoting EU policies, sanctions to incentivize human rights reform.
- Engagement with Arab human rights mechanisms like Arab Charter, Arab Court.

However, the effectiveness of these efforts is often constrained by geopolitical interests of different actors.

## Criticism and Controversies

Key criticisms of France's approach include:

- Accusations of neo-colonial attitudes, double standards in dealing with allied regimes.
- Concerns over ethnic/religious discrimination against Arab/Muslim minorities in France itself.
- Debates around freedom of speech vs. hate speech in the French context.

## Current Trends and Future Directions

Some current and potential future developments:

- Continued human rights dialogues, democracy support initiatives with Arab partners.
- Managing tensions between security, counter-terrorism policies and human rights.
- Increasing focus on emerging issues like online freedom, tech surveillance, climate justice.
- Calls for a more consistent, value-based foreign policy not compromised by economic interests.

Overall, Franco-Arab relations on human rights and democracy remain complex, requiring France to balance its principles with pragmatic interests, while cooperating with Arab nations and international actors to make progress on this agenda.

# References For Further Reading

Matthews, Thandwive. "To be Equal and Free: The Nexus Between Human Rights and Democracy". A Publication of Heinrich Böll Foundation, December 2019. https://www.boell.de/sites/default/files/2020-01/200128_Human%20Rights%20and%20Democracy%20Paper%20%28UPDATEv004%29.pdf

Laurent Fabius, Minister of Foreign Affairs, "France and the New Arab World". Paris, 27 June 2012. https://au.ambafrance.org/IMG/pdf/120704_France_and_the_New_Arab_World.pdf

Boniface, Pascal. "Beyond Islamophobia: France's Policies toward the Arab World." IRIS, December 22, 2020. https://www.iris-france.org/153125-beyond-islamophobia-frances-policies-toward-the-arab-world/.

Day, Jonathan. "Liberté, Égalité, Fraternité: The Meaning and History of France's National Motto." Liberties.eu, May 18, 2021. https://www.liberties.eu/en/stories/liberte-egalite-fraternite/43532.

Duryea, Catherine. "Human Rights Movements in the Middle East." E-International Relations, May 20, 2019. https://www.e-ir.info/2019/05/20/human-rights-movements-in-the-middle-east/.

France Diplomacy - Ministry for Europe and Foreign Affairs. "Middle-East," September 2020. https://www.diplomatie.gouv.fr/en/french-foreign-policy/security-disarmament-and-non-proliferation/crises-and-conflicts/israel-palestine/.

Hadad, Dina. "Human Rights in the Arab World: A Regional Legacy in Crisis."

ATHENS JOURNAL of LAW 5, no. 3 (July 1, 2019): 275–302. https://doi.org/10.30958/ajl.5-3-4.

Human Rights Watch. "France: Events of 2023." Human Rights Watch, December 16, 2023. https://www.hrw.org/world-report/2024/country-chapters/france.

Lequesne, Christian. "Support for Democracy and Human Rights in France," February 21, 2022. https://sciencespo.hal.science/hal-03582139/document.

"Liberty -Equality -Fraternity," n.d. https://et.ambafrance.org/IMG/pdf/2022-11-21_traduction_anglais_125_ferensay_legasion_2212_-2.pdf.

Mikail, Barah. "France and the Arab Spring: An Opportunistic Quest for Influence," 2011. https://www.files.ethz.ch/isn/133447/WP110_France_and_arab_spring.pdf.

Ministère de l'Europe et des Affaires étrangères. "Liberty, Equality, Fraternity." France Diplomatie :: Ministry for Europe and Foreign Affairs. France Diplomatie - MEAE, 2023. https://www.diplomatie.gouv.fr/en/coming-to-france/france-facts/symbols-of-the-republic/article/liberty-equality-fraternity.

Permanent Mission of France. "14 July and Symbols of France," September 29, 2023. https://onu-geneve.delegfrance.org/14-July-and-symbols-of-France.

Présidence de la République . "Liberty, Equality, Fraternity." elysee.fr, December 14, 2022. https://www.elysee.fr/en/french-presidency/liberty-equality-fraternity.

"The Arab Human Rights System Annex to the ABC of Human Rights for Development Cooperation," 2017. https://www.institut-fuer-menschenrechte.de/fileadmin/user_upload/Publikationen/E-Info-Tool/e-info-tool_abc_of_hr_for_dev_coop_the_arab_hr-system.pdf.

Ufheil-Somers, Amanda. "The Middle East and Human Rights." MERIP, December 1, 1987. https://merip.org/1987/11/the-middle-east-and-human-rights/.

Weston, Burns H. "Human Rights - Human Rights in the Arab World | Britannica." www.britannica.com, n.d. https://www.britannica.com/topic/human-rights/Human-rights-in-the-Arab-world.

Williamson, Lucy. "What Do Liberty, Equality, Fraternity Mean to France Now?" BBC News, July 13, 2016. https://www.bbc.com/news/world-europe-36775634.

# XII

# Peacekeeping and Conflict Resolution Efforts

## Introduction to Peacekeeping Initiatives

French peacekeeping operations have been pivotal in maintaining peace and stability in conflict-affected regions across the Arab world. These operations serve a dual purpose: to protect civilians from violence and to create an environment conducive to long-lasting peace and development. The goals of French peacekeeping initiatives are deeply rooted in the principles of international law, human rights, and the maintenance of global security. Through these initiatives, France aims to facilitate dialogue, prevent conflicts, and build the capacity of local institutions to manage societal tensions and transition towards sustainable peace effectively. The importance of these objectives cannot be overstated, as they are essential for promoting stability, fostering reconciliation, and encouraging socio-economic progress in war-torn areas. By engaging in peacekeeping activities, France demonstrates its commitment to upholding international norms and supporting vulnerable populations in times of crisis. These initiatives also emphasize the country's proactive approach to addressing complex security challenges and contributing to the broader global peace agenda.

## *Historical Context of French Involvement*

France has a long history of involvement in peacekeeping and conflict resolution efforts in the Arab world, stemming from its colonial legacy and diplomatic interests. The historical context of French participation in this domain can be traced back to the decolonization era when France sought to maintain influence and presence in its former colonies while also shaping the geopolitical landscape in the post-colonial Arab states. This period marked a significant transition for French foreign policy, as it sought to navigate the complexities of maintaining ties with newly independent nations while safeguarding its strategic interests. French involvement in peacekeeping initiatives in the Middle East and North Africa can be viewed through various lenses, including military interventions, diplomatic negotiations, and cooperation with international organizations. Throughout the decades, France has actively addressed conflicts and promoted stability in the region, often leveraging its historical ties and cultural understanding to engage with regional stakeholders. The historical context also encompasses France's role during critical junctures such as the Arab-Israeli conflicts, civil wars, and geopolitical realignments, which have shaped the trajectory of its involvement in peacekeeping and conflict resolution efforts. Moreover, the evolution of French involvement reflects broader shifts in global politics, including the impact of the Cold War, regional power dynamics, and changes in international norms related to peace and security. By delving into the historical context of French involvement, we gain insight into its diplomatic strategies' continuity, its adaptation of its peacekeeping approaches, and the enduring commitment to enhancing stability and reconciliation in the Arab world.

## Key Frameworks and International Mandates

Key frameworks and international mandates are foundational in shaping France's involvement in peacekeeping and conflict resolution efforts in the Arab world. Drawing upon historical precedents and evolving global dynamics, these frameworks provide the essential guidelines and legal basis for French interventions in conflict zones. At the heart of this framework lies the United Nations Security Council, which is primarily responsible for maintaining international peace and security. Under Chapter VII of the UN Charter, the authorization of peacekeeping missions through UN Security Council Resolutions forms the legal bedrock upon which French engagements are predicated. This grants legitimacy to France's participation in addressing conflicts and upholding stability in the Arab world. Additionally, critical international mandates such as the Responsibility to Protect (R2P) doctrine and the Geneva Conventions serve as guiding principles for France's commitments to preventing mass atrocities, protecting civilians, and ensuring compliance with international humanitarian law. In tandem with these frameworks, diplomatic engagement and negotiation strategies within the framework of international law are paramount in fostering cooperation and consensus among diverse stakeholders. Utilizing mediation, conflict prevention, and peacebuilding initiatives underscores France's proactive approach to promoting sustainable peace in the region. Moreover, adherence to multilateral conventions and treaties, including the Arms Trade Treaty and the Ottawa Treaty banning anti-personnel landmines, showcases France's commitment to advancing arms control and disarmament efforts. Recognizing the complex nature of these mandates, France continuously seeks to enhance its capacity and expertise by collaborating with regional and international partners, contributing to training, and strengthening the capabilities of peacekeeping forces. By embracing a holistic approach that encompasses legal and normative frameworks, France endeavors to fulfill its obligations as a responsible actor in advancing peace and stability across the Arab world.

## Case Studies: Successful Missions in the Arab World

In the Arab world, France has undertaken numerous peacekeeping missions to promote stability and conflict resolution. One notable success story is the mission in Lebanon, where French troops played a pivotal role in implementing UN Security Council Resolution 1701. This resolution aimed to end the 2006 Israel-Lebanon conflict and resulted in significant progress towards peace and stability in the region. As part of the United Nations Interim Force in Lebanon (UNIFIL), the French contingent demonstrated exceptional professionalism and adaptability in navigating complex political and security challenges.

Another compelling case study is France's involvement in the Darfur region of Sudan. The French peacekeeping forces contributed to the African Union-United Nations Hybrid Operation in Darfur (UNAMID), which aimed to protect civilians and facilitate humanitarian assistance amid a prolonged conflict. Through strategic engagement and coordination with international partners, France made meaningful contributions to mitigating the impact of the crisis and laying the groundwork for sustainable peace-building efforts.

A critical success was also achieved in Côte d'Ivoire, where French forces supported the United Nations Operation in Côte d'Ivoire (UNOCI) in stabilizing the country after political turmoil and conflict. Through their commitment to upholding the principles of peacekeeping and their respect for local communities, French troops effectively advanced the cause of peace and reconciliation.

Furthermore, France's participation in the Multinational Force and Observers (MFO) in the Sinai Peninsula stands as a testament to its enduring commitment to peacekeeping in the Arab world. France has played a constructive role in preserving regional peace and security by deploying military personnel to monitor compliance with the Egypt-Israel Peace Treaty.

These case studies underscore France's proactive engagement and unwavering dedication to fostering peace and stability in the Arab world through its peacekeeping missions. The lessons learned from these successful endeavors continue to inform France's strategic approach to addressing present and future challenges in conflict zones.

## *Challenges and Obstacles in Conflict Zones*

One of the most formidable challenges in conflict zones is the complex political, ethnic, and religious tensions that often underpin the conflicts. These factors can exacerbate existing grievances and create persistent obstacles to lasting peace. Additionally, the presence of extremist groups and non-state actors further complicates the situation, as their agendas may diverge from the interests of the local population and the broader goals of international peacekeeping efforts.

In conflict zones, humanitarian crises are often widespread, with populations facing dire food, water, shelter, and healthcare shortages. This poses immediate threats to life and well-being and hampers the prospects of establishing stable governance and rebuilding infrastructure. Moreover, the presence of landmines and unexploded ordnance adds another layer of danger for both civilians and peacekeeping forces, impeding safe access to essential areas for aid delivery and reconstruction efforts.

Another critical challenge lies in the intricate dynamics of post-conflict reconstruction. Reintegrating former combatants, reconciling divided communities, and rebuilding trust between conflicting factions require careful navigation and sustained commitment. Furthermore, the process of justice and accountability for human rights abuses presents a delicate balancing act, with the need to address past injustices without inciting further discord.

The role of external actors, such as neighboring countries or global powers, can also complicate peacekeeping efforts. Their geopolitical interests, economic entanglements, or historical alliances can influence the trajectory of the conflict, sometimes hindering the establishment of a sustainable peace. Moreover, the influx of refugees and internally displaced persons into neighboring regions can strain already fragile social and economic systems, creating ripple effects that can exacerbate tensions and instability.

Finally, while peacekeepers aim to maintain impartiality and neutrality, navigating local power dynamics and establishing legitimacy among diverse stakeholders presents an ongoing challenge. Building trust and cooperation with local authorities, civil society organizations, and grassroots leaders is essential for effective peacekeeping, yet this requires a nuanced understanding of the intricate socio-political fabric of the conflict-affected region.

Navigating these multifaceted challenges demands strategic coordination, adaptability, and perseverance from all actors involved in peacekeeping and conflict resolution efforts.

## *Role of Diplomacy in Conflict Resolution*

Effective diplomacy plays a crucial role in resolving conflicts within the complex landscape of international relations. In Franco-Arab relations, diplomatic efforts mitigate tensions and foster peaceful resolutions. Diplomacy leverages dialogue, negotiation, and mediation to navigate conflicting interests and facilitate meaningful engagement between the parties involved. By employing diplomatic channels, France has sought to build bridges and establish common ground with Arab states to address historical grievances and constructively resolve contentious issues. Through principled negotiation and skilled mediation, diplomats work towards creating an environment conducive to peace and stability in conflict-affected regions. The role of diplomacy extends beyond mere political negotiations; it encompasses cultural sensitivity, respect for human rights, and commitment to upholding international laws and conventions. This approach underscores the importance of fostering trust and understanding between conflicting parties, laying the groundwork for sustained peace and reconciliation. French diplomats actively engage in backchannel diplomacy, confidential communication, and shuttle diplomacy, utilizing these methods to defuse tensions, build consensus, and encourage constructive dialogue. Their efforts are underpinned by a commitment to upholding humanitarian principles and promoting justice, often involving multilateral diplomacy through collaborative initiatives with international organizations such as the United Nations and the European Union and regional bodies like the Arab League. This collaborative approach enhances the efficacy of conflict resolution measures by pooling diverse resources, expertise, and perspectives. France's diplomatic corps also emphasizes the significance of long-term relationship-building and preventive diplomacy, seeking to address the root causes of conflict before they escalate into crises. Diplomats endeavor to foster enduring stability and create a conducive environment for post-conflict reconstruction and development by addressing underlying grievances and investing in sustainable peacemaking strategies. The adroit practice of diplomacy requires an astute understanding of cultural nuances, historical contexts, and socio-political dynamics. As such, diplomats undergo rigorous training and continuous professional development to handle intricate diplomatic engagements effectively. Moreover, the digital age has expanded diplomatic frontiers, demanding innovative digital diplomacy and public engagement approaches, enabling broader societal participation in conflict resolution efforts. When employed judiciously, diplomacy serves as a force for positive transformation, nurturing mutual respect, fostering cooperation, and paving the path for durable peace in conflicted regions.

## Interactions with Global and Regional Organizations

France's engagement in peacekeeping and conflict resolution efforts is deeply intertwined with its interactions with global and regional organizations. At the global level, France has actively participated in United Nations (UN) peacekeeping missions, providing troops, logistical support, and expertise to promote stability in conflict-stricken regions. The country has consistently emphasized the importance of multilateral cooperation and partnerships to address complex security challenges. This commitment to collaborative action is evident in France's extensive involvement in UN Security Council deliberations and decision-making processes related to peace and security matters. French diplomats have played a pivotal role in shaping UN resolutions and initiatives to ease tensions and foster sustainable peace in the Arab world and beyond. Moreover, France's membership in vital regional organizations such as the European Union (EU) and the Organization for Security and Cooperation in Europe (OSCE) has enabled it to effectively leverage collective resources and expertise to support conflict resolution efforts. The EU, in particular, has served as a platform for France to coordinate diplomatic endeavors and provide humanitarian assistance in crisis-affected areas in close coordination with other member states. Additionally, through the OSCE, France has contributed to conflict prevention and post-conflict rehabilitation initiatives, signaling its commitment to upholding international norms and principles of peaceful coexistence. Furthermore, France has actively engaged with regional bodies such as the Arab League and the African Union to align its peacekeeping strategies with the specific geopolitical dynamics of the Arab region and Africa. By fostering dialogue and collaboration with these organizations, France has been able to tailor its interventions to address local socioeconomic and political complexities, thereby enhancing the efficacy of peacekeeping operations. The interconnected nature of these global and regional interactions underscores France's dedication to creating a harmonious and secure environment through sustained engagement with diverse stakeholders.

## *Impact Assessment: Social and Political Outcomes*

In assessing the impact of France's peacekeeping and conflict resolution efforts in the Arab world, it is crucial to analyze the social and political outcomes comprehensively. French forces and diplomatic interventions have had wide-ranging effects on the affected societies and their political landscapes. The most notable social outcome has been restoring stability and security in post-conflict areas. Through peacekeeping missions, France has played a significant role in providing humanitarian aid, protecting civilians, and rebuilding essential infrastructure, thereby improving living conditions for local populations. This has often resulted in re-establishing social order, fostering an environment conducive to further development and reconciliation. Furthermore, the involvement of French peacekeepers has also led to enhanced intercommunal dialogue and facilitated the return of displaced persons, contributing to the gradual normalization of societal dynamics. From a political perspective, France's peacekeeping efforts have influenced the governance structures and power dynamics within conflict-affected regions. By maintaining peace and security, France has created opportunities to establish and consolidate democratic institutions and the rule of law. Moreover, the support provided by French diplomatic initiatives has enabled the mediation of conflicts, leading to the formulation of inclusive political agreements and transitional arrangements. This has often paved the way for restoring legitimate governance and initiating political reforms, promoting long-term stability. However, it is essential to recognize that the impact assessment also encompasses challenges and unintended consequences. Despite positive outcomes, there have been instances where the application of peacekeeping strategies has faced resistance from local factions, complicating the attainment of sustained stability. Additionally, there have been concerns regarding the potential interference with sovereignty and the risk of inadvertently perpetuating dependency on external assistance. Furthermore, political outcomes have exhibited complexities, including negotiating power-sharing agreements and addressing historical grievances. These complexities highlight the intricate nature of peacekeeping and underscore the need for continued evaluation and adaptation of approaches. Moving forward, an inclusive and thorough impact assessment is indispensable for informing future peacekeeping endeavors, ensuring that the social and political outcomes drive sustainable progress and contribute to achieving lasting peace and stability.

## *France's Future Strategy in Peacekeeping*

As France continues to navigate the complex landscape of peacekeeping and conflict resolution, it is imperative to outline a comprehensive strategy for future engagements. The shifting dynamics in conflict zones call for a proactive approach integrating traditional peacekeeping efforts with evolving geopolitical realities. Firstly, France must prioritize multilateral collaboration and consensus-building within international organizations such as the United Nations and the European Union. By leveraging its diplomatic prowess, France can advocate for more inclusive and effective peacekeeping mandates that address the root causes of conflicts and promote sustainable peace. Moreover, investing in innovative technological solutions for monitoring and intervention will enhance France's operational capabilities in peacekeeping missions. Embracing advancements in surveillance, communication, and rapid response mechanisms will bolster the effectiveness of interventions and minimize risks to peacekeeping personnel. Additionally, France's future strategy should emphasize a holistic approach that encompasses both military operations and socioeconomic and humanitarian initiatives. Engaging with local communities and empowering grassroots peacebuilding efforts will foster long-term stability and resilience in conflict-affected regions. Furthermore, greater emphasis on capacity-building and training programs for local security forces will contribute to the sustainable transfer of responsibilities and ensure a smooth transition towards indigenous peacekeeping capacities. France must adapt its strategy to address non-traditional security threats, including cyber warfare, terrorism, and transnational crime, which have become intertwined with modern conflicts. By integrating expertise from diverse fields such as cybersecurity, counter-terrorism, and law enforcement, France can enhance its contributions to global peace and security. Lastly, an integral part of France's future strategy in peacekeeping involves active engagement with regional stakeholders and the implementation of tailored approaches that reflect the distinct sociopolitical dynamics of each conflict zone. This nuanced approach will enable France to build trust and credibility within the local population, fostering cooperation and ownership of peacebuilding efforts. In conclusion, France's future strategy in peacekeeping should embrace a forward-looking, adaptive, and multidimensional approach that accounts for the intricacies of contemporary conflicts. France can play a pivotal role in promoting sustainable peace and security in conflict-affected regions by aligning its efforts with international partners, focusing on holistic interventions, and adapting to emerging challenges.

## *Summary and Transitional Insights*

As France continues to navigate its future strategy in peacekeeping, it is imperative to summarize the key insights and transitional considerations. The French approach to peacekeeping has evolved significantly over the years, reflecting the dynamic nature of conflicts in the Arab world and beyond. In summary, this chapter has shed light on the historical context of French involvement in peacekeeping efforts in the region, highlighting the multifaceted dimensions of these missions. From the early colonial era to contemporary engagements, France has endeavored to uphold its international peace and security commitments.

The transitional insights from this analysis point towards a nuanced understanding of the challenges and opportunities ahead. France must continue to adapt its peacekeeping strategies to effectively address evolving conflict dynamics, considering the asymmetrical nature of contemporary warfare and the complexities of regional geopolitics. Moreover, as the global landscape transforms, there is an increasing need for collaborative frameworks and multilateral approaches to peacekeeping. France should leverage its diplomatic acumen and historical ties in the Arab world to foster partnerships with regional stakeholders and international organizations.

Furthermore, the impact assessment conducted in this chapter underscores the significance of evaluating peacekeeping missions' social and political outcomes. France must critically assess the efficacy of its interventions, considering the implications for local communities and broader stabilization efforts. By prioritizing the do-no-harm principle and actively engaging with grassroots actors, France can enhance the legitimacy and sustainability of its peacekeeping endeavors.

In light of the foregoing, the future of French peacekeeping in the Arab world hinges upon a comprehensive and adaptive approach. This involves integrating lessons from past experiences, harnessing innovative technologies for conflict prevention and management, and fostering inclusive dialogue among diverse stakeholders. As France embarks on this trajectory, it should remain committed to upholding human rights, promoting sustainable peace, and championing conflict resolution through diplomacy and dialogue.

In conclusion, the transitional insights gleaned from this chapter provide a roadmap for France's continued engagement in peacekeeping and conflict resolution efforts. By incorporating these insights into its strategic framework, France can contribute meaningfully to pursuing enduring peace and stability in the Arab world.

## IN A NUTSHELL

France has a long history of involvement in peacekeeping and conflict resolution efforts in the Arab world, driven by its strategic interests, historical ties, and commitment to international peace and security. Here's a summary of the various aspects of this engagement:

## Historical Context of French Involvement

France's role in peacekeeping missions in the Arab region can be traced back to the post-colonial era when many Arab nations gained independence. Some key historical milestones include:

- 1956: France participated in the first UN peacekeeping operation, the United Nations Emergency Force (UNEF I), deployed in Egypt during the Suez Crisis.
- 1978: France joined the United Nations Interim Force in Lebanon (UNIFIL) following the outbreak of the Lebanese Civil War.
- 1992-1995: France contributed troops to the UN Protection Force (UNPROFOR) in the former Yugoslavia, including Bosnia and Herzegovina.
- 2013: France intervened militarily in Mali under a UN mandate to counter Islamist rebels, leading to the establishment of the UN Multidimensional Integrated Stabilization Mission in Mali (MINUSMA).

France's involvement was often shaped by its desire to maintain influence in its former colonies and project power in regions of strategic importance, especially in North Africa and the Levant.

## Key Frameworks and International Mandates

France's peacekeeping efforts have been conducted under various international frameworks and mandates, primarily through the United Nations but also in cooperation with other organizations:

- UN Security Council Resolutions: France, as a permanent member, has played a key role in drafting and approving resolutions that authorize and define the mandates of UN peacekeeping missions.
- NATO Operations: France has contributed troops to NATO-led missions, such as the Implementation Force (IFOR) and Stabilization Force (SFOR) in Bosnia and Herzegovina.
- EU Missions: France has participated in EU-led civilian and military missions, like the EU Training Mission in Mali (EUTM Mali), complementing UN efforts.
- Ad-hoc Coalitions: In some cases, like the 2011 intervention in Libya, France joined ad-hoc coalitions under a UN mandate to protect civilians.

## Case Studies: Successful Missions in the Arab World

While challenges persist, France has contributed to several peacekeeping missions in the Arab world that have achieved notable outcomes:

- Lebanon (UNIFIL): France has been a major contributor to UNIFIL since its inception, helping to maintain a fragile peace and facilitate humanitarian aid delivery.
- Mali (MINUSMA): The French-led intervention and subsequent UN mission have helped counter terrorist threats and support political stabilization efforts, despite ongoing challenges.
- Libya (2011): The NATO-led intervention, with French participation, helped protect civilians and contributed to the overthrow of Muammar Gaddafi's regime, although the country remains unstable.

## Challenges and Obstacles in Conflict Zones

However, French peacekeeping efforts have also faced significant challenges in various conflict zones:

- Complex Security Situations: Missions often operate in volatile environments with active armed groups, terrorism threats, and civilian protection concerns, as seen in Mali and Lebanon.
- Political Instability: Lack of progress in political processes and governance reforms can undermine peacekeeping efforts, as witnessed in Libya and Lebanon.
- Resource Constraints: Ensuring adequate funding, equipment, and personnel for long-term deployments can be a challenge, especially in protracted conflicts.
- Mandate Limitations: Restrictive mandates or rules of engagement can limit the effectiveness of peacekeeping forces in responding to evolving situations.

## Role of Diplomacy in Conflict Resolution

France has complemented its military contributions with diplomatic efforts to facilitate conflict resolution and promote political solutions:

- Peace Negotiations: France has hosted or participated in various peace conferences and initiatives, such as the 2016 Middle East Peace Initiative in Paris.
- Mediation Efforts: French diplomats have engaged in mediation efforts, often in coordination with regional partners like the Arab League, to resolve conflicts like those in Lebanon and Libya.
- Capacity Building: France provides training and support to build the capacities of local security forces and institutions in conflict-affected countries.

## Interactions with Global and Regional Organizations

France's peacekeeping efforts have involved close cooperation with global and regional organizations:

- United Nations: France works closely with the UN Secretariat, Security Council, and various UN agencies in planning, deploying, and supporting peacekeeping missions.
- NATO: France has contributed to NATO-led

operations, leveraging the alliance's military capabilities and coordination mechanisms.
- European Union: France collaborates with EU institutions and other member states in civilian and military crisis management missions.
- Arab League: France engages with the Arab League and its member states to coordinate efforts and seek regional buy-in for peacekeeping initiatives.
- African Union: France supports AU-led peace operations, such as the AU Mission in Somalia (AMISOM), through capacity building and logistical assistance.

## *Impact Assessment: Social and Political Outcomes*

The impact of French peacekeeping efforts in the Arab world has been mixed, with both positive outcomes and ongoing challenges:

- Positive Outcomes: Missions have contributed to protecting civilians, facilitating humanitarian aid, supporting political transitions, and capacity building in some contexts.
- Ongoing Challenges: However, lasting peace and stability remain elusive in many conflict zones, with issues like terrorism, governance deficits, and human rights concerns persisting.
- Criticism: France has faced criticism from human rights groups over perceived prioritization of strategic interests over human rights concerns in some cases.

## France's Future Strategy in Peacekeeping

Looking ahead, France is likely to continue its engagement in peacekeeping and conflict resolution efforts in the Arab world, while adapting its approach to address evolving challenges:

- Emphasis on Political Solutions: France is expected to place greater emphasis on facilitating political processes and inclusive governance as prerequisites for lasting peace.
- Burden-Sharing: France may seek to share the burden of peacekeeping through enhanced cooperation with regional organizations and partners, given resource constraints.
- Human Rights and Accountability: There may be increased pressure on France to prioritize human rights, accountability, and the protection of civilians in its peacekeeping efforts.
- Counterterrorism and Stabilization: Countering terrorism and supporting stabilization efforts are likely to remain priorities, especially in the Sahel region and the Levant.

Overall, while France's peacekeeping efforts have yielded mixed results, its continued engagement in the Arab world reflects its strategic interests, historical ties, and commitment to international peace and security. Adapting to evolving challenges and fostering regional cooperation will be crucial for the effectiveness of future peacekeeping endeavors.

# References For Further Reading

Amb. DE RIVIÈRE, NICOLAS . "France Voted in Favor of the Draft Resolution Providing New Rights to the Observer State of Palestine within the United Nations." France ONU, May 10, 2024. https://onu.delegfrance.org/france-voted-in-favor-of-the-draft-resolution-providing-new-rights-on-the.

Tardy, Thierry, '5 France', in Alex J. Bellamy, and Paul D. Williams (eds), Providing Peacekeepers: The Politics, Challenges, and Future of United Nations Peacekeeping Contributions (Oxford, 2013; online edn, Oxford Academic, 23 May 2013), https://doi.org/10.1093/acprof:oso/9780199672820.003.0006, accessed 22 May 2024.

———. "Strengthening Cooperation between the Arab League and the UN Remains Essential." France ONU, June 8, 2023. https://onu.delegfrance.org/strengthening-cooperation-between-the-arab-league-and-the-un-remains-essential.

Amb. NICOLAS DE RIVIERE, NICOLAS . "France Voted in Favor of the Resolution Presented on Behalf of the Arab Group." France ONU, October 27, 2023. https://onu.delegfrance.org/france-voted-in-favor-of-the-resolution-presented-on-behalf-of-the-arab-group.

Boniface, Pascal . "Beyond Islamophobia: France's Policies toward the Arab World." IRIS, December 22, 2020. https://www.iris-france.org/153125-beyond-islamophobia-frances-policies-toward-the-arab-world/.

El Karoui , Hakim. "A New Strategy for France in a New Arab World." Institut Montaigne, August 2017. https://www.institutmontaigne.org/en/publications/new-strategy-france-new-arab-world.

Fayet, Héloïse. "What Strategic Posture Should France Adopt in the Middle East?," November 2022. https://www.ifri.org/sites/default/files/atoms/files/fayet_focus112_pmo_us_2023.pdf.

France Diplomacy - Ministry for Europe and Foreign Affairs. "France and UN Peacekeeping Operations," September 2020. https://www.diplomatie.gouv.fr/en/french-foreign-policy/france-and-the-united-nations/france-and-the-united-nations/france-and-un-peacekeeping-operations/.

France Diplomacy - Ministry for Europe and Foreign Affairs. "Initiative for the Middle East Peace Process," January 15, 2017. https://www.diplomatie.gouv.fr/en/country-files/israel-palestinian-territories/peace-process/initiative-for-the-middle-east-peace-process/.

France Diplomacy - Ministry for Europe and Foreign Affairs. "United Nations – 75th Anniversary of the Blue Helmets and Peacekeeping Operations (29.05.23)," 2023. https://www.diplomatie.gouv.fr/en/french-foreign-policy/france-and-the-united-nations/news-and-events/news/news-2023/article/united-nations-75th-anniversary-of-the-blue-helmets-and-peacekeeping-operations.

France ONU. "United Nations Peacekeeping," n.d. https://onu.delegfrance.org/united-nations-peacekeeping.
La France aux Émirats arabes unis. "Middle East Peace Process Initiative," June 7, 2016. https://ae.ambafrance.org/Middle-east-Peace-process-initiative.

L'IHEDN : Institut des hautes études de défense nationale. "Opérations Extérieures : Quand La France Se Met Au Service de L'ONU," August 21, 2023. https://ihedn.fr/en/2023/08/21/operations-exterieures-quand-la-france-se-met-au-service-de-lonu/.

onu.delegfrance.org. "France ONU," n.d. https://onu.delegfrance.org/-France-at-the-United-Nations-.

Ricard, Philippe. "French Diplomats Frustrated by Macron's Decisions in the Middle East." Le Monde.fr, November 9, 2023. https://www.lemonde.fr/en/international/article/2023/11/09/french-diplomats-frustrated-by-macron-s-decisions-in-the-middle-east_6240340_4.html.

Uysal , Selin . "France's Diplomatic Role in the Middle East Post-October 7 | the Washington Institute." www.washingtoninstitute.org, February 2, 2024. https://www.washingtoninstitute.org/policy-analysis/frances-diplomatic-role-middle-east-post-october-7.

www.cheminsdememoire.gouv.fr. "The History of the Overseas Operations of the French Armed Forces since 1963 | Chemins de Mémoire." Ministère des Armées, n.d. https://www.cheminsdememoire.gouv.fr/en/history-overseas-operations-french-armed-forces-1963.

# XIII

# Environmental Cooperation and Sustainable Development

## Introduction to Franco-Arab Environmental Initiatives

The onset of environmental initiatives between France and Arab countries marks a significant milestone in the shared commitment to sustainable development and ecological preservation. This cooperative effort can be traced to the early influencers who recognized the interdependence between environmental stewardship and long-term socio-economic prosperity. Historical interactions between France and Arab states laid the groundwork for mutual understanding and collaboration on environmental issues. Early pioneers and thought leaders from both regions were instrumental in fostering an awareness of the need for concerted action to address environmental challenges. Their efforts sowed the seeds for future joint endeavors and set the stage for establishing enduring partnerships. Within this context, the foundational principles of Franco-Arab environmental cooperation took root, guided by a sense of responsibility towards the planet and a collective vision for sustainable development. The historical overview of cooperation provides invaluable insights into the evolution of shared environmental values and the shaping of collaborative strategies to safeguard the natural world while advancing societal progress.

## Historical Overview of Cooperation

The historical cooperation between France and the Arab world in the environmental arena dates back to the mid-20th century, following decolonization. During this time, both regions recognized the pressing need for collaborative efforts to address environmental challenges. Creating organizations such as the Union for the Mediterranean and the Arab League provided platforms for dialogue and action on environmental issues, laying the foundation for future collaboration. French-Arab environmental cooperation gained momentum in the 1970s with the emergence of global environmental movements and the recognition of environmental degradation as a transnational issue requiring coordinated responses. This era saw the signing of several bilateral and multilateral agreements to promote sustainable development, biodiversity conservation, and climate resilience across the Franco-Arab region. The 1990s marked a turning point in environmental cooperation, with an increasing focus on sustainable development goals and integrating environmental considerations into economic and social policies. Initiatives such as the Marseille Declaration on Environment and Development reaffirmed the commitment of both France and Arab countries to pursue sustainable practices while addressing poverty and inequality. The early 21st century witnessed a deepening of cooperation in response to the growing threats of climate change and natural resource depletion. Joint initiatives focused on renewable energy, water management, and ecosystem preservation have been instrumental in strengthening the ties between France and Arab states. As the world faces unprecedented environmental challenges, the historical overview of Franco-Arab environmental cooperation is a testament to the enduring commitment to preserving the planet for future generations.

## *Key Agreements and Multilateral Treaties*

In Franco-Arab environmental cooperation and sustainable development, key agreements and multilateral treaties have played a pivotal role in shaping collaborative efforts and fostering mutual commitment to address pressing environmental challenges. Over the years, both France and various Arab states have actively engaged in formalizing their environmental aspirations through a series of landmark agreements and treaties that underscore the importance of collective action and shared responsibility. These accords serve as legal frameworks and signify a solid political will to prioritize environmental conservation and adopt sustainable practices. One such significant agreement is the Paris Agreement, which aims to limit global temperature rise and mitigate climate change's impact. France and several Arab countries have ratified this pact, demonstrating their joint commitment to combatting climate change and transitioning towards low-carbon economies. Additionally, the Mediterranean Action Plan (MAP), orchestrated by the United Nations Environment Programme (UNEP), has been pivotal in promoting environmental sustainability and addressing pollution in the Mediterranean region. This multilateral treaty has provided a platform for France and its Arab counterparts to collaboratively tackle marine pollution, coastal degradation, and biodiversity loss, thereby advancing the cause of environmental protection in the Mediterranean. Moreover, bilateral partnerships between France and individual Arab states have led to the signing of specific agreements focused on marine conservation, wildlife protection, and forest management. These accords have laid the groundwork for coordinated efforts in preserving natural habitats, promoting biodiversity, and ensuring ecosystem resilience. The involvement of governmental and non-governmental stakeholders in upholding these agreements reflects a multi-faceted approach to environmental diplomacy, emphasizing the need for inclusive participation and diverse expertise in sustainable development initiatives. Continuous dialogue and periodic reassessment of these agreements will be crucial to adapt to evolving environmental challenges and leverage innovative solutions to benefit present and future generations.

## *Renewable Energy Projects and Collaboration*

Renewable energy projects and collaboration between France and Arab countries have become increasingly significant in addressing the global challenge of transitioning towards sustainable and low-carbon energy systems. This sector has witnessed a growing focus on fostering cooperation in renewable energy technologies, policy frameworks, and investment opportunities. Both regions recognize the potential for mutual benefits in advancing renewable energy development, from reducing reliance on fossil fuels to driving economic growth and creating green jobs.

France has been promoting renewable energy innovation and has established itself as a leader in wind, solar, hydro, and biomass energy sectors. Its expertise in clean energy technologies presents valuable opportunities for collaboration with Arab states seeking to diversify their energy mix and expand their renewable energy capacity. Through joint initiatives and partnerships, both parties can leverage their respective strengths to accelerate the deployment of renewable energy projects, improve energy efficiency, and promote sustainable practices.

The collaboration extends beyond the exchange of knowledge and technology transfer. It encompasses strategic investments in renewable energy infrastructure, research and development, and cross-border energy trade. By fostering an environment conducive to public and private sector engagement, France and Arab countries can enhance the attractiveness of renewable energy investments and promote co-investment in large-scale projects that contribute to energy security and environmental sustainability. Additionally, fostering collaboration through financial mechanisms, such as green bonds, can mobilize capital for renewable energy ventures, laying the groundwork for sustainable development.

Furthermore, this collaboration offers a platform to address shared challenges in scaling up renewable energy, including grid integration, storage capabilities, and regulatory frameworks. Both regions can identify innovative solutions to optimize renewable energy systems, address intermittency concerns, and enable seamless integration into the existing energy infrastructure by working in tandem. Furthermore, collaboration in research and development can drive technological advancements, leading to cost reductions and improved performance of renewable energy systems, ultimately benefiting both regions economically and environmentally.

Partnership initiatives extend to capacity building and skill enhancement programs to cultivate a skilled workforce to drive the renewable energy transition. Educational exchanges, training workshops, and joint academic programs foster the development of expertise in renewable energy technologies, project management, and policy formulation, laying the foundation for long-term sustainability and self-reliance in energy development.

As the world navigates the complexities of energy transition and strives to meet climate targets, the collaboration between France and Arab countries in renewable energy projects holds immense promise. By leveraging collective resources, expertise, and ambition, these collaborative efforts have the potential to reshape energy landscapes, unlock new markets, and demonstrate the viability of sustainable energy solutions on a global scale.

## Water Resource Management and Conservation Efforts

Effective water resource management and conservation efforts are critical to the Franco-Arab environmental collaboration. Water scarcity and competition for limited water resources pose significant challenges to both regions, necessitating a comprehensive and coordinated approach to address these issues.

In Franco-Arab relations, water resource management initiatives have focused on various aspects, including sustainable irrigation practices, integrated water resource management, and the development of efficient water supply systems. Both France and Arab countries have actively engaged in knowledge sharing, technical cooperation, and capacity-building programs aimed at improving water governance and tackling water-related challenges.

Promoting water conservation measures has been a key priority in the partnership between France and Arab states. This includes raising awareness about the value of water, promoting the use of water-saving technologies, and implementing policies to reduce wastage and misuse of water resources. Furthermore, joint research and innovation projects have aimed to enhance water efficiency and optimize water use across different sectors, such as agriculture, industry, and domestic consumption.

Addressing transboundary water issues, especially in shared river basins and aquifers, is integral to water resource management. Cooperation in this area involves the establishment of legal frameworks, joint monitoring mechanisms, and dispute resolution protocols to ensure equitable and sustainable utilization of transboundary water resources. Through multilateral forums and diplomatic channels, France and Arab states have actively promoted cross-border cooperation and negotiated agreements to manage shared water resources responsibly.

Implementing green infrastructure and nature-based solutions has also emerged as a significant focus in the joint efforts towards water resource management. This encompasses the restoration of wetlands, reforestation projects, and the preservation of aquatic ecosystems, contributing to improved water quality, flood control, and biodiversity conservation. Such initiatives support ecological sustainability and enhance communities' resilience to climate-related water challenges.

Beyond conservation, France and Arab countries have collaborated to enhance access to safe drinking water and sanitation services, particularly in underserved and vulnerable communities. Investments in water infrastructure, including decentralized and nature-based solutions, have improved water accessibility, better hygiene practices, and reduced health risks, contributing to overall human well-being and social development.

Continued emphasis on water resource management and conservation will require sustained political commitment, institutional capacity building, and public engagement. By fostering a shared sense of responsibility and promoting inclusive and holistic approaches, Franco-Arab cooperation in this domain can lead to lasting improvements in water security, environmental sustainability, and the well-being of present and future generations.

## *Climate Change Adaptation and Mitigation Strategies*

Climate change poses a significant threat to the environment and ecosystems of both France and the Arab world. Effective adaptation and mitigation strategies are crucial to address the challenges posed by rising global temperatures, extreme weather events, and sea-level rise. In Franco-Arab relations, cooperation in climate change adaptation and mitigation is essential for ensuring sustainable development and long-term environmental protection. This section delves into the key aspects of climate change response strategies and the collaborative efforts between France and Arab states.

One fundamental approach to mitigating climate change is reducing greenhouse gas emissions. France has been at the forefront of promoting clean energy technologies and renewable power sources while advocating for international agreements to limit carbon emissions. Through diplomatic channels, France has engaged in dialogue with Arab countries to foster commitments to reduce emissions, invest in renewable energy infrastructure, and embrace sustainable practices across industries.

In tandem with emission reduction efforts, adaptation strategies are imperative to address the impacts of climate change that are already being felt. These strategies encompass diverse measures, including enhancing coastal defense systems, implementing flood control measures, and supporting agricultural practices resilient to changing weather patterns. The exchange of best practices and technical expertise between France and Arab states is vital in strengthening the adaptive capacity of vulnerable communities and ecosystems.

Furthermore, promoting sustainable land use and forest conservation constitutes a critical climate change mitigation and adaptation component. Both France and Arab countries have rich ecosystems and biodiversity that require protection from the adverse effects of climate change. Collaboration in afforestation, reforestation, and sustainable land management can contribute to carbon sequestration, biodiversity conservation, and the preservation of natural habitats.

Another crucial aspect of climate change response is fostering public awareness and education. Educational programs on climate change impacts, solutions, and capacity-building initiatives are central to equipping individuals and communities with the knowledge and skills necessary to adapt to and mitigate climate change. France and Arab states have initiated joint projects to promote environmental education, train professionals in climate science, and raise awareness about sustainable lifestyles.

In conclusion, the looming threat of climate change necessitates an unwavering commitment to collaborative action. By prioritizing climate change adaptation and mitigation strategies through cooperation, France and Arab states can chart a course toward a sustainable future.

This collective endeavor safeguards the environment and fosters resilience, innovation, and shared prosperity across borders.

## *Sustainable Urban Development Programs*

Urban development plays a pivotal role in environmental sustainability and the promotion of livable, resilient cities. Sustainable urban development programs aim to integrate social, economic, and environmental aspects to create harmonious and inclusive urban spaces for current and future generations. In the Franco-Arab context, these programs are characterized by a commitment to balancing economic growth with environmental protection while addressing the unique challenges posed by rapid urbanization. This section examines sustainable urban development programs' key components and strategies within the Franco-Arab collaboration framework.

One of the fundamental aspects of sustainable urban development is urban planning, which prioritizes smart growth, efficient land use, and the preservation of green spaces. This involves comprehensive zoning regulations, mixed-use development, and the establishment of public transportation networks to reduce reliance on private vehicles and lower carbon emissions. Additionally, integrating nature-based solutions such as green roofs, urban gardens, and permeable pavements helps mitigate the urban heat island effect and enhances biodiversity within the cityscape.

Furthermore, sustainable infrastructure development is crucial in promoting eco-friendly practices. Implementation of energy-efficient buildings, renewable energy sources, and sustainable waste management systems is integral to reducing urban areas' ecological footprint. Investment in modernizing water and sewage systems ensures efficient resource utilization and minimizes pollution, contributing to the overall environmental health of urban communities. Moreover, fostering resilient infrastructure to withstand the impacts of climate change, such as extreme weather events and sea-level rise, is imperative for safeguarding urban inhabitants and assets.

Another significant aspect of sustainable urban development is the enhancement of public spaces and promoting healthy lifestyles. Access to parks, recreational facilities, and pedestrian-friendly pathways enhances the quality of life and encourages social interaction and community engagement. Prioritizing green corridors and urban forestry initiatives facilitates air purification, noise reduction, and wildlife habitat conservation, creating a more ecologically balanced urban environment. Moreover, promoting active transportation modes such as walking and cycling reduces greenhouse gas emissions and fosters healthier communities.

In conclusion, sustainable urban development programs in the Franco-Arab context are designed to address the complex interplay between urbanization, environmental conservation, and societal well-being. By embracing comprehensive urban planning, sustainable infrastructure, and public space enhancement, these programs seek to foster vibrant, resilient, and ecologically responsible cities that can thrive in global environmental challenges.

## *Education and Capacity Building in Environmental Sciences*

Education and capacity building in environmental sciences are fundamental in fostering the necessary knowledge and expertise to address complex ecological challenges within the Franco-Arab context. Through a concerted effort to enhance scholastic curriculum and promote research initiatives, both France and Arab states have strived to cultivate a new generation of environmentally conscious scholars and professionals. This section explores the multidimensional strategies employed to advance environmental education and reinforce capacity building within this critical domain. Firstly, it is imperative to underscore the proliferation of joint academic programs and knowledge exchange platforms between educational institutions in France and Arab countries. This collaborative framework facilitates the exchange of best practices and nurtures a sense of cultural understanding and solidarity, key ingredients for effective global environmental stewardship. Moreover, capacity-building initiatives encompass a spectrum of activities ranging from specialized training workshops on biodiversity conservation to promoting cross-disciplinary research projects aimed at tackling regional environmental peculiarities. Engaging with indigenous knowledge systems and integrating traditional ecological wisdom into modern scientific curricula represent an innovative approach to imbibing a holistic perspective on sustainable environmental practices. Furthermore, investments in state-of-the-art laboratory infrastructures and access to cutting-edge technological advancements exemplify the commitment to nurturing a competitive cohort of environmental scientists and researchers. Equally significant, establishing mentorship programs led by eminent environmental experts fosters an enabling environment for aspiring scholars to benefit from invaluable insights and guidance. Complementing formal education, outreach programs targeted at schools and local communities catalyze environmental consciousness among future decision-makers and citizens. Environmental education bridges the chasm between knowledge dissemination and tangible environmental impact by accentuating the interplay between theoretical insight and practical application. To this end, policymakers and educational authorities must conjoin efforts to develop curricular content that integrates sustainable principles across diverse academic disciplines, thereby imprinting a collective ecological conscience that transcends national boundaries. In conclusion, education and capacity building in environmental sciences represent the cornerstone for cultivating a community of proficient environmental custodians equipped to confront ecological dilemmas with erudition and innovation.

## Challenges and Barriers to Implementation

Achieving effective implementation of environmental cooperation and sustainable development initiatives between France and the Arab world is challenging. One of the primary barriers to successful implementation is the complex and diverse nature of environmental issues, which often require a multidisciplinary approach to mitigation and management. Furthermore, differing regulatory frameworks and policy priorities among participating nations can create inconsistencies and hinder the alignment of efforts. This lack of harmonization necessitates extensive stakeholder coordination and negotiation to establish common goals and strategies. Additionally, financial constraints and resource limitations can impede the execution of comprehensive environmental programs, particularly in developing nations within the Arab world. Addressing these disparities through innovative funding mechanisms and strategic partnerships is essential to ensure equitable access to resources and technology. Another significant challenge relates to socio-cultural factors and varying public perceptions of environmental conservation and sustainability. Cultural norms, attitudes, and behavioral patterns influence community engagement and participation in green initiatives, highlighting the importance of tailored communication and outreach strategies. Moreover, addressing geopolitical tensions and security concerns in conflict-affected regions presents inherent obstacles to sustained environmental cooperation. Armed conflicts and political instability can disrupt environmental projects and exacerbate ecological damage, necessitating conflict-sensitive approaches and peace-building interventions. Lastly, the rapid pace of technological advancements poses both opportunities and challenges in environmental cooperation. Keeping abreast of emerging technologies while navigating potential ethical and privacy considerations requires continuous adaptation and ethical foresight. Overcoming these barriers demands a collaborative and adaptive approach, leveraging expertise from diverse sectors and fostering inclusive participation at local, national, and international levels.

## *Future Outlook for Green Diplomacy*

As we move forward into the future, the prospects for green diplomacy in Franco-Arab relations appear promising yet challenging. The evolving global environmental landscape demands a more concerted effort in diplomatic endeavors to address pressing ecological issues. The future of green diplomacy between France and the Arab world hinges on multifaceted strategies encompassing policy innovation, technological collaboration, and societal engagement.

One key aspect of the future outlook is the need for strengthened international cooperation and partnerships. This entails fostering alliances with public and private stakeholders, leveraging diverse expertise, and sharing best practices to establish a structured framework for sustainable development. Cross-border cooperation will become increasingly pivotal in addressing transnational environmental challenges like climate change, biodiversity loss, and natural resource management.

Furthermore, advancements in eco-friendly technologies and renewable energy solutions will shape the future trajectory of green diplomacy. Coordinated research and development initiatives can lead to breakthrough innovations, facilitating the transition towards cleaner and more sustainable energy sources. This technological diplomacy will bolster environmental conservation efforts and create economic opportunities through the proliferation of green industries and job creation.

Education and capacity building will play a pivotal role in shaping the future of green diplomacy. Investing in environmental literacy and scientific research will empower future generations to become conscientious stewards of the planet. By integrating environmental studies into academic curricula and promoting knowledge exchange programs, Franco-Arab cooperation can nurture a cadre of experts equipped to tackle complex environmental issues with ingenuity and foresight.

Nevertheless, the emerging future of green diplomacy is not devoid of challenges. Geopolitical complexities, resource competition, and divergent national interests pose significant hurdles to seamless environmental collaboration. Striking a balance between sovereignty and shared responsibility will necessitate adept diplomatic negotiations and a convergence of long-term visions shared by all involved parties.

In conclusion, the future of green diplomacy in Franco-Arab relations holds immense potential for fostering sustainable development, environmental stewardship, and collective well-being. By embracing an integrated approach that harmonizes political, economic, and environmental dimensions, France and the Arab world can coalesce towards a greener future marked by resilience, harmony, and prosperity.

## IN A NUTSHELL

### Franco-Arab Environmental Initiatives

France and Arab states have engaged in numerous environmental initiatives aimed at fostering cooperation and sustainable development. These initiatives span various sectors, including energy, water management, and climate change mitigation.

### Overview of Cooperation

The cooperation between France and Arab states is characterized by strategic partnerships and agreements that focus on mutual benefits and shared goals. These collaborations are often formalized through high-level dialogues, such as the UAE-France High-Level Business Council and the Comprehensive Strategic Energy Partnership (CSEP).

## Key Agreements and Multilateral Treaties

1. **Comprehensive Strategic Energy Partnership (CSEP)**: This agreement between France and the UAE focuses on energy cooperation, including renewable energy, hydrogen, and nuclear energy.
2. **Paris Agreement**: Both France and Arab states are signatories to the Paris Agreement, committing to climate action and the reduction of greenhouse gas emissions.
3. **Memorandum of Understanding (MoU) on Climate Action**: France and the UAE signed a MoU to enhance cooperation on climate action, including support for COP28.

## Renewable Energy Projects and Collaboration

France and Arab states have launched several renewable energy projects, focusing on solar, wind, and hydrogen energy:

1. **TotalEnergies and Masdar**: Collaboration on developing renewable energy projects in emerging markets, including solar and wind energy initiatives in Central Asia and Africa.
2. **Sustainable Aviation Fuel**: Partnerships between TotalEnergies, Masdar, and Airbus to develop sustainable aviation fuel.
3. **Geothermal Energy**: ADNOC and Tabreed's collaboration on the first Geothermal Cooling Plant in the UAE.

## Water Resource Management and Conservation Efforts

France's approach to water resource management emphasizes sustainable and inclusive practices:

1. **French Water Partnership**: Active in promoting water security and sustainable management practices, including at COP28.
2. **Water Governance in the Arab Region**: Arab states, including the UAE, have adopted various water management strategies, such as cloud seeding and the reuse of irrigation drainage waters.

## Climate Change Adaptation and Mitigation Strategies

France and Arab states are working together to address climate change through various strategies:

1. **Decarbonization Initiatives**: Joint efforts to decarbonize hard-to-abate industries and promote clean hydrogen as a fuel.
2. **Climate Resilience**: Projects like "Project Prosperity" are supported by the UAE, which facilitates the exchange of desalinated water for solar energy.

## Sustainable Urban Development Programs

France and Arab states are also focusing on sustainable urban development:

1. **Louvre Abu Dhabi and Sorbonne University Abu Dhabi**: These institutions are part of broader cultural and educational cooperation that includes sustainable development initiatives.
2. **Urban Growth Centers**: Efforts to ensure sustainable essential services in urban areas, focusing on water and waste management.

## Education and Capacity Building in Environmental Sciences

Educational initiatives and capacity-building programs are crucial components of Franco-Arab environmental cooperation:

1. **Sorbonne University Abu Dhabi**: Offers programs that include environmental sciences and sustainability.
2. **Training Programs**: Various initiatives to train professionals in water management, renewable energy, and climate resilience.

## Challenges and Barriers to Implementation

Despite significant progress, several challenges remain:

1. **Political and Social Barriers**: Issues such as political instability and social inequalities can hinder the implementation of environmental projects.
2. **Funding and Resources**: Securing adequate funding and resources for large-scale projects remains a challenge.

## Future Outlook for Green Diplomacy

The future of Franco-Arab environmental cooperation looks promising, with several key areas of focus:

1. **Enhanced Cooperation**: Continued emphasis on strategic partnerships and high-level dialogues to address environmental challenges.
2. **Innovative Solutions**: Development and implementation of innovative technologies and practices in renewable energy and water management.
3. **Global Leadership**: Joint efforts to lead global climate action, particularly through platforms like COP28.

In conclusion, the collaboration between France and Arab states in environmental initiatives is multifaceted and dynamic, addressing critical issues such as energy security, water management, and climate change. The ongoing and future projects highlight the potential for significant advancements in sustainable development and green diplomacy.

# References For Further Reading

Guterres, António. "Letter dated 8 May 2023 from the Secretary-General addressed to the President of the Security Council". https://www.securitycouncilreport.org/atf/cf/%7B65BFCF9B-6D27-4E9C-8CD3-CF6E4FF96FF9%7D/s_2023_331.pdf

Amal Bourhrous and Emelie Poignant Khafagi. "ENVIRONMENTAL POLITICS IN GULF COOPERATION COUNCIL STATES: STRENGTHENING THE ROLE OF CIVIL SOCIETY". SIPRI Research Policy Paper, November 2023. https://www.sipri.org/sites/default/files/2023-11/rpp2311_environmental_politics_in_gcc_states.pdf

Arab News. "Saudi Arabia, France Sign MoU on Energy Cooperation," July 9, 2023. https://www.arabnews.com/node/2334546/business-economy.

arabwaterconvention.org. "Arab Water Convention – Non-Conventional Water Resources : Business Opportunities." Accessed May 23, 2024. https://arabwaterconvention.org.

Bianco, Cinzia. "A New Climate for Peace: How Europe Can Promote Environmental Cooperation between the Gulf Arab States and Iran – European Council on Foreign Relations." ECFR, October 11, 2022. https://ecfr.eu/publication/a-new-climate-for-peace-how-europe-can-promote-environmental-cooperation-between-the-gulf-arab-states-and-iran/.

Business France. "UAE-France Energy Days: Edition 7 Brings Energy Industry Leaders Together for Collaborative Exchange." Business France Middle East, September 22, 2023. https://world.businessfrance.fr/middle-east/uae-france-energy-days-edition-7-brings-energy-industry-leaders-together-for-collaborative-exchange/.

Chandak, Pooja. "UAE-France Business Council Ignites Clean Energy Collaboration in Paris." SolarQuarter, February 21, 2024. https://solarquarter.com/2024/02/21/uae-france-business-council-ignites-clean-energy-collaboration-in-paris/.

COP28 in Dubai. "COP28 in Dubai." Accessed May 23, 2024. https://www.partenariat-francais-eau.fr/en/cop28/.

El Karoui, Hakim. "A New Strategy for France in a New Arab World." Institut Montaigne, August 2017. https://www.institutmontaigne.org/en/publications/new-strategy-france-new-arab-world.

FRANCE 24. "France, UAE Sign Strategic Deal to Partner on Energy Projects," July 18, 2022. https://www.france24.com/en/france/20220718-energy-deals-top-agenda-as-uae-president-meets-macron-in-paris.

France Diplomacy, Ministry for Europe and Foreign Affairs. "15th Session of the UAE-France Strategic Dialogue Discusses Growing Cooperation between UAE & France (19.06.23)." France Diplomacy, 2019. https://www.diplomatie.gouv.fr/en/country-files/united-arab-emirates/events/article/15th-session-of-the-uae-france-strategic-dialogue-discusses-growing-cooperation.

France in the UK. "France and UAE Extend Their Strategic Partnership," July 21, 2022. https://uk.ambafrance.org/France-and-UAE-extend-their-strategic-partnership.

Ministry for Europe and Foreign Affairs. "French Policy on Water and Sanitation." France Diplomacy , February 2020. https://www.diplomatie.gouv.fr/en/french-foreign-policy/development-assistance/other-major-sectors/french-policy-on-water-and-sanitation/.

———. "Resumption of Diplomatic Relations between the Member States of the Cooperation Council for the Arab States of the Gulf (06.01.21)." France Diplomacy , January 6, 2021. https://www.diplomatie.gouv.fr/en/country-files/north-africa-and-middle-east/news/article/resumption-of-diplomatic-relations-between-the-member-states-of-the-cooperation.

Schaefer, Paula . "Climate Change as an Opportunity for Cooperation in the Middle East | Heinrich-Böll-Stiftung | Tel Aviv - Israel." il.boell.org, March 30, 2023. https://il.boell.org/en/2023/03/30/climate-change-opportunity-cooperation-middle-east.

"THE FRENCH POLICY APPROACH for the MANAGEMENT of WATER RESOURCES and AQUATIC BIODIVERSITY a Source of Inspiration for the Implementation of the 2030 Agenda," October 2019. https://www.oieau.fr/eaudoc/system/files/34225-eng.pdf.

TotalEnergies.com. "UAE – France High-Level Business Council 2nd Plenary Meeting in Paris," February 19, 2024. https://totalenergies.com/media/news/press-releases/uae-france-high-level-business-council-2nd-plenary-meeting-paris.

treaties.un.org. "United Nations Treaty Collection," December 12, 2015. https://treaties.un.org/pages/ViewDetails.aspx?chapter=27&clang=_en&mtdsg_no=XXVII-7-d&src=TREATY.

UNDP. "Water Governance in the Arab Region Managing Scarcity and Securing the Future United Nations Development Programme Regional Bureau for Arab States," 2013. https://www.undp.org/sites/g/files/zskgke326/files/migration/arabstates/ARAB_WATER_REPORT_December_Final_Eng.pdf.

# XIV

# France's Role in Arab Spring Revolutions

## Overview of the Arab Spring

The Arab Spring, a series of pro-democracy uprisings and grassroots movements that swept across the Arab world in the early 2010s, has significantly reshaped the political landscape in the region. Originating in Tunisia with Mohamed Bouazizi's self-immolation in December 2010, the fervor for change quickly spread to other Arab countries, including Egypt, Libya, Yemen, Syria, and Bahrain. The catalyst for these uprisings was a confluence of socioeconomic grievances, high unemployment rates, corruption, and demands for greater political freedom and human rights.

France, as a key player in global politics and with historical ties to several Arab countries, closely monitored the tumultuous events of the Arab Spring. Recognizing the potential for significant geopolitical shifts, France sought to navigate the rapidly evolving situations in these countries while safeguarding its strategic interests in the region. The prospect of democratic transitions in various Arab states presented opportunities and challenges for French diplomacy and foreign policy.

As the Arab Spring unfolded, France faced complex considerations regarding its relationships with incumbent regimes, opposition groups, and revolutionary forces. Attentive to the unique dynamics in each country, France adopted nuanced approaches tailored to the specific contexts and developments in Tunisia, Egypt, Libya, and beyond. The French government engaged in diplomatic initiatives to promote stability, facilitate peaceful transitions, and advocate for respect for human rights and democratic values.

Moreover, France's response to the Arab Spring was influenced by its economic interests, particularly in energy resources and trade relations with Arab countries. The transformations brought about by the uprisings necessitated careful recalibration of economic partnerships and assessments of potential risks and opportunities for French businesses and investors operating in the region. This reevaluation mirrored France's broader efforts to align its foreign policy with the evolving geopolitical realities shaped by the Arab Spring.

The eruption of the Arab Spring precipitated a reconfiguration of power dynamics and societal aspirations in the Arab world, compelling France to navigate an ever-changing regional landscape. As the chapters of this transformative period continue to unfold, the interplay between France's geopolitical interests and the enduring impact of the Arab Spring remains an essential dimension of contemporary international relations.

## *Initial French Response to Uprisings*

The Arab Spring, a series of uprisings and protests that swept across the Middle East and North Africa, presented a significant challenge to the established order in the region. As these movements unfolded, France grappled with formulating a response that balanced its strategic interests with its commitment to democratic values and human rights. The French government faced the dilemma of engaging with the evolving political landscape in a manner that upheld stability while also aligning with the aspirations of the people seeking greater freedom and representation. At the onset of the uprisings, France initially approached the situation cautiously, emphasizing the importance of stability in the region while expressing support for peaceful transitions towards democracy. President Nicolas Sarkozy's administration sought to engage diplomatically with the leaders of affected countries, urging them to initiate political reforms and uphold fundamental rights to address their citizens' grievances. Simultaneously, French officials underscored the need for dialogue and reconciliation to avert further escalation of violence and instability. This measured approach aimed to navigate the delicate balance between promoting democratic change and safeguarding regional stability, reflecting the complexities inherent in France's role as a key actor in the Arab world. Moreover, the initial French response involved close coordination with European partners and international organizations to assess the situation and devise collective strategies for engagement. France actively participated in diplomatic initiatives to address the crisis, including through the European Union and the United Nations, underscoring its commitment to multilateral cooperation in shaping the regional dynamics. As the uprisings continued to unfold, France recalibrated its stance, recognizing the legitimate demands of the protesters and advocating for inclusive political processes that respected the people's will. This transition in approach underscored France's recognition of the changing realities on the ground and its acknowledgement of the need to adapt its policies in response to the evolving situation. In summary, the initial French response to the Arab Spring revolutions unfolded against careful deliberation, diplomatic engagement, and recalibration of policy stances, reflecting the complexities and challenges inherent in navigating a rapidly transforming regional landscape.

## *Diplomatic Strategies and International Coordination*

With the onset of the Arab Spring revolutions, France found

itself in a crucial position to craft diplomatic strategies and engage in international coordination to address the unfolding political developments in the Arab world. Understanding the significance of these events, French diplomacy focused on aligning with international partners to formulate a unified response that prioritized stability, human rights, and democratic aspirations. At the core of France's diplomatic efforts was the recognition of the historic transformations shaking the region and the need to carefully navigate the complexities of each situation. Diplomatic strategies were meticulously crafted, emphasizing promoting dialogue, fostering peaceful transitions, and advocating for inclusive political processes. France actively participated in international forums such as the United Nations, European Union, and the Arab League to coordinate joint actions and share perspectives on the evolving situations in various countries affected by the Arab Spring. Through multilateral engagements, France sought consensus on approaches to support the people's aspirations while balancing regional and global geopolitical considerations. The adherence to diplomatic norms and principles of international law underscored France's commitment to upholding shared values and safeguarding peace and stability in the region. Furthermore, proactive engagement by French diplomats leveraged the country's historical ties and cultural understanding of the Arab world to navigate the complexities of the revolution and post-revolutionary scenarios. This involved recognizing the diversity of actors and interests within each country and engaging with various stakeholders, including governments, opposition groups, civil society, and regional powers, to influence outcomes towards peaceful resolutions constructively. France's ability to translate these diplomatic strategies into impactful actions was pivotal in shaping international responses to the Arab Spring revolutions, demonstrating its commitment to supporting democratic transitions and contributing to regional stability.

## Humanitarian Aid and Support Initiatives

In the wake of the Arab Spring uprisings, France took proactive measures to provide humanitarian aid and support to the affected regions in collaboration with international organizations and local partners. As chaos and instability gripped several Arab countries, the plight of civilians became a primary concern for the international community. France swiftly mobilized its resources to address the urgent humanitarian needs arising from the conflicts. Humanitarian aid efforts encompassed diverse initiatives, including providing displaced populations with food, medical assistance, and shelter. The French government, working with non-governmental organizations (NGOs) and the United Nations, coordinated massive relief operations to ensure that essential supplies reached those in dire need. Moreover, France played a pivotal role in facilitating the evacuation of foreign nationals and vulnerable individuals from conflict zones, demonstrating a commitment to protecting human lives amidst the turmoil. This comprehensive approach underscored France's dedication to alleviating the suffering inflicted by the upheavals of the Arab Spring. Furthermore, France extended support to host countries grappling with the influx of refugees, emphasizing the importance of international solidarity in addressing complex humanitarian crises. Beyond immediate aid assistance, France also engaged in long-term development projects to rebuild infrastructure, enhance healthcare systems, and promote sustainable livelihoods in post-conflict environments. These endeavors reflected France's enduring commitment to promoting stability, resilience, and prosperity in the Arab Spring-affected regions while fostering lasting partnerships for positive change. The multifaceted humanitarian aid and support initiatives exemplified France's recognition of the interconnectedness of global challenges and its active role in advancing collective responses to humanitarian crises.

## France's Communication Strategy and Media Role

In the wake of the Arab Spring revolutions, France's communication strategy and media role played a pivotal part in shaping public perception and international discourse surrounding the events unfolding in the Arab world. Recognizing the significance of effective communication during times of crisis, France utilized its diplomatic channels and media platforms to convey its stance on the uprisings and provide nuanced insights to global audiences. French officials engaged in strategic messaging, emphasizing the country's commitment to supporting democratic transitions and advocating for peaceful resolutions to the challenges arising from the Arab Spring. Through carefully crafted speeches by political leaders and ambassadors, France sought to align its rhetoric with its foreign policy objectives, emphasizing the importance of stability, human rights, and inclusive governance in the region. Moreover, France leveraged its media resources to facilitate open dialogues, promote cross-cultural understanding, and counter misinformation regarding the Arab Spring movements. The French government collaborated with reputable journalists, scholars, and analysts to provide comprehensive coverage and insightful analysis of the developments in the affected Arab countries. This proactive engagement aimed to counter disinformation and foster informed public discourse on the complex sociopolitical dynamics. Additionally, France actively utilized social media, press conferences, and interviews to communicate its diplomatic initiatives and partnerships aimed at addressing the multifaceted challenges posed by the Arab Spring. By leveraging digital platforms and traditional media outlets, France endeavored to ensure transparency in its approach and demonstrate its solidarity with the aspirations of the Arab people for dignity, freedom, and justice. This concerted effort underscored France's commitment to upholding democratic values and fostering constructive international dialogue amid the turbulence of the Arab Spring. As the narrative around the events unfolded, France continually adapted its communication strategies to uphold its credibility and influence global narratives as the Arab Spring continued to unfold.

## *Military Involvement and Security Measures*

In response to the Arab Spring revolutions, France implemented a multifaceted approach to address the escalating security concerns in the region. Military involvement and security measures became pivotal to France's response to the evolving geopolitical landscape. Recognizing the potential threats to regional stability and the spread of extremism, France strategically deployed military assets and personnel to support allied governments and mitigate the risks posed by the unrest. This proactive stance aimed to uphold vital national interests, protect French citizens, and contribute to global peace and security efforts. France navigated a delicate balance between respecting sovereignty and enforcing international norms to address security challenges effectively. Collaborating with regional partners, France engaged in joint military exercises, intelligence sharing, and capacity-building programs to enhance the capabilities of Arab states in countering emerging security threats. The coordination of efforts sought to foster sustainable security solutions and promote collective resilience against destabilizing forces. Moreover, France prioritized bolstering border security, maritime surveillance, and counterterrorism operations to safeguard vital infrastructure and prevent illicit activities from jeopardizing regional stability. In light of the complex dynamics, France also invested in diplomatic initiatives to facilitate dialogue and conflict resolution while safeguarding human rights and upholding international law. Through its military involvement and security measures, France was committed to upholding stability and fostering cooperation within the Franco-Arab partnership. The evolving security landscape necessitated adaptive responses that underscored the interconnectedness of regional security and its implications for global peace. As the tumultuous aftermath of the Arab Spring subsided, France engaged constructively with

Arab countries to shape a secure and prosperous future for both regions. The lessons learned from this pivotal period informed strategic recalibrations and laid the foundation for enduring security partnerships that endure to this day.

## Economic Impacts on Franco-Arab Relations

The Arab Spring revolutions had significant economic impacts on France's relations with the Arab world. The turmoil and unrest in several Arab countries had reverberating effects on trade, investment, and economic cooperation. As traditional economic ties were disrupted and geopolitical landscapes shifted, France was compelled to reassess its economic engagement strategies with the Arab states.

One of the primary repercussions was the fluctuation in energy markets. Several Arab countries, including major oil and gas producers, experienced disruptions in their energy sectors due to domestic instability and political transitions. This affected global energy markets and posed challenges to France's energy security and economic stability. Diversification of energy sources and supply routes became a crucial consideration for France to mitigate potential vulnerabilities arising from the Arab Spring upheavals.

Furthermore, the economic fallout of the Arab Spring prompted France to reevaluate its trade partnerships and investment initiatives in the region. The uncertainty and volatility following the uprisings led to shifts in market dynamics and investment climates. French businesses in the Arab world faced new risks and uncertainties, requiring strategic adjustments to navigate the evolving economic landscape. Additionally, balancing economic interests with socio-political developments in the aftermath of the Arab Spring presented complex challenges for France's foreign policy and economic diplomacy.

In response to these economic implications, France sought to engage in dialogue and partnership with the Arab states to address the challenges and opportunities arising from the post-Arab Spring era.

Economic cooperation and development assistance emerged as key pillars of Franco-Arab relations, focusing on promoting inclusive growth, job creation, and sustainable economic reforms. Moreover, France leveraged its economic expertise and resources to support the recovery and reconstruction efforts in Arab countries affected by the upheavals, emphasizing the importance of stability and prosperity for fostering enduring bilateral relations.

The economic impacts of the Arab Spring on Franco-Arab relations underscored the interconnectedness of global economies and the imperative of adapting to evolving geopolitical circumstances. This period of transformation propelled France to recalibrate its economic engagement strategies and deepen collaboration with the Arab world, laying the groundwork for resilient and mutually beneficial economic ties amidst the challenges and opportunities presented by the post-Arab Spring environment.

## *Post-Arab Spring Recovery and Reconstruction Efforts*

Following the dramatic events of the Arab Spring, the affected countries faced the daunting task of rebuilding their societies and economies. France recognized the significant challenges and actively supported the region's post-conflict recovery and reconstruction efforts. This section will delve into the multifaceted initiatives undertaken by France and its partners to contribute to the stabilization and revitalization of the post-Arab Spring nations.

One key aspect of post-conflict recovery was the emphasis on infrastructure rehabilitation and economic development. France leveraged its expertise in urban planning, transportation, and energy sectors to assist in rebuilding critical infrastructure damaged during the uprisings. This comprehensive approach aimed to lay the foundation for sustainable economic growth and social stability in the affected countries.

Moreover, France played a pivotal role in facilitating humanitarian aid and providing essential services to the displaced populations and refugees. Collaborating with international organizations and local NGOs, France worked tirelessly to address the immediate needs of the affected communities, including access to food, healthcare, and shelter. The commitment to humanitarian assistance reflected France's dedication to alleviating the suffering caused by the conflicts and fostering long-term resilience.

In addition to physical reconstruction, France prioritized advancing democratic governance and institution-building in the post-Arab Spring societies. France sought to empower local governments and civil society organizations through diplomatic channels and capacity-building programs, promoting accountability, transparency, and inclusivity. By nurturing these democratic foundations, France aimed to foster a conducive political reconciliation and social cohesion environment.

Furthermore, recognizing the vital role of education in societal transformation, France allocated resources to support educational initiatives in post-conflict environments. Collaboration with local educational institutions and the implementation of scholarship programs aimed to provide opportunities for the youth, empowering them to become agents of positive change and contribute to the future prosperity of their nations.

The recovery and reconstruction process after the Arab Spring was undoubtedly complex and challenging. France's unwavering commitment to these efforts underscored its determination to stand in solidarity with the affected nations and contribute to their sustainable recovery. This comprehensive approach embodied France's vision for a stable, prosperous, and harmonious future for the post-Arab Spring societies, rooted in enduring partnerships and mutual respect.

## Analysis of Policy Effectiveness and Lessons Learned

The period following the Arab Spring revolutions marked a crucial juncture in Franco-Arab relations, prompting a comprehensive evaluation of the policies adopted by France and the broader international community. Analyzing the effectiveness of these policies and drawing valuable lessons from the turbulent events of the Arab Spring is instrumental in shaping future diplomatic strategies. This analysis delves into various political, economic, and humanitarian domains.

At the outset, it is imperative to assess France's and the international community's immediate responses to the Arab Spring uprisings. The efficacy of diplomatic interventions and the synchronization of efforts with regional and global stakeholders form pivotal aspects of this evaluation. Moreover, a critical examination of the humanitarian aid and support initiatives deployed during the crises sheds light on their impact and areas for improvement.

In conducting this analysis, proactive communication strategies and media engagement were influential in shaping the narrative and garnering international support. The utilization of these channels, including social media platforms, warrants a careful review to discern the most effective means of disseminating information and influencing public opinion.

Furthermore, the security implications and military involvement during the Arab Spring revolutions necessitate meticulous scrutiny. It is essential to assess the balance between humanitarian assistance and security measures, gauging the long-term ramifications of such interventions on stability and trust within the affected regions.

Economically, France's role in post-Arab Spring recovery and reconstruction efforts warrants an in-depth examination. Analyzing the impacts of economic partnerships and development initiatives is indispensable to ascertain the efficacy of leveraging economic opportunities amidst the transitory phase following the uprisings.

As this analysis progresses, emphasizing lessons learned from policy implementation emerges as integral. Identifying shortcomings, acknowledging successes, and distilling best practices are crucial in fortifying future diplomatic endeavors' resilience and adaptability. Furthermore, conducting a comprehensive assessment allows for a holistic understanding of Franco-Arab relations' complexities, laying the groundwork for informed decision-making and strategic foresight.

Ultimately, analyzing policy effectiveness and lessons learned serves as a compass for navigating future challenges and opportunities within the dynamic landscape of Franco-Arab relations. The insights gleaned from this introspective evaluation are invaluable in calibrating diplomatic approaches, fostering mutual understanding, and advancing shared objectives to benefit France and its Arab counterparts.

## *Prospects for Future Cooperation*

As the dust settled after the Arab Spring, the prospects for future cooperation between France and the countries affected by the uprisings came into focus. One key aspect of this cooperation is the promotion of democratic governance and human rights. France has an opportunity to work closely with these nations to support democratic transitions, build institutions, and ensure the respect of fundamental rights. This may involve providing technical assistance, capacity building, and promoting inclusive political processes that empower marginalized voices.

Moreover, economic cooperation holds significant potential for fostering regional stability and development. France can explore avenues for trade, investment, and economic partnerships that contribute to job creation, infrastructure development, and sustainable growth. Strengthening economic ties can also serve as a means to address underlying grievances and disparities that contributed to the social unrest during the Arab Spring.

Security collaboration is another critical area for future cooperation. Given the complex security challenges that emerged in the aftermath of the uprisings, France can engage in dialogue and joint initiatives with these nations to address common threats such as terrorism, extremism, and regional instability. This may involve sharing expertise and intelligence and conducting training programs to enhance the security capacities of partner countries.

Cultural and educational exchanges present an avenue for deepening mutual understanding and fostering people-to-people connections. France can leverage its rich cultural heritage and academic resources to facilitate exchange programs, language teaching, and knowledge-sharing initiatives. France can help bridge cultural divides and nurture a sense of shared identity and solidarity by promoting cultural dialogue and academic cooperation.

Furthermore, environmental and sustainable development cooperation offers a platform to address pressing environmental concerns and promote regional green initiatives. Collaborative efforts in climate change mitigation, renewable energy deployment, and water resource management can contribute to long-term environmental sustainability and resilience.

In conclusion, the prospects for future cooperation between France and the Arab Spring-affected countries are multifaceted and hold immense potential for cultivating enduring partnerships. By prioritizing democratic governance, economic prosperity, security, cultural exchange, and environmental sustainability, France can play a pivotal role in contributing to the region's peace, stability, and progress.

# IN A NUTSHELL

## France's Role in the Arab Spring Revolutions

### 1. Overview of the Arab Spring

The Arab Spring was a series of protests and uprisings that began in December 2010 in Tunisia and quickly spread across the Middle East and North Africa (MENA). The movement was driven by widespread dissatisfaction with authoritarian regimes, economic hardship, and demands for greater political rights and government accountability. Key events included the ousting of Tunisia's President Zine El Abidine Ben Ali, Egypt's President Hosni Mubarak, Libya's Muammar Gaddafi, and Yemen's Ali Abdullah Saleh. The uprisings led to varying degrees of political change, civil unrest, and in some cases, prolonged conflict and instability.

### 2. Initial French Response to Uprisings

France's initial response to the Arab Spring was marked by hesitation and a degree of miscalculation. Initially, France supported the authoritarian regimes in Tunisia and Egypt, reflecting its long-standing relationships with these governments. For instance, French Foreign Minister Michèle Alliot-Marie offered French security assistance to help quell the protests in Tunisia, a move that was widely criticized and later retracted. However, as the uprisings gained momentum and the scale of the protests became apparent, France shifted its stance, eventually supporting the movements for democratic change.

## 3. Diplomatic Strategies and International Coordination

France played a significant role in international diplomatic efforts during the Arab Spring. French President Nicolas Sarkozy was proactive in coordinating with other international leaders, particularly within the European Union and NATO. France was instrumental in advocating for and leading the NATO intervention in Libya, which aimed to protect civilians from Gaddafi's forces. This intervention was a turning point in the conflict, leading to the eventual overthrow of Gaddafi. France also pushed for financial aid packages for post-revolutionary Egypt and Tunisia, highlighting its commitment to supporting democratic transitions.

## 4. Humanitarian Aid and Support Initiatives

France provided substantial humanitarian aid to countries affected by the Arab Spring. The French government, through the Territorial Communities External Action Fund (FACECO), supported numerous projects aimed at providing emergency assistance and stabilizing affected regions. These projects included housing, healthcare, education, and vocational training for displaced persons and refugees, particularly in Iraq, Jordan, Lebanon, and Syria. France also supported the documentation of human rights violations and the protection of cultural heritage in conflict zones.

## 5. France's Communication Strategy and Media Role

France's communication strategy during the Arab Spring involved a mix of public diplomacy and media engagement. French leaders, including Foreign Minister Alain Juppé, publicly acknowledged the surprise and challenges posed by the uprisings, emphasizing France's support for human rights and democratic transitions. Juppé's speeches highlighted a tone of humility and a commitment to backing democratic movements in North Africa . French media, including France 24, played a crucial role in covering the events, providing international audiences with real-time updates and analyses .

## 6. Military Involvement and Security Measures

France's military involvement was most notable in Libya, where it led the NATO intervention to enforce a no-fly zone and protect civilians from Gaddafi's forces. This military action was a significant aspect of France's strategy to support the Arab Spring movements and prevent mass atrocities. The intervention was coordinated with the United Kingdom and the United States, marking a significant moment of international military cooperation . France also provided training and support to local forces in the region to enhance security and stability .

## 7. Economic Impacts on Franco-Arab Relations

The Arab Spring had significant economic implications for Franco-Arab relations. The instability and conflicts disrupted trade and investment flows between France and the MENA region. However, France also saw opportunities to support economic recovery and development in post-revolutionary states. Initiatives included promoting economic reforms, supporting small and medium-sized enterprises, and encouraging French businesses to invest in the region . France's economic strategy aimed to foster stability and growth, which were seen as essential for long-term peace and development.

## *8. Post-Arab Spring Recovery and Reconstruction Efforts*

France has been actively involved in post-Arab Spring recovery and reconstruction efforts. This involvement includes financial aid, technical assistance, and support for governance reforms. France has focused on rebuilding infrastructure, supporting democratic institutions, and promoting social and economic development. In Iraq, for example, France has provided significant funding for reconstruction projects and humanitarian assistance . The French Development Agency (AFD) has also been instrumental in implementing projects aimed at improving living conditions and fostering resilience in affected communities .

## *9. Policy Effectiveness and Lessons Learned*

The effectiveness of France's policies during the Arab Spring has been mixed. While France played a crucial role in supporting democratic movements and providing humanitarian aid, its initial hesitation and support for authoritarian regimes were criticized. The intervention in Libya, while successful in toppling Gaddafi, led to prolonged instability and conflict, raising questions about the long-term impacts of military interventions.

France has learned the importance of timely and consistent support for democratic movements and the need for comprehensive strategies that include political, economic, and social dimensions.

## 10. Prospects for Future Cooperation

Looking ahead, France aims to strengthen its cooperation with Arab states by focusing on shared challenges such as security, economic development, and climate change. France's future strategy involves promoting inclusive governance, supporting economic reforms, and enhancing regional stability through diplomatic and development initiatives. The lessons learned from the Arab Spring highlight the need for a balanced approach that combines support for democratic transitions with efforts to address underlying socio-economic issues. France's commitment to multilateralism and international cooperation will be crucial in fostering sustainable and resilient partnerships in the region. In conclusion, France's role in the Arab Spring revolutions was multifaceted, involving diplomatic, military, humanitarian, and economic dimensions. While there were initial missteps, France ultimately played a significant role in supporting democratic movements and providing aid to affected regions. The experiences and lessons from the Arab Spring will continue to shape France's foreign policy and its approach to cooperation with the Arab world.

# France's Role in the Arab Spring Revolutions

## 1. Overview of the Arab Spring

The Arab Spring was a series of protests and uprisings that began in December 2010 in Tunisia and quickly spread across the Middle East and North Africa (MENA). The movement was driven by widespread dissatisfaction with authoritarian regimes, economic hardship, and demands for greater political rights and government accountability. Key events included the ousting of Tunisia's President Zine El Abidine Ben Ali, Egypt's President Hosni Mubarak, Libya's Muammar Gaddafi, and Yemen's Ali Abdullah Saleh. The uprisings led to varying degrees of political change, civil unrest, and in some cases, prolonged conflict and instability .

## 2. Initial French Response to Uprisings

France's initial response to the Arab Spring was marked by hesitation and a degree of miscalculation. Initially, France supported the authoritarian regimes in Tunisia and Egypt, reflecting its long-standing relationships with these governments. For instance, French Foreign Minister Michèle Alliot-Marie offered French security assistance to help quell the protests in Tunisia, a move that was widely criticized and later retracted . However, as the uprisings gained momentum and the scale of the protests became apparent, France shifted its stance, eventually supporting the movements for democratic change .

## 3. Diplomatic Strategies and International Coordination

France played a significant role in international diplomatic efforts during the Arab Spring. French President Nicolas Sarkozy was proactive in coordinating with other international leaders, particularly within the European Union and NATO. France was instrumental in advocating for and leading the NATO intervention in Libya, which aimed to protect civilians from Gaddafi's forces. This intervention was a turning point in the conflict, leading to the eventual overthrow of Gaddafi . France also pushed for financial aid packages for post-revolutionary Egypt and Tunisia, highlighting its commitment to supporting democratic transitions .

## 4. Humanitarian Aid and Support Initiatives

France provided substantial humanitarian aid to countries affected by the Arab Spring. The French government, through the Territorial Communities External Action Fund (FACECO), supported numerous projects aimed at providing emergency assistance and stabilizing affected regions. These projects included housing, healthcare, education, and vocational training for displaced persons and refugees, particularly in Iraq, Jordan, Lebanon, and Syria . France also supported the documentation of human rights violations and the protection of cultural heritage in conflict zones .

## 5. France's Communication Strategy and Media Role

France's communication strategy during the Arab Spring involved a mix of public diplomacy and media engagement. French leaders, including Foreign Minister Alain Juppé, publicly acknowledged the surprise and challenges posed by the uprisings, emphasizing France's support for human rights and democratic transitions. Juppé's speeches highlighted a tone of humility and a commitment to backing democratic movements in North Africa . French media, including France 24, played a crucial role in covering the events, providing international audiences with real-time updates and analyses.

## 6. Military Involvement and Security Measures

France's military involvement was most notable in Libya, where it led the NATO intervention to enforce a no-fly zone and protect civilians from Gaddafi's forces. This military action was a significant aspect of France's strategy to support the Arab Spring movements and prevent mass atrocities. The intervention was coordinated with the United Kingdom and the United States, marking a significant moment of international military cooperation. France also provided training and support to local forces in the region to enhance security and stability.

## 7. Economic Impacts on Franco-Arab Relations

The Arab Spring had significant economic implications for Franco-Arab relations. The instability and conflicts disrupted trade and investment flows between France and the MENA region. However, France also saw opportunities to support economic recovery and development in post-revolutionary states. Initiatives included promoting economic reforms, supporting small and medium-sized enterprises, and encouraging French businesses to invest in the region. France's economic strategy aimed to foster stability and growth, which were seen as essential for long-term peace and development.

## 8. Post-Arab Spring Recovery and Reconstruction Efforts

France has been actively involved in post-Arab Spring recovery and reconstruction efforts. This involvement includes financial aid, technical assistance, and support for governance reforms. France has focused on rebuilding infrastructure, supporting democratic institutions, and promoting social and economic development. In Iraq, for example, France has provided significant funding for reconstruction projects and humanitarian assistance . The French Development Agency (AFD) has also been instrumental in implementing projects aimed at improving living conditions and fostering resilience in affected communities .

## 9. Policy Effectiveness and Lessons Learned

The effectiveness of France's policies during the Arab Spring has been mixed. While France played a crucial role in supporting democratic movements and providing humanitarian aid, its initial hesitation and support for authoritarian regimes were criticized. The intervention in Libya, while successful in toppling Gaddafi, led to prolonged instability and conflict, raising questions about the long-term impacts of military interventions. France has learned the importance of timely and consistent support for democratic movements and the need for comprehensive strategies that include political, economic, and social dimensions .

## 10. Prospects for Future Cooperation

Looking ahead, France aims to strengthen its cooperation with Arab states by focusing on shared challenges such as security, economic development, and climate change. France's future strategy involves promoting inclusive governance, supporting economic reforms, and enhancing regional stability through diplomatic and development initiatives. The lessons learned from the Arab Spring highlight the need for a balanced approach that combines support for democratic transitions with efforts to address underlying socio-economic issues. France's commitment to multilateralism and international cooperation will be crucial in fostering sustainable and resilient partnerships in the region . In conclusion, France's role in the Arab Spring revolutions was multifaceted, involving diplomatic, military, humanitarian, and economic dimensions. While there were initial missteps, France ultimately played a significant role in supporting democratic movements and providing aid to affected regions. The experiences and lessons from the Arab Spring will continue to shape France's foreign policy and its approach to cooperation with the Arab world.

# References For Further Reading

Al Jazeera. "What Is the Arab Spring, and How Did It Start?" Al Jazeera, December 17, 2020. https://www.aljazeera.com/news/2020/12/17/what-is-the-arab-spring-and-how-did-it-start.

Benkirane, Reda . "The Role of Social Networks and New Media in the Arab Spring – Reda Benkirane Home Page." archipress.org , July 2012. https://www.archipress.org/reda/?page_id=507.

Bidart, Sawsan. "How International News Is Constructed : The Case of Arab Spring," March 29, 2019. https://theses.hal.science/tel-03276314/file/These_Sawsan_ATALLAH_BIDART.pdf.

Britannica, T. Editors of Encyclopaedia. "Arab Spring summary." Encyclopedia Britannica, April 29, 2021. https://www.britannica.com/summary/Arab-Spring.

Cavatorta, Francesco . "Arab Spring: The Awakening of Civil Society. A General Overview." www.iemed.org, n.d. https://www.iemed.org/publication/arab-spring-the-awakening-of-civil-society-a-general-overview/.

El Karoui , Hakim . "A New Strategy for France in a New Arab World."

Institut Montaigne, August 2017. https://www.institutmontaigne.org/en/publications/new-strategy-france-new-arab-world.

France Diplomacy . "France's Action to Help the Victims of Ethnic and Religious Persecution in the Middle East." Ministry for Europe and Foreign Affairs, January 2020. https://www.diplomatie.gouv.fr/en/country-files/north-africa-and-middle-east/france-s-action-to-help-the-victims-of-ethnic-and-religious-persecution-in-the/.

FRANCE24.English. "Arab Spring: The First Smartphone Revolution." France 24, November 30, 2020. https://www.france24.com/en/live-news/20201130-arab-spring-the-first-smartphone-revolution.

Lakomy, Miron. "THE 'ARAB SPRING' in FRENCH FOREIGN POLICY," 2012. https://www.cejiss.org/images/issue_articles/2012-volume-6-issue-3-4/article-04-0.pdf.

Martin, Boris. "Interview with Rachid Lahlou: 'within French Diversity, I Wanted to Address Muslim Humanitarian Aid' - Alternatives Humanitaires." Humanitarian Alternatives, July 5, 2018. https://www.alternatives-humanitaires.org/en/2018/07/05/within-french-diversity-i-wanted-to-address-muslim-humanitarian-aid/.

Mikail, Barah. "France and the Arab Spring: An Opportunistic Quest for Influence," 2011. https://www.files.ethz.ch/isn/133447/WP110_France_and_arab_spring.pdf.

MoveMe. "ArabSpring and Mobilisation through Social Media." https://moveme.studentorg.berkeley.edu/. Accessed May 23, 2024. https://moveme.studentorg.berkeley.edu/project/arab-spring.

Robinson, Kali, and Will Merrow. "The Arab Spring at Ten Years: What's the Legacy of the Uprisings?" Council on Foreign Relations. Council on Foreign Relations, December 3, 2020. https://www.cfr.org/article/arab-spring-ten-years-whats-legacy-uprisings.

Skupin, Lucas. "To What Extent Did the Arab Spring Trigger a Transformation of

Dominant Paradigms in French Foreign Policy?," June 20, 2011. https://www.ie-ei.eu/IE-EI/Ressources/file/memoires/2011/LSKUPIN.pdf.

University of Illinois Library. "LibGuides: Arab Spring: Background." guides.library.illinois.edu, July 26, 2023. https://guides.library.illinois.edu/c.php?g=348276&p=2346883.

# XV

# Macron's Presidency: A New Era in Franco-Arab Relations

### The Macron Era Begins

In May 2017, Emmanuel Macron was elected as the President of France at a time when the country faced significant challenges, both domestically and in its international relations, including the Franco-Arab partnerships. His victory marked a departure from traditional political norms, as he emerged as a centrist figure with a progressive vision for the future. Macron's ascent to power generated widespread anticipation and a sense of optimism regarding his potential to bring about positive change within France and its relationships with Arab states. The new French president's background as a former investment banker and his role as the Minister of Economy, Industry, and Digital Affairs under President François Hollande lent credence to his pro-business and reform-oriented agenda. Additionally, Macron's outreach to diverse communities and his engagement with Arab leaders before assuming office hinted at his commitment to revitalizing Franco-Arab ties on multiple fronts. As such, his presidency was expected to usher in a new era of diplomacy, economic cooperation, and cultural exchange between France and the Arab world. The early days of Macron's tenure were characterized by ambitious promises and high international visibility, setting the stage for dynamic shifts in France's foreign policy focus and strategic engagements with Arab states.

## Strategic Vision for Franco-Arab Relations under Macron

President Emmanuel Macron's approach to Franco-Arab relations has been marked by a strategic vision that seeks to redefine and strengthen the historical ties between France and the Arab world. With an understanding of the evolving geopolitical landscape, Macron aims to establish a mutually beneficial and forward-looking partnership that addresses contemporary challenges while leveraging shared opportunities. Central to this vision is the recognition of the Arab region's significance in global affairs and the commitment to engaging with Arab states on various political, economic, and cultural fronts. Macron's strategic vision prioritizes multilateralism and dialogue as key pillars for fostering trust and cooperation with Arab states. By advocating for a proactive and inclusive approach, he seeks to position France as a reliable and constructive partner in addressing regional and international issues. Macron's emphasis on a balanced foreign policy framework underscores the importance of maintaining open channels of communication and collaboration while respecting the sovereignty and diverse interests of Arab states. Moreover, his strategic vision promotes stability, security, and sustainable development in the Arab world through diplomatic engagement, trade partnerships, and capacity-building initiatives. Macron's commitment to addressing complex regional dynamics through a nuanced and principled approach reflects a recognition of the interconnectedness of global challenges and the need for joint efforts to achieve lasting solutions. Macron's strategic vision also encompasses a comprehensive understanding of the cultural and social dimensions of Franco-Arab relations, aiming to build bridges of understanding and solidarity through educational, artistic, and intercultural exchanges. This holistic approach underscores Macron's commitment to nurturing a more profound and enduring relationship with Arab societies based on mutual respect, empathy, and shared values. Overall, Macron's strategic vision for Franco-Arab relations signals a departure from traditional paradigms and embraces a dynamic, forward-thinking outlook that resonates with the aspirations and realities of the contemporary Arab world.

## *Policy Changes and Diplomatic Initiatives*

During the Macron era, Franco-Arab relations witnessed significant policy changes and diplomatic initiatives aimed at fostering a new phase of engagement and cooperation. One pivotal policy shift was in France's approach towards the Middle East, adopting a more balanced and nuanced stance to engage with a diverse set of regional actors effectively. Macron's administration demonstrated a commitment to multilateralism and dialogue, emphasizing diplomacy as the linchpin of its foreign policy in the Arab world.

This strategic reorientation led to diplomatic initiatives to enhance ties with key Arab states while addressing complex regional challenges. Macron's proactive engagement in the Israeli-Palestinian conflict exemplified this approach, as France sought to revive stalled peace negotiations and promote a two-state solution. Additionally, heightened efforts were made to expand ties with the Gulf Cooperation Council (GCC) countries, solidifying economic partnerships and joint security measures.

Moreover, France undertook decisive steps to address pressing humanitarian issues in the region, such as the Syrian civil war and the Yemeni crisis. Macron's proactive involvement in advocating for peace and stability underscored the importance of humanitarian diplomacy in Franco-Arab relations. This renewed focus on conflict resolution and mediation positioned France as a key influencer in shaping regional discourse and seeking sustainable solutions to protracted conflicts.

Furthermore, the Macron government prioritized comprehensive engagement with North African nations, particularly Algeria, Tunisia, and Morocco. France aimed to bolster people-to-people connections and foster mutual understanding by implementing dynamic outreach programs and cultural exchange initiatives. Educational exchanges and youth empowerment programs were central in shaping a positive narrative and cultivating long-term partnerships across various sectors.

Beyond bilateral engagements, France took assertive steps in aligning its foreign policy with the wider European Union (EU) framework, advocating for a unified EU strategy towards the Arab world. Macron's leadership in promoting EU integration in the Mediterranean region aimed to harness collective efforts to address common challenges and advance shared interests. The collaborative approach envisioned an inclusive and interconnected future underpinned by robust diplomatic endeavors transcending traditional geopolitical divides.

In conclusion, Macron's presidency's policy changes and diplomatic initiatives underscored a paradigm shift in Franco-Arab relations, characterizing a proactive and pragmatic foreign policy agenda. These initiatives redefined the dynamics of engagement and reflected France's unwavering commitment to upholding international norms, fostering mutual respect, and promoting sustainable development in its interactions with the Arab world.

## *Key Bilateral Engagements and Summits*

In Franco-Arab relations during the Macron presidency, key bilateral engagements and summits have played a pivotal role in shaping the strategic direction of the relationship between France and Arab states. Macron's proactive approach to multilateral diplomacy has seen a series of high-level meetings and engagements with leaders from across the Arab world, focusing on fostering cooperation and mutual understanding. One such landmark summit was the 2018 intergovernmental meeting with Arab League members, which underscored France's commitment to engaging with its Arab partners on various issues, including security, economic development, and cultural exchange.

Additionally, bilateral engagements at the head-of-state level have been instrumental in strengthening ties between France and individual Arab countries. As evidenced by President Macron's visits to key Arab states and reciprocal visits by Arab leaders to France, these high-profile encounters have served as platforms for dialogues on pressing regional and global challenges. Furthermore, the establishment of joint commissions and strategic partnerships between France and select Arab states has facilitated ongoing dialogues on areas such as defense cooperation, counter-terrorism measures, and energy security.

The significance of these bilateral engagements extends beyond mere diplomatic exchanges, as they paved the way for concrete agreements and memoranda of understanding (MoUs) between France and Arab counterparts. These agreements have spanned diverse sectors, including trade, investment, education, and cultural collaboration, thus reinforcing the multifaceted nature of the Franco-Arab relationship under Macron's leadership. Moreover, through these summits and bilateral engagements, France has actively promoted its vision for sustainable economic growth and innovation in the Arab world, seeking to position itself as a strategic partner in the region's socio-economic development.

It is important to note that these engagements and summits have focused on political and economic affairs and prioritized cultural and societal exchange. Promoting cultural diplomacy and people-to-people connections has been a recurring theme in these interactions, reflecting France's dedication to fostering greater mutual understanding and tolerance between French and Arab societies. This has encompassed initiatives such as educational exchanges, cultural showcases, and collaborative research projects, all aimed at nurturing long-term bonds between the people of France and Arab states.

As the Macron era unfolds, the legacy of these bilateral engagements and summits will undoubtedly leave a lasting imprint on the fabric of Franco-Arab relations, setting new benchmarks for future collaborations and solidifying the foundation for a dynamic partnership built on shared values and aspirations.

## *Trade Agreements and Economic Impact*

France's engagement in trade agreements with Arab states has been a cornerstone of its foreign policy, fostering economic interdependence and mutual growth. The Macron administration keenly prioritized strengthening trade ties with Arab countries, recognizing the immense potential for collaboration in diverse sectors. Establishing strategic partnerships and negotiating comprehensive trade agreements have played a pivotal role in shaping the economic landscape of Franco-Arab relations. These agreements have facilitated the flow of goods and services and paved the way for enhanced investment, technological exchange, and knowledge transfer. Moreover, they have fostered a climate of cooperation that transcends mere economic transactions, promoting cultural understanding and diplomatic harmony. One notable agreement is the Euro-Mediterranean Partnership (EUROMED), which aims to create a free trade area encompassing the EU and 16 Mediterranean partner countries, including several Arab states. This initiative has contributed significantly to boosting trade volumes, creating employment opportunities, and driving socio-economic development within the participating nations. France's proactive involvement in supporting the modernization and diversification of Arab economies has yielded substantial economic impact, leading to heightened prosperity and stability in the region. Furthermore, exchanging expertise in renewable energy, infrastructure development, and digital innovation has reinforced sustainable economic growth and catalyzed the emergence of new industry clusters. The mutually beneficial nature of these trade agreements has fostered a climate conducive to long-term economic partnerships, positioning France and Arab states as strategic allies in a rapidly evolving global economy. The economic impact of these collaborations extends beyond bilateral trade statistics, influencing broader geopolitical dynamics and contributing to the consolidation of a robust Franco-Arab economic axis. As France continues to play a pivotal role in facilitating economic integration and fostering innovation across the Arab world, the enduring legacy of these trade agreements is poised to shape the future trajectory of Franco-Arab relations, ushering in an era of shared prosperity and economic resilience.

## *Military Cooperation and Defense Strategy*

In the Macron era, military cooperation has taken center stage in France's approach to Franco-Arab relations. The strategic partnership between France and Arab states has focused on traditional defense assistance and evolved to encompass broader security challenges in the region. Under President Macron's leadership, a concerted effort has been made to strengthen defense ties with Arab countries, prioritizing collaborative strategies to address shared threats and promote stability. This has manifested in joint military exercises, intelligence sharing, and capacity-building initiatives designed to enhance the capabilities of Arab partner forces. Macron's administration has emphasized the importance of leveraging military cooperation to counter terrorism and extremism, particularly in the context of ongoing conflicts in the Middle East and North Africa. France has provided technical expertise, training, and equipment to support its Arab allies in confronting these complex security threats. Additionally, discussions on defense strategy have delved into addressing non-traditional security concerns such as cybersecurity and hybrid warfare, reflecting the evolving nature of contemporary challenges. The coordination of efforts in these domains has contributed to fostering a comprehensive defense framework that aligns with the broader objectives of Franco-Arab relations. Underpinning this military collaboration is the mutual recognition of the imperative to uphold regional stability and safeguard common interests. Through sustained engagement and dialogue, France has sought to establish a cohesive defense strategy that not only bolsters the security of individual Arab states but also reinforces collective security architectures. Macron's presidency has also underscored the significance of promoting transparency and accountability in arms sales and defense partnerships, affirming a commitment to responsible arms transfers and ethical conduct in military engagements. The defense strategy has also focused on developing interoperability among armed forces, enabling seamless coordination and joint operations when addressing emergent threats or participating in peacekeeping missions. This emphasis on interoperability reflects a pragmatic approach to enhancing the effectiveness of multilateral efforts and strengthening the defense capabilities of Arab countries. Furthermore, Macron's government has articulated a vision for fostering sustainable, mutually beneficial defense partnerships founded on the principles of sovereignty, mutual respect, and shared responsibilities. Therefore, military cooperation and defense strategy stand as pivotal elements in the contemporary landscape of Franco-Arab relations, serving as critical pillars in shaping a future characterized by enhanced security collaboration, proactive risk mitigation, and robust deterrence mechanisms.

## *Cultural Diplomacy and Educational Exchanges*

Cultural diplomacy is a vital tool in fostering understanding, building trust, and strengthening relationships between nations. Under Macron's presidency, France has placed significant emphasis on leveraging cultural diplomacy to enhance Franco-Arab relations. Educational exchanges form a key component of this strategy, aiming to promote mutual understanding and collaboration between the two regions.

France has actively engaged in cultural diplomacy programs encompassing various artistic and intellectual exchange forms. This includes promoting the French language and culture through alliances such as the Institut Français and Alliance Française, which aim to provide educational and cultural resources to individuals worldwide. Additionally, initiatives such as promoting French literature, cinema, music, and visual arts enrich cultural dialogue and exchange between France and Arab countries.

Educational exchanges play a crucial role in fostering cross-cultural understanding and academic cooperation. The exchange of students, scholars, and researchers between France and Arab states facilitates sharing of knowledge, expertise, and ideas. These exchanges enrich the academic environments and nurture lasting personal connections that contribute to the overall diplomatic relationship. Moreover, joint research projects, academic partnerships, and collaborative educational programs motivate innovation, creativity, and the advancement of shared goals.

Furthermore, with a focus on multicultural challenges, educational exchanges play an integral role in promoting intercultural dialogue and diversity. They enable individuals to experience different perspectives and embrace multiculturalism, enriching both societies. By facilitating opportunities for exposure to diverse cultural and intellectual traditions, educational exchanges foster an environment of inclusion and respect for diversity.

In conclusion, promoting cultural diplomacy and educational exchanges became a cornerstone of Franco-Arab relations during Macron's presidency. By emphasizing the importance of cultural understanding, France is committed to nurturing enduring partnerships based on mutual respect, collaboration, and shared values. Through these initiatives, France aims to build bridges that transcend cultural differences, leading to a more interconnected and harmonious global community.

## Immigration, Integration, and Multicultural Challenges

France's approach to immigration, integration, and multiculturalism represents a significant dimension of its evolving engagement with the Arab world. The issue of immigration has been a complex and contentious one, deeply intertwined with social, economic, and political considerations. Under President Macron's leadership, the French government has sought to address the multifaceted challenges posed by migration and diversity with a combination of pragmatism and commitment to upholding the country's values. Macron's administration acknowledges the historical presence of Arab communities in France and recognizes the need for inclusive policies that promote successful integration while preserving cultural diversity. Efforts to create a cohesive society have involved dialogues with representatives of various cultural and religious backgrounds to foster mutual understanding and respect. These initiatives have emphasized the importance of language acquisition, employment opportunities, and access to education as crucial elements in facilitating the integration of immigrants. Additionally, the government has implemented measures to combat discrimination and enhance social cohesion, focusing on combating prejudices and stereotypes. While navigating these interconnected challenges, the French authorities have also worked to address security concerns and maintain public order, striving to strike a delicate balance between national security and civil liberties. The complex nature of integration dynamics requires continuous adaptation and response, necessitating ongoing dialogue and policy refinement. As France grapples with the complexities of immigration, the nation's approach under Macron's presidency reflects a nuanced understanding of multicultural coexistence and emphasizes the imperative of unity within diversity.

## Assessing the Response to Regional Conflicts

Under President Macron's leadership, France has taken a proactive stance in addressing regional conflicts in the Franco-Arab context. Conflict and instability in the Middle East and North Africa pose considerable challenges to global peace and security, and France has been actively seeking diplomatic solutions and promoting stability. Assessing the response to regional conflicts entails examining France's approach to specific situations such as the Syrian Civil War, Yemen crisis, and Libyan conflict. In each case, France has worked closely with regional and international partners to mitigate the impacts of these conflicts and advance towards sustainable peace. Macron's administration has emphasized the importance of multilateralism and international cooperation in resolving these conflicts, recognizing that unilateral actions often fail to deliver lasting solutions. France has collaborated with Arab states, the United Nations, and the European Union to address the root causes of conflicts, support humanitarian efforts, and facilitate political dialogue. Furthermore, through its military presence and participation in peacekeeping missions, France has contributed to stabilizing volatile regions and providing much-needed assistance to affected populations. The evaluation of France's response to regional conflicts also involves an analysis of diplomatic negotiations and mediation efforts. President Macron's administration has demonstrated a willingness to engage with diverse actors and bring conflicting parties to the negotiating table. France's longstanding ties with many Arab states have positioned it as a credible mediator in the region, enabling it to play a constructive role in conflict resolution. Additionally, France has consistently advocated for adherence to international law and the protection of human rights in conflict zones, aligning its policies with fundamental principles of justice and humanitarianism. As France navigates the complexities of regional conflicts, it adapts its strategies and approaches to address evolving challenges effectively. Through ongoing assessment and adaptation, France aims to contribute meaningfully to promoting peace and stability in the Franco-Arab context. Looking ahead, the lessons learned from past engagements are instrumental in shaping France's future response to regional conflicts, reinforcing its commitment to upholding the values of diplomacy, cooperation, and peacebuilding.

## Prospects for Future Franco-Arab Relations in the Macron Era

As we look to the future of Franco-Arab relations under the leadership of President Macron, it becomes crucial to assess the opportunities and challenges that lie ahead. The evolving geopolitical landscape demands a reevaluation of diplomatic strategies and the identification of potential areas for collaboration. One key aspect is the need for sustained dialogue and engagement with Arab states to address common concerns and aspirations. Macron's presidency marks a significant juncture in redefining the bilateral ties, opening doors for innovation and cooperation.

In the economic sphere, there exists vast potential for increased trade partnerships and investment ventures between France and Arab countries. Initiatives such as diversifying economic interests, promoting sustainable development, and harnessing technological advancements can foster mutual prosperity. Strengthening these economic linkages can contribute to both regions' growth and facilitate greater interdependence and understanding.

Furthermore, a proactive approach to addressing security challenges is imperative for ensuring stability in the Franco-Arab relationship. With the rise of global threats, including terrorism and cyber warfare, collaborative efforts in intelligence sharing, counter-terrorism measures, and cybersecurity protocols are essential. By bolstering joint defense initiatives and fostering a united front in combating extremism, the Macron administration can lay the groundwork for sustainable peace and security.

Cultural diplomacy and educational exchanges also hold promise for nurturing long-term relationships. Programs promoting cultural understanding, language studies, and academic collaborations can bridge societal divides and promote mutual respect. By facilitating people-to-people interactions, France and Arab states can build enduring bonds based on shared knowledge and appreciation of diverse cultures.

Addressing migration and integration challenges within Europe forms another crucial aspect of future Franco-Arab relations. Collaborative frameworks geared towards effective integration policies, social cohesion, and immigrant empowerment can pave the way for a cohesive society. Embracing diversity and inclusivity while acknowledging the contributions of Arab communities can set a positive precedent for the region.

Lastly, leveraging France's historical ties with Arab countries to mediate in regional conflicts stands as a beacon of hope for fostering lasting peace. Macron's administration can position itself as a credible mediator and peace facilitator through active diplomacy and interventions. France can significantly influence regional dynamics and alleviate tensions by promoting dialogue and conflict resolution mechanisms.

In conclusion, the Macron era presents an opportune moment to forge a new chapter in Franco-Arab relations predicated on mutual respect, cooperation, and progress. By charting a course that prioritizes economic partnerships, security collaboration, cultural exchanges, integration efforts, and conflict resolution, France can carve out a forward-looking trajectory for sustained and harmonious engagement with Arab states.

# IN A NUTSHELL

> **Macron's Era: Continuities and Changes in France's Arab Policy**
>
> ### 1. Strategic Vision for Franco-Arab Relations under Macron
>
> Under President Emmanuel Macron, France's strategic vision for Franco-Arab relations has been characterized by a blend of continuity and change. Macron has emphasized a multilateral approach, seeking to position France as a key player in the Middle East while balancing traditional alliances and new partnerships. This vision includes promoting stability, security, and economic cooperation, as well as addressing global challenges such as climate change and terrorism.
>
> ### 2. Policy Changes and Diplomatic Initiatives
>
> Macron's era has seen several notable policy changes and diplomatic initiatives:
>
> - **Multilateralism and Strategic Dialogues**: Macron has reinforced France's commitment to multilateralism, engaging in strategic dialogues with key Arab states such as the UAE and Saudi Arabia. These dialogues have

focused on a wide range of issues, including energy security, climate change, and regional stability.
- **Humanitarian and Development Aid**: France has increased its humanitarian aid and development assistance to conflict-affected regions, particularly in Syria, Iraq, and Lebanon. This includes support for reconstruction efforts and addressing the needs of refugees and displaced persons.

### 3. Key Bilateral Engagements and Summits

Macron has prioritized high-level bilateral engagements and summits to strengthen Franco-Arab relations:

- **State Visits and Strategic Partnerships**: Macron has hosted and visited leaders from the UAE, Saudi Arabia, and other Arab states, resulting in the signing of strategic partnerships and agreements. For example, the Comprehensive Strategic Energy Partnership with the UAE aims to enhance cooperation in the energy sector.
- **Baghdad Conference**: Macron has been actively involved in the Baghdad Conference on Partnership and Cooperation, which aims to support Iraq's sovereignty and regional stability.

### 4. Trade Agreements and Economic Impact

Trade and economic cooperation have been central to Macron's Arab policy:

- **Bilateral Trade Agreements**: France has signed

several trade agreements with Arab states, focusing on sectors such as energy, defense, and technology. The agreements aim to boost economic ties and create new opportunities for French businesses.
- **Economic Partnerships**: Macron has promoted economic partnerships through initiatives like the UAE-France High-Level Business Council, which seeks to enhance bilateral trade and investment.

## 5. Military Cooperation and Defense Strategy

Military cooperation and defense strategy have remained key components of France's Arab policy:

- **Military Presence and Operations**: France maintains a significant military presence in the Middle East, including operations in Iraq, Syria, and the UAE. The Chammal operation, for instance, involves French troops in the fight against terrorism.
- **Defense Agreements**: France has signed defense agreements with several Arab states, providing military training, equipment, and support. This includes the deployment of Rafale fighters and defense systems in the UAE.

## 6. Cultural Diplomacy and Educational Exchanges

Cultural diplomacy and educational exchanges have been important tools in strengthening Franco-Arab relations:

- **Cultural Institutions**: France has established cultural

institutions such as the Louvre Abu Dhabi and Sorbonne University Abu Dhabi, which serve as symbols of Franco-Arab cooperation in culture and education.
- **Educational Programs**: France has promoted educational exchanges and capacity-building programs, including the teaching of the French language in Emirati schools and cooperation in higher education.

## 7. Immigration, Integration, and Multicultural Challenges

Immigration and integration have posed significant challenges for France:

- **Immigration Policies**: Macron's administration has faced criticism for its handling of immigration and integration issues, particularly concerning the treatment of Muslim communities and the rise of Islamophobia.
- **Multiculturalism**: The French government's approach to multiculturalism has been contentious, with debates over secularism and the integration of immigrants into French society.

## 8. Assessing the Response to Regional Conflicts

France's response to regional conflicts under Macron has been multifaceted:

- **Humanitarian Aid**: France has provided substantial humanitarian aid to conflict zones, including Syria and

Iraq, focusing on emergency assistance and reconstruction.
- **Diplomatic Efforts**: Macron has engaged in diplomatic efforts to mediate conflicts and promote peace, such as supporting the Abraham Accords and calling for a ceasefire in Gaza.

## 9. Prospects for Future Franco-Arab Relations in the Macron Era

The future of Franco-Arab relations under Macron looks promising, with several key areas of focus:

- **Enhanced Cooperation**: Continued emphasis on strategic partnerships and high-level dialogues to address shared challenges.
- **Innovative Solutions**: Development and implementation of innovative technologies and practices in renewable energy and water management.
- **Global Leadership**: Joint efforts to lead global climate action and promote multilateralism, particularly through platforms like COP28.

In conclusion, Macron's era has seen both continuities and changes in France's Arab policy. While maintaining traditional alliances and military cooperation, Macron has also introduced new diplomatic initiatives and economic partnerships. The focus on multilateralism, cultural diplomacy, and addressing global challenges reflects a comprehensive approach to strengthening Franco-Arab relations.

# References For Further Reading

Ronja Kempin (ed.) "France's Foreign and Security Policy under President Macron". SWP Research Paper 4 May 2021, Berlin. https://www.swp-berlin.org/publications/products/research_papers/2021RP04_PolicyUnderMacron_DASEP.pdf

Alkinani, Zeidon . "Maghreb-France Relations as Macron Begins Second Term." Arab Center Washington DC, May 26, 2022. https://arabcenterdc.org/resource/maghreb-france-relations-as-macron-begins-second-term/.

Boniface , Pascal . "The Geopolitical Significance of Macron's Re-Election in France." IRIS, May 20, 2022. https://www.iris-france.org/167631-the-geopolitical-significance-of-macrons-re-election-in-france/.

Caulcutt , Clea . "Macron's Rift with Diplomats Deepens after Missteps on Israel-Hamas War." POLITICO, November 22, 2023. https://www.politico.eu/article/in-wake-of-setbacks-on-israel-hamas-war-macron-seeks-second-wind/.

Dagres, Holly. "Under Macron's Leadership, France Is Leading a Middle Power Strategy in the Gulf. Here's How." Atlantic Council, August 16, 2022. https://www.atlanticcouncil.org/blogs/menasource/under-macrons-leadership-france-is-leading-a-middle-power-strategy-in-the-gulf-heres-how/.

Duclos , Michel . "Macron in Beirut and Baghdad: A New French Approach to the Middle East?" Institut Montaigne, September 11, 2020. https://www.institutmontaigne.org/en/expressions/macron-beirut-and-baghdad-new-french-approach-middle-east.

Duclos, Michel . "Tracing French Diplomacy: A Brief History of Macron's Foreign

Policy." Institut Montaigne, October 12, 2021. https://www.institutmontaigne.org/en/expressions/tracing-french-diplomacy-brief-history-macrons-foreign-policy.

elysee.fr. "France-United Arab Emirates Joint Statement on the Occasion of the State Visit to France of Sheikh Mohamed Bin Zayed al Nahyan, President of the UAE 18-19 July 2022," July 20, 2022. https://www.elysee.fr/en/emmanuel-macron/2022/07/20/france-united-arab-emirates-joint-statement-on-the-occasion-of-the-state-visit-to-france-of-sheikh-mohamed-bin-zayed-al-nahyan-president-of-the-uae-18-19-july-2022.

elysee.fr. "Speech of the President of the Republic on the Defense and Deterrence Strategy," February 7, 2020. https://www.elysee.fr/en/emmanuel-macron/2020/02/07/speech-of-the-president-of-the-republic-on-the-defense-and-deterrence-strategy.

France Diplomacy - Ministry for Europe and Foreign Affairs. "15th Session of the UAE-France Strategic Dialogue Discusses Growing Cooperation between UAE & France (19.06.23)." France Diplomacy, 2019. https://www.diplomatie.gouv.fr/en/country-files/united-arab-emirates/events/article/15th-session-of-the-uae-france-strategic-dialogue-discusses-growing-cooperation.

France Diplomacy - Ministry for Europe and Foreign Affairs. "Speech by President Emmanuel Macron - Ambassadors' Conference 2018," August 27, 2018. https://www.diplomatie.gouv.fr/en/the-ministry-and-its-network/news/ambassadors-week/ambassadors-week-edition-2018/article/speech-by-president-emmanuel-macron-ambassadors-conference-2018.

France Diplomatie. "The French Government's Trade Policy." Ministry for Europe and Foreign Affairs, 2017. https://www.diplomatie.gouv.fr/en/french-foreign-policy/economic-diplomacy-foreign-trade/the-french-government-s-trade-policy/.

France in the UK. "France and UAE Extend Their Strategic Partnership," July 21, 2022. https://uk.ambafrance.org/France-and-UAE-extend-their-strategic-partnership.

La France aux Émirats arabes unis. "14th Session of the UAE-France Strategic Dialogue," August 4, 2022. https://ae.ambafrance.org/14th-session-of-the-UAE-France-Strategic-Dialogue.

Secrétariat général de la défense et de la sécurité nationale. "National Strategic Review 2022," 2022. https://www.sgdsn.gouv.fr/files/files/rns-uk-20221202.pdf.

"SPEECH by the PRESIDENT of the REPUBLIC at the CONFERENCE of AMBASSADORS," August 28, 2023. https://www.elysee.fr/admin/upload/default/0001/15/68ca793aaf44c90fd79cbf1bc3a234e71c3e1d57.pdf.

Trinquet, Thibaut. "With a New U.S. Administration, What Is next for Macron's Middle East Ambitions? | German Marshall Fund of the United States." www.gmfus.org. Accessed May 23, 2024. https://www.gmfus.org/news/new-us-administration-what-next-macrons-middle-east-ambitions.

Uysal, Selin . "France's Diplomatic Role in the Middle East Post-October 7 | the Washington Institute." www.washingtoninstitute.org, February 2, 2024. https://www.washingtoninstitute.org/policy-analysis/frances-diplomatic-role-middle-east-post-october-7.

Vincent, Elise . "France's Strategic Thinking in the Middle East Is at a Standstill." www.ifri.org, December 20, 2022. https://www.ifri.org/en/espace-media/lifri-medias/frances-strategic-thinking-middle-east-standstill.

# XVI

# Economic Reforms and Investment Opportunities

## Overview of Economic Reforms in France

France's economic reforms have evolved significantly, particularly in the pre-Macron era. Historically, economic policies in France were characterized by a strong focus on state intervention, labor market regulations, and a relatively high public spending-to-GDP ratio. The decades leading up to Macron's presidency were marked by a climate of slow economic growth, high unemployment rates, and complex bureaucratic hurdles that impeded entrepreneurial innovation and foreign investment. Policymakers and economists increasingly recognized the need for substantial reforms to revitalize the French economy and ensure its competitive position in the global market.

The election of Emmanuel Macron as President in 2017 ushered in a new era of economic reforms in France. Macron's vision was centered on liberalizing the economy, enhancing labor market flexibility, reducing public expenditure, and fostering a more business-friendly environment. His administration embarked on transformative measures, including labor law revisions, corporate tax cuts, and initiatives to streamline bureaucracy. These initiatives sought to create a more attractive investment landscape and stimulate economic growth.

Moreover, Macron's economic agenda also encompassed institutional reforms such as overhauling the pension system, redefining the state's role in the economy, and addressing structural inefficiencies. This comprehensive approach aimed to improve France's overall economic resilience and agility, positioning the country as an appealing destination for domestic and foreign investors. The intent was to bolster the competitive strengths of French industries, stimulate entrepreneurship, and foster a culture of innovation.

The evolving economic reforms also placed considerable emphasis on sustainability and environmental consciousness. Macron's government is committed to advancing sustainable development goals, promoting clean energy solutions, and aligning economic policies with environmental considerations. These efforts underscored the broader objective of creating a more resilient and environmentally conscious economy capable of addressing global challenges while fostering economic prosperity.

In conclusion, the economic reforms preceding Macron's presidency reflect a period of introspection and recognition of the need for substantial changes. Macron's tenure brought about a shift towards liberalization, modernization, and sustainability, positioning France as a more globally competitive and attractive investment destination.

## Impact of Macron's Policies on Franco-Arab Economic Ties

President Emmanuel Macron's economic reforms have significantly influenced Franco-Arab economic ties. Macron's pro-business policies and commitment to fostering trade and investment have facilitated a positive shift in the economic partnership between France and the Arab region. Through bold initiatives such as labor market reforms, tax cuts, and deregulation efforts, Macron has aimed to enhance France's economic competitiveness and attractiveness to foreign investors, including those from Arab countries. This proactive approach has revitalized the French economy and bolstered its position as an appealing investment destination for Arab businesses and entrepreneurs. Macron's emphasis on innovation and technology has further catalyzed collaborations in renewable energy, digital infrastructure, and sustainable development sectors. His advocacy for closer economic integration within the European Union has provided a solid foundation for expanded economic engagement with Arab countries. Moreover, Macron's diplomatic outreach and strategic partnerships with key Arab states have fostered a conducive environment for enhanced economic cooperation. By championing multilateralism and advocating for inclusive economic growth, Macron has effectively elevated the profile of Franco-Arab economic relations on the global stage. Furthermore, his commitment to addressing societal challenges, such as youth unemployment and socioeconomic disparities, resonates with many Arab countries facing similar issues. This shared vision for social progress and economic prosperity has fortified the bond between France and its Arab partners, paving the way for mutually beneficial economic ventures. As a result, Macron's policies have not only stimulated economic activity and trade between France and Arab countries but have also encouraged a renewed sense of collaboration, trust, and optimism in economic diplomacy.

## *Investment Opportunities in the Arab Region*

As economic ties between France and the Arab region continue to strengthen, exploring the vast investment opportunities available in this dynamic area is crucial. The Arab region offers a diverse and rapidly growing market with a young, tech-savvy population and a strong appetite for innovation. With an expanding middle class and strategic geographic positioning, the Arab region presents an array of investment prospects across various sectors, including technology, renewable energy, infrastructure, healthcare, and education.

One of the key areas ripe for investment is the technology sector. Arab countries are experiencing a digital transformation, with a burgeoning startup ecosystem and increasing adoption of digital technologies. This presents an opportunity for French companies to invest in these emerging ventures or engage in technology transfer partnerships to leverage the Arab region's innovative potential. Additionally, the renewable energy sector, encompassing solar and wind energy projects, has seen significant growth in the Arab region as governments prioritize sustainable energy solutions. French expertise in renewable energy technologies positions the country to play a vital role in supporting and investing in these initiatives.

Furthermore, infrastructure development in the Arab region offers substantial investment avenues. With ambitious transportation and urban development projects underway, there is a high demand for foreign expertise and capital. From high-speed rail networks to smart city initiatives, French companies can contribute to and benefit from these large-scale infrastructure projects. Similarly, the healthcare and education sectors present compelling investment opportunities driven by a desire to improve public services and enhance human capital in the region.

Navigating these investment opportunities requires an understanding of the unique regulatory and cultural aspects of each Arab country. While the region offers promising prospects, French investors must conduct thorough market research and establish local partnerships to ensure successful and sustainable investments. Embracing a long-term perspective and committing to social responsibility can further solidify the mutually beneficial relationships between France and the Arab region.

In conclusion, the Arab region is an attractive destination for French investment, offering economic potential, innovation, and demographic advantages. By identifying and seizing the diverse investment opportunities present in the Arab region, France can enhance its economic engagement and contribute to the region's growth and prosperity, fostering enduring partnerships built on mutual benefit and shared success.

## *Technological Advancements and Innovations*

The evolving landscape of Franco-Arab economic relations is deeply influenced by the rapid technological advancements and the wave of innovation sweeping across various industries. In recent years, technological progress has played a pivotal role in reshaping the economic ecosystem, fostering more excellent connectivity, and propelling bilateral trade and investment between France and the Arab region.

Renewable energy is one of the key areas where technological advancements have made significant strides. The Arab countries, endowed with abundant solar resources, have been at the forefront of harnessing solar power through large-scale projects and initiatives. The integration of French expertise in renewable energy technologies has not only accelerated the shift towards sustainable and clean energy sources but has also underpinned collaborative efforts to address environmental challenges and climate change.

Furthermore, digital transformation and Industry 4.0 technologies have revolutionized traditional business models and operational frameworks. The widespread adoption of cutting-edge solutions such as artificial intelligence, big data analytics, and the Internet of Things (IoT) has not only bolstered productivity and efficiency. Still, it has also created new avenues for cross-border investments and partnerships. This convergence of tech-driven innovation presents an opportune moment for France and the Arab states to leverage synergies and propel economic growth in strategic sectors, including manufacturing, healthcare, and logistics.

In addition, breakthroughs in financial technology (fintech) have paved the way for seamless payment systems, digital banking services, and innovative investment platforms, stimulating financial inclusion and driving entrepreneurship. By embracing fintech solutions, Franco-Arab collaborations can unlock new pathways for capital mobilization, venture funding, and cross-border transactions, ultimately enhancing the overall competitiveness of the economic landscape.

It is imperative to underscore the transformative potential of technological advancements in nurturing an ecosystem conducive to entrepreneurship and innovation. The integration of incubators, research hubs, and technology parks has catalyzed the development of a vibrant startup culture, fostering creativity and propelling cross-border knowledge exchange. The coalescence of disruptive technologies with proactive policy frameworks has laid the groundwork for a thriving innovation ecosystem that will invariably shape the trajectory of Franco-Arab economic cooperation in the digital age.

## *Public-Private Partnerships: A Strategic Approach*

In Franco-Arab economic relations, public-private partnerships (PPPs) have emerged as a strategic mechanism for leveraging resources and expertise to foster sustainable growth and development. These collaborative ventures bring together governmental entities and private enterprises in a shared effort to address pressing socioeconomic challenges and capitalize on emerging opportunities. By pooling resources and sharing risks, PPPs can yield substantial benefits for France and Arab countries. Through a carefully orchestrated approach, these partnerships facilitate the mobilization of private sector capital, knowledge, and innovation while tapping into the public sector's regulatory and developmental capacities. Moreover, PPPs are pivotal in driving infrastructural developments, technology transfer, and capacity building across diverse energy, healthcare, transportation, and urban planning sectors. The strategic alignment of interests between government and industry stakeholders catalyzes fostering sustainable economic activities and enhancing the overall business environment within the Franco-Arab context.

Effective PPPs necessitate clear governance structures, transparent legal frameworks, and equitable risk-sharing arrangements. Establishing a conducive legislative environment becomes imperative to instill investor confidence and attract private capital. In this regard, sound regulatory mechanisms and streamlined approval processes are essential for the smooth execution and implementation of PPP projects. Governments can mitigate potential risks by institutionalizing accountability, enacting comprehensive legal safeguards, and ensuring fair competition among market players. Furthermore, proactive measures aimed at enhancing transparency and combating corruption bolster the integrity of PPPs, thus fostering a conducive atmosphere for long-term investments and sustained economic prosperity.

The success of PPPs hinges on meticulous project planning, rigorous risk assessment, and robust performance monitoring mechanisms. Through stringent due diligence and feasibility studies, it is crucial to identify viable projects with clear economic viability and social impact. Subsequently, structuring PPP agreements that delineate roles, responsibilities, and performance targets is pivotal to aligning stakeholder interests and ensuring project deliverables. Regular assessments and performance evaluations throughout the project lifecycle enable timely intervention, course correction, and optimal resource allocation to achieve predefined outcomes.

Moreover, knowledge sharing and capacity development constitute integral components of successful PPP endeavors. Building local expertise and fostering technology transfer through skill development programs and knowledge exchange initiatives enriches the human capital base and spurs entrepreneurial activities and indigenous innovation. Additionally, collaboration with academic and research institutions further strengthens the partnership's technological and intellectual assets, laying the foundation for sustainable advancements and competitiveness within the Franco-Arab economic landscape.

In conclusion, public-private partnerships (PPPs) epitomize a strategic framework for catalyzing dynamic economic cooperation and sustainable growth between France and the Arab region. Leveraging complementary strengths and resources collaboratively, PPPs hold immense potential in shaping both parties' resilient, inclusive, and prosperous future. As the landscape of international business evolves, the strategic embrace of PPPs as a vehicle for transformative economic engagements stands to herald a new era of mutually beneficial collaborations and enduring socio-economic progress.

## *Taxation and Regulatory Changes*

Taxation and regulatory frameworks are pivotal in shaping the economic landscape and fostering sustainable growth in Franco-Arab relations. This section delves into the intricate domain of taxation policies and regulatory changes, aiming to understand their impact on cross-border investments and bilateral trade comprehensively.

France's commitment to enhancing its tax laws and regulatory environment has been instrumental in attracting foreign direct investment (FDI) from Arab countries. Implementing competitive tax rates and investor-friendly regulations has significantly bolstered Arab investors' confidence in the French market. Furthermore, ongoing efforts to simplify administrative procedures and streamline regulatory processes have further augmented France's attractiveness as a favorable investment destination for Arab businesses.

Conversely, regulatory changes within the Arab region have presented opportunities and challenges for French enterprises seeking to expand their operations in these markets. A detailed analysis of recent regulatory reforms in key Arab economies sheds light on the evolving business landscape and the implications for French companies looking to penetrate these markets. Understanding the nuances of local tax systems and regulatory requirements is imperative for French businesses to navigate the complexities and capitalize on emerging opportunities.

In addition to tax and regulatory reforms at the national level, bilateral initiatives aimed at harmonizing tax policies and resolving regulatory discrepancies between France and Arab countries are paramount. Collaborative efforts to establish clear and consistent taxation guidelines for cross-border transactions facilitate smoother trade relations and instill confidence in investors by minimizing uncertainty and mitigating potential risks associated with tax ambiguity.

Moreover, the dialogue surrounding tax treaties and double taxation avoidance agreements between France and Arab countries underscores the commitment to fostering a conducive environment for economic collaboration. Such agreements nurture trust and stability in cross-border transactions by providing a framework for resolving tax-related issues and preventing fiscal evasion, thereby catalyzing sustained economic partnerships.

This section will offer insights into the dynamic interplay between taxation policies and regulatory changes and their ramifications on the Franco-Arab economic landscape. It will analyze case studies illustrating the impact of tax and regulatory dynamics on specific industries, shedding light on best practices and potential pitfalls to equip readers with a nuanced understanding of the evolving fiscal and regulatory framework governing Franco-Arab economic engagements.

## *Sustainable Development Goals and Economic Growth*

Sustainable development lies at the heart of modern economic cooperation, serving as a foundation for long-term prosperity and stability in Franco-Arab relations. Pursuing sustainable development goals (SDGs) encompasses a broad spectrum of interconnected objectives, including economic growth, social inclusion, and environmental sustainability. As France and Arab countries seek to deepen their economic ties, a collective commitment to advancing SDGs is imperative for fostering resilience and shared prosperity.

How France and Arab countries can leverage their economic ties to advance SDGs, fostering resilience and shared prosperity? Here are some clues:

## Economic Growth

### France's Role in Economic Development

France has a long-standing commitment to sustainable development, as evidenced by its support for the United Nations' 2030 Agenda for Sustainable Development. The country has implemented various policies to promote economic growth while ensuring environmental sustainability and social inclusion. For instance, France's development cooperation focuses on sectors such as health, education, and infrastructure, which are crucial for sustainable economic growth.

### Arab Region's Economic Opportunities

The Arab region, while facing significant challenges, also presents numerous opportunities for economic growth. Countries in the region are increasingly focusing on diversifying their economies and investing in sectors such as renewable energy, digital infrastructure, and education. The 2023 Arab SDG Index highlights positive trends in areas like digital infrastructure and basic health outcomes, which are essential for sustainable economic development.

## Social Inclusion

### Addressing Inequality and Promoting Inclusion

Social inclusion is a vital aspect of sustainable development. Both France and Arab countries face challenges related to social inequality and the inclusion of marginalized groups. For example, Tunisia's youth employment landscape reveals significant regional and gender disparities, with rural areas and women being particularly disadvantaged. Addressing these disparities requires targeted policies that promote education, vocational training, and access to finance for marginalized groups.

## Collaborative Initiatives

France and Arab countries can collaborate on initiatives aimed at promoting social inclusion. For instance, the European Social Inclusion Initiative by J-PAL Europe focuses on using rigorous evidence to promote the social inclusion of migrants, which can be adapted and implemented in the Arab region to address similar challenges.

# Environmental Sustainability

## Renewable Energy and Environmental Protection

Environmental sustainability is a cornerstone of the SDGs. France has made significant strides in promoting renewable energy and environmental protection. The country's commitment to reducing $CO_2$ emissions through the use of alternative and nuclear energy sources is a testament to its dedication to environmental sustainability.

## Arab Region's Environmental Challenges and Opportunities

The Arab region faces unique environmental challenges, including water scarcity and vulnerability to climate change. However, there are also opportunities for progress. For example, some Arab countries have made advancements in scaling up renewable energy and transitioning to low-carbon societies. Collaborative efforts, such as the Buildings and Climate Global Forum organized by France and UNEP, highlight the importance of international cooperation in addressing environmental challenges.

## Enhancing Public-Private Partnerships

Public-private partnerships (PPPs) are crucial for achieving the SDGs. The 2030 Agenda emphasizes the role of the private sector in sustainable development, and both France and Arab countries can benefit from enhanced PPPs. These partnerships can drive innovation, create jobs, and mobilize resources for sustainable development projects.

## Leveraging Financial Mechanisms

Innovative financial mechanisms, such as debt-for-nature swaps, can help address both environmental and economic challenges. These mechanisms allow countries to reduce their debt in exchange for commitments to environmental protection, thereby promoting both financial stability and environmental sustainability.

## Strengthening Data and Monitoring

Effective implementation of the SDGs requires robust data and monitoring systems. Both France and Arab countries need to invest in improving data availability and quality to track progress and make informed policy decisions. This includes developing comprehensive indicators and leveraging technologies for data collection and analysis.

Ultimately, the pursuit of sustainable development goals is essential for fostering long-term prosperity and stability in Franco-Arab relations. By focusing on economic growth, social inclusion, and environmental sustainability, France and Arab countries can deepen their economic ties and work towards shared prosperity. Collaborative initiatives, innovative financial mechanisms, and robust data systems are key to advancing the SDGs and building resilient, inclusive, and sustainable societies.

## Challenges to Foreign Investment

Foreign investment is crucial in strengthening economic ties between France and the Arab region. However, various challenges often hinder the smooth flow of foreign investment into these economies. One of the primary challenges is the complex regulatory environment, characterized by differing legal frameworks, administrative procedures, and bureaucratic hurdles. Navigating these regulations can be daunting for foreign investors and may lead to delays or uncertainties in the investment process.

Another significant challenge is the lack of transparency and potential corruption within certain business practices. Fluctuating political landscapes and governance issues in some Arab countries can create an unpredictable investment climate, deterring potential foreign investors from committing to long-term projects or partnerships. Furthermore, the region's varying political stability and security threats pose significant concerns for investors, impacting their risk assessment and overall investment decisions.

Economic volatility and fluctuating currency exchange rates also pose challenges to foreign investment. The impact of global economic trends, regional conflicts, and geopolitical tensions can create uncertainty and affect the financial viability of investment initiatives. Additionally, cultural differences and language barriers may present communication challenges and hinder the effective execution of investment strategies and negotiations.

Furthermore, the lack of sufficient infrastructure and logistical support in some areas of the Arab region can impede the efficient operation of businesses, affecting the overall attractiveness of the investment environment. Limited access to financing options and credit facilities may also constrain the ability of foreign investors to mobilize capital and expand their presence in the region.

Addressing these challenges requires proactive measures and collaborative efforts between governmental bodies, regulatory authorities, and private sector stakeholders. Initiatives to enhance transparency, streamline regulatory processes, and implement anti-corruption measures are essential in creating a conducive environment for foreign investment. Enhanced political stability, security measures, and risk mitigation strategies can instill confidence in potential investors and contribute to a more stable investment climate.

Moreover, fostering open dialogue and cultural exchange can bridge the gap created by cultural differences and improve cross-border business relations. Investing in developing infrastructure, transportation networks, and reliable energy sources is critical for establishing a robust foundation to support foreign investment initiatives.

By addressing these challenges and implementing strategic reforms, France and the Arab region can unlock the full potential of foreign investment, furthering economic integration and mutual prosperity.

## *Case Studies: Successful Franco-Arab Economic Collaborations*

In recent decades, Franco-Arab economic collaborations have yielded numerous successful case studies demonstrating bilateral cooperation's potential and benefits. These case studies highlight the tangible outcomes of joint ventures and provide valuable insights into the factors that contribute to successful partnerships between France and the Arab region. One notable case study is the partnership between a leading French energy company and an Arab state in developing renewable energy projects. This collaboration resulted in the establishment of cutting-edge wind and solar power facilities, contributing significantly to the sustainable energy goals of the Arab country while providing the French company with access to new markets and opportunities for technological innovation. Another compelling case study revolves around the joint efforts of French and Arab financial institutions in supporting infrastructure development projects in the Arab world. Through strategic investment and financing arrangements, these collaborative initiatives have facilitated the construction of vital transportation networks, urban infrastructure, and industrial facilities, fostering economic growth and enhancing regional connectivity. Furthermore, successful Franco-Arab joint ventures in telecommunications and digital technology have showcased the value of leveraging expertise and resources to drive innovation and address the evolving needs of both markets. These partnerships have led to implementing advanced communication systems and stimulated job creation and skills development, strengthening the socio-economic fabric of the participating Arab countries. The success stories of Franco-Arab economic collaborations serve as compelling examples of the mutual benefits derived from strategic alliances and shared endeavors. They underscore the importance of fostering long-term relationships based on trust, innovation, and a commitment to sustainable development. By analyzing these case studies, policymakers, business leaders, and stakeholders can gain valuable insights into the diverse avenues for cooperation and the best practices that underpin successful partnerships between France and the Arab world.

## *Future Trends in Economic Cooperation*

The future of economic cooperation between France and the Arab region holds immense potential for growth and innovation. As both regions adapt to the changing global economic landscape, it is essential to anticipate and prepare for the upcoming trends that will shape their economic engagement. A key trend expected to drive economic cooperation is the emphasis on sustainable development and green initiatives. With increasing awareness of environmental challenges, there is a growing demand for eco-friendly technologies and renewable energy solutions. This presents an opportunity for collaborative ventures focusing on clean energy, sustainable infrastructure, and environmental conservation.

Another significant trend is the digital transformation of industries. The Fourth Industrial Revolution has ushered in an era of technological advancements, artificial intelligence, and big data analytics. Both France and the Arab countries are embracing digitalization to enhance productivity and efficiency across various sectors. Future economic cooperation will likely revolve around digital innovation, smart cities, and technology-driven solutions that foster economic growth and competitiveness.

Furthermore, diversifying investment portfolios is anticipated to shape future economic collaboration. Traditional sectors such as oil and gas will continue to play a vital role, but there is a growing interest in expanding investments into healthcare, education, technology, and hospitality. This strategic diversification will mitigate risks associated with commodity dependence and create new avenues for economic prosperity and cross-border partnerships.

In addition, integrating small and medium-sized enterprises (SMEs) into the economic landscape is a pivotal trend. SMEs are recognized as engines of growth and innovation, and fostering an environment supportive of SME development can enhance bilateral trade and investment. Collaboration in nurturing entrepreneurship, promoting startups, and facilitating access to finance will be crucial in driving economic cooperation between France and the Arab region.

Moreover, the evolving geopolitical dynamics and regional alliances are poised to influence economic ties. With shifting global equations, stakeholders must navigate the geopolitical landscape effectively to leverage emerging opportunities and address challenges. Adapting to geopolitical shifts and fostering robust diplomatic relations will be instrumental in sustaining and expanding economic cooperation in the future.

Overall, the future trends in economic cooperation between France and the Arab region underscore the need for sustained dialogue, innovation, and strategic alignment. By recognizing and proactively responding to these trends, both regions can fortify their economic partnership and foster mutual prosperity in an evolving global economy.

# IN A NUTSHELL

> **List of inventions in the medieval Islamic world**
>
> *Innovations during the Islamic Golden Age and beyond*
>
> **Time Period:** 8th to 16th century
> **Cultural and Scientific Flourishing:** The Islamic Golden Age marked a period of significant achievements in various fields of science, culture, and economy.
> **Significant Developments:** Inventions and advancements spanned numerous areas including mathematics, astronomy, medicine, engineering, and agriculture.
> **Inception of the Golden Age:** Inaugurated by the Abbasid caliph Harun al-Rashid through the establishment of the House of Wisdom in Baghdad.
> **Preservation and Innovation:** Adopted and preserved knowledge from Persia, Egypt, India, China, and Greco-Roman antiquity while making numerous improvements.
> **Impact on Later States:** Inventions continued in the Ottoman and Mughal empires during the Age of the Islamic Gunpowders.

> *1. Overview of Economic Reforms in France*
>
> Since taking office in 2017, French President Emmanuel Macron has implemented a series of economic reforms aimed at

liberalizing the labor market, reducing taxes, and making France more attractive to foreign investors. Key reforms include:

- Reducing the corporate tax rate from 33.3% to 25%.
- Abolishing the wealth tax and introducing a flat tax on capital gains to stimulate investment
- Simplifying labor laws to make it easier for businesses to hire and fire employees.
- Introducing stricter unemployment benefit rules to encourage job acceptance.

## 2. Impact of Macron's Policies on Franco-Arab Economic Ties

Macron's economic policies have had a significant impact on Franco-Arab economic relations. His administration has focused on strengthening ties with Arab countries through various initiatives:

- France has deepened its economic and strategic relationships with Gulf countries, particularly Saudi Arabia and the UAE, leveraging opportunities presented by their economic transformations.
- Macron's government has also maintained strong economic ties with North African countries like Tunisia and Morocco, focusing on trade, investment, and security cooperation.

## 3. Investment Opportunities in the Arab Region

The Arab region offers numerous investment opportunities across various sectors:

- **UAE**: Real estate, renewable energy, technology, and tourism are key sectors attracting foreign investment.
- **Qatar**: Opportunities in the Halal economy, pharmaceuticals, cleantech, electric vehicles, 3-D printing, agritech, e-gaming, and cybersecurity.
- **Saudi Arabia**: Vision 2030 has opened up sectors like infrastructure, tourism, and technology for foreign investment.

## 4. Technological Advancements and Innovations

Technological advancements in the Arab region are creating new investment opportunities:

- The UAE is becoming a hub for innovation in artificial intelligence, blockchain, and fintech.
- Qatar is investing heavily in technology sectors such as 3-D printing and electric vehicles.
- Historical contributions from the medieval Islamic world have laid the foundation for modern technological advancements in the region.

## 5. Public-Private Partnerships: A Strategic Approach

Public-Private Partnerships (PPPs) are crucial for infrastructure development in the MENA region. The OECD highlights the importance of PPPs in overcoming barriers to successful project completion. These partnerships can drive innovation, create jobs, and mobilize resources for sustainable development projects.

## 6. Taxation and Regulatory Changes

Macron's administration has introduced several taxation and regulatory changes to boost economic growth:
- A €2 billion tax cut for the middle class is planned for 2025.
- Simplification of administrative processes to reduce bureaucratic hurdles for businesses.
- Regulatory changes to support industrial projects and improve financial appeal.

## 7. Sustainable Development Goals and Economic Growth

Both France and Arab countries are committed to advancing Sustainable Development Goals (SDGs):

- France's "France Relance" recovery plan aims to achieve carbon neutrality by 2050, focusing on green hydrogen, cleaner transport, and decarbonizing industry.
- Arab countries are investing in renewable energy and sustainable technologies to meet global sustainability goals.

## 8. Challenges to Foreign Investment

Despite the opportunities, there are challenges to foreign investment in the Arab region:

- Political instability and regulatory uncertainties can deter investors.
- Economic disparities and technological gaps between countries in the region.
- Complex bureaucratic processes and lack of transparency in some countries.

## 9. Case Studies: Successful Franco-Arab Economic Collaborations

Several successful collaborations highlight the potential of Franco-Arab economic ties:

- The establishment of the Louvre Abu Dhabi and Sorbonne University in the UAE.
- France's strategic partnerships with Saudi Arabia in sectors like defense and infrastructure.
- Joint efforts in Tunisia to tackle radicalization and promote economic stability.

## 10. Future Trends in Economic Cooperation

Future trends in Franco-Arab economic cooperation are likely to focus on:

- Increased investment in technology and innovation sectors.

- Strengthening public-private partnerships to drive infrastructure development.
- Continued efforts to achieve sustainable development goals and address environmental challenges.
- Expanding trade and investment ties to foster economic growth and stability in both regions.

By leveraging these opportunities and addressing the challenges, France and Arab countries can deepen their economic ties and work towards shared prosperity and resilience.

# References For Further Reading

Ronja Kempin (ed.) "France's Foreign and Security Policy under President Macron". SWP Research Paper 4 May 2021, Berlin. German Institute for International and Security Affairs. https://www.swp-berlin.org/publications/products/research_papers/2021RP04_PolicyUnderMacron_DASEP.pdf

Elizabeth Pineau and Tassilo Hummel. "Macron promises wide array of reforms for France as he seeks reset". REUTERS. January 17, 2024. https://www.reuters.com/world/europe/macron-urges-french-be-united-promises-wide-array-reforms-2024-01-16/

Alkinani, Zeidon . "Maghreb-France Relations as Macron Begins Second Term." Arab Center Washington DC, March 1, 2023. https://arabcenterdc.org/resource/maghreb-france-relations-as-macron-begins-second-term/.

Arab Authority for Agricultural Investment and Development. "Home." Accessed May 23, 2024. https://www.aaaid.org/en/.

BRUNET, Romain . "Five Years of Macron: France's Economy Trickles down in Drips and Drops (Part 2 of 4)." France 24, March 11, 2022. https://www.france24.com/en/france/20220311-trickle-down-in-drips-and-drops-the-french-economy-after-five-years-under-macron.

Cafiero, Giorgio. "What's Driving France and Saudi Arabia's Deepening Ties?" https://www.newarab.com/, June 20, 2023. https://www.newarab.com/analysis/whats-driving-france-and-saudi-arabias-deepening-ties.

Duclos , Michel . "Macron in Beirut and Baghdad: A New French Approach to the Middle East?" Institut Montaigne, September

11, 2020. https://www.institutmontaigne.org/en/expressions/macron-beirut-and-baghdad-new-french-approach-middle-east.

elysee.fr. "7th Edition of the Choose France Summit.," May 13, 2024. https://www.elysee.fr/en/emmanuel-macron/2024/05/13/7th-edition-of-the-choose-france-summit.

France Diplomacy - Ministry for Europe and Foreign Affairs. "France Relance Recovery Plan: Building the France of 2030," 2020. https://www.diplomatie.gouv.fr/en/french-foreign-policy/economic-diplomacy-foreign-trade/promoting-france-s-attractiveness/france-relance-recovery-plan-building-the-france-of-2030/.

Garcia, Anthon . "Top UAE Investment Opportunities in 2023." Economy Middle East, February 22, 2024. https://economymiddleeast.com/news/best-investments-in-uae/.

Leali , Giorgio . "Macron Vows More Liberal Reforms to Shake France's Economy." POLITICO, January 17, 2024. https://www.politico.eu/article/france-president-emmanuel-macron-liberal-reforms-economy/.

Leclerc, Aline , and Thibaud Métais. "Macron Looks to Boost Growth and Liberalize France's Labor Market, Again." Le Monde.fr, January 18, 2024. https://www.lemonde.fr/en/economy/article/2024/01/18/macron-looks-to-boost-growth-and-liberalize-france-s-labor-market-again_6442516_19.html.

Sugiura, Alexander. "Bloomberg - Are You a Robot?" www.bloomberg.com, May 14, 2024. https://www.bloomberg.com/news/articles/2024-05-13/france-s-president-emmanuel-macron-s-plan-to-transform-europe-big-take-podcast.

Thomas GOMART and Marc HECKER. "MACRON, DIPLOMAT a New French Foreign Policy? Études de L'Ifri," 2018. https://www.ifri.org/sites/default/files/atoms/files/gomart_hecker_macron_diplomat_new_french_foreign_policy_2018.pdf.

Urvoy, Heloise . "Macron Speech: What Economic Changes Should French People Expect?" euronews, January 17, 2024. https://www.euronews.com/business/2024/01/17/macron-speech-what-economic-changes-should-french-people-expect.

www.invest.qa. "Business and Investment Opportunities in Qatar | Invest Qatar." Accessed May 23, 2024. https://www.invest.qa/en/sectors-and-opportunities/opportunities.

www.pbs.org. "Global Connections . Science and Technology | PBS." Accessed May 23, 2024. https://www.pbs.org/wgbh/globalconnections/mideast/themes/science/index.html.

# XVII

# Immigration Policies and Integration Challenges

## Historical Overview of French Immigration Policies

The roots of French immigration policy can be traced back to the late 19th century when France faced a labor shortage, particularly in its industrial sector. This necessitated the influx of foreign workers from Italy, Spain, and other European countries. The first major legislative milestone in this domain was the 1889 law, which laid the groundwork for regulating the entry and residence of foreigners in France. Subsequent laws, such as the 1927 Aliens Act, further cemented the legal framework for immigration.

Following the aftermath of World War II, France witnessed a wave of immigration from its former colonies in North Africa, mainly Algeria, due to economic incentives and historical ties. This influx led to the passing of the 1945 law, which provided special provisions for these colonial subjects. However, it was the 1970s that marked a significant turning point, with the oil crisis resulting in a surge of migration from

North Africa and Turkey, leading to the adoption of the 1974 law that aimed to control and limit immigration.

The 1980s heralded a paradigm shift in French immigration policies, marked by the passage of the 1984 Pasqua laws, which focused on controlling family reunification and combating illegal immigration. However, the 1990s saw a more liberal approach, exemplified by the introduction of the Martine Aubry Law in 1998, which granted amnesty to a significant number of undocumented immigrants and facilitated their integration.

In the early 21st century, legislative developments reshaped French immigration policies. The 2003 Sarkozy law reinforced border controls and introduced the notion of

## *Legislative Developments Post-2000*

In the post-2000 era, France has witnessed significant legislative developments in response to the challenges and opportunities posed by immigration. The passage of significant laws, such as the 2003 Lellouche Law and the 2006 Immigration and Integration Act, reflect the evolving nature of French immigration policy. These legislations aimed to streamline and regulate immigration flows while addressing integration and social cohesion issues. Additionally, the introduction of the famous 'CESEDA' (Code of Entry and Residence of Foreign Nationals and the Right to Asylum) in 2007 consolidated various immigration-related provisions under a single legal framework, laying down stringent regulations and procedural norms for immigration and asylum. Furthermore, the Sarkozy government's 2011 Immigration Law brought about significant changes, including introducing new residency permit categories based on labor market needs and reinforcing deportation measures for irregular migrants. This legislative overhaul has not only reshaped the legal landscape. Still, it has also framed the public discourse on immigration, fostering debates on national identity, cultural diversity, and the socioeconomic implications of immigration.

Moreover, the recent Macron administration has continued this trend with the 2018 Asylum and Immigration Law, which sought to address refugee protection, security, and the management of migratory flows. These legislative developments post-2000 underscore the multifaceted nature of immigration in France and highlight the complex interplay between legal frameworks, political discourse, and societal dynamics.

## *Demographic Impact of Immigration*

The demographic impact of immigration on French society has been a subject of considerable debate and analysis. At the outset, it is crucial to recognize that immigration has played a significant role in shaping the population dynamics of France over the past several decades. The influx of immigrants, mainly from former colonies and other countries, has contributed to French society's diversity and multicultural fabric. This demographic transformation has not only influenced the ethnic and cultural composition of the population but has also had far-reaching implications for various aspects of socio-economic life. As of today, people with immigrant backgrounds or belonging to foreign-born communities constitute a substantial proportion of the French population. Understanding the demographic impact of immigration involves examining patterns of settlement, population distribution, fertility rates, age structure, and labor force participation among immigrant and non-immigrant groups. These dynamics have implications for public policy, social cohesion, and the future trajectory of French society. Moreover, the interplay between immigration and demographic trends has led to discussions about the aging population, labor market dynamics, and the sustainability of welfare systems. Exploring these issues necessitates a nuanced understanding of the intersection between immigration, demography, and national identity. Additionally, analyzing the demographic impact of immigration requires a multidimensional approach encompassing statistical data, sociological research, and policy evaluations. It involves assessing the spatial concentration of immigrant populations, their incorporation into local communities, and the challenges and opportunities arising from the diversification of the populace. Furthermore, comprehending the demographic impact enables policymakers, researchers, and civil society organizations to grasp the evolving nature of migration trends and to develop informed strategies for inclusive development and social integration. Overall, the demographic impact of immigration in France underscores the complexity and dynamism of contemporary societies, necessitating a holistic approach to understanding and managing diversity.

### Immigration to France
*Immigration trends and demographics in France*

**Population of Immigrants (2021)**
Nearly 7 million immigrants, representing 10.3% of the total population

**Major Immigrant Regions**
Parisian urban area (40% of immigrants), Rhône-Alpes (Lyon), and Provence-Alpes-Côte d'Azur (Marseille)

**Newborns with Immigrant Background (2010)**
27.3% had at least one foreign-born parent; 23.9% had one or both parents born outside of Europe

**Significant European Immigrant Increase (2009-2012)**
The number of Spanish, Portuguese, and Italian immigrants doubled due to the financial crisis

**New Foreigners (2012 vs 2022)**
229,000 new foreigners in 2012; Over 320,000 in 2022 with a majority from Africa

**Most Common Nationalities of Newcomers (2012)**
Portuguese (8%), British (5%), Spanish (5%), Italians (4%), Germans (4%), Romanians (3%), Belgians (3%)

**Migration Increase Under Macron**

> Significant increase in students, family reunification, and labor migration under President Emmanuel Macron

## *Government and Community Integration Initiatives*

Government and community integration initiatives in France have been crucial in addressing the challenges posed by immigration and fostering social cohesion. The French government has implemented various policies and programs to facilitate the integration of immigrant communities into the broader society. One key initiative is the establishment of integration contracts, which outline rights and responsibilities for immigrants, including language courses and civic education. These contracts have been instrumental in promoting the active participation of immigrants in French society. Additionally, the government has invested in vocational training and job placement programs to support the economic integration of immigrants, helping them secure employment and contribute to the country's workforce. Alongside these efforts, various community-based organizations and non-governmental entities have also played a pivotal role in fostering integration. These entities often provide valuable support services, such as cultural orientation, language assistance, and social engagement activities, all of which are essential for newcomers to adapt and thrive in their new environment. Furthermore, initiatives focused on intercultural dialogue and mutual understanding have been instrumental in bridging the gap between immigrant communities and the wider society, promoting empathy and collaboration. Collaborative projects involving immigrants and native-born citizens have helped build solidarity and facilitate the exchange of diverse perspectives. While challenges persist, the collaborative approach taken by the government and community actors underscores a shared commitment to promoting social inclusion and creating an environment where immigrants can fully participate and contribute to the richness of French society.

## Challenges Faced by Immigrant Communities

Immigrant communities in France encounter a myriad of challenges that impact their socio-economic integration and overall well-being. One of the primary challenges stems from the disparities in access to quality education and employment opportunities. Many immigrants, especially those from non-EU countries, face barriers to securing stable and fulfilling jobs due to language barriers, lack of recognition of foreign qualifications, and discriminatory hiring practices. This often leads to high levels of unemployment or underemployment within immigrant communities, contributing to socio-economic marginalization.

Moreover, cultural integration poses a significant challenge as immigrants navigate the complexities of adapting to a new societal framework while preserving their cultural identity. Cultural differences may lead to social segregation, whereby immigrant communities experience isolation and struggle to integrate into mainstream society fully. Additionally, systemic discrimination and prejudice further exacerbate the challenges faced by immigrant communities, impacting their access to housing, healthcare, and public services.

The issue of legal status and residency rights also looms large over immigrant communities, particularly for undocumented migrants. These individuals often live in precarious situations, facing constant fear of deportation and limited access to essential services. The legal limbo they find themselves in amplifies the vulnerability of this population and hinders their ability to participate in and contribute to society fully.

Furthermore, generational disconnect poses unique challenges as second and third-generation immigrants grapple with identity, belonging, and societal acceptance issues. This intergenerational tension can lead to feelings of alienation and a sense of not fully belonging to either the culture of their parents or that of the host country.

Lastly, the rise of anti-immigrant sentiments and xenophobic attitudes in specific segments of the French population creates a hostile environment for immigrant communities, leading to social tensions and a fraying social fabric. These challenges underscore the multifaceted nature of immigrant communities' obstacles in France and necessitate comprehensive policy responses and community-driven interventions to foster inclusive and cohesive societies.

## *Role of Civil Society in Immigrant Integration*

Civil society plays a crucial role in facilitating the integration of immigrant communities within the French social fabric. Non-governmental organizations, community groups, religious institutions, and advocacy networks actively engage in initiatives aimed at supporting and empowering immigrants as they navigate the challenges of settling in a new country. Civil society organizations promote social cohesion and inclusion through service provision, advocacy, and community-building efforts. One key aspect of the role of civil society in immigrant integration is the provision of essential services such as language classes, employment assistance, housing support, and cultural orientation programs. These services are instrumental in helping newcomers adapt to their new environment, gain access to opportunities, and develop a sense of belonging. Additionally, civil society organizations often advocate for immigrant rights and participate in policy discussions related to immigration and integration. By amplifying the voices of immigrant communities and championing inclusive policies, these entities contribute to shaping a more supportive and equitable environment for immigrants. Moreover, civil society initiatives foster community engagement and intercultural dialogue, creating platforms for meaningful interaction between immigrants and the broader society. These interactions foster mutual understanding and enable the sharing of diverse perspectives and experiences, enriching the societal tapestry. Furthermore, civil society interventions in immigrant integration promote empowerment by providing platforms for leadership development, skill-building, and civic participation among immigrants. By encouraging active involvement in civic life, these initiatives help immigrants become active contributors to their new communities, thereby enhancing social cohesion and collective resilience. The role of civil society in immigrant integration extends beyond immediate settlement needs, encompassing long-term efforts to address systemic barriers and promote societal inclusion. Through research, grassroots mobilization, and public awareness campaigns, civil society organizations work towards fostering an environment where diversity is celebrated and where all individuals have equal opportunities to thrive. Through the collaborative efforts of government agencies, civil society, and other stakeholders, comprehensive and sustainable solutions to integration challenges can be developed, ensuring that France embraces its identity as a diverse and inclusive nation.

## Impact of EU Policies on French Immigration

The impact of EU policies on French immigration has been a pivotal aspect of the country's immigration framework. As a member of the European Union, France is subject to various EU regulations and directives that significantly influence its immigration policies and practices. One of the most influential aspects of EU policy on French immigration is the concept of free movement within the Schengen Area. This agreement allows for the free movement of EU citizens within the participating countries, leading to significant immigration flows into France from other EU member states.

Furthermore, EU policies on border control and external migration management have also affected French immigration. The EU's efforts to manage external borders and control irregular migration have led to collaborative measures, including joint border patrols and information sharing among member states. These initiatives directly affect France in managing immigration flows and ensuring compliance with EU standards.

Additionally, EU regulations regarding asylum and refugee policies have shaped French immigration practices. The Common European Asylum System (CEAS) seeks to harmonize asylum procedures and standards across EU member states, impacting France's reception and integration of refugees. The Dublin Regulation, which determines the EU member state responsible for examining an asylum application, has placed significant pressure on countries like France, particularly in managing large numbers of asylum seekers.

Moreover, the EU's emphasis on promoting integration and combating discrimination has influenced France's approach to immigrant integration. Through funding programs and initiatives, the EU has encouraged member states to develop inclusive integration policies and support measures for immigrant communities. This has prompted France to align its integration efforts with EU guidelines, focusing on language learning, employment opportunities, and social inclusion.

At the same time, EU policies on migration and security have raised challenges for France, particularly in the context of terrorism and border management. The EU's responses to security threats and the securitization of migration have influenced French immigration policies, leading to increased border controls and enhanced security measures.

Overall, the impact of EU policies on French immigration has been multifaceted, shaping various aspects of immigration legislation, border management, asylum procedures, and integration strategies. Understanding this influence is crucial in comprehending the broader dynamics of French immigration within the context of European Union frameworks and objectives.

## *Future Policy Directions in the Context of Global Migration*

As global migration continues to shape societies and influence demographics, France must adopt innovative policy directions to address the challenges and opportunities presented by this phenomenon. A holistic understanding of the economic, social, and cultural dynamics at play on a global scale must inform the future of immigration policies. Recognizing the intricate interconnectedness of global migration, policy frameworks should emphasize cooperation and collaboration with international partners and multilateral organizations such as the United Nations and the European Union to confront shared migration-related concerns. Furthermore, future policy directions should balance humanitarian imperatives and national interests, ensuring that migration policies are comprehensive, fair, and sustainable. This entails a nuanced approach that considers the rights and needs of migrants while also safeguarding national security and societal cohesion. Embracing flexibility and adaptability is crucial in navigating the evolving landscape of global migration, with policies capable of responding to emergent challenges and accommodating shifting migratory patterns. Moreover, future policies should prioritize the promotion of inclusive societies and the respectful integration of diverse cultures, fostering an environment where immigrants can contribute meaningfully to the fabric of their adoptive nation. Enhancing opportunities for education, employment, and civic engagement for migrants is essential to harnessing the potential benefits of immigration, propelling economic growth, and nurturing vibrant, multicultural communities. Emphasizing the significance of evidence-based policymaking, future directions should leverage data-driven insights to inform decision-making and measure the impact of immigration policies. This necessitates robust monitoring and evaluation mechanisms to ensure policies remain responsive to evolving societal needs and aspirations. Lastly, anticipatory planning for future migration trends is paramount, encompassing scenario analysis and risk assessment to preemptively address potential challenges and capitalize on favorable opportunities. By envisaging proactive and forward-looking policy directives, France can position itself as a trailblazer in cultivating a progressive, inclusive approach to immigration, setting a compelling example for the world as it confronts the complex realities of global migration.

## *Comparative Analysis with Other European Countries*

France's approach to immigration and integration can be enriched through a comparative analysis with other European countries facing similar challenges. By examining the policies and practices of countries such as Germany, the United Kingdom, Sweden, and the Netherlands, valuable insights can be gained to inform and improve France's strategies in this critical area. These nations have distinct historical, social, and political contexts that have influenced their immigration and integration policies. For instance, Germany has experienced significant labor migration and has implemented various programs to integrate migrant workers into society. The United Kingdom has dealt with issues related to post-colonial immigration and has grappled with debates surrounding multiculturalism. Sweden has been known for its progressive approach to refugee acceptance and has focused on supporting new arrivals. Similarly, the Netherlands has implemented innovative community engagement and language learning models for immigrant populations. Through a comparative lens, France can evaluate the strengths and weaknesses of its current approach, identify promising practices from other countries, and adapt successful strategies to the French context. This process can help French policymakers design more effective and inclusive immigration and integration policies that align with global best practices while considering the specific needs and dynamics within France.

## *Policy Recommendations for Improved Integration*

Integrating immigrant communities into French society is a multifaceted challenge that requires comprehensive and proactive policy measures. As discussed in the previous section, drawing on the experiences of other European countries and considering the unique dynamics of immigration in France, a set of targeted policy recommendations can be proposed to enhance the integration framework.

Firstly, a holistic approach that addresses the economic and social aspects of integration and the cultural dimension is needed. Policies should promote intercultural understanding and foster a sense of belonging among immigrants and the native population. This could involve initiatives such as multicultural education in schools, diversity promotion in public institutions, and community-based cultural exchange programs.

Secondly, the labor market plays a crucial role in integration. Efforts should be made to ensure equal access to employment opportunities for immigrants, including recognition of foreign qualifications and skills. Implementing affirmative action measures and incentivizing diverse hiring practices by employers can help combat discrimination and promote inclusive economic participation.

Additionally, language acquisition is essential for social integration and economic mobility. Government-funded language training programs should be expanded, and support should be provided for immigrants to improve their language proficiency. This, coupled with vocational and job-specific training, can enhance immigrants' employability and facilitate their integration into the workforce.

Furthermore, access to housing is pivotal for stable integration. Housing policies must address the specific needs of immigrant communities, providing affordable and culturally sensitive accommodation options. Preventing housing discrimination and promoting neighborhood diversity can contribute to cohesive and inclusive communities.

Social cohesion can be bolstered through community engagement and civic participation. Encouraging active involvement in local decision-making processes and providing platforms for dialogue between different cultural groups can foster mutual respect and understanding. Strengthening social support networks and community centers can also facilitate the social integration of immigrant populations.

Lastly, the legal framework surrounding immigration and citizenship should be reviewed to ensure streamlined procedures for residency and naturalization. Simplifying administrative processes, improving transparency, and providing legal assistance to immigrants can alleviate bureaucratic hurdles and uncertainties, promoting a sense of security and belonging.

In conclusion, successful integration requires synergistic efforts across various policy domains encompassing education, employment, housing, social cohesion, and legal frameworks. By implementing these recommendations, France can strive towards a more inclusive and harmonious societal fabric, enriching the nation's cultural tapestry and leveraging the contributions of its diverse population.

# IN A NUTSHELL

## Historical Overview of French Immigration Policies

French immigration policies have evolved significantly over the years, shaped by economic needs, geopolitical events, and social dynamics. In the 19th and early 20th centuries, France experienced waves of immigration from European countries such as Italy, Spain, and Portugal, driven by economic opportunities in the growing industrial sectors. Post-World War II, France established a guest-worker program to address labor shortages, inviting workers from former colonies in North Africa. The 1970s marked a shift with the oil crisis leading to stricter immigration controls and the suspension of permanent worker immigration in 1974. The 1980s saw a mix of restrictive and liberal policies, including the "Exceptional Regularization" under President François Mitterrand, which granted legal status to many undocumented immigrants.

## *Legislative Developments Post-2000*

Since 2000, French immigration policy has seen numerous reforms aimed at balancing control and integration. Key legislative changes include the 2003 law on immigration control and integration, which introduced measures to combat illegal immigration and promote the integration of legal immigrants. The 2006 law further emphasized "chosen immigration," focusing on attracting skilled workers while tightening family reunification rules. Recent developments include the controversial 2023 immigration law, which introduced quotas, stricter conditions for social benefits, and new measures for regularizing undocumented workers in short-staffed professions.

## *Demographic Impact of Immigration*

Immigration has significantly impacted France's demographic landscape. As of 2021, immigrants made up 10.3% of the French population, with a notable increase in diversity over the decades. The immigrant population has shifted from predominantly European origins to a more diverse mix, including significant numbers from Africa and Asia. This demographic shift has implications for social services, labor markets, and cultural integration.

## *Government and Community Integration Initiatives*

France has implemented various integration initiatives, primarily targeting education, employment, and social cohesion. The concept of "mainstreaming" has been central, where integration needs are addressed through general social policies rather than targeted programs. The Office for Integration, Reception, and Citizenship (DAIC) and the Agency for Social Cohesion and Equal Opportunity (Acsé) are key institutions in this effort. However, the effectiveness of these initiatives is often debated, given the challenges of measuring their impact due to the prohibition of ethnic statistics.

## Challenges Faced by Immigrant Communities

Immigrant communities in France face several challenges, including higher unemployment rates, social exclusion, and discrimination. Immigrants are more vulnerable to economic downturns and often live in disadvantaged urban areas with limited access to quality education and healthcare. The integration process is further complicated by societal attitudes and political rhetoric that can stigmatize immigrants.

## Role of Civil Society in Immigrant Integration

Civil society organizations play a crucial role in supporting immigrant integration in France. These organizations provide essential services such as language training, legal assistance, and social support. They also advocate for immigrant rights and work to combat discrimination and xenophobia. The involvement of civil society is vital in bridging gaps left by government policies and fostering community cohesion.

## Impact of EU Policies on French Immigration

EU policies have significantly influenced French immigration, particularly through the principles of free movement and asylum regulations. France's integration into the EU has facilitated easier movement across borders, impacting immigration patterns and policy responses. EU directives and regulations also shape national policies on asylum seekers and refugees, adding layers of complexity to France's immigration framework.

## *Future Policy Directions in the Context of Global Migration*

Future French immigration policies are likely to continue balancing control with integration, influenced by global migration trends and domestic political dynamics. The focus may shift towards more selective immigration, prioritizing skilled migrants while imposing stricter controls on asylum seekers and family reunification. The ongoing debates over national identity and social cohesion will also shape future policy directions.

## *Comparative Analysis with Other European Countries*

Compared to other European countries, France's immigration policies have been relatively restrictive, particularly since the 1970s. While countries like Germany and the UK have seen higher growth rates in their immigrant populations, France has maintained a more controlled approach. However, France shares common challenges with its European counterparts, such as integrating diverse immigrant populations and addressing social tensions related to immigration.

In summary, French immigration policies and integration efforts reflect a complex interplay of historical, economic, and social factors. The ongoing evolution of these policies will continue to shape the demographic and cultural landscape of France in the context of broader European and global migration trends.

# References For Further Reading

"March 2007 French immigration policy". March 2007. Ministère des Affaires étrangères. https://au.ambafrance.org/IMG/pdf/immigration_policy.pdf

Boubtane, Ekrame. "France Reckons with Immigration amid Reality of Rising Far Right." Migration Policy Institute, May 4, 2022. https://www.migrationpolicy.org/article/france-immigration-rising-far-right.

Britannica. "France - Immigration." In Encyclopædia Britannica, 2019. https://www.britannica.com/place/France/Immigration.

Deley, M. "French Immigration Policy since May 1981." The International Migration Review 17, no. 2 (1983): 196–211. https://pubmed.ncbi.nlm.nih.gov/12339130/.

Escafré-Dublet, Angéline. "Mainstreaming Immigrant Integration Policy in France Education, Employment, and Social Cohesion Initiatives Education, Employment, and Social Cohesion Initiatives," August 2014. https://www.migrationpolicy.org/sites/default/files/publications/Mainstreaming-France-FINAL.pdf.

———. "Mainstreaming Immigrant Integration Policy in France: Education, Employment, and Social Cohesion Initiatives." migrationpolicy.org, August 19, 2014. https://www.migrationpolicy.org/research/mainstreaming-immigrant-integration-policy-france-education-employment-and-social-cohesion.

INED. "How Many Immigrants Are There in France?" Ined - Institut national d'études démographiques, April 6, 2020. https://www.ined.fr/en/everything_about_population/demographic-facts-sheets/faq/how-many-immigrants-france/.

Le Monde.fr. "What's in France's Controversial Immigration Law?" December 20, 2023. https://www.lemonde.fr/en/france/article/2023/12/20/what-s-in-france-s-controversial-immigration-law_6361995_7.html.

MENA Research Center . "France S History of Immigration - MENA Research Center," February 2, 2024. https://www.mena-researchcenter.org/frances-history-of-immigration/.

Ofii. "Our History," n.d. https://www.ofii.fr/en/notre-histoire/.

Pascual, Julia. "Immigrants in France Are Becoming More Diverse but Still Face Greater Economic Challenges." Le Monde.fr, March 31, 2023. https://www.lemonde.fr/en/france/article/2023/03/31/immigrants-in-france-are-becoming-more-diverse-but-still-face-greater-economic-challenges_6021311_7.html.

Rygiel, Philippe. "France: Immigration since 1945." The Encyclopedia of Global Human Migration, February 4, 2013. https://doi.org/10.1002/9781444351071.wbeghm239.

Soleil, Johanna. "Integrated or Excluded: The Effects of French Integration Policies on Immigrant Communities from 2000 to 2020." Claremont-UC Undergraduate Research Conference on the European Union 2022, no. 1 (2022): 93–101. https://doi.org/10.5642/urceu.dkiz3846.

"THE IMPACT of IMMIGRATION on the LABOUR MARKET, PUBLIC FINANCES and ECONOMIC GROWTH Literature Review PRESENTATION FILE," July 10, 2019. https://www.strategie.gouv.fr/sites/strategie.gouv.fr/files/atoms/files/report-immigration-juillet-2019.pdf.

"The Measurement of Foreign and Immigrant Populations." Accessed May 23, 2024. https://www.insee.fr/en/statistiques/fichier/2563032/17-819_Insee-En-Bref-Immigration-vUK-Interactif.pdf.

Vickstrom, E.R. (2019). Evolution of Immigration-Control Policies in France, Italy, and Spain. In: Pathways and Consequences of Legal Irregularity. IMISCOE Research Series. Springer, Cham. https://doi.org/10.1007/978-3-030-12088-7_2

Virginie Guiraudon. "Immigration Policy in France." Brookings. Brookings, July 2001. https://www.brookings.edu/articles/immigration-policy-in-france/.

WENDEN, CATHERINE WIHTOL. "The Evolution of French Immigration Policy after May 1981." International Migration 22, no. 3 (July 1984): 199–213. https://doi.org/10.1111/j.1468-2435.1984.tb00997.x.

# XVIII

# France's Role in the Middle East Conflicts

## Historical Context and Early Involvements

French colonialism left a profound impact on its engagements in the Middle East. The legacy of colonization shaped France's military and political involvements in the region during the 19th and early 20th centuries. By establishing territories such as French Algeria, French Tunisia, and French Morocco, France asserted its influence in North Africa while extending its reach into the Levant, including modern-day Lebanon and Syria. This colonial presence facilitated economic exploitation and entrenched French political interests, creating lasting repercussions for its role in the Middle East.

The strategic significance of these territories was underscored by their geopolitical positioning and access to key trade routes. French ambitions to maintain control over these areas often led to entanglements in regional conflicts and power struggles. These early involvements laid the foundation for France's future interventions and diplomatic pursuits in the Middle East. Furthermore, the French Mandate period following World War I reinforced France's authority and involvement in shaping the political landscape of the Levant.

Moreover, the intertwined economic and political interests in the Levant and North Africa drew France into confrontations and collaborations with other major powers, notably the United Kingdom. The competition and cooperation between these colonial powers in the region had far-reaching consequences and significantly influenced the trajectory of Middle Eastern affairs. By examining this historical context, it becomes evident that French colonial legacy and early involvements were pivotal in shaping the complexities of its role in the Middle East conflicts, setting the stage for subsequent diplomatic endeavors and military interventions.

## *The Suez Crisis of 1956: A Pivotal Moment*

The Suez Crisis of 1956 is a pivotal and defining moment in the history of Franco-Arab relations. The crisis emerged against the backdrop of escalating tensions between Egypt, Israel, France, and the United Kingdom, ultimately leading to a complex web of international conflict and power play. At its core, the crisis was sparked by Egyptian President Gamal Abdel Nasser's announcement of the nationalization of the Suez Canal Company. This move directly challenged the interests of France and Britain, which had significant stakes in the canal's operation. In response to Nasser's actions, France and the UK initiated a secret military alliance with Israel, setting the stage for a coordinated attack on Egypt. This dramatic turn of events exposed the deeply entrenched colonial legacies and highlighted the fragile nature of post-World War II global politics. The ensuing military confrontation led to a swift and decisive international intervention, as the United States and the Soviet Union played critical roles in mediating the conflict and ensuring a ceasefire. For France, the Suez Crisis represented both a reaffirmation of its imperialist ambitions and a sobering realization of its diminished influence on the world stage. The aftermath of the crisis prompted a reevaluation of French foreign policy and a strategic shift towards forging closer ties with its former colonies in North

Africa and the Middle East. From a broader geopolitical perspective, the Suez Crisis marked the declining influence of traditional colonial powers and the emergence of new dynamics in the Middle East. This defining episode serves as a lens to examine the intricate interplay of nationalism, imperialism, and superpower rivalries during a profound global transformation. Ultimately, the Suez Crisis of 1956 reshaped the trajectory of Franco-Arab relations and left an indelible imprint on the region's geopolitics for decades.

## *Lebanon Interventions in the 1980s*

Lebanon was the focus of international attention in the 1980s due to its complex and protracted civil war. France's interventions in Lebanon during this tumultuous period reflected its historical ties to the region and its commitment to mitigating the conflict. Under President François Mitterrand, the French government sought to assert its influence and promote stability in Lebanon through diplomatic efforts and military deployments.

France's involvement in Lebanon was multifaceted, encompassing both political and military dimensions. Diplomatically, France was pivotal in mediating negotiations between various Lebanese factions and external stakeholders. Its diplomatic initiatives aimed to foster reconciliation and pave the way for a lasting peace agreement. Concurrently, France maintained a military presence in Lebanon as part of an international peacekeeping force deployed under the auspices of the United Nations. The participation of French troops underscored France's commitment to upholding peace and security in Lebanon.

However, France's intervention in Lebanon was not without controversy and challenges. The complexities of the Lebanese civil war, characterized by sectarian divisions and geopolitical rivalries, presented formidable obstacles to achieving a comprehensive resolution. Additionally, the presence of foreign military forces in Lebanon engendered tensions and raised questions about the extent of their effectiveness in quelling the violence.

Moreover, France grappled with the tragic ramifications of the 1983 Beirut barracks bombing, which resulted in significant casualties among French military personnel. This tragic event underscored the risks and sacrifices associated with France's intervention in Lebanon while also reaffirming its resolve to confront terrorist threats and safeguard stability in the region.

In retrospect, France's interventions in Lebanon during the 1980s epitomized the complexities and challenges inherent in navigating the intricate dynamics of Middle Eastern conflicts. The experiences and outcomes of its involvement in Lebanon continue to inform and shape France's approach to regional crises, underscoring the enduring significance of its role in the Middle East.

## *French Diplomacy during the Gulf War*

During the Gulf War, France pursued a nuanced diplomatic approach to balance its alliance with the United States and its historical ties with Arab states in the region. As the international community grappled with Iraq's invasion of Kuwait in 1990, France opted for a combination of diplomatic efforts and military contributions to address the escalating crisis. French President François Mitterrand, acknowledging the need to prevent Iraq's aggression and preserve regional stability, worked tirelessly to secure a peaceful resolution through international diplomacy while recognizing the strategic importance of maintaining unity within the Western coalition. France's stance was characterized by its advocacy for a multilateral approach and pursuing a UN-led diplomatic solution. Amid the mounting tensions, France's then-Foreign Minister Roland Dumas engaged in extensive shuttle diplomacy in the Middle East, reinforcing the necessity of finding a diplomatic exit strategy to avoid a full-scale military conflict. Additionally, French diplomats played a pivotal role in advocating for a peaceful resolution through UN Security Council resolutions and diplomatic channels, emphasizing the primacy of diplomacy and international law in resolving the crisis. Simultaneously, France contributed military assets to the coalition forces, including providing aircraft and naval forces, while remaining cautious about the prospect of a full-fledged ground invasion. This approach reflected France's commitment to upholding its international obligations while prioritizing diplomatic solutions over unilateral military action. Furthermore, France's diplomatic endeavors during the Gulf War underscored its determination to promote peace and stability in the Middle East, demonstrating its capacity to navigate complex geopolitical landscapes while fostering constructive dialogue among conflicting parties. The Gulf War thus epitomized France's pragmatic and principled approach to addressing regional conflicts, encapsulating its multifaceted roles as a global diplomatic actor and a proponent of inclusive and consensus-based solutions.

## *Collaboration and Conflict in the Israeli-Palestinian Affairs*

The Israeli-Palestinian conflict has been a significant factor in shaping French foreign policy in the Middle East. France has historically maintained close ties with both Israelis and Palestinians, aiming to balance the complexities of this profoundly entrenched dispute. Throughout the years, France has sought to mediate, advocating for a two-state solution and promoting dialogue between the two parties. However, this pursuit has not been without challenges, as the conflict is steeped in a long history of territorial disputes, security concerns, and divergent national aspirations. Despite these obstacles, France has consistently reaffirmed its commitment to finding a peaceful resolution to the Israeli-Palestinian conflict. During heightened tensions, France has utilized its diplomatic channels to engage with regional and international stakeholders, emphasizing the importance of de-escalation, humanitarian aid, and respect for international law. French leaders have worked to foster a balanced approach, acknowledging the legitimate rights and grievances of both Israelis and Palestinians while condemning acts of violence and human rights abuses on all sides. In recent years, France has actively supported initiatives aimed at reviving stalled peace talks, reinforcing the need for mutual recognition, security guarantees, and the establishment of viable Palestinian statehood alongside a secure Israel. This position has resonated with various regional actors and beyond, reflecting France's enduring determination to contribute positively to the quest for a lasting, just, and comprehensive resolution to the Israeli-Palestinian conflict.

## *Israel/Palestine: France's Official Position*

France's official position on the Israel-Palestine conflict, as outlined by the French Ministry for Europe and Foreign Affairs, is detailed in nine key points. Here is a comprehensive summary:

### 1. *Friendship with Both Israelis and Palestinians*

France maintains strong historical, cultural, and human ties with both Israel and Palestine. It was one of the first countries to recognize Israel in 1949 and has consistently supported Israel's right to exist and live in security. Simultaneously, France supports the creation of a Palestinian state with secure and recognized borders, advocating for Jerusalem to be the capital of both states. France has also taken significant steps to recognize Palestinian rights, such as voting in favor of the PLO's observer status at the UN and upgrading the status of the Palestinian delegation in France.

## 2. Adherence to International Law

France calls for strict compliance with international law and relevant UN resolutions. It promotes a two-state solution based on the 1967 borders, a fair solution for refugees, and the end of Israeli occupation. France condemns Israeli settlement activities in the West Bank and East Jerusalem as illegal under international law and an obstacle to peace. It supports measures like the EU's labeling of products from Israeli settlements to distinguish between Israeli territory and occupied Palestinian territories.

## 3. Commitment to Regional Stability

France condemns all acts of violence and terrorism and urges all parties to combat incitement to hatred. It emphasizes the need for proportionality in the use of force and calls for the protection of civilians. France is committed to Israel's security as a key principle of its regional policy.

## 4. Advocacy for a Two-State Solution

France believes that a two-state solution is the only viable resolution to the conflict, addressing the legitimate aspirations of both Israelis and Palestinians for security, independence, recognition, and dignity. It supports borders based on the 1967 lines with land swaps, security arrangements, a fair solution for refugees, and Jerusalem as the capital of both states.

## 5. Jerusalem as the Capital of Both States

France holds that the status of Jerusalem should be determined through peace negotiations, with the city serving as the capital of both Israel and Palestine. Pending a negotiated resolution, France does not recognize any sovereignty over Jerusalem and opposes unilateral actions that alter the status quo of holy sites.

## 6. Support for Palestinian Statehood

France supports the establishment of an independent, viable, and sovereign Palestinian state. It provides significant financial assistance to the Palestinian Territories and supports the development of strong and democratic Palestinian institutions through various cooperation projects.

## 7. Humanitarian Assistance

France is deeply concerned about the living conditions of Palestinians and is committed to addressing humanitarian emergencies. It contributes to humanitarian agencies and organizations, including significant support to UNRWA. France also supports various development projects in Gaza and the West Bank, particularly in water and sanitation.

## 8. Encouragement of Inter-Palestinian Reconciliation

France supports efforts for inter-Palestinian reconciliation, which it views as essential for improving living conditions in Gaza and ensuring the security of the territory. It calls on Hamas to recognize Israel, adhere to past agreements, and renounce violence.

## 9. Readiness to Support Political Processes

France is prepared to support any initiative that complies with international law and aims for a negotiated two-state solution. It maintains contact with both Israeli and Palestinian parties to

> facilitate the resumption of negotiations and ensure the viability of the two-state solution.
>
> In summary, France's position is firmly rooted in the principles of international law, advocating for a two-state solution with Jerusalem as the capital of both states, and supporting humanitarian and development efforts in the Palestinian Territories. France condemns violence and illegal settlement activities and calls for a negotiated resolution to the conflict.

## *France's Role in the Iraq War and Aftermath*

France's involvement in the Iraq War and its aftermath has been a significant aspect of its foreign policy in the Middle East. In the lead-up to the war, France took a pivotal stance against the military intervention in Iraq, opposing the Bush administration's decision to engage in armed conflict without explicit authorization from the United Nations Security Council. This position was rooted in France's commitment to multilateralism and international law, emphasizing the importance of diplomatic solutions and peaceful resolutions to conflicts. Despite facing criticism from some quarters, France remained steadfast in its opposition to the invasion of Iraq, advocating for continued weapons inspections and non-military interventions to address concerns about the regime of Saddam Hussein.

Following the toppling of the Ba'athist government and the subsequent occupation of Iraq by coalition forces, France's stance on the reconstruction efforts and governance of post-war Iraq became a subject of scrutiny and debate. The French government prioritized the restoration of sovereignty to the Iraqi people and called for greater involvement of the United Nations in the political transition and nation-building processes. This approach was informed by France's aspirations for a unified and democratic Iraq, free from external influence and sectarian strife.

Moreover, France played a crucial role in promoting dialogue between different factions within Iraq and sought to bridge divides among the country's diverse population. Through diplomatic channels and engagement with regional stakeholders, France endeavored to construct avenues for reconciliation and inclusive governance, recognizing the complexities of Iraq's sociopolitical landscape.

In the subsequent years, as Iraq grappled with insurgency, internal divisions, and the rise of extremist groups, France extended support to the Iraqi government in countering security threats and fostering stability. This assistance encompassed training programs for Iraqi security forces, provision of humanitarian aid, and collaboration on intelligence-sharing to address the evolving security challenges in the country.

As the conflict in Iraq evolved into a multifaceted struggle with implications for regional security and global geopolitics, France reaffirmed its commitment to standing by the Iraqi people and supporting the quest for sustainable peace and prosperity. The complexities and consequences of France's role in the Iraq War and its aftermath underscored the complexities of international interventions and the imperative of pursuing holistic approaches to post-conflict rehabilitation and geopolitical realignments.

## *Influence and Engagement in Syria's Civil War*

France's involvement in the Syrian Civil War has been multifaceted, driven by a complex web of strategic, humanitarian, and geopolitical considerations. Since the onset of the conflict in 2011, France has been actively seeking a resolution to the crisis while simultaneously addressing its national security interests and commitment to international human rights and humanitarian law. This chapter delves into the multifaceted nature of France's influence and engagement in the

Syrian Civil War, examining the various dimensions that have shaped the country's approach and impact on the conflict. As one of the critical Western powers involved in the conflict, France's position on Syria has evolved in response to the changing dynamics within the war-torn country and the broader regional context. From supporting opposition forces to participating in international peace initiatives, France has sought to play a constructive role in shaping the outcome of the conflict and addressing its devastating humanitarian consequences. The chapter scrutinizes France's diplomatic efforts to build consensus among international actors, including its engagement with other European Union members and the United Nations, to push for a peaceful resolution to the conflict and alleviate the suffering of the Syrian population. Furthermore, it explores France's stance on the Assad regime and its efforts to counter extremist groups operating within Syrian borders, as well as the implications of these policies on regional stability and global security. In addition, the chapter assesses France's provision of humanitarian aid and its contribution to addressing the refugee crisis resulting from the conflict, shedding light on the country's commitment to upholding humanitarian principles amidst the complexities of the conflict. Lastly, given the ongoing nature of the Syrian Civil War and its repercussions, the chapter considers the future trajectory of France's involvement, analyzing potential strategies and challenges in effectively influencing the conflict's outcome and contributing to the pursuit of sustainable peace and stability in Syria and the wider region.

## *Negotiating Nuclear Tensions with Iran*

As an influential global player, France has been deeply involved in the negotiations surrounding Iran's nuclear program. The issue of Iran's nuclear ambitions has posed a significant challenge to international security and stability. France has consistently advocated for a diplomatic solution to address the concerns over Iran's nuclear activities. Diplomatic efforts have focused on preventing Iran from acquiring nuclear weapons while respecting its rights to the peaceful use of nuclear technology. France has been actively engaged in multilateral negotiations, including the P5+1 talks, to reach a comprehensive agreement with Iran. These negotiations have required a delicate balancing of interests and rigorous diplomacy to navigate complex geopolitical dynamics. French diplomats have emphasized the importance of verifiable mechanisms to ensure Iran's compliance with its international obligations. Furthermore, France has underscored the need for transparent monitoring and inspections to prevent any potential military dimension to Iran's nuclear program. The negotiations have also highlighted the interconnectedness of regional security concerns, including the implications of a nuclear Iran on neighboring countries. France has sought to engage with regional partners to address shared security challenges and build consensus on the approach towards Iran's nuclear aspirations. Moreover, the negotiations have underscored the significance of maintaining unity among the international community in addressing proliferation risks. France has been instrumental in aligning diverse perspectives and fostering cooperation among the P5+1 members, demonstrating leadership and commitment to finding a sustainable resolution. The complexities of the negotiations have demanded nuanced diplomacy, requiring France to uphold its principled stance while remaining flexible and open to constructive dialogue. Throughout this process, French leaders have underscored the imperative of achieving a comprehensive and lasting solution that upholds non-proliferation norms and contributes to regional stability. This chapter delves into the intricacies of France's engagement in negotiating nuclear tensions with Iran, highlighting the multifaceted diplomatic strategies employed to pursue a constructive and durable resolution.

## *Military Presence and Strategic Alliances*

Complex geopolitical dynamics and regional security challenges have shaped France's military presence and strategic alliances in the

Middle East. The country has a historical legacy of military involvement in the region, stemming from its colonial past and subsequent efforts to maintain influence and protect its interests. Over the years, France has established strategic alliances with various countries in the Middle East, contributing to its multifaceted approach towards security and stability. One key aspect of France's military presence is its participation in multinational operations aimed at countering terrorism and maintaining peace in the region. The French military often joins international coalitions and undertakes joint military exercises with regional partners to address shared security threats. This collaborative approach reflects France's commitment to upholding global security and combating transnational security challenges. Furthermore, France's military engagements in the Middle East are driven by the need to safeguard vital economic interests, particularly energy resources and maritime trade routes. As a permanent member of the United Nations Security Council, France plays a significant role in shaping international security policies, including those related to the Middle East. Its military presence in the region is often coordinated with diplomatic efforts to de-escalate conflicts and promote peacebuilding initiatives. Additionally, France has established defense cooperation agreements with several Middle Eastern countries, facilitating the exchange of military technology, joint training programs, and intelligence sharing. These partnerships strengthen France's military capabilities and foster greater interoperability with regional security forces. However, France's military presence and strategic alliances in the Middle East have also faced scrutiny and criticism, particularly regarding perceived interference in internal conflicts and allegations of violating sovereignty. Balancing the need for security cooperation with respect for national sovereignty remains a delicate challenge for France as it navigates its military involvement in the region. Moreover, evolving regional dynamics, such as the rise of non-state actors and proxy conflicts, continuously shape France's approach to maintaining military presence and nurturing strategic alliances in the Middle East. Consequently, France continues to reassess its military strategy and engagement in the region to adapt to shifting security realities and contribute to sustainable peace and stability.

## *Evaluating Impact: Humanitarian Aid versus Military Action*

As France continues to navigate its role in the complex web of Middle East conflicts, the debate over the effectiveness and repercussions of humanitarian aid versus military action has become increasingly pertinent. Humanitarian aid, focusing on providing relief and support to affected populations, aims to mitigate immediate suffering and address pressing needs. France has historically played a significant role in providing humanitarian assistance to war-torn regions and displaced communities, often working in collaboration with international organizations and NGOs to deliver essential supplies, medical care, and other urgent aid. This approach underscores France's commitment to alleviating human suffering and fostering regional stability. However, the efficacy of humanitarian aid is subject to limitations, especially in protracted conflicts where underlying political, social, and economic grievances persist. While crucial for addressing immediate crises, humanitarian aid alone may not address the root causes of conflict or bring about sustainable peace. In contrast, military action, whether in the form of peacekeeping missions, targeted interventions, or strategic alliances, has been leveraged by France to directly confront security threats, deter aggression, and stabilize volatile situations. France's military involvement in the Middle East has been multifaceted, from supporting counterterrorism efforts to participating in international coalition operations. The decision to deploy military forces is often fraught with complexities and ethical considerations, as it can give rise to unintended consequences, civilian casualties, and geopolitical tensions. Moreover, the long-term impact of military interventions and the potential for mission creep raises critical questions about the overall effectiveness and strategic outcomes. As such, the juxtaposition of humanitarian aid and military action signifies a balancing act for France, requiring careful assessment of short-term relief objectives against broader regional security imperatives. Ultimately, navigating the dichotomy between humanitarian aid and military action demands a holistic approach that integrates diplomatic initiatives, political dialogue, and multilateral cooperation to address the Middle East's interconnected challenges. France's evolving stance reflects a deliberative engagement with the complex dynamics of conflict resolution, acknowledging the intricate interplay between humanitarian imperatives and security interests in shaping sustainable solutions.

## IN A NUTSHELL

### Suez Crisis

*1956 military conflict in Egypt*

**Date:** 29 October 1956 - 7 November 1956.
**Location:** Egypt, from the Gaza Strip to the Suez Canal.
**Participants:** United Kingdom, France, Israel vs Egypt.
**Primary Objective:** To overthrow Egyptian president Gamal Abdel Nasser and regain control of the Suez Canal.
**Outcome:** Military withdrawal under international pressure, territorial occupation, Suez Canal closure, and international humiliation of Britain and France.
**Significance:** Marked the decline of British and French global influence; rise of the United States and Soviet Union as superpowers; strengthened Nasser's position.

## France's Role in the Middle East Conflicts

### 1. Historical Context and Early Involvements

France's involvement in the Middle East dates back centuries, with significant influence during the colonial era. In the 19th century, France established a strong presence in regions like Lebanon and Syria, which were under its mandate after World War I. This period was marked by both cooperation and conflict with local populations, as France sought to maintain control and influence over these territories.

### 2. The Suez Crisis of 1956: A Pivotal Moment

The Suez Crisis of 1956 was a significant turning point in Franco-Middle Eastern relations. When Egyptian President Gamal Abdel Nasser nationalized the Suez Canal, France, along with Britain and Israel, launched a military intervention to regain control. The crisis ended in a diplomatic defeat for France, as international pressure, particularly from the United States and the Soviet Union, forced a withdrawal. This event marked the decline of French and British influence in the region and highlighted the emerging dominance of the United States and the Soviet Union.

### 3. Lebanon Interventions in the 1980s

France's involvement in Lebanon during the 1980s was part of a broader multinational effort to stabilize the country amidst its civil war. French troops participated in peacekeeping missions under the United Nations Interim Force in Lebanon (UNIFIL) and later as part of the Multinational Force in Lebanon (MNF) following the 1982 Israeli invasion. Despite these efforts, the interventions were marred by violence, including the tragic bombing of French barracks in Beirut in 1983, which resulted in significant French casualties.

## 4. French Diplomacy during the Gulf War

During the Gulf War of 1990-1991, France played a crucial diplomatic and military role as part of the international coalition against Iraq's invasion of Kuwait. Operation Daguet saw the deployment of over 20,000 French troops, marking one of France's largest military engagements since World War II. France's participation underscored its commitment to international security and its strategic interests in the Middle East.

## 5. Collaboration and Conflict in the Israeli-Palestinian Affairs

France has historically maintained a complex relationship with both Israel and the Palestinian territories. Initially a close ally of Israel, France's stance shifted over the decades, particularly after the Six-Day War in 1967 when it imposed an arms embargo on the region. In recent years, France has sought to balance its support for Israel's security with advocacy for Palestinian statehood, often positioning itself as a mediator in the conflict.

## 6. France's Role in the Iraq War and Aftermath

France famously opposed the 2003 U.S.-led invasion of Iraq, a stance that strained its relations with the United States and the United Kingdom. Despite this opposition, France has remained engaged in Iraq, particularly in efforts to combat terrorism and support reconstruction efforts in the post-Saddam era.

## 7. Influence and Engagement in Syria's Civil War

France has been actively involved in the Syrian Civil War, primarily through diplomatic efforts and support for opposition groups. France has also participated in international coalitions targeting ISIS and has provided humanitarian aid to Syrian refugees. The conflict has highlighted France's strategic interests in maintaining stability in the region and combating extremism.

## 8. Negotiating Nuclear Tensions with Iran

France has played a significant role in negotiations over Iran's nuclear program, participating in the P5+1 talks that led to the 2015 Joint Comprehensive Plan of Action (JCPOA). France's involvement underscores its commitment to non-proliferation and regional security, although the future of the JCPOA remains uncertain following the U.S. withdrawal from the agreement.

## 9. Military Presence and Strategic Alliances

France maintains a strategic military presence in the Middle East, including bases in the United Arab Emirates and participation in various international coalitions. These alliances are crucial for France's broader security strategy and its efforts to project power and influence in the region.

## 10. Evaluating Impact: Humanitarian Aid versus Military Action

France's approach to the Middle East has often balanced military intervention with humanitarian efforts. While military actions have been significant, France has also been a major provider of humanitarian aid, particularly in conflict zones like Syria and

Lebanon. This dual approach aims to address both immediate security concerns and long-term stability through development and support for affected populations. In summary, France's role in the Middle East is characterized by a blend of historical ties, strategic interests, and a commitment to both military and humanitarian efforts. The country's actions in the region reflect its broader foreign policy goals of maintaining influence, ensuring security, and promoting stability amidst complex geopolitical dynamics.

# References For Further Reading

Bbc.co.uk. "BBC NEWS | Europe | France's Own Lesson from Suez," 2009. http://news.bbc.co.uk/2/hi/europe/6102536.stm.

Benraad, Myriam. "France's Fascination with Israel and Palestine – European Council on Foreign Relations." ECFR, July 21, 2014. https://ecfr.eu/article/commentary_frances_fascination_with_israel_and_palestine290/.

France Diplomacy - Ministry for Europe and Foreign Affairs. "Israel/Palestinian Territories - Q&a (08.12.23)," December 8, 2023. https://www.diplomatie.gouv.fr/en/country-files/israel-palestinian-territories/news/2023/article/israel-palestinian-territories-q-a-08-12-23.

France Diplomacy - Ministry for Europe and Foreign Affairs. "Middle-East," September 2020. https://www.diplomatie.gouv.fr/en/french-foreign-policy/security-disarmament-and-non-proliferation/crises-and-conflicts/israel-palestine/.

Imperial War Museum. "Why Was the Suez Crisis so Important?" Imperial War Museums, 2018. https://www.iwm.org.uk/history/why-was-the-suez-crisis-so-important.

Les Chemins de la Mémoire . "The Era of Overseas Operations ." www.cheminsdememoire.gouv.fr, April 2013. https://www.cheminsdememoire.gouv.fr/en/era-overseas-operations.

Office of the Historian. "The Suez Crisis, 1956." State.gov, 2019. https://history.state.gov/milestones/1953-1960/suez.

Qiujun, Zhou . "France's High-Profile Involvement in Middle East Turmoil - China

Military." eng.chinamil.com.cn, October 23, 2023. http://eng.chinamil.com.cn/WORLD_209198/WorldMilitaryAnalysis/16261159.html.

Rapnouil, Manuel Lafont. "Alone in the Desert? How France Can Lead Europe in the Middle East." ECFR, April 10, 2018. https://ecfr.eu/publication/alone_in_the_desert_how_france_can_lead_europe_in_the_middle_east/.

Spagnolo, John P. "France and the Middle East | Encyclopedia.com." www.encyclopedia.com, n.d. https://www.encyclopedia.com/humanities/encyclopedias-almanacs-transcripts-and-maps/france-and-middle-east.

Tara Varma and Kevin Huggard. "France Responds to the Israel-Gaza Crisis." Brookings, December 15, 2023. https://www.brookings.edu/articles/france-responds-to-the-israel-gaza-crisis/.

U.S. Department of State. "Suez Crisis, 1956." State.gov, 2019. https://2001-2009.state.gov/r/pa/ho/time/lw/97179.htm.

Uysal, Selin. "France's Diplomatic Role in the Middle East Post-October 7 | the Washington Institute." www.washingtoninstitute.org, February 2, 2024. https://www.washingtoninstitute.org/policy-analysis/frances-diplomatic-role-middle-east-post-october-7.

www.cvce.eu. "The Conflicts in the near and Middle East - Research Corpora - CVCE Website." Accessed May 23, 2024. https://www.cvce.eu/en/collections/unit-content/-/unit/56d70f17-5054-49fc-bb9b-5d90735167d0/eaf57e8d-185a-4e7c-ad09-65d6de928359.

www.cvce.eu. "The Suez Crisis - Historical Events in the European Integration Process (1945–2014) - CVCE Website," n.d. https://www.cvce.eu/en/education/unit-content/-/unit/02bb76df-d066-4c08-a58a-d4686a3e68ff/178e0373-75b1-4c85-bf6b-81c444b33c26.

# XIX

# Security Threats and Regional Stability

## Overview of Current Security Threats in the Arab Region

The Arab region faces many complex security threats that significantly affect regional stability and global security. Longstanding territorial disputes are at the heart of these challenges, fueled by historical grievances and competing claims to land and resources. The unresolved conflicts in Palestine, Yemen, Syria, and other areas continue to destabilize the region, exacerbating tensions and perpetuating cycles of violence. Furthermore, the rise of extremism and terrorist organizations poses a grave threat to the Arab world, with groups like ISIS and Al-Qaeda exploiting political instability and societal vulnerabilities to advance their radical agendas. Their influence has transcended national borders, leading to widespread fear and insecurity among the populace. The proliferation of weapons, including chemical and biological agents, further compounds these security concerns, posing significant risks to both state and human security. The region's strategic importance, particularly its vast energy reserves and critical maritime routes, makes it a focal point for geopolitical competition and power struggles, adding another layer of complexity to the security landscape. Geopolitical rivalries and regime changes often intensify security threats, leading to proxy wars and interventions that prolong the suffering of civilians and strain international relations. The intricate web of interrelated security challenges demands a comprehensive and nuanced approach that addresses the root causes while embracing multilateral cooperation and conflict resolution mechanisms. As France and other international stakeholders navigate these pressing security threats, the need for concerted efforts to promote dialogue, build trust, and uphold the principles of sovereignty and non-interference becomes increasingly vital. A deeper understanding of the historical context and evolving dynamics in the Arab region is essential for devising effective strategies to mitigate security risks and foster enduring peace.

## *Historical Context and Evolution of Regional Conflicts*

The historical roots of regional conflicts in the Arab world run deep, shaped by a complex interplay of political, economic, and cultural factors. The early 20th century saw the collapse of the Ottoman Empire, leading to the redrawing of borders and the creation of artificial states, often without regard for ethnic or religious divisions. This legacy of colonial intervention sowed the seeds of discord that continue to influence regional dynamics. Post-independence struggles for power and influence further fueled instability as newly formed nations grappled with fragile institutions and competing interests. The Arab-Israeli conflict, with its enduring territorial disputes and geopolitical significance, has been a primary source of tension, shaping alliances and animosities across the region. Moreover, the Cold War rivalry between superpowers exacerbated existing fault lines, leading to proxy wars and interventions that heightened regional fragility. The rise of nationalist and Islamist movements, spurred by disenchantment with incumbent regimes and external interference, added new dimensions to the evolving conflict landscape. The prolonged power struggles in countries like Iraq, Syria, and Yemen, combined with pervasive socio-economic disparities, have deepened the fault lines, creating fertile ground for violence and radicalization. The historical evolution of regional conflicts underscores their intricate nature, reflecting a confluence of historical grievances, identity politics, and external influences. Understanding this complex backdrop is essential for devising effective strategies to promote stability and address security threats in the Arab world.

## *Analysis of Terrorist Organizations and Their Impact*

Terrorist organizations have played a significant role in shaping the security landscape of the Arab region for decades, posing severe threats to stability and peace. This section comprehensively analyzes the various terrorist groups operating in the region and their far-reaching impact on regional dynamics. These organizations have exploited historical grievances, political instability, and socio-economic disparities to advance their agendas through violence and intimidation. Examining these groups' ideologies, strategies, and modus operandi is crucial in understanding the root causes of conflicts and devising effective counterterrorism measures. The emergence and proliferation of groups such as Al-Qaeda, ISIS, Hezbollah, and Hamas have not only destabilized individual countries but also had transnational repercussions, posing challenges to global security. Moreover, their influence extends beyond conventional warfare, as they harness modern communication and propaganda tools for radicalization and recruitment, amplifying their impact on vulnerable populations. Furthermore, the diverse nature of these organizations demands a nuanced approach, considering factors such as domestic support, external financing, and ideological affiliations. Understanding the complex web of alliances and rivalries within and among these groups is essential for crafting tailored responses that address specific threats without exacerbating broader tensions. Additionally, the evolving nature of terrorism, including cyber-based attacks and unconventional tactics, necessitates continuous adaptation of security frameworks and intelligence capabilities. The indiscriminate targeting of civilians, infrastructure, and cultural heritage by these organizations has inflicted widespread suffering and undermined prospects for sustainable development and progress. As France confronts these challenges, it must balance robust counter-terrorism operations with efforts to address underlying grievances and vulnerabilities that fuel extremist ideologies. By fostering collaboration with regional partners and international stakeholders, France can bolster collective efforts to combat terrorism while promoting avenues for dialogue and reconciliation. Emphasizing the protection of human rights and the rule of law is integral to countering the narratives propagated by terrorist groups while upholding democratic values and societal resilience. Ultimately, comprehensive analysis and proactive measures are imperative in mitigating the impact of terrorist organizations and safeguarding regional stability.

## *France's Military and Diplomatic Initiatives in the Region*

As a critical player in the Arab region, France has been deeply involved in various military and diplomatic initiatives to address the complex security challenges and promote regional stability. The country has maintained a strong military presence in strategic areas, conducting counter-terrorism operations and supporting regional allies. France also actively participates in peacekeeping missions and contributes troops to multinational efforts to maintain stability in conflict-ridden areas. In addition to its military engagements, France has pursued a proactive diplomatic approach, engaging with regional governments, international organizations, and other stakeholders to foster dialogue, facilitate conflict resolution, and promote cooperation. France seeks to build consensus on pressing security issues through its diplomatic missions and high-level dialogues and encourages multilateral efforts to address common threats. Furthermore, France has played a pivotal role in brokering and supporting peace agreements, leveraging its historical ties and diplomatic influence to mediate between conflicting parties. The country's commitment to enhancing regional security is also reflected in its provision of training and technical assistance to local security forces, reinforcing their capacity to combat terrorism and maintain law and order. Moreover, France collaborates closely with regional partners to strengthen border security, intelligence-sharing capabilities, and counter-radicalization measures, contributing to a more robust and coordinated response to security threats. France's military and diplomatic initiatives in the region underscore its enduring commitment to advancing peace, stability, and security, aligning with its broader foreign policy objectives and pursuing strategic interests. By combining military force with diplomatic finesse, France continues to play a constructive and influential role in shaping the security landscape of the Arab region, navigating complex dynamics, and striving to mitigate the multifaceted challenges that impact regional stability.

## *Role of International Alliances and Partnerships*

International alliances and partnerships are pivotal in addressing security threats and maintaining regional stability in the Arab region. As a key player in global diplomacy, France recognizes the significance of collaborative efforts with international actors to address complex security challenges in the Arab world. International alliances provide a framework for collective action, information sharing, and resource pooling to combat transnational security threats effectively. Additionally, partnerships with regional and global entities enable coordinated responses to crises and contribute to conflict resolution efforts. International alliances and partnerships also facilitate the exchange of best practices, capacity-building initiatives, and joint training exercises, which are essential for enhancing the capabilities of regional security forces. France has actively engaged in strategic alliances with countries such as the United States, United Kingdom, Germany, and other European Union members to foster multilateral cooperation in addressing security threats in the Arab region. These partnerships encompass a range of initiatives, including intelligence-sharing, counter-terrorism operations, and joint military exercises. Furthermore, France values its collaboration with regional organizations such as the Arab League, the Gulf Cooperation Council (GCC), and the African Union to promote stability and security in the Middle East and North Africa. The synergistic efforts between France and these regional bodies facilitate diplomatic negotiations and conflict mediation while addressing broader socio-economic and humanitarian concerns. Beyond governmental alliances, France has also forged partnerships with non-governmental organizations, academia, and civil society groups to engage in dialogue, share expertise, and support grassroots initiatives that contribute to long-term stability in the Arab region. These networks offer platforms for knowledge exchange, cultural understanding, and social cohesion programs integral to countering radicalization and promoting inclusive governance. In conclusion, international alliances and partnerships cannot be overstated in addressing security threats and fostering regional stability in the Arab region. France's commitment to forging collaborative relationships with international and regional actors underscores the importance of collective action and solidarity in confronting multifaceted security challenges. Through concerted efforts and mutual support, international alliances and partnerships serve as catalysts for sustaining peace, countering extremism, and safeguarding the well-being of nations in the Arab world.

## Cybersecurity Challenges and Information Warfare

The modern era has witnessed a significant rise in cyber threats and information warfare, posing complex challenges to the security and stability of the Arab region. Cybersecurity threats encompass a wide array of malicious activities, including hacking, data breaches, and cyber espionage, which have the potential to inflict severe damage on critical infrastructure, governmental institutions, and private enterprises. This chapter delves into the multifaceted nature of cybersecurity challenges and the increasing relevance of information warfare in shaping regional dynamics. As technological advancements continue to reshape the geopolitical landscape, it has become imperative for nations to bolster their cybersecurity mechanisms and counter disinformation campaigns effectively. The Arab region, with its diverse geopolitical interests and complex security environment, is particularly susceptible to cyber threats. State-sponsored cyber-attacks and non-state actors leveraging digital platforms for propaganda and psychological warfare have magnified the region's vulnerability. Moreover, the prevalence of socio-political tensions and regional conflicts has created fertile ground for malicious actors to exploit existing fault lines through online manipulation and subversive activities. France, in its engagement with the Arab world, is at the forefront of addressing cybersecurity challenges and countering information warfare. The country has been actively fostering cybersecurity capacities within Arab countries, providing technical assistance, and facilitating knowledge exchange to mitigate emerging threats. Furthermore, France's proactive stance in advocating for international norms and protocols governing cyberspace reflects its commitment to upholding global cybersecurity standards and preventing destabilizing cyber incidents. Information warfare, characterized by disseminating misleading narratives and false information, has become a potent tool for influencing public opinion and sowing discord. The interconnected nature of digital communication platforms has amplified the reach and impact of information warfare tactics, necessitating a concerted effort to safeguard against manipulative content. France recognizes the nuanced interplay between cybersecurity and information warfare, emphasizing the importance of building resilience against disinformation campaigns and promoting digital literacy to inoculate societies from malicious influence. As the Arab region grapples with evolving security paradigms, the convergence of cyber threats and information warfare demands an integrated approach encompassing diplomatic, technological, and societal dimensions. By forging collaborative initiatives and sharing best practices, France and its Arab partners can strive to fortify their collective defenses and safeguard regional stability amidst the burgeoning challenges presented by the cyber domain.

## *Humanitarian Issues and Their Implications for Stability*

The humanitarian landscape in the Arab region is marked by complex challenges that have significant implications for regional stability. The protracted conflicts, internal displacements, and refugee crises have created a profound humanitarian crisis with far-reaching consequences. This section will delve into the multifaceted issues and their repercussions on the broader security dynamics of the region.

At the heart of the humanitarian crisis is the displacement of millions of people within and across national borders. This has strained the capacity of host countries and heightened socio-economic vulnerabilities among displaced populations and the host communities. The strain on primary resources such as water, food, and shelter has increased competition and tension, exacerbating existing fault lines and the potential for instability.

Furthermore, the collapse of essential infrastructure, including healthcare and education systems, has had a crippling impact on the well-being and prospects of entire generations. The lack of access to education and healthcare perpetuates poverty cycles and undermines the potential for long-term peace and prosperity. Addressing these issues is paramount for the restoration of stability and sustainable development.

The humanitarian crisis also intersects with security concerns, as vulnerable populations become susceptible to exploitation and recruitment by extremist groups. The absence of essential services and economic opportunities renders affected communities susceptible to radical ideologies and criminal networks, posing a direct threat to regional stability. Moreover, the influx of displaced persons can strain the social fabric of host societies, leading to social tensions and potentially violent confrontations.

Moreover, the humanitarian crisis poses significant challenges to international humanitarian law, human rights, and the protection of civilians. The erosion of fundamental human rights and the breakdown of the rule of law undermine the prospects for peaceful coexistence and reconciliation, further entrenching fragility in the region. It is imperative to uphold international norms and standards to mitigate the humanitarian fallout and safeguard the dignity and rights of affected populations.

In conclusion, the humanitarian issues plaguing the Arab region are intricately linked to the broader questions of stability and security. Addressing these challenges requires a comprehensive approach encompassing immediate relief efforts and long-term strategies for sustainable development, conflict resolution, and peacebuilding. By prioritizing humanitarian action and placing it at the forefront of regional agendas, stakeholders can work towards mitigating the adverse implications and fostering a more stable and resilient Arab region.

## *Future Scenarios: Predicting Regional Dynamics*

The future of the Arab region is subject to a complex web of political, economic, and social dynamics that have the potential to shape its trajectory in numerous ways. As we analyze the regional landscape and envision possible scenarios, it becomes evident that several factors will significantly impact the course of events. One such factor is emerging powers' role and influence on regional alliances and conflicts. The evolving geopolitical dynamics, including the shifting balance of power among key players, will undeniably contribute to shaping the region's future. Moreover, the impact of technological advancements and their ramifications for security and warfare cannot be overlooked. The intersection of cyber capabilities, artificial intelligence, and information warfare will likely transform the nature of conflicts and pose new challenges to stability and governance. Another critical aspect that warrants consideration is the demographic trends and their potential implications for regional dynamics. Population growth, urbanization, and youth bulges are all factors that can fuel socio-political changes and demand proactive governance strategies. Furthermore, the ever-present issue of resource scarcity and competing interests over water, energy, and mineral reserves is poised to remain a defining factor in regional dynamics. As we delve into future scenarios, it is imperative to consider the possibility of transformative events, such as popular uprisings, regime changes, or unexpected geopolitical realignments. These unforeseen developments can have far-reaching consequences and require agile and adaptive policy responses from regional and global actors. Lastly, the impact of climate change on the region cannot be underestimated, as rising temperatures, extreme weather events, and environmental degradation hold the potential to exacerbate existing challenges and trigger new security threats. Converging these multifaceted variables requires a holistic and nuanced approach to predicting regional dynamics, acknowledging the interconnectedness of various factors, and embracing the fluidity of future scenarios.

## Policy Recommendations for Enhancing Security and Stability

As we navigate the complex landscape of security threats and regional instability in the Arab region, developing comprehensive policy recommendations that can effectively enhance stability and mitigate security challenges becomes imperative. Firstly, France must prioritize diplomatic engagements and multilateral collaborations to foster trust and cooperation among regional stakeholders. This could involve proactive mediation, conflict resolution initiatives, and peace-building measures to address deep-rooted conflicts and promote sustainable peace. Moreover, strengthening intelligence-sharing mechanisms and cybersecurity frameworks will be crucial to counter emerging threats such as cyber warfare, disinformation campaigns, and radicalization through online platforms. Emphasizing investment in education, vocational training, and economic development can address underlying socio-economic grievances that often fuel instability and extremism. Additionally, France should devise targeted strategies for countering organized crime, illicit arms trafficking, and border security challenges that pose significant threats to regional stability. Furthermore, prioritizing humanitarian aid and refugee assistance and mitigating the impact of climate change will also contribute to long-term stability in the region. Cooperation with other global powers and international organizations to bolster peacekeeping operations, promote good governance, and uphold human rights will reinforce stability. Empowering local civil society organizations, women's groups, and youth networks can ensure inclusive participation in decision-making, promoting social cohesion and resilience. Developing and implementing a robust and coherent policy framework, underpinned by a nuanced understanding of the regional dynamics and context-specific approaches, are vital for sustaining lasting security and stability. These recommendations serve as a strategic roadmap for France to effectively contribute to enhancing security and stability in the Arab region, fostering a conducive environment for sustainable peace and prosperity.

## Conclusion: France's Strategic Outlook and Next Steps

France's engagement in addressing security threats and enhancing regional stability in the Arab world has been shaped by a multifaceted approach that integrates diplomatic, military, and humanitarian dimensions. As the region grapples with complex challenges, France must refine its strategic outlook and chart a course for future action. The following section analyzes France's strategic outlook and outlines critical next steps for consolidating its role in promoting security and stability in the Arab region. Assessing the evolving security landscape in the Arab world, France must reaffirm its commitment to fostering peace and mitigating conflicts while acknowledging the diverse factors that contribute to instability. By leveraging its diplomatic expertise, France can play a pivotal role in mediating regional disputes and advancing peaceful resolutions. Moreover, aligning with international alliances and partners will be instrumental in collectively addressing common security threats and bolstering regional stability. Embracing a proactive approach to cybersecurity and information warfare is paramount for safeguarding against emerging threats in the digital domain. Additionally, France's military engagements and capacity-building efforts should be calibrated to combat extremist groups and contribute to long-term stability effectively. In light of the humanitarian crises that persist in the region, France must prioritize empathy and support for vulnerable populations, recognizing the interconnectedness of humanitarian issues and overall regional stability. Looking ahead, France's strategic outlook should emphasize adaptability and foresight, positioning itself to anticipate and respond to evolving security dynamics. Proactive intelligence-gathering and scenario planning will identify potential risks and formulate preemptive measures. Furthermore, enacting sustainable policies that foster economic development and socio-political reforms will create resilient societies and sustainable stability. France's next steps should encompass sustained dialogue and collaboration with regional stakeholders, embracing a holistic approach that integrates diverse perspectives in addressing security challenges and fostering lasting peace. By upholding its dedication to multilateralism and global cooperation, France can leverage its influence to shape a more secure and stable Arab region. Through effective leadership and unwavering commitment, France can navigate the complexities of the Arab world's security landscape, contributing to a future defined by peace, stability, and prosperity.

# IN A NUTSHELL

## France's Arab Policy and Security Threats and Regional Stability

### 1. Overview of Current Security Threats in the Arab Region

The Arab region faces a multitude of security threats, including ongoing conflicts, terrorism, and geopolitical rivalries. Key areas of concern include the civil wars in Syria and Yemen, the instability in Libya, and the persistent threat of terrorism from groups like ISIS and Al-Qaeda. Additionally, regional power struggles, particularly between Saudi Arabia and Iran, exacerbate tensions and contribute to instability.

### 2. Historical Context and Evolution of Regional Conflicts

The modern Middle East has been shaped by a series of conflicts, many of which have roots in the colonial era and the arbitrary borders drawn by Western powers post-World War I. The Arab-Israeli conflict, the Iranian Revolution, the Iran-Iraq War, and the

Gulf Wars are significant historical events that have shaped the region's current dynamics. The Arab Spring uprisings in 2011 further disrupted the region, leading to civil wars and increased instability.

## 3. Analysis of Terrorist Organizations and Their Impact

Terrorist organizations such as ISIS, Al-Qaeda, and their affiliates have had a profound impact on the Arab region. These groups have exploited political vacuums and social grievances to establish footholds, particularly in Iraq, Syria, and Yemen. Their activities have led to significant loss of life, displacement of populations, and destabilization of entire regions. France has been directly affected by terrorism, with several high-profile attacks linked to these groups.

## 4. France's Military and Diplomatic Initiatives in the Region

France has been actively involved in the Middle East through both military and diplomatic means. Militarily, France has participated in international coalitions against ISIS and has maintained a military presence in countries like Iraq, Syria, and Lebanon. Diplomatically, France has sought to mediate conflicts and promote stability through initiatives such as the International Alliance for the Protection of Heritage in Conflict (ALIPH) and various humanitarian efforts.

## 5. Role of International Alliances and Partnerships

France's efforts in the Middle East are bolstered by its alliances and partnerships with regional and international actors. Key partners include the United States, the United Arab Emirates, and Saudi

Arabia. France also works closely with the European Union and the United Nations to address security and humanitarian challenges in the region.

## 6. Cybersecurity Challenges and Information Warfare

The Middle East is increasingly vulnerable to cybersecurity threats, including cyberattacks on critical infrastructure and government systems. These threats are compounded by the region's rapid digitization and the strategic importance of its energy resources. France, along with its allies, is working to enhance cybersecurity measures and protect against information warfare.

## 7. Humanitarian Issues and Their Implications for Stability

Humanitarian crises in the Arab region, driven by conflicts and displacement, pose significant challenges to stability. Countries like Syria, Yemen, and Lebanon face severe humanitarian conditions, with millions of people in need of aid. France has been active in providing humanitarian assistance and advocating for international support to address these crises.

## 8. Future Scenarios: Predicting Regional Dynamics

The future of the Arab region is likely to be shaped by ongoing conflicts, geopolitical rivalries, and the outcomes of current diplomatic efforts. Potential scenarios include continued instability and conflict, gradual stabilization through international mediation, or significant geopolitical shifts driven by changes in leadership or external interventions. The role of non-state actors and the impact of climate change on resources like water and food security will also be critical factors.

## 9. Policy Recommendations for Enhancing Security and Stability

To enhance security and stability in the Arab region, France and its partners should focus on:

Strengthening diplomatic efforts to mediate conflicts and promote political solutions.

Enhancing support for counter-terrorism initiatives and capacity-building for local security forces.

Increasing humanitarian aid and development assistance to address the root causes of instability.

Promoting regional cooperation and dialogue to address shared security challenges.

Investing in cybersecurity measures to protect critical infrastructure and counter information warfare.

## Conclusion: France's Strategic Outlook and Next Steps

France's strategic outlook in the Arab region involves a balanced approach of military engagement, diplomatic initiatives, and humanitarian support. Moving forward, France aims to continue its efforts to combat terrorism, support regional stability, and address humanitarian needs. Strengthening alliances and partnerships, particularly within the framework of the European Union and the United Nations, will be crucial for France to effectively navigate the complex dynamics of the Middle East. In summary, France's policy towards the Arab region is multifaceted, addressing immediate security threats while also working towards long-term stability and development. The evolving geopolitical landscape and the persistent challenges of terrorism and humanitarian crises will require sustained and adaptive strategies.

# References For Further Reading

Cammack, Perry. "Fueling Middle East Conflicts—or Dousing the Flames." Carnegie Endowment for International Peace, 2011. https://carnegieendowment.org/2018/10/23/fueling-middle-east-conflicts-or-dousing-flames-pub-77548.

El Karoui , Hakim . "A New Strategy for France in a New Arab World." Institut Montaigne, August 2017. https://www.institutmontaigne.org/en/publications/new-strategy-france-new-arab-world.

ESCWA Publication. "Arab Risk Monitor: Assessing Vulnerability and Resilience in the Region." United Nations Economic and Social Commission for Western Asia, 2023. https://www.unescwa.org/publications/arab-risk-monitor-assessing-vulnerability-resilience-region.

Europa.eu. "Lutte de l'UE Contre Le Terrorisme - Consilium," 2017. https://www.consilium.europa.eu/fr/policies/fight-against-terrorism.

France Diplomacy - Ministry for Europe and Foreign Affairs. "Fight against Terrorism - Meeting on Combating Hamas (Paris, 13 Dec. 2023)," December 13, 2023. https://www.diplomatie.gouv.fr/en/country-files/israel-palestinian-territories/news/2023/article/fight-against-terrorism-meeting-on-combating-hamas-paris-13-dec-2023.

France Diplomatie - Ministère de l'Europe et des Affaires étrangères. "Terrorisme : L'action Internationale de La France," November 2019. https://www.diplomatie.gouv.fr/fr/politique-etrangere-de-la-france/securite-desarmement-et-non-proliferation/terrorisme-l-action-internationale-de-la-france/.

Gayubas, Augusto . "Conflicts in the Middle East: History and Characteristics." https://humanidades.com/, January 17, 2024. https://humanidades.com/en/conflicts-in-the-middle-east/.

Positive Technologies. "Cybersecurity Threatscape in the Middle East: 2022-2023." ptsecurity.com. Positive Technologies, July 17, 2023. https://www.ptsecurity.com/ww-en/analytics/middle-east-cybersecurity-threatscape-2022-2023/.

Représentation permanente de la France auprès des Organisations Internationales et des Nations unies à Vienne. "La France et La Lutte Contre Le Terrorisme," July 5, 2022. https://onu-vienne.delegfrance.org/La-France-et-la-lutte-contre-le-terrorisme.

Shah, Anup. "The Middle East Conflict—a Brief Background — Global Issues." www.globalissues.org, July 30, 2006. https://www.globalissues.org/article/119/the-middle-east-conflict-a-brief-background.

Uysal, Selin . "France's Diplomatic Role in the Middle East Post-October 7 | the Washington Institute." www.washingtoninstitute.org, February 2, 2024. https://www.washingtoninstitute.org/policy-analysis/frances-diplomatic-role-middle-east-post-october-7.

Vincent, Elise . "France's Strategic Thinking in the Middle East Is at a Standstill." www.ifri.org, December 20, 2022. https://www.ifri.org/en/espace-media/lifri-medias/frances-strategic-thinking-middle-east-standstill.

Wright, Robin. "Explainer: The Roots and Realities of 10 Conflicts in the Middle East | Wilson Center." www.wilsoncenter.org, February 5, 2024. https://www.wilsoncenter.org/article/explainer-roots-and-realities-10-conflicts-middle-east.

www.cvce.eu. "The Conflicts in the near and Middle East - Research Corpora - CVCE Website." Accessed May 24, 2024. https://www.cvce.eu/en/collections/unit-content/-/unit/56d70f17-5054-49fc-bb9b-5d90735167d0/eaf57e8d-185a-4e7c-ad09-65d6de928359.

www.mofa.gov.ae. "UAE Embassy in Paris-Bilateral Relationship." Accessed May 24, 2024. https://www.mofa.gov.ae/en/Missions/Paris/UAE-Relationships/Bilateral-Relationship.

# XX

# France's Influence in North Africa

## Historical Overview of Franco-North African Relations

The colonial legacy and the subsequent political transitions in the region have profoundly influenced the historical relationship between France and North Africa. Since colonial times, when various North African countries were subject to French rule, the relationship dynamics have evolved significantly. The struggle for independence and the decolonization process profoundly shaped the nature of Franco-North African relations. The transition from colonialism to independence marked a pivotal juncture in the historical context of this relationship, as it led to significant adjustments in political power structures and diplomatic engagements. The post-independence era saw a complex interplay of economic, political, and cultural factors that continued to influence the dynamics between France and North African nations. The historical overview encompasses the periods of cooperation, conflict, and negotiation, reflecting the intricate evolution of Franco-North African relations. It provides crucial insights into the enduring complexities and nuances that have characterized this relationship, offering a comprehensive understanding of the contextual backdrop for analyzing contemporary interactions and prospects.

## Economic Impact and Trade Agreements

The economic impact of Franco-North African relations has been profound, shaping the trajectory of both regions and fostering interdependence. Trade agreements between France and North African countries have driven economic growth, facilitated commerce, and bolstered regional integration. With historical ties dating back to colonial periods, these trade agreements have evolved to reflect contemporary economic priorities and geopolitical realities.

France has long been a key trading partner for North African nations, with significant investments in diverse sectors such as energy, infrastructure, agriculture, and manufacturing. The exchange of goods and services has spurred economic development and cultivated mutual prosperity. At the same time, trade agreements have provided avenues for technology transfer, skills enhancement, and knowledge sharing, contributing to the modernization of North African economies.

Moreover, these economic linkages have resulted in cultural and social exchanges, enriching the fabric of both French and North African societies. The impact of trade agreements goes beyond mere commercial transactions, serving as catalysts for broader collaboration in education, innovation, and entrepreneurship.

Trade agreements have also enabled North African countries to leverage their natural resources and human capital, fostering sustainable development and diversification of their economies. Meanwhile, France has benefited from access to critical markets, resources, and strategic partnerships in the region, further solidifying its position as a principal player in North African economic affairs.

Challenges, however, persist within the context of economic impact and trade agreements. Market access, regulatory harmonization, and labor mobility require sustained dialogue and concerted efforts to ensure trade benefits are equitably distributed. Furthermore, global dynamics, technological advancements, and shifting consumer preferences continually shape the economic landscape, necessitating adaptive trade policies and agile economic strategies.

It is imperative to recalibrate trade agreements to address emerging challenges and tap into new opportunities. This entails fostering inclusive growth, promoting sustainable practices, and harnessing the potential of digital economies. Strengthening economic partnership frameworks can catalyze innovation, spur job creation, and enable North African economies to compete effectively in the global marketplace. By nurturing robust trade relations, France and North African nations can chart a mutually beneficial course toward shared prosperity underpinned by equitable economic interdependence.

## *Political Influence and Diplomatic Engagements*

In the complex web of Franco-North African relations, political influence, and diplomatic engagements play a pivotal role in shaping the dynamics between France and the nations of North Africa. Since the colonial era, France has sought to maintain and cultivate political influence in the region through various channels, including bilateral partnerships, multilateral diplomacy, and active engagement in regional and international forums.

One key aspect of France's political influence in North Africa lies in its historical ties and shared interests with these countries. French leaders have utilized their relationships with North African counterparts to assert their influence on matters of mutual concern, such as security, counterterrorism, migration, and economic cooperation. Through high-level diplomatic visits, strategic dialogues, and partnership agreements, France continues to assert its presence in the political landscape of North Africa.

French diplomatic engagements in the region extend beyond traditional state-to-state interactions. France has actively promoted regional stability, mediated conflicts, and supported democratic transitions in North African countries. In doing so, France has aimed to project itself as a responsible and reliable partner committed to the region's peace, security, and development.

Moreover, France's involvement in North African affairs is closely linked to its broader strategic interests at the regional level and within the context of European and global politics. As a member of the European Union and a permanent member of the United Nations Security Council, France wields significant diplomatic clout, which it leverages to shape agendas and policies concerning North Africa on the international stage.

However, it is essential to acknowledge that France's political influence in North Africa is not without complexities and challenges. The historical legacy of colonialism, diverging national interests, and evolving geopolitical dynamics pose inherent obstacles to ensuring enduring political influence. Moreover, the rise of new global players and non-traditional security threats further complicates the landscape within which France seeks to maintain its political relevance in the region.

Looking ahead, the effectiveness of France's political influence in North Africa will hinge upon its ability to adapt to shifting power dynamics, address the aspirations of North African societies, and engage in diplomatic efforts mutually beneficial and respectful of the region's sovereignty. While navigating these intricacies, France can continue to harness its diplomatic expertise and historical ties to advance a balanced and inclusive approach toward its political influence in North Africa, fostering cooperative and constructive relations for all parties involved.

## *Military Cooperation and Security Alliances*

Military cooperation and security alliances have been pivotal in shaping the relationship between France and North African nations. The historical ties between France and countries such as Algeria,

Morocco, and Tunisia have created strong military bonds that have endured for decades. These relationships have been characterized by collaboration on defense capabilities, joint military exercises, and arms trade, all of which have contributed to regional stability and security. France's military presence in the region has also been driven by its historical colonial influence and strategic geopolitical interests. The French military has cooperated with North African states, including training programs, intelligence sharing, and counter-terrorism efforts. In recent years, the focus has expanded to encompass broader security challenges such as border control, maritime security, and peacekeeping operations. Additionally, France has facilitated security alliances among North African countries and supported their efforts to combat transnational threats and insurgencies. This approach has not only strengthened bilateral relations but has also reinforced multilateral security cooperation within the region. France has sought to foster trust and mutual understanding through military cooperation and security alliances while addressing common security concerns. However, these partnerships have also faced criticism and scrutiny, particularly regarding sovereignty, human rights, and the impact on regional power dynamics. Furthermore, evolving security threats, including terrorism, cyber warfare, and organized crime, continue to test the resilience and effectiveness of these alliances. Therefore, it becomes essential for France and North African nations to adapt their security cooperation strategies to address emerging challenges and ensure long-term stability. The future of military cooperation and security alliances between France and North Africa will depend on the ability of both parties to navigate complexities, uphold shared values, and adapt to changing security dynamics in the region.

## *Cultural Ties and Linguistic Influence*

Cultural exchange and mutual influence across the Mediterranean have long characterized the relationship between France and North

Africa. The historical entwinement of cultures, languages, and traditions has created a rich tapestry of shared heritage that continues to shape the social fabric of both regions. French colonial rule in North Africa left an enduring imprint on the local cultures, introducing elements of the French language, customs, and institutions. This influence persists today, with French as a widely spoken second language in many North African countries, particularly Algeria, Tunisia, and Morocco. Notably, the intermingling of French and Arabic has produced a unique hybrid known as 'Franco-Arabic,' reflecting the linguistic fusion between the two regions.

Furthermore, the literary, artistic, and culinary contributions from North Africa have greatly enriched the cultural landscape of France. From iconic works of literature by Algerian-born author Albert Camus to the vibrant North African music and cuisine celebrated across French cities, the impact of North African cultural expressions on French society is profound. This cross-pollination of ideas has engendered a dynamic and diverse cultural milieu, fostering a cosmopolitan identity and transcending national boundaries. Moreover, the proliferation of North African art, music, and cinema in France has significantly shaped the country's cultural discourse, highlighting the interconnectedness of these two regions.

Linguistic influence extends beyond mere communication; it encompasses transmitting values, perspectives, and modes of expression. The intertwining of French and Arabic languages symbolizes the intricate interplay between tradition and modernity, offering a lens through which to examine the complex dynamics of acculturation and adaptation. This linguistic fusion underscores the resilience of cultural identities and the adaptive nature of language in capturing the essence of shared experiences. Moreover, the prevalent bilingualism in this context reflects a nuanced form of cultural diplomacy as a bridge for dialogue and understanding between France and North Africa.

In conclusion, the cultural ties and linguistic influence between France and North Africa underscore a legacy of interconnectedness, reciprocity, and enduring collaboration. The amalgamation of languages, customs, and artistic expressions has fostered a sense of shared heritage and laid the foundation for multifaceted partnerships in various domains. Embracing this intercultural dialogue enriches both societies, contributing to a globalized world where diversity is celebrated, and unity is forged through interweaving distinct traditions and narratives.

## *Education and Academic Collaborations*

Education and academic collaborations have played a vital role in shaping Franco-North African relations. The exchange of knowledge, ideas, and expertise has strengthened bilateral ties and contributed to the socio-economic development of North African nations. French universities and research institutions have been pivotal in fostering academic partnerships with their counterparts in North Africa, facilitating student exchange programs, joint research initiatives, and faculty collaboration. This has not only provided North African students with access to quality education but has also allowed for the transfer of skills and knowledge back to their home countries. Furthermore, academic collaborations have promoted cultural understanding and intercultural dialogue, encouraging a deeper appreciation of each other's societal values and traditions. The emphasis on language acquisition, mainly French, has been a bridging tool, enabling enhanced communication and academic exchanges. Additionally, scholarships and grants provided by the French government and international organizations have supported talented individuals from North Africa to pursue higher education in France, further strengthening the academic ties between the two regions. These collaborations have extended beyond the traditional academic realm to encompass areas such as vocational training, capacity building, and scientific cooperation. By investing in education and academic collaborations, France has sought to contribute to North African countries' human capital development and knowledge-based economy. As a result, these partnerships have improved the quality of education and research in the region and fostered innovation, entrepreneurship, and sustainable development. France and North African nations must continue prioritizing and expanding education and academic collaborations to empower future generations, promote cross-cultural understanding, and address contemporary global challenges.

## Development Aid and Infrastructure Projects

France's engagement in development aid and infrastructure projects in North Africa has been a significant aspect of its regional foreign policy. The historical ties between France and North African countries, coupled with strategic geopolitical interests, have led to various development initiatives to foster economic growth, sustainability, and socio-economic well-being. Development aid from France to North Africa encompasses a wide range of sectors, including but not limited to education, healthcare, agriculture, water resource management, renewable energy, and transportation infrastructure. These initiatives are usually carried out through bilateral agreements, multilateral partnerships, and collaboration with international organizations such as the United Nations and the European Union. One of the primary objectives of French development aid is to support the socio-economic development of North African nations by addressing key challenges such as poverty, unemployment, and inadequate infrastructure. Through financial assistance, technical expertise, and capacity-building programs, France aims to contribute to improving living conditions and creating sustainable opportunities for the local population. Furthermore, France has played a pivotal role in implementing infrastructure projects in North Africa, focusing on sectors such as transportation, energy, telecommunications, and urban development. These projects aim to enhance connectivity and mobility within the region and promote economic integration and trade. Examples of such initiatives include the construction of highways, ports, and airports and the development of renewable energy sources. Additionally, France has supported the modernization and expansion of urban centers, contributing to the creation of smart cities and sustainable urban planning. The impact of these projects extends beyond mere physical infrastructure, as they also facilitate technological transfer, job creation, and the establishment of conducive environments for business and investment. Overall, France's commitment to development aid and infrastructure projects in North Africa underscores its dedication to fostering long-term partnerships and sustainable development in the region, all while reinforcing its presence and influence as a key player in promoting progress and stability.

## *Immigration Policies and Diaspora Dynamics*

The historical ties between France and North Africa have significantly impacted immigration policies and diaspora dynamics. As a former colonial power, France has long attracted North African immigrants seeking economic opportunities and a better quality of life. This influx of migrants has played a crucial role in shaping contemporary French society's cultural landscape and socio-economic fabric. French immigration policies towards North Africans have evolved over time, reflecting the changing geopolitical and domestic realities. Integrating the North African diaspora into French society has been a complex and, at times, contentious issue. The challenges surrounding immigration, cultural assimilation, and social cohesion continue to be subjects of intense debate and scrutiny. Diversity and inclusion are essential aspects of France's identity, and managing immigration from North Africa presents opportunities and obstacles. The diaspora dynamics encompass a broad spectrum of experiences, ranging from successful integration and upward mobility to marginalization and discrimination. Understanding the diverse trajectories of individuals within the North African diaspora is crucial for policymakers, community leaders, and social researchers. Economic, educational, and linguistic factors significantly influence the diaspora's interactions with the host society and their transnational connections. The Franco-North African diaspora encompasses a rich tapestry of cultural expressions, traditions, and collective memories contributing to modern-day France's multicultural essence. Moreover, the diaspora bridges France and North Africa, fostering cross-border collaborations, trade linkages, and people-to-people exchanges. Addressing the complexities of immigration policies and diaspora dynamics requires a comprehensive and nuanced approach that recognizes the multi-faceted nature of this relationship. Striking a balance between safeguarding national interests, promoting social cohesion, and respecting individual rights is paramount. Furthermore, engaging in constructive dialogues and fostering mutual understanding can help alleviate tensions and foster a more inclusive society for all inhabitants of France.

## *Challenges in Contemporary Relations*

The contemporary relations between France and North Africa have been marked by many complex challenges that have significantly impacted the two regions' diplomatic, economic, and socio-cultural dynamics. One of the foremost challenges is the historical and colonial legacy, which engendered resentment and skepticism in North African countries toward French policies and interventions. The lingering effects of colonization continue to influence the perception of France's role in the region, posing a significant obstacle to building trust and fostering mutually beneficial partnerships. Additionally, the socio-economic disparities and unequal power dynamics have contributed to tensions and friction in contemporary relations. These disparities manifest in economic inequalities, lack of development opportunities, and divergent political interests, leading to strains in diplomatic and bilateral engagements. Another pivotal challenge is the evolving security landscape, characterized by transnational threats such as terrorism, extremism, and organized crime. The spread of radical ideologies and the proliferation of armed groups across the Sahel region pose a direct security threat to both France and North African nations, necessitating robust cooperation and coordinated efforts to address the shared security concerns. Moreover, the issue of migration continues to be a contentious point in contemporary relations. Managing migrant flows, asylum policies, and integration processes has elicited discord and debate, reflecting the divergent approaches and differing national priorities in addressing this complex humanitarian and societal issue. Cultural misunderstandings and misconceptions also present a formidable challenge. Perceptions of cultural superiority, stereotypes, and biases shape interactions and create barriers to effective communication and collaboration. Overcoming these challenges requires a nuanced approach that acknowledges historical grievances, addresses socio-economic disparities, enhances security cooperation, and fosters inclusive dialogue. Navigating the contemporary challenges in Franco-North African relations demands a comprehensive and multi-faceted strategy prioritizing mutual respect, understanding, and the pursuit of common ground for sustained cooperation and partnership.

## *Future Prospects and Strategic Objectives*

As France continues to navigate its complex relationship with North Africa, it is crucial to look ahead and consider the prospects and strategic objectives for this evolving partnership. The shifting geopolitical landscape, economic dynamics, and sociocultural factors compel French policymakers to reassess their approach and identify key priorities. One of the primary strategic objectives for France is to foster long-term stability and security in North Africa, as these are foundational prerequisites for sustained cooperation and prosperity. This entails addressing immediate security challenges and supporting socio-political reforms that promote inclusive governance and minimize conflict potential. Moreover, sustainable economic development and trade diversification represent critical prospects for the region. France aims to deepen economic ties and investment in North Africa, leveraging its expertise in various sectors such as energy, infrastructure, and technology. By fostering an environment conducive to business growth and innovation, France and North African countries benefit from enhanced economic opportunities. A critical future objective also involves continued cultural exchange and academic collaborations to strengthen people-to-people ties and mutual understanding. Education and linguistic programs, alongside cultural initiatives, can contribute to nurturing an interconnected Franco-North African community, thereby cementing lasting bonds that transcend national borders. An integral part of France's strategic vision for North Africa lies in engaging proactively in environmental sustainability and climate change mitigation. Given the shared ecological challenges faced by the Mediterranean region, France envisions collaborative efforts to promote sustainable development, eco-friendly practices, and resource management to safeguard the natural heritage of North Africa. Furthermore, proactive managing migration and diaspora issues is central to shaping future relations. France seeks to develop coherent immigration policies that uphold humanitarian values while addressing practical concerns and providing pathways for integration and social cohesion. By recognizing the contributions of the North African diaspora and fostering meaningful dialogue, France endeavors to build a more inclusive society and bolster transnational connections. In conclusion, as France charts the course for its engagement with North Africa, the pursuit of shared prosperity, stability, and cultural exchange underscores the multifaceted nature of its strategic goals. By forging a path forward based on these objectives, France can reinforce its position as a valuable partner in the region, contributing to the collective advancement of Franco-North African interests.

# IN A NUTSHELL

## France's Influence in North Africa

### 1. Economic Impact and Trade Agreements

France has a significant economic presence in North Africa, primarily through trade agreements and investments. The EU-North Africa Association Agreements, initiated in the late 1990s, have been pivotal in fostering economic, trade, and financial cooperation between the EU and North African countries such as Tunisia, Morocco, Egypt, and Algeria. These agreements aimed to establish a Euro-Mediterranean free trade area, boosting trade in sectors like automotive and aerospace. However, the rise of emerging markets like China and Turkey has challenged the EU's market share in North Africa, leading to a deterioration in the trade balance for North African countries with the EU.

### 2. Political Influence and Diplomatic Engagements

France's political influence in North Africa is deeply rooted in its colonial history and continues through active diplomatic engagements. France maintains strong ties with countries like Morocco, Tunisia, and Algeria, although these relationships have faced challenges. For instance, tensions with Morocco over visa restrictions and diplomatic disputes have strained relations, while efforts to improve ties with Algeria have been met with mixed results. France's diplomatic strategy often involves balancing its historical ties with contemporary geopolitical interests, such as energy needs and regional stability.

## 3. Military Cooperation and Security Alliances

France has a robust military presence and security cooperation framework in North Africa. This includes military bases in countries like Djibouti and Senegal, and active participation in regional security initiatives. France's military strategy in the region focuses on counter-terrorism, peacekeeping, and supporting local security forces through training and joint operations. The recent shift towards "Africanisation" of military bases aims to increase the involvement of African troops and enhance local capabilities.

## 4. Cultural Ties and Linguistic Influence

Cultural and linguistic ties between France and North Africa are profound, stemming from the colonial era. French remains a significant language in countries like Morocco, where it is widely used in governance, commerce, and education. These cultural ties are reinforced through institutions like the Alliance Française and various cultural exchange programs that promote French language and culture in the region.

## 5. Education and Academic Collaborations

France has established numerous educational and academic collaborations with North African countries. These include partnerships between universities, research institutions, and academic exchange programs. Initiatives like the Erasmus+ program and the Marie Skłodowska-Curie actions support mobility and collaboration between European and African researchers, enhancing academic ties and capacity building in North African universities.

## 6. Development Aid and Infrastructure Projects

France is a major provider of development aid and infrastructure support in North Africa. Through the Agence Française de Développement (AFD), France funds various projects aimed at improving infrastructure, healthcare, education, and economic development in the region. These efforts are part of a broader strategy to promote stability and development, addressing the root causes of migration and economic disparity.

## 7. Immigration Policies and Diaspora Dynamics

France's immigration policies significantly impact its relations with North African countries. The large North African diaspora in France, particularly from Algeria, Morocco, and Tunisia, plays a crucial role in bilateral relations. Immigration policies have sometimes been a source of tension, as seen with the recent visa restrictions that affected diplomatic ties with Morocco. The diaspora also contributes to cultural and economic exchanges, maintaining strong transnational connections.

## 8. Challenges in Contemporary Relations

Contemporary relations between France and North Africa face several challenges, including geopolitical rivalries, economic competition, and social tensions. Issues like the Western Sahara conflict, visa policies, and the influence of other global powers like China and Russia complicate France's diplomatic efforts in the region. Additionally, internal political dynamics in North African countries, such as the rise of nationalist movements, pose challenges to maintaining stable and cooperative relations.

## 9. Future Prospects and Strategic Objectives

Looking ahead, France aims to strengthen its strategic objectives in North Africa through enhanced economic cooperation, deeper security alliances, and robust diplomatic engagements. The focus will likely be on fostering sustainable development, supporting regional stability, and addressing shared security threats like terrorism and cybercrime. France's strategy will also involve balancing its historical ties with the evolving geopolitical landscape, ensuring that its influence remains relevant and effective in the region.

In summary, France's influence in North Africa is multifaceted, encompassing economic, political, military, cultural, and educational dimensions. While there are significant challenges, the prospects for continued cooperation and strategic engagement remain strong, driven by mutual interests and historical ties.

# References For Further Reading

Aboderin, Isabella, Divine Fuh, Eyob Balcha Gebremariam, and Puleng Segalo. "Beyond 'Equitable Partnerships': The Imperative of Transformative Research Collaborations with Africa." Global Social Challenges Journal 2, no. 2 (December 1, 2023): 212–28. https://doi.org/10.1332/27523349Y2023D000000002.

Ahipeaud, Evelyne, Olivier Besson, Camille Bortolini, and Vincent Michel. "EU-North Africa Association Agreements and Trade Integration," December 2021. https://www.tresor.economie.gouv.fr/Articles/be8e5f08-ed3d-4060-ad72-cd7b9e32a152/files/bb2f4e83-f673-49f1-817b-8c210143e5fa.

Arab Center Washington DC. "Maghreb-France Relations as Macron Begins Second Term," March 1, 2023. https://arabcenterdc.org/resource/maghreb-france-relations-as-macron-begins-second-term/.

Berriault, Lea. "France Torn between Morocco and Algeria." GIS Reports, November 17, 2023. https://www.gisreportsonline.com/r/france-morocco-algeria/.

Direction générale du Trésor. "EU-North Africa Association Agreements and Trade Integration," December 21, 2021. https://www.tresor.economie.gouv.fr/Articles/2021/12/21/eu-north-africa-association-agreements-and-trade-integration.

Dworkin, Anthony. "The Maghreb Maze: Harmonising Divergent European Policies in North Africa." ECFR, January 30, 2024. https://ecfr.eu/publication/the-maghreb-maze-harmonising-divergent-european-policies-in-north-africa/.

Fontagné, Lionel, Nadia Rocha, Michele Ruta, and Gianluca Santoni. "The Economic Impact of Deepening Trade Agreements." Banque de France, February 14, 2022. https://www.banque-france.fr/en/publications-and-statistics/publications/economic-impact-deepening-trade-agreements.

France Diplomacy - Ministry for Europe and Foreign Affairs. "French Diplomacy in Africa: Global Issues," May 2021. https://www.diplomatie.gouv.fr/en/country-files/africa/french-diplomacy-in-africa-global-issues/.

France Diplomacy - Ministry for Europe and Foreign Affairs. "Security and Defence Cooperation Directorate (DCSD)," November 2021. https://www.diplomatie.gouv.fr/en/french-foreign-policy/security-disarmament-and-non-proliferation/security-and-defence-cooperation-directorate-dcsd/.

France Diplomacy - Ministry for Europe and Foreign Affairs. "Statement before the National Assembly by the Government on Renewed Partnerships between France and African Countries, Followed by a Debate, in Accordance with Article 50-1 of the Constitution – Address by Ms Catherine Colonna, Minister for Europe and Foreign Affairs (21.11.23)," November 21, 2023. https://www.diplomatie.gouv.fr/en/country-files/africa/news/article/statement-before-the-national-assembly-by-the-government-on-renewed.

France Diplomatie :: Ministry for Europe and Foreign Affairs. "The French Government's Trade Policy," 2017. https://www.diplomatie.gouv.fr/en/french-foreign-policy/economic-diplomacy-foreign-trade/the-french-government-s-trade-policy/.

IHEDN. "Afrique-France : Vers Un Nouveau Modèle de Partenariat Militaire." Institut des hautes études de défense nationale, March 22, 2023. https://ihedn.fr/en/2023/03/22/afrique-france-vers-un-nouveau-modele-de-partenariat-militaire/.

Maassen, Peter. "Recommendations for a New European Collaboration Strategy," February 2020. https://www.the-guild.eu/publications/insight-papers/insight-paper-one.pdf.

Ministry for Europe and Foreign Affairs. "Indo-Pacific Strategy." Accessed April 23, 2023. https://franceintheus.org/IMG/pdf/Indopacifique_web.pdf.

Secrétariat général de la défense et de la sécurité national. "National Strategic Review 2022," 2022. https://www.sgdsn.gouv.fr/files/files/rns-uk-20221202.pdf.

# XXI

# Soft Power and Public Diplomacy

## Introduction to Soft Power in International Relations

Soft power, a term coined by Joseph Nye, refers to the ability of a country to influence others through non-coercive means, such as culture, political values, and foreign policies. In contemporary international relations, soft power has powerfully shaped global perceptions and built sustainable diplomatic relationships. Unlike hard power, which relies on military force and economic coercion, soft power leverages a nation's attractiveness and persuasive appeal to achieve its foreign policy objectives. Countries can effectively project their values and ideas onto the international stage by strategically deploying cultural assets, media presence, and collaborative initiatives. Additionally, soft power encompasses the capacity to shape norms and influence the behavior of other states without resorting to overt aggression or punitive measures. As globalization continues to blur geographical boundaries and interconnect societies, the significance of soft power as a tool for international influence has become increasingly pronounced. It plays a pivotal role in fostering cross-cultural understanding, promoting dialogue, and mitigating conflicts, thereby maintaining global peace and stability. The effectiveness of soft power lies in its ability to engender goodwill and trust among target audiences, ultimately facilitating diplomatic breakthroughs and productive engagements. In an era characterized by complex geopolitical dynamics and transnational challenges, nations with robust soft power capabilities are better positioned to navigate the intricacies of modern statecraft and secure mutually beneficial partnerships. Moreover, aligning soft power strategies with ethical principles and respect for diversity enhances a country's standing in the international community, elevating its reputation as a responsible global actor. Therefore, grasping the nuances of soft power and harnessing its potential offers substantial advantages in achieving strategic objectives and advancing national interests within the evolving landscape of international relations.

> ## *Soft power*
> ## *The ability to influence without coercion*
> **Definition:** The capacity to shape the preferences of others through appeal and attraction, using culture, political values, and foreign policies.
> **Contrasted With:** Hard power, which involves coercion and the use of force.
> **Popularized by:** Joseph Nye of Harvard University in his 1990 book 'Bound to Lead: The Changing Nature of American Power'.
> **Further Development:** Joseph Nye expanded on the concept in his 2004 book, 'Soft Power: The Means to Success in World Politics'.
> **Key Insight:** "The best propaganda is not propaganda," and in the Information Age, "credibility is the scarcest resource."

## Historical Evolution of France's Public Diplomacy

France has a rich history of employing public diplomacy as a strategic tool to influence global affairs. The historical evolution of French public diplomacy can be traced back to the era of colonial expansion, where cultural and linguistic ties were established with various regions worldwide. During this period, France utilized its colonial networks to promote the French language, culture, and values, laying the foundation for its future soft power endeavors. Additionally, establishing French cultural institutions such as the Alliance Française and cultural centers abroad greatly contributed to disseminating French culture and ideas. As France emerged from the shadows of colonialism and World War II, it sought to redefine its international image by emphasizing cultural diplomacy and cooperation. The post-war period witnessed the concept of 'cultural exception,' wherein France aimed to safeguard its cultural heritage while simultaneously projecting it on the global stage. This led to the promotion of French literature, arts, cinema, and intellectual discourse as tools of diplomacy. Furthermore, creating institutions like the Institut Français and TV5 Monde reinforced French cultural presence worldwide. The evolution of media played a pivotal role in shaping France's public diplomacy efforts. With the advent of television and later digital media, France strategically utilized platforms like France 24, RFI (Radio France Internationale), and other media entities to broadcast its perspectives to international audiences. These initiatives enhanced France's global outreach and facilitated cross-cultural dialogue. Moreover, the collaborative efforts of French and international media organizations contributed to the exchange of diverse viewpoints, thereby advancing France's diplomatic goals. Over time, France has expanded its public diplomacy through educational exchanges and academic partnerships. Promoting French language and culture in educational curricula abroad and scholarship programs such as the Eiffel scholarships and Erasmus+ has solidified France's influence in education and knowledge sharing. In summary, the historical evolution of France's public diplomacy underscores its continuous adaptation to global changes, leveraging cultural, educational, and media assets to strengthen its soft power and public image.

## *Key Tools and Mechanisms of French Soft Power*

French soft power leverages various tools and mechanisms to shape international perceptions, build influence, and forge strong diplomatic ties. At the core of France's soft power strategy lies its commitment to promoting the French language and culture to foster connections with people around the world. The Alliance Française network, comprising over 800 establishments globally, plays a pivotal role in this endeavor by offering French language courses, cultural events, and exchanges, bolstering cross-cultural understanding and cooperation.

In addition to linguistic outreach, France capitalizes on its rich cultural heritage and artistic expressions to engage global audiences. The Institut Français, under the purview of the Ministry of Foreign Affairs, serves as a vital platform for showcasing French creativity and innovation through various initiatives such as exhibitions, screenings, and performances. These cultural showcases serve as a conduit for dialogue and mutual appreciation, cultivating lasting bonds between France and other nations.

Moreover, France recognizes the profound influence of its media and communication channels in shaping international narratives. Media entities like France 24 and TV5 Monde not only disseminate French perspectives but also offer a window into diverse cultural narratives, underscoring the country's commitment to open dialogue and exchange of ideas across borders. France's prowess in the film industry, marked by the Cannes Film Festival and world-renowned auteurs, amplifies its soft power projection, capturing global imagination and fostering admiration for French cinematic artistry.

Educational diplomacy is another keystone of France's soft power arsenal, as evidenced by the robust network of French international schools and renowned universities that attract students worldwide.

France nurtures the next generation of global leaders through academic partnerships, research collaborations, and student mobility programs. It fosters enduring intellectual exchange, solidifying its standing as an academic powerhouse and incubator of multicultural knowledge.

Furthermore, France's engagement in sports, particularly football, is a unifying force transcending geographical boundaries and promoting goodwill. France amplifies its soft power reach by hosting prestigious sporting events and nurturing athletic talent, underscoring shared values and camaraderie across nations.

The multifaceted nature of French soft power, encompassing language, culture, media, education, and sports, underscores its efficacy in building bridges and nurturing enduring relationships. By harnessing these key tools and mechanisms, France continues to carve a distinctive imprint on the global stage, embodying the profound impact of soft power in contemporary statecraft.

## *Cultural Institutes and Language Promotion Abroad*

Cultural institutes and language promotion programs are pivotal in globalizing French soft power. These institutions, such as the Alliance Française and Institut Français, act as hubs for cultural exchange, educational outreach, and linguistic immersion. Through these entities, France showcases its rich cultural heritage, fosters cross-cultural understanding, strengthens diplomatic ties, and promotes the French language as a vehicle for international communication.

The Alliance Française, with its extensive network of branches worldwide, serves as a platform for promoting French language and culture through language courses, cultural events, and exchange programs. It enables individuals from diverse backgrounds to immerse themselves in the French language and engage with the country's arts, literature, and traditions. In doing so, it facilitates meaningful people-to-people connections and nurtures an appreciation for French culture beyond national borders.

Simultaneously, the Institut Français, operating under the aegis of the French Ministry of Foreign Affairs, conducts various activities to bolster France's cultural influence on the global stage. These initiatives encompass artistic collaborations, film festivals, literary events, and exhibitions, which contribute to projecting France's contemporary and dynamic image abroad. Furthermore, the Institut Français actively supports cultural cooperation projects, fostering dialogue and mutual understanding between French and international artists, intellectuals, and thought leaders.

Moreover, the Alliance Française and Institut Français serve as platforms for diplomatic outreach, often organizing events and forums that bring together influential stakeholders from governmental, academic, and cultural spheres. By providing spaces for dialogue and collaboration, these institutions play a crucial role in advancing France's soft power through cultural diplomacy, ultimately shaping positive perceptions of France and its values.

Additionally, the proliferation of French cultural institutes and language promotion programs in the Arab world signifies France's commitment to enhancing its presence and influence in the region. Pursuing cultural and linguistic exchanges with Arab states facilitates intercultural dialogue and fosters enduring relationships based on shared cultural appreciation. This cultural bridge-building nurtures goodwill and lays the groundwork for deeper diplomatic engagement and collaboration.

In conclusion, cultural institutes and language promotion abroad are indispensable elements of the French soft power strategy. They serve as conduits for cultural diplomacy, foster mutual understanding, and project an alluring image of France globally.

## Media, Communication Channels, and Brand Image

In international relations, projecting a nation's image holds immense significance. France, with its rich cultural heritage and influential intellectual productions, has strategically utilized media and communication channels to bolster its brand image on the global stage. Through a carefully crafted narrative, France positions itself as a hub of creativity, innovation, and sophistication, leveraging soft power to enhance its diplomatic influence.

The strategic deployment of media plays a pivotal role in shaping public perception and fostering positive relationships with foreign audiences. French public diplomacy extensively employs television, radio, print publications, and digital platforms to disseminate diverse narratives encapsulating the country's multifaceted identity. From showcasing the allure of Parisian haute couture to highlighting avant-garde artistic movements and technological advancements, these media channels serve as conduits for projecting a contemporary and dynamic French identity.

Furthermore, France harnesses its communication outreach to amplify its commitment to global issues such as sustainability, human rights, and cultural diversity. Collaborations with international media outlets and hosting high-profile events exemplify France's endeavor to showcase its dedication to progressive values and contribute to meaningful discourse on a global scale.

Central to France's public diplomacy strategy is cultivating a distinctive brand image that resonates across borders. 'Brand France' encompasses the country's renowned luxury brands and culinary expertise and its achievements in science, technology, and architecture. By consistently presenting this cohesive narrative, France builds an enduring and recognizable brand associated with excellence and cultural refinement.

Moreover, using communication channels to highlight collaborative ventures and partnerships with Arab states amplifies the notion of France as an inclusive and engaged diplomatic actor. Emphasizing mutual respect and understanding, France fosters long-term relationships through media diplomacy, forging bonds based on reciprocal cooperation and shared values. This proactive engagement lays the foundation for sustained dialogue and collaboration, underscoring the robust nature of Franco-Arab relations.

In conclusion, the thoughtful integration of media and communication channels and the cultivation of a compelling brand image are integral components of France's public diplomacy toolbox. Through purposeful storytelling and strategic messaging, France asserts its position as a global influencer, weaving a narrative that amplifies its cultural, artistic, and intellectual prowess while affirming its commitment to collaborative partnerships. Through these mediums, France continues to shape narratives, strengthen diplomatic ties, and cultivate enduring connections with the international community.

## *Educational Outreach and Scholar Exchanges*

Educational outreach and scholar exchanges are crucial aspects of France's public diplomacy strategy, as powerful tools for fostering mutual understanding and cooperation with Arab states. Through targeted initiatives and partnerships, France has successfully promoted its rich cultural heritage and academic expertise while engaging in constructive dialogue and knowledge exchange. The French government, academic institutions, and educational organizations have developed comprehensive programs to enhance educational ties and nurture future leaders. The focus on educational outreach encompasses various activities, including student exchange programs, joint research ventures, and academic collaborations. These initiatives facilitate the transfer of knowledge and expertise and cultivate a global mindset among participants. By providing opportunities for Arab students and scholars to study in France and vice versa, these exchanges create invaluable cross-cultural experiences and forge lasting personal and professional connections.

France's active involvement in educational outreach extends beyond higher education and includes efforts to enhance curriculum development, promote language learning, and support vocational training in Arab countries. Through strategic investments in educational infrastructure and capacity-building projects, France aims to empower local institutions and contribute to advancing education systems in the region. Moreover, the emphasis on promoting the French language as a tool for intellectual and cultural exchange underscores France's commitment to nurturing linguistic diversity and fostering multilingualism. As part of its engagement in scholar exchanges, France encourages collaborative research initiatives, academic conferences, and joint publications to facilitate the sharing of ideas and best practices. By harnessing the intellectual capital of both French and Arab scholars, these endeavors enrich academic discourse, drive innovation, and address shared societal challenges. Additionally, visiting professorships, academic chairs, and research grants promote sustained academic partnerships and knowledge transfer between France and Arab states. In essence, educational outreach and scholar exchanges serve as foundational building blocks in enhancing Franco-Arab relations, shaping a positive narrative of academic collaboration, and laying the groundwork for a prosperous and interconnected future. Embracing diversity, fostering intellectual curiosity, and investing in human capital are essential tenets of France's enduring commitment to leveraging education for positive change and mutual prosperity.

## Influence Through Arts, Literature, and Cinema

France's rich cultural heritage has significantly driven its worldwide soft power and public diplomacy efforts. Through promoting its arts, literature, and cinema, France has showcased its values, creativity, and intellectual prowess to global audiences, including those in the Arab states. The enduring appeal of French literary giants such as Victor Hugo, Albert Camus, and Marcel Proust continues to captivate readers worldwide, fostering an appreciation for the French language and thought. France's iconic artistic movements, from Impressionism to Surrealism, have left an indelible mark on the international art scene, serving as a testament to the country's enduring cultural influence. Furthermore, French cinema, with masterpieces from luminaries like Jean-Luc Godard, François Truffaut, and Agnès Varda, has entertained and enlightened audiences globally, providing a lens into French society and values. In Franco-Arab relations, the exchange of artistic and literary works has served as a bridge for mutual understanding and dialogue between the two cultures. France's cultural diplomacy initiatives have facilitated collaborative projects that have brought together artists, writers, and filmmakers from France and Arab states, resulting in the cross-pollination of ideas, storytelling traditions, and creative expressions. Through film festivals, literary exchanges, and art exhibitions, France has showcased the diversity and vibrancy of Arab culture to French audiences while also introducing the richness of French artistic and literary traditions to audiences in Arab states. These cultural exchanges have bolstered people-to-people ties and fostered a deeper appreciation for the shared human experiences that transcend geographical and cultural boundaries. Moreover, by nurturing cultural collaborations, France has sought to underscore the universal values of liberty, equality, and fraternity that underpin its cultural ethos, thereby forging enduring connections with the Arab world based on mutual respect and appreciation. Exploring and celebrating arts, literature, and cinema have become instrumental drivers of French public diplomacy, facilitating meaningful intercultural dialogue and engendering a sense of solidarity and interconnectedness between France and the Arab states.

## *Partnerships and Collaborations with Arab States*

France has a long history of fostering partnerships and collaborations with Arab states, recognizing the strategic importance of these relationships in various domains. In the political arena, France has worked closely with Arab states on matters of mutual concern, such as regional stability, counterterrorism, and conflict resolution. This collaboration has often taken the form of high-level dialogues, joint initiatives, and diplomatic mediation efforts to address complex geopolitical challenges. The economic ties between France and Arab states have also been robust, encompassing trade relations, investment ventures, and energy partnerships. French companies have actively engaged in sectors such as infrastructure development, energy production, and technology transfer, contributing to the economic growth and modernization of Arab countries. Additionally, France has promoted cultural exchanges and educational cooperation as essential pillars of its engagement with Arab states. This includes initiatives to preserve and promote Arab cultural heritage, facilitate academic interchanges, and foster linguistic exchanges through educational programs and scholarships. Furthermore, France has endeavored to strengthen scientific and technological collaborations, particularly in areas such as research and innovation, aiming to harness collective expertise for addressing contemporary global challenges. In the realm of security and defense, France has cooperated with Arab states to enhance defense capabilities, conduct joint military exercises, and bolster security mechanisms to counter shared threats effectively. This collaboration has included intelligence-sharing, capacity-building efforts, and military training programs, reflecting a commitment to safeguarding regional peace and stability. Moreover, France has actively participated in multilateral forums and institutions alongside Arab states, advocating for common interests, promoting dialogue, and advancing cooperative frameworks to address global issues collectively. Overall, the enduring partnerships and collaborations between France and Arab states underscore the multifaceted nature of their relationship, demonstrating a commitment to mutual prosperity, peace, and progress.

## Case Studies: Successful Diplomatic Engagements

In examining Franco-Arab relations, it becomes apparent that the successful diplomatic engagements between France and Arab states have been pivotal in shaping the broader landscape of international affairs. One notable case study pertains to the partnership between France and the United Arab Emirates (UAE). This collaborative alliance has transcended traditional diplomatic ties and delved into extensive cooperation within various sectors, including defense, technology, and cultural exchange. The establishment of the Louvre Abu Dhabi, a groundbreaking cultural project, is a testament to the fruitful collaboration between the two nations. Furthermore, the joint efforts in counterterrorism initiatives and security cooperation showcase the depth of their diplomatic engagement, exemplifying effective bilateral relations. Another compelling case study is the enduring partnership between France and Morocco. This diplomatic alliance encompasses multifaceted cooperation, from economic trade and investment to shared commitment toward sustainable development and environmental conservation. The strategic alignment on key regional and global issues underscores the strength and resilience of their diplomatic endeavors. Moreover, France's support for Morocco's modernization and education reform initiatives has reinforced the bilateral relations, fostering mutual trust and understanding. Additionally, the collaborative efforts in addressing migration challenges and promoting socio-economic development further underscore the successful diplomatic engagements between the two nations. These case studies not only exemplify the effectiveness of French diplomacy in the Arab world but also shed light on the tangible benefits of such robust alliances, emphasizing the significance of successful diplomatic engagements in fostering long-term partnerships and mutual prosperity.

## Challenges and Future Prospects

As France continues to wield its soft power and engage in public diplomacy with the Arab world, it faces many challenges and must consider prospects for sustaining its influence. One significant challenge is the ever-evolving geopolitical landscape, characterized by shifting alliances and power dynamics. The rise of non-state actors and the increasing influence of emerging global powers present complexities that can impact France's diplomatic endeavors. Additionally, the digital age has transformed the nature of communication and information dissemination, posing opportunities and challenges in shaping public opinion and maintaining a positive image abroad.

Another area of concern relates to cultural diplomacy. While France has a rich cultural heritage, ensuring its cultural outreach remains relevant and resonates with diverse audiences is a continuous challenge. Adapting to the changing preferences and interests of younger generations, especially in the digital realm, presents an ongoing task for French public diplomacy officials. Moreover, language barriers and nuances in cultural contexts require a nuanced approach to convey the desired message without misinterpretation effectively.

Furthermore, France's ability to align its soft power initiatives with these priorities will be crucial as the international community grapples with pressing issues such as climate change, sustainable development, and global health crises. Navigating the intersection of diplomatic objectives and broader global challenges while addressing societal expectations and demands necessitates strategic planning and adaptability.

Looking toward the future, France must consider opportunities to leverage its strengths and innovation in technology, education, and sustainability to shape its public diplomacy strategies. Embracing advancements in digital diplomacy, harnessing the potential of social media, and fostering partnerships with civil society organizations can enhance France's visibility and engagement in the Arab world. Investing in educational and cultural exchanges, promoting intercultural dialogue, and supporting youth empowerment initiatives can position France for a more inclusive and impactful public diplomacy approach.

In conclusion, while challenges persist in public diplomacy, France has the potential to pursue enduring and mutually beneficial relationships with the Arab world. By addressing these challenges proactively and seizing prospects, France can continue to exercise soft power that fosters understanding, collaboration, and sustainable partnerships across borders.

# IN A NUTSHELL

## Soft Power and Public Diplomacy

### 1. Introduction to Soft Power in International Relations

Soft power, a term coined by Joseph Nye, refers to the ability to influence others through attraction and persuasion rather than coercion or payment. It involves shaping the preferences of others through appeal and attraction, leveraging cultural values, political ideals, and foreign policies to achieve foreign policy objectives. Unlike hard power, which relies on military and economic might, soft power uses non-coercive means to build networks, communicate compelling narratives, and establish international norms.

### 2. Historical Evolution of France's Public Diplomacy

France has a long history of using public diplomacy to enhance its global influence. During the 17th and 18th centuries, France promoted its culture throughout Europe, making French the language of diplomacy. The French Revolution further expanded France's soft power by promoting revolutionary ideals across Europe. In the modern era, France has continued to leverage its cultural and linguistic heritage through institutions like the Alliance Française and the Institut Français, which promote French language and culture worldwide.

## 3. Key Tools and Mechanisms of French Soft Power

France employs a variety of tools and mechanisms to project its soft power, including cultural diplomacy, educational exchanges, and media outreach. Cultural diplomacy involves promoting French culture through festivals, exhibitions, and artistic exchanges. Educational diplomacy includes scholarships, academic partnerships, and student exchanges that enhance France's global reputation. Media and digital diplomacy leverage platforms like social media to shape public opinion and promote French values.

## 4. Cultural Institutes and Language Promotion Abroad

Institutions like the Alliance Française and the Institut Français play a crucial role in promoting French language and culture abroad. These institutes offer language courses, cultural events, and educational programs that foster a positive image of France and strengthen cultural ties with other countries. The extensive network of these institutes ensures a broad reach, enhancing France's cultural influence globally.

## 5. Media, Communication Channels, and Brand Image

France utilizes various media and communication channels to enhance its brand image and influence. Traditional media, such as television and radio, along with digital platforms like social media, are used to disseminate French culture, values, and policies. Public diplomacy efforts include broadcasting French news and cultural programs internationally, which helps shape global perceptions of France. The strategic use of media ensures that France remains visible and influential in global conversations.

## 6. *Educational Outreach and Scholar Exchanges*

Educational outreach is a cornerstone of France's soft power strategy. Programs like Erasmus+ and partnerships with international universities facilitate student and scholar exchanges, promoting French education and fostering international collaboration. Scholarships and academic grants attract international students to French institutions, enhancing France's reputation as a center of learning and innovation.

## 7. *Influence Through Arts, Literature, and Cinema*

France's rich cultural heritage in arts, literature, and cinema is a powerful tool of soft power. French films, literature, and art are celebrated worldwide, contributing to France's cultural prestige. Events like the Cannes Film Festival and the promotion of French literature and art exhibitions abroad help maintain France's cultural influence and attract global admiration.

## 8. *Partnerships and Collaborations with Arab States*

France has established strong cultural and educational partnerships with Arab states, leveraging historical ties and mutual interests. These collaborations include cultural exchanges, joint educational programs, and support for cultural institutions in Arab countries. Such partnerships enhance France's influence in the Arab world and promote mutual understanding and cooperation.

## 9. Case Studies: Successful Diplomatic Engagements

Several case studies highlight the success of France's soft power and public diplomacy. For instance, the Alliance Française's extensive network in North Africa has significantly promoted French language and culture, strengthening France's ties with the region. Another example is France's role in the UNESCO World Heritage program, where it has successfully advocated for the preservation of cultural sites, enhancing its global cultural leadership.

## 10. Challenges and Future Prospects

Despite its successes, France faces challenges in maintaining and expanding its soft power. Global competition from other cultural powers, political tensions, and economic constraints can hinder France's public diplomacy efforts. However, by continuing to innovate in cultural diplomacy, expanding educational outreach, and leveraging digital platforms, France can sustain and enhance its influence. Future prospects include deepening cultural and educational ties with emerging markets and adapting to the evolving global landscape. In conclusion, France's strategic use of soft power and public diplomacy has been instrumental in maintaining its global influence. By leveraging its cultural heritage, educational excellence, and media presence, France continues to shape international perceptions and foster global cooperation.

# References For Further Reading

Yolanda Smits, Clémentine Daubeuf, Philippe Kern. (2016) "European Cultural Institutes Abroad".the European Parliament's Committee on Culture and Education. https://www.europarl.europa.eu/RegData/etudes/STUD/2016/563418/IPOL_STU%282016%29563418_EN.pdf

Abratis, Julien. "PUBLIC POLICY MASTER THESIS the Role of EU Delegations in Public Diplomacy Challenges and Opportunities," 2020. https://www.sciencespo.fr/public/sites/sciencespo.fr.public/files/ABRATIS%20Julien%20-%20Thesis%20EAP.pdf.

Ens-lyon.fr. "Soft Power (Puissance Douce) — Géoconfluences," 2019. http://geoconfluences.ens-lyon.fr/glossaire/soft-power.

Grix, Jonathan, and Paul Michael Brannagan. "Of Mechanisms and Myths: Conceptualising States' 'Soft Power' Strategies through Sports Mega-Events." Diplomacy & Statecraft 27, no. 2 (April 2, 2016): 251–72.

MARTIN, Virginie . "French Revolution and Diplomatic Practice (The)." Encyclopédie d'histoire numérique de l'Europe. Accessed May 24, 2024. https://ehne.fr/en/encyclopedia/themes/european-humanism/diplomatic-practices/french-revolution-and-diplomatic-practice.

Matteucci, Aldo. "Soft Power: The Means to Success in World Politics." Diplo, 2005. https://www.diplomacy.edu/resource/soft-power-the-means-to-success-in-world-politics/.

Meierding, Emily, and Rachel Sigman. "Understanding the Mechanisms of

International Influence in an Era of Great Power Competition." Journal of Global Security Studies 6, no. 4 (April 8, 2021). https://doi.org/10.1093/jogss/ogab011.

Nye Jr, Joseph . "» Soft Power." International Relations, n.d. http://internationalrelations.org/soft-power/.

Nye, Joseph. "Soft Power: The Origins and Political Progress of a Concept." Palgrave Communications 3, no. 17008 (February 21, 2017). https://doi.org/10.1057/palcomms.2017.8.

Siracusa, Joseph M., 'Evolution of diplomacy', Diplomatic History: A Very Short Introduction, 2nd edn, Very Short Introductions (Oxford, 2021; online edn, Oxford Academic, 22 July 2021), https://doi.org/10.1093/actrade/9780192893918.003.0001, accessed 24 May 2024.

Soft Power 30. "What Is Soft Power?" The Soft Power 30. Portland, 2015. https://softpower30.com/what-is-soft-power/.

UNESCO. "Cutting Edge | from Standing out to Reaching Out: Cultural Diplomacy for Sustainable Development | UNESCO." www.unesco.org, January 27, 2022. https://www.unesco.org/en/articles/cutting-edge-standing-out-reaching-out-cultural-diplomacy-sustainable-development.

Wagner, Jan-Philipp. "The Effectiveness of Soft & Hard Power in Contemporary International Relations." E-International Relations, May 14, 2014. https://www.e-ir.info/2014/05/14/the-effectiveness-of-soft-hard-power-in-contemporary-international-relations/.

# XXII

# Gender Equality and Women's Rights

## Historical Context of Gender Issues in Franco-Arab Relations

In exploring the historical context of gender issues in Franco-Arab relations, it is essential to delve into the intricate tapestry of cultural, societal, and political factors that have shaped the status of women in both regions. A complex interplay of traditions, religious influences, and evolving ideologies marks the history of gender relations in France and Arab countries. In the Arab world, traditional social structures often relegated women to subordinate roles, defined by domestic duties and limited access to education and employment opportunities. However, it is crucial to acknowledge that the historical experiences of gender relations across the diverse Arab countries are multifaceted and not monolithic. Similarly, in the context of France, gender dynamics have been shaped by historical events, such as the French Revolution, which sparked discussions on equality and citizenship rights. The evolution of gender relations in France was also influenced by colonial legacies and interactions with its former Maghreb and Middle East colonies. It is imperative to recognize the profound impact of these historical trajectories on contemporary policies and attitudes toward gender equality. Influential moments, such as the feminist movements in France and the Arab world, have played pivotal roles in challenging patriarchal norms and advocating for women's rights. These movements have contributed to the formulation of legislative frameworks aimed at addressing gender disparities and promoting equality. Furthermore, historical milestones, including landmark legal reforms and women's participation in political and societal spheres, have significantly influenced gender issues in Franco-Arab relations. This historical analysis provides valuable insights into the complexities of gender dynamics in both regions and underscores the need for nuanced approaches to promote gender equality and women's empowerment.

## *Legislative Frameworks for Women's Rights in France and Arab Countries*

The legislative frameworks for women's rights in France and Arab countries reflect the complex intersection of culture, tradition, and international human rights standards. In France, significant strides have been made to ensure gender equality and women's empowerment through a series of legislative measures. These include laws addressing equal pay, gender-based discrimination, reproductive rights, and domestic violence. The landmark legislation, such as the Parity Law of 2000, which mandates gender balance in political representation, has reshaped the political landscape and paved the way for increased female participation in decision-making processes. Moreover, the 2014 Gender Equality Law reinforced efforts to combat gender-based violence and promote workplace equality.

Contrastingly, the legislative landscape in Arab countries varies considerably due to diverse cultural, religious, and legal systems. While some nations have introduced progressive reforms, others continue to grapple with deeply entrenched patriarchal structures and discriminatory practices. For instance, Tunisia stands out as a trailblazer in the region, enacting robust laws to safeguard women's rights and promote gender parity. Its 1956 Code of Personal Status abolished polygamy and instituted key provisions guaranteeing women's rights to education, employment, and inheritance. Similarly, Morocco's 2004 Family Code represented a significant leap forward in recognizing women's rights within a legal framework, albeit challenges persist in its effective enforcement.

However, in some conservative jurisdictions, existing laws may perpetuate gender disparities and restrict women's autonomy. Legal provisions relating to inheritance, marriage, divorce, and child custody often raise concerns about unequal treatment and undermine women's agency. Moreover, societal norms and customary practices can exert substantial influence, sometimes overshadowing legal protections and hindering the realization of gender equality.

At the international level, conventions such as the Convention on the Elimination of All Forms of Discrimination Against Women (CEDAW) provide a crucial framework for monitoring and advocating for legislative reforms that uphold women's rights. By examining the varied legislative landscapes in France and Arab countries, we gain insights into the multifaceted approaches and persistent challenges surrounding women's rights. While legislative reforms are essential, their impactful implementation and alignment with societal attitudes remain integral to fostering lasting change and achieving true gender equality.

## *Comparative Analysis of Gender Equality Measures*

Gender equality measures in France and Arab countries have been the subject of intense scrutiny and comparison as they reflect these societies' broader social, cultural, and political dynamics. In France, the evolution of gender equality measures has been shaped by a legacy of feminist activism, the impact of Enlightenment ideals, and a strong emphasis on laïcité, or secularism. This has led to progressive legislation such as the right to vote (1944), access to birth control (1967), and the legal recognition of reproductive rights. Additionally, France has implemented affirmative action policies and gender quotas to promote women's representation in politics and corporate leadership roles. In contrast, Arab countries vary significantly in their approaches to gender equality measures, influenced by Islamic jurisprudence, tribal traditions, and historical legacies of colonialism. While some nations have made strides in guaranteeing women's rights through constitutional amendments and legal reforms, others continue to grapple with gender disparities in areas such as inheritance, divorce, and custody laws. The comparative analysis examines the nuances and complexities of gender equality measures across these diverse contexts, shedding light on the interplay between religion, culture, and modernization. It considers the role of international conventions and human rights frameworks in influencing policy reforms and fostering dialogue on gender issues. Moreover, the analysis delves into the socio-economic implications of gender disparities, highlighting how unequal access to employment, education, and healthcare perpetuates systemic inequalities. By juxtaposing the experiences of French and Arab women, this comparative analysis aims to challenge stereotypes and misconceptions, emphasizing the shared aspirations for dignity, autonomy, and equality. It underscores the importance of cross-cultural exchanges and collaborative initiatives to advance gender equality globally, transcending geographical boundaries and ideological divides.

## Impact of Educational Initiatives on Women's Empowerment

Educational initiatives are pivotal in fostering women's empowerment within Franco-Arab relations. By providing access to quality education, young women are equipped with the necessary knowledge and skills to engage in various spheres of society actively. Across both France and Arab countries, efforts to bolster educational opportunities for girls and women have yielded profound impacts on gender equality and women's rights. In France, implementing policies to enhance educational inclusivity has significantly contributed to narrowing the gender gap. Through reforms in curriculum design and the promotion of STEM subjects, the educational landscape has become more conducive for young women to pursue traditionally male-dominated fields, thus challenging societal stereotypes and promoting gender parity. Similarly, in Arab countries, targeted initiatives to improve female literacy rates and expand educational resources have catalyzed socio-economic changes. As more girls gain access to education, traditional gender roles are being redefined, paving the way for increased female participation in the labor market and political arena. Furthermore, educational programs emphasizing leadership development and civic engagement nurture a new generation of empowered women poised to effect positive change in their respective societies. However, despite significant progress, challenges persist, such as disparities in educational access based on geographic location or socio-economic status. In some conservative communities, resistance to co-educational systems and limited secondary education options for girls hinder the realization of educational equity. Therefore, a multi-faceted approach involving government interventions, community partnerships, and international collaboration is essential to address these impediments and ensure that educational initiatives continue to be powerful in advancing women's empowerment. Looking ahead, it is imperative to sustain the momentum of educational reforms and expand efforts to promote lifelong learning opportunities for women, thereby creating a more equitable and inclusive society.

## *Economic Opportunities and the Gender Gap*

The economic landscape is pivotal in shaping gender equality within Franco-Arab relations. As countries strive for socioeconomic progress, it is essential to address the existing gender gap in economic opportunities. In France and Arab countries, women have made notable strides in pursuing higher education and professional careers. However, disparities in access to leadership positions, equal pay, and entrepreneurship persist. This section delves into the multifaceted dimensions of the gender gap within the economic sphere.

Economic opportunities for women are intricately linked to labor force participation and representation in decision-making roles. Despite the increased presence of women in the workforce, specific sectors continue to be dominated by males, perpetuating unequal access to career growth and remuneration. Similarly, the prevalence of glass ceilings hinders women from ascending to upper management and executive positions, thereby amplifying the gender disparity in leadership roles.

Furthermore, the gender pay gap remains a poignant issue, with women earning less than their male counterparts for similar work. This phenomenon undermines financial security and contributes to long-term wealth discrepancies. Consequently, addressing pay inequity is paramount in ensuring fair and just economic empowerment for women across both French and Arab societies.

In addition to traditional employment, fostering an environment conducive to female entrepreneurship is imperative in bridging the gender gap. Supporting women-led startups, access to capital, and tailored mentorship programs can unlock a wave of innovation and economic potential. By encouraging entrepreneurial ventures, governments, and private entities can actively contribute to narrowing the economic disparities between men and women.

Moreover, the impact of cultural and societal factors on economic opportunities cannot be understated. Social norms, stereotypes, and biases often create barriers for women seeking to enter non-traditional fields or pursue ambitious career paths. Addressing these embedded cultural obstacles is crucial in effecting substantial change and dismantling the systemic constraints that impede women's economic advancement.

In conclusion, achieving gender equality in economic opportunities necessitates a holistic approach encompassing legislative reforms, corporate policies, educational initiatives, and societal evolution. By mitigating the gender gap in economic empowerment, Franco-Arab relations can harness the full potential of their collective workforce and drive sustainable progress.

## *Cultural Barriers and Societal Shifts*

Cultural barriers and societal shifts play a pivotal role in shaping the landscape of gender equality within the context of Franco-Arab relations. The deeply rooted cultural norms, traditional values, and societal expectations often create significant barriers to women's empowerment and gender equality. In many Arab societies, patriarchal structures have been ingrained for generations, leading to inherent bias and discrimination against women in various aspects of life, including education, employment, and political participation. These deep-seated cultural barriers perpetuate gender disparities and hinder progress toward achieving equal rights for women. However, it is crucial to acknowledge that societal shifts occur at varying paces across different regions and communities. There is an ongoing evolution in attitudes and perceptions towards gender roles, driven by urbanization, globalization, and increased access to education and information. These shifts reflect a gradual change in societal mindset, particularly among younger generations, who are increasingly challenging traditional gender norms and advocating for greater gender equality. With the emergence of social movements and activism, there is a growing momentum for redefining cultural narratives and promoting inclusivity and diversity. Moreover, global interconnectedness has facilitated the exchange of ideas and values, contributing to the diffusion of progressive attitudes regarding gender equality. This interplay between cultural barriers and societal shifts underscores the complex dynamics at play within Franco-Arab relations. It calls for a multifaceted approach that recognizes the importance of respecting cultural diversity while simultaneously championing women's rights and fostering inclusive societies. Embracing these societal shifts and addressing deeply entrenched cultural barriers are integral to advancing gender equality and empowering women in both French and Arab contexts. By strategically navigating these intricate dynamics, stakeholders can work towards fostering a more equitable and progressive environment where women have the opportunity to thrive and contribute meaningfully to society.

## *Role of NGOs and International Bodies*

Non-governmental organizations (NGOs) and international bodies are crucial in promoting gender equality and women's rights in Franco-Arab relations. These entities often catalyze change by advocating for policy reforms, conducting research, and directly supporting marginalized women and communities. In the Franco-Arab context, several prominent NGOs such as Oxfam, Human Rights Watch, and UN Women have been actively addressing gender disparities and promoting women's empowerment initiatives. These organizations collaborate with local partners and governments to implement impactful programs that address specific challenges faced by women in diverse cultural and social settings. Their efforts range from advocating for legal reforms to providing essential services such as healthcare, education, and economic opportunities for women. Additionally, these NGOs work towards awareness-raising and capacity-building to foster a more inclusive and equitable society. Furthermore, international bodies like the United Nations (UN) and the European Union (EU) play a pivotal role in shaping policies and frameworks that promote gender equality on a global scale. Agencies such as UN Women and the UN Population Fund (UNFPA) provide technical assistance and financial support to projects aimed at improving the status of women in the Arab world and enhancing their participation in socio-economic development. Through various initiatives, the EU supports gender mainstreaming efforts and advocates for women's rights as an integral part of its foreign policy agenda. The collaborative efforts of NGOs and international bodies contribute to advancing gender equality by fostering dialogue, sharing best practices, and mobilizing resources to address systemic challenges. Their involvement strengthens diplomatic ties and fosters cross-cultural understanding, ultimately working towards a more egalitarian and inclusive Franco-Arab partnership.

## *Case Studies: Success Stories of Gender Equality*

In exploring the realm of gender equality and women's rights within Franco-Arab relations, it is indispensable to delve into specific case studies that highlight successful initiatives and pioneering efforts in bridging the gender gap. These case studies exemplify progress and illustrate the transformative impact of dedicated programs and policies. One such case study revolves around the innovative gender parity measures implemented by a leading French multinational corporation in the Arab world. Through targeted recruitment strategies, mentorship programs, and internal policies promoting work-life balance, the company achieved remarkable advancements in female representation at all organizational levels, thus fostering an inclusive corporate culture and redefining workplace dynamics. Furthermore, the company's proactive approach to addressing gender inequality has garnered accolades from governmental and non-governmental entities, positioning it as a trailblazer in promoting women's empowerment. Another compelling case study emanates from a collaborative educational initiative jointly undertaken by France and select Arab countries. This groundbreaking program aimed to enhance education access for girls in marginalized communities, thereby nurturing future generations of empowered female leaders. This initiative successfully transcended cultural barriers and traditional norms by providing scholarships, building schools, and implementing outreach efforts, significantly increasing female enrollment and fostering an environment conducive to gender equality. Additionally, the profound impact of this endeavor extended beyond academics, positively influencing community perceptions and instigating conversations on the pivotal role of women in societal progress. These case studies underscore the instrumental role of public-private partnerships, cross-cultural collaboration, and policy innovation in effecting tangible change and dismantling systemic obstacles to gender equality. They offer invaluable insights into best practices, practical strategies, and the transformative potential of concerted efforts in advancing women's rights within the Franco-Arab context.

## *Challenges and Controversies in Policy Implementation*

Implementing gender equality policies in Franco-Arab relations is a complex endeavor fraught with numerous challenges and controversies. One of the most prominent issues is the clash between traditional cultural values and progressive legislation. Many Arab societies have deeply ingrained patriarchal structures that have historically subordinated women, making it difficult to enact and enforce policies that seek to elevate their status. This often leads to resistance from conservative elements within these societies, further complicating the implementation process. Additionally, differences in legal systems and interpretations of religious doctrines pose significant hurdles in ensuring consistent application of gender equality laws across Arab countries. The lack of standardized enforcement mechanisms undermines the efficacy of these policies and perpetuates disparities in women's rights. Another contentious area is the intersection of gender equality with broader geopolitical dynamics. France's historical involvement in the Middle East and North Africa region has created intricate power dynamics that can impede meaningful progress in advancing women's rights. Political sensitivities and strategic considerations may overshadow the prioritization of gender equality initiatives, leading to diluted efforts and compromised outcomes. Moreover, economic factors play a pivotal role in shaping the success of gender equality policies.

Limited access to resources and opportunities for women, exacerbated by socio-economic disparities, hinders the realization of substantive change. Addressing economic inequalities and empowering women economically remains a persistent challenge in bridging the gender gap. Furthermore, the digital age introduces new complexities in policy implementation. The interplay of technology, social media, and cyber discourse creates opportunities and threats for gender equality efforts. While digital platforms can amplify advocacy and awareness, they also serve as battlegrounds for opposing narratives and disinformation, posing challenges in shaping constructive public discourse on women's rights. Lastly, navigating the diverse landscape of feminist movements and ideologies adds another layer of complexity to policy implementation. Striking a balance between respecting indigenous feminist perspectives and promoting universal human rights principles is a delicate task that requires nuanced understanding and inclusive engagement. This necessitates fostering dialogue and collaboration among various stakeholders, including governmental bodies, civil society organizations, and grassroots initiatives, to mitigate potential frictions and ensure equitable representation. Addressing these multifaceted challenges and controversies demands a holistic approach integrating cultural sensitivity, legislative harmonization, strategic diplomacy, and sustained commitment to engendering lasting transformation in Franco-Arab relations.

## *Prospects and Policy Recommendations*

As we look ahead to the future of gender equality and women's rights in Franco-Arab relations, it is imperative to recognize the progress made thus far while also acknowledging the persistent challenges that require attention and strategic action. The prospects for advancing gender equality hinge on a multi-faceted approach encompassing legislative reforms, cultural shifts, economic empowerment, and social advocacy. Policymakers, civil society organizations, and international bodies need to work collaboratively towards the following policy recommendations. Firstly, fostering meaningful dialogue and cooperation between France and Arab countries can lead to the exchange of best practices and policies regarding gender equality, augmenting mutual learning and understanding. Secondly, implementing targeted educational programs and awareness campaigns aimed at dispelling gender stereotypes and promoting inclusive values within communities will be pivotal in effecting long-term change. Moreover, supporting entrepreneurship and vocational training for women in both France and the Arab world can contribute to narrowing the economic gender gap and enabling financial independence. Policy focus should address the cultural barriers hindering women's advancement, including empowering women to challenge traditional gender roles and promoting societal acceptance of gender diversity. To further support these efforts, it is crucial to allocate resources and funding to initiatives that combat gender-based violence, provide legal aid, and establish support networks for marginalized women. Additionally, ongoing monitoring and evaluation mechanisms should be implemented to assess the effectiveness of policies and programs, ensuring that progress is sustained and responsive to evolving societal needs. Enhancing the participation and leadership of women in decision-making processes across all sectors is essential for driving sustainable socio-economic development and fostering inclusive societies. By embracing an intersectional approach to gender equality, inclusive of diverse ethnic, religious, and social backgrounds, the potential for impactful transformation grows exponentially. Through a collective commitment to advancing the status of women in Franco-Arab relations, there exists a tremendous opportunity to shape a brighter, more equitable future for generations to come.

# IN A NUTSHELL

### 1. Historical Context of Gender Issues in Franco-Arab Relations

The historical context of gender issues in Franco-Arab relations is deeply rooted in centuries of shared history, cultural exchange, and colonialism. France's colonial past in the Arab world, particularly in North Africa, has significantly influenced gender dynamics. The colonial period saw the imposition of French legal and social norms, which often conflicted with local traditions and practices. Post-colonial relations have continued to shape gender issues, with France often promoting its model of secularism and gender equality, sometimes clashing with the more conservative gender norms prevalent in many Arab countries.

### 2. Legislative Frameworks for Women's Rights in France and Arab Countries

**France**

France has a robust legislative framework promoting gender equality. Key legal instruments include the 1979 Convention on the Elimination of All Forms of Discrimination Against Women (CEDAW), which France ratified, and various national laws aimed at ensuring gender parity in political representation, combating domestic violence, and promoting equal pay. France's feminist foreign policy, adopted in 2019, further underscores its commitment to gender equality globally.

**Arab Countries**

In contrast, many Arab countries have more complex and varied legislative frameworks. While some countries like Tunisia and Morocco have made significant strides in reforming personal status laws to improve women's rights, others maintain more restrictive laws influenced by traditional and religious norms. For instance, Tunisia's 1956 personal status code was a pioneering reform, but issues like inheritance laws still reflect gender inequality. The region's legal frameworks often lack comprehensive protections against gender-based violence and discrimination.

## 3. Comparative Analysis of Gender Equality Measures

France ranks high on gender equality indices, with significant progress in political representation, legal protections, and economic participation for women. In contrast, the Arab region generally lags behind, with lower female labor force participation, higher rates of gender-based violence, and significant legal and social barriers to gender equality. However, there are notable exceptions, such as Tunisia and Morocco, which have implemented progressive reforms.

## 4. Impact of Educational Initiatives on Women's Empowerment

Educational initiatives have been crucial in empowering women in both France and the Arab world. In France, women have higher educational attainment rates than men, which has translated into better employment opportunities and political representation. In the Arab world, initiatives like Morocco's conditional cash transfers for girls' education and Egypt's digital skills training programs have shown positive impacts, although challenges remain in changing societal norms and ensuring equal access to education.

## 5. Economic Opportunities and the Gender Gap

The gender gap in economic opportunities remains a significant issue. In France, women still face a gender pay gap and under-representation in senior management positions. In the Arab world, the situation is more pronounced, with very low female labor force participation rates and high unemployment among women. Efforts to promote women's economic empowerment, such as legal reforms and support for women-led businesses, are ongoing but face significant cultural and structural barriers.

## 6. Cultural Barriers and Societal Shifts

Cultural barriers play a significant role in hindering gender equality. In France, issues like the hijab ban highlight the tension between secularism and religious freedom, disproportionately affecting Muslim women. In the Arab world, patriarchal norms and stereotypes continue to restrict women's roles in society. However, there are signs of societal shifts, with increasing advocacy for women's rights and gradual changes in public attitudes towards gender equality.

## 7. Role of NGOs and International Bodies

NGOs and international bodies have been instrumental in promoting gender equality. In France, organizations like Amnesty International and the High Council for Equality between Women and Men advocate for women's rights and monitor government policies. In the Arab world, international organizations like the UN and the OECD work with local NGOs to implement gender equality programs and provide technical assistance for legal reforms.

## 8. Case Studies: Success Stories of Gender Equality

**France**

France's feminist foreign policy and the Generation Equality Forum are notable success stories, showcasing France's leadership in global gender equality initiatives. Domestically, the increase in women's political representation and legal protections against gender-based violence are significant achievements.

**Arab Countries**

Tunisia's personal status code reforms and Morocco's Moudawana are often cited as successful case studies in the Arab world. These reforms have improved women's legal rights and social status, although implementation challenges remain.

## 9. Challenges and Controversies in Policy Implementation

Despite progress, both France and the Arab world face challenges in implementing gender equality policies. In France, controversies over secularism and religious freedom, particularly regarding Muslim women's attire, highlight ongoing tensions. In the Arab world, resistance to legal reforms, entrenched patriarchal norms, and inadequate enforcement of existing laws pose significant obstacles.

## 10. Prospects and Policy Recommendations

**France**

To further gender equality, France should continue to address the gender pay gap, promote women's representation in senior management, and ensure that secular policies do not disproportionately affect religious minorities. Strengthening support for women's rights organizations and increasing transparency in feminist foreign policy initiatives are also crucial.

**Arab Countries**

In the Arab world, continued legal reforms, enhanced enforcement of gender equality laws, and targeted educational and economic empowerment programs are essential. International cooperation and support from global organizations can help sustain momentum for change. Addressing cultural barriers through public awareness campaigns and engaging men in gender equality efforts are also important strategies. In conclusion, while significant progress has been made in promoting gender equality in both France and the Arab world, ongoing efforts are needed to address remaining challenges and ensure that all women can fully enjoy their rights and opportunities.

# References For Further Reading

Sofia Papastamkou. French-Egyptian Relations Before the Suez Crisis (1954-1956). Philippe Vial; Georges-Henri Soutou; Robert Frank ; Martin Alexander. Les Occidentaux et la crise de Suez : une relecture politico-militaire, Publications de la Sorbonne, pp.77-94, 2015, 978-2-85944-769-4. halshs-01346429 https://shs.hal.science/halshs-01346429/document

Gender in Geopolitics Institute, Americans for Democracy & Human Rights in Bahreïn, "France's Feminist Diplomacy and Women's Rights in the Gulf: Rhetoric over Reality", 29.04.2021. https://igg-geo.org/?p=3237&lang=en

OECD/ILO/CAWTAR (2020), Changing Laws and Breaking Barriers for Women's Economic Empowerment in Egypt, Jordan, Morocco and Tunisia, Competitiveness and Private Sector Development, OECD Publishing, Paris, https://doi.org/10.1787/ac780735-en.

Amnesty International. "France: Ensure Muslim Women and Girls Can Play Sports," March 8, 2024. https://www.amnesty.org/en/latest/news/2024/03/france-ensure-muslim-women-and-girls-can-play-sports/.

Arab Center Washington DC. "Women's Rights and 'State Feminism' in the Arab World," May 1, 2023. https://arabcenterdc.org/resource/womens-rights-and-state-feminism-in-the-arab-world/.

Blanchard, Pascal. "The Paradox of Arab France." The Cairo Review of Global Affairs, June 27, 2016. https://www.thecairoreview.com/essays/the-paradox-of-arab-france/.

data.unwomen.org. "Country Fact Sheet | UN Women Data Hub." Accessed May 24, 2024. https://data.unwomen.org/country/france.

El Ghoul, Bernard . "Émile Magazine - for Michèle Ramis, 'France Is One of the Very First Countries to Adopt a Feminist Foreign Policy.'" Émile Magazine, February 19, 2024. https://www.emilemagazine.fr/article/2024/2/19/-michle-ramis-france-is-one-of-the-very-first-countries-to-adopt-a-feminist-foreign-policy.

European Institute for Gender Equality. "Gender Equality Index | 2022 | France," n.d. https://eige.europa.eu/gender-equality-index/2022/country/FR.

fcc.uchicago.edu. "The Franco-Arab Thing: Exploring Centuries of Franco-Arab Relations | France Chicago Center," March 29, 2014. https://fcc.uchicago.edu/the-franco-arab-thing-exploring-centuries-of-franco-arab-relations/.

Filiu, Jean-Pierre. "Women's Freedom of Movement Still Impeded in Arab World." Le Monde.fr, August 28, 2023. https://www.lemonde.fr/en/international/article/2023/08/28/women-s-freedom-of-movement-still-impeded-in-the-arab-world_6111549_4.html.

Fougières, Mahaut de. "The French Brief - the Road to Gender Equality in France's Labor Market." Institut Montaigne, April 7, 2021. https://www.institutmontaigne.org/en/expressions/french-brief-road-gender-equality-frances-labor-market.

Jahangeer, Roshan Arah. "In France, Abortion Rights and Hijab Bans Highlight a Double Standard on Women's Rights." The Conversation, March 14, 2024. https://theconversation.com/in-france-abortion-rights-and-hijab-bans-highlight-a-double-standard-on-womens-rights-225418.

Ministry for Europe and Foreign Affairs . " FRANCE and WOMEN RIGHTS," September 16, 2010. https://cn.ambafrance.org/IMG/pdf/women_rights_eng_16_09_2010-1-2.pdf.

Ministry for Gender Equality, Diversity and Equal Opportunities. "TOWARDS REAL GENDER EQUALITY KEY FIGURES -2022 EDITION the ESSENTIALS," November 30, 2022. https://www.egalite-femmes-hommes.gouv.fr/sites/efh/files/2023-03/Chiffres_cl%C3%A9s_de_l_%C3%A9galit%C3%A9_2021_ed2022_EN.pdf.

OECD. "On 5 July, over 200 Participants from 13 MENA and 26 OECD Countries Came Together to Discuss Gender-Sensitive Education and Skills Development Policies in the MENA Region with a Focus on Developing Girls'

'Gender-Sensitive Education and Skills Development Policies in the MENA Region: Developing Girls' Digital Skills in the Post-COVID-19 World' CONCLUSIONS," July 5, 2021. https://www.oecd.org/mena/competitiveness/WEEF-Webinar-Conclusions-5-July-2021-Digital-skills.pdf.

UNDP. "Gender Justice & the Law in the Arab Region | United Nations Development Programme." Accessed May 24, 2024. https://www.undp.org/arab-states/gender-justice-law-arab-region.

www.ilo.org. "Gender Equality and Non-Discrimination in the Arab States | International Labour Organization." Accessed May 24, 2024. https://www.ilo.org/regions-and-countries/arab-states/ilo-arab-states/areas-work/gender-equality-and-non-discrimination-arab-states.

www.oecd.org. "MENA-OECD Competitiveness Programme on Gender - Organisation for Economic Co-Operation and Development," 2024. https://www.oecd.org/mena/competitiveness/gender-equality-women-economic-empowerment/.

# XXIII

# France's Role in Refugee Crises

## Historical Context and Origins of the Crises

The refugee crisis in France is deeply embedded in the historical events and conflicts that have plagued the Middle East and Africa. The Post-World War II era witnessed significant geopolitical shifts, with colonial empires dismantling and new nation-states emerging. However, this decolonization process was fraught with unrest and power struggles, leading to enduring political instability across regions. Furthermore, the Cold War rivalry between the United States and the Soviet Union fueled proxy wars and interventions in these areas, perpetuating social upheaval and conflict. The lasting impact of these conflicts has been the displacement of millions of individuals seeking refuge from violence, persecution, and economic deprivation. The ongoing turmoil in the Middle East, particularly the Syrian civil war and the rise of extremist groups, such as ISIS, has led to massive refugee outflows, with neighboring countries overwhelmed by the sheer scale of humanitarian needs. Similarly, in Africa, protracted conflicts in countries like South Sudan, Somalia, and the Democratic Republic of Congo have created waves of displaced populations struggling for survival and basic rights. These historical trajectories shed light on the multifaceted origins of the refugee crisis, reflecting the interplay of political, economic, and social factors that have shaped migration patterns and forced displacement. Understanding these dynamics is crucial in formulating effective policy responses and addressing the complex challenges of the refugee crisis.

## Policy Framework and Legislative Responses

Like many other European countries, France has been grappling with the refugee crisis that has unfolded in recent years. In response to this complex humanitarian challenge, the French government has developed a multifaceted policy framework combined with legislative responses to address the crisis's various dimensions. The fundamental cornerstone of France's approach lies in aligning its domestic legislation with international norms and treaties while recognizing the need for responsive and adaptive policies to manage the influx of asylum seekers and refugees effectively. As part of this effort, the French government has implemented comprehensive legislative measures covering asylum procedures, rights of refugees, integration policies, and security considerations.

One significant aspect of the policy framework is the establishment of legal pathways for asylum seekers to access protection in France. This includes robust refugee status determination procedures by international law and the provision of adequate resources to streamline the processing of applications. Additionally, the government has promulgated legislation outlining the rights and entitlements of refugees within the country, encompassing access to education, healthcare, and employment opportunities.

Furthermore, the legislative responses have focused on enhancing social cohesion and integration through targeted programs and initiatives. These policies seek to empower refugees to become self-reliant and contribute meaningfully to French society, emphasizing language acquisition, job training, and community support networks. To address potential security concerns, the government has also introduced measures to ensure effective monitoring and screening processes without compromising the humanitarian principles underlying refugee protection.

France has actively shaped the European Union's collective response to the refugee crisis in tandem with domestic efforts. This involves advocating for a harmonized approach to burden-sharing among EU member states, reinforcing common standards for asylum procedures, and facilitating coordinated resettlement programs. France's commitment to multilateral cooperation has extended to collaborating with international organizations such as the United Nations High Commissioner for Refugees (UNHCR) and other relevant bodies to leverage expertise and resources in addressing the protracted challenges posed by the crisis.

As the refugee crisis evolves, ongoing dialogue and evaluation of policy effectiveness remain critical. The French government's approach underscores the importance of balancing humanitarian imperatives with national security considerations and social integration dynamics. It also highlights the necessity of adopting a forward-looking legislative framework that aligns with evolving global realities and explores innovative solutions to support and protect those forcibly displaced from their homes.

## *Humanitarian Efforts and Aid Distribution*

France has long been committed to upholding its humanitarian obligations to address the refugee crisis. Humanitarian efforts encompass a wide range of activities, including providing direct assistance to refugees, implementing relief operations in conflict zones, and collaborating with international organizations to alleviate the suffering of displaced populations. Central to France's approach is promoting respect for human rights and safeguarding human dignity in all facets of aid distribution. Through diplomatic channels and partnerships, France strives to ensure that humanitarian aid reaches those in need, irrespective of political or military considerations.

A significant aspect of France's humanitarian efforts is providing refugees with essential healthcare, education, and shelter services. This entails working closely with NGOs and local authorities to establish and maintain camps and centers where refugees can access vital resources. Additionally, France actively contributes to international funds and initiatives to tackle the root causes of displacement and address the immediate needs of affected communities. France mobilizes global solidarity and support for humanitarian causes by leveraging its diplomatic influence and financial resources.

Aid distribution is carefully orchestrated to optimize impact and efficiency. Coordination with international agencies and local partners ensures that resources are allocated prudently and transparently, with stringent monitoring mechanisms to prevent misuse or diversion. Furthermore, France emphasizes engaging with host communities to foster harmonious relations and mitigate potential social tensions. This inclusive approach is instrumental in promoting long-term stability and facilitating the integration of refugees into their new environments.

In addition to addressing the immediate needs of refugees, France remains dedicated to advocating for durable solutions to displacement. This involves engaging in diplomatic efforts to resolve conflicts, promote peace-building initiatives, and create conditions conducive to safe and voluntary repatriation. Moreover, France actively participates in international forums and multilateral negotiations to strengthen legal frameworks and institutional capacities to protect refugees' rights and ensure their welfare.

Ultimately, France's humanitarian efforts and aid distribution reflect a steadfast commitment to upholding the principles of solidarity, compassion, and collective responsibility in the face of human suffering. By adhering to these values, France endeavors to make a meaningful difference in the lives of refugees and contribute to the broader global effort to address the complexities of forced displacement.

## *Integration and Settlement Programs*

As France grapples with the challenges posed by the refugee crisis, implementing effective integration and settlement programs has emerged as a crucial aspect of comprehensive response strategies. Integration encompasses the provision of necessities such as housing, education, and healthcare and extends to the cultural, linguistic, and social assimilation of refugees into French society. This process is instrumental in promoting their autonomy, fostering positive social cohesion, and mitigating the risk of marginalization.

The integration and settlement programs implemented in France are designed to facilitate the smooth transition of refugees into their new environment while respecting their backgrounds and identities. These initiatives focus on providing language courses, vocational training, and employment opportunities to enhance refugees' economic self-sufficiency. Furthermore, specialized support services are offered to address mental health concerns, trauma, and other psychosocial needs resulting from their displacement experiences.

In tandem with facilitating integration, settlement programs strive to create inclusive spaces that celebrate diversity and encourage intercultural dialogue. Local community engagement and grassroots initiatives foster mutual understanding and acceptance. Collaboration with non-governmental organizations, religious institutions, and volunteer networks enhances the effectiveness of these programs by building a support network for refugees and promoting cross-cultural exchange.

Moreover, establishing mentorship programs and peer support networks provides refugees with vital guidance and community connections. This empowers them to navigate the complexities of their new environment and fosters a sense of belonging and solidarity. Such initiatives are instrumental in reducing the sense of alienation that often accompanies forced displacement and demonstrate a commitment to upholding the values of compassion and empathy.

While notable progress has been made, challenges persist in ensuring refugees' successful integration and settlement. Issues such as bureaucratic hurdles, limited access to resources, and societal prejudices hinder the efficacy of these programs. Addressing these barriers requires a multifaceted approach that involves policy reforms, educational campaigns to combat misinformation, and the active involvement of civil society in advocating for refugees' rights.

In conclusion, implementing robust integration and settlement programs demonstrates France's commitment to providing refugees with the tools and support necessary to rebuild their lives and contribute positively to society. By embracing the principles of inclusivity, empowerment, and solidarity, France endeavors to create a welcoming environment where refugees can thrive and enrich the nation's cultural tapestry.

## *Cooperation with EU and International Agencies*

France's role in addressing the refugee crisis is intricately tied to its cooperation with the European Union (EU) and various international agencies. As a member of the EU, France actively participates in collective efforts to manage and respond to the challenges posed by large-scale migration and forced displacement. This cooperation extends to collaboration on policy development, resource allocation, and joint initiatives to support refugees and asylum seekers. Furthermore, France engages with international agencies such as the United Nations High Commissioner for Refugees (UNHCR), the International Organization for Migration (IOM), and various NGOs to leverage expertise, facilitate coordination, and mobilize resources to address the multifaceted dimensions of the refugee crisis. Through these partnerships, France seeks to align its strategies with broader regional and global frameworks, ensuring that its efforts are integrated into comprehensive and cohesive responses to the crisis. Within the EU, France advocates for burden-sharing and solidarity among member states to uphold shared values regarding refugee protection and humanitarian principles. The country also plays an active role in shaping EU asylum, resettlement, and border management policies to promote more effective and humane approaches to refugee reception and integration. Beyond its regional commitments, France collaborates with international organizations to contribute to capacity-building, advocacy, and emergency response mechanisms. This includes participating in multilateral forums to discuss best practices, share experiences, and contribute to developing normative standards guiding the treatment of refugees. By leveraging its influence within the EU and engaging with international agencies, France reinforces its commitment to upholding human rights, offering protection to those in need, and fostering greater global cooperation in addressing the complexities of the refugee crisis.

## *Challenges in Asylum Seeker Processing*

Processing asylum-seekers presents a multifaceted challenge for French authorities, encompassing legal, logistical, and humanitarian considerations. The influx of asylum seekers requires efficient and fair processing to ensure timely access to protection for those fleeing persecution and conflict. However, the complexity of verifying claims, ensuring compliance with international refugee law, and managing administrative procedures poses significant challenges.

One key challenge lies in the capacity and resources of immigration authorities tasked with assessing asylum applications. The volume of incoming applications often exceeds the available personnel and infrastructure, leading to backlogs and delays in the processing timeline. This strain on resources can compromise the thoroughness and accuracy of assessments, potentially impacting the safety and well-being of individuals awaiting decisions on their status.

Another critical issue is consistent and standardized application procedures across different regional offices. Discrepancies in decision-making processes can result in unequal treatment of asylum seekers and undermine the integrity of the overall system. Addressing this challenge requires robust oversight, regular staff training, and clear guidelines to promote uniformity in decision-making.

Furthermore, the diverse backgrounds and experiences of asylum seekers necessitate culturally sensitive and trauma-informed approaches to processing. Many applicants have endured traumatic events and may exhibit signs of psychological distress, requiring compassionate and specialized support during interviews and assessments. Training immigration officials to recognize and respond to these needs is crucial to upholding ethical standards and ensuring fair treatment.

Additionally, the evolving nature of geopolitical conflicts and persecution worldwide demands constant adaptation of asylum policies and procedures. Keeping abreast of global developments and integrating updated information into the decision-making process is essential for accurately evaluating the legitimacy of asylum claims.

Moreover, effective coordination with partner organizations and legal representatives adds another layer of complexity to the processing of asylum applications. Ensuring transparent communication and collaboration while upholding data privacy and security standards presents an ongoing challenge for immigration authorities.

Overcoming these challenges requires a comprehensive approach, including increased resources for immigration agencies, streamlined and harmonized procedures, ongoing training and professional development for staff, and robust oversight mechanisms. By addressing these challenges, France can enhance the efficiency, fairness, and integrity of its asylum-seeker processing system, further demonstrating its commitment to protecting and supporting those seeking refuge within its borders.

## *Public Perception and Societal Impact*

Public perception and societal impact of the refugee crisis in France have been crucial in shaping policy decisions and social dynamics. The influx of asylum seekers has sparked polarized public discourse, with voices both advocating for welcoming refugees and expressing concerns about security and integration. This has significantly influenced the political landscape and broader societal attitudes towards immigration and multiculturalism. From a grassroots level to the highest echelons of government, the issue of refugees has been a topic of intense debate, reflecting the diverse perspectives within French society.

The portrayal of refugees in media and popular culture has also played a pivotal role in shaping public opinion. Misinformation and stereotypes often perpetuate negative narratives, contributing to fear and xenophobia, while positive stories of resilience and successful integration efforts can foster empathy and understanding. This media influence has underscored the necessity of responsible reporting and accurate representation of refugee experiences to counter misconceptions and prejudice.

Additionally, the societal impact of the refugee crisis extends beyond mere opinion, influencing community cohesion and social dynamics. Localities that host refugee populations may experience strains on resources and services, leading to tensions and integration challenges. However, these communities also witness heartwarming stories of solidarity and compassion as individuals and organizations come together to address the needs of newcomers. The interaction between refugees and host communities shapes the cultural fabric of these areas, creating opportunities for cross-cultural exchange while presenting real-world challenges.

Moreover, the integration of refugees into the labor market and educational institutions has wide-ranging implications for the economy and social welfare. Understanding and addressing the barriers refugees face in attaining employment and education is essential for promoting inclusivity and harnessing the potential contributions of a diverse population. It also necessitates a reevaluation of existing social policies to ensure equitable access to opportunities for all residents, irrespective of their background.

Ultimately, public perception and societal impact are intricately intertwined, reflecting the complex interplay of cultural attitudes, political discourses, and everyday interactions. Examining these dynamics with nuance and sensitivity makes it possible to navigate the challenges posed by the refugee crisis in a manner that promotes empathy, cooperation, and sustainable integration.

## Case Studies: Successes and Failures

In examining the role of France in addressing the refugee crisis, it is imperative to delve into specific case studies that highlight both successful initiatives and notable shortcomings. One such case study revolves around the temporary housing program implemented in collaboration with local municipalities, where refugees were provided with essential services and support to facilitate their integration. This initiative witnessed commendable success as it not only ensured dignified living conditions for the displaced individuals but also fostered a sense of community and solidarity within the host society. Additionally, the provision of language and vocational training yielded positive outcomes, enabling refugees to secure employment and contribute meaningfully to their new environment.

Conversely, an area of failure stems from the bureaucratic hurdles encountered by asylum seekers during the application process. Lengthy waiting periods and administrative inefficiencies often led to frustration and disenchantment among the refugee population. These challenges inadvertently resulted in social exclusion and hindered the realization of their full potential within French society. Furthermore, instances of discrimination and stigmatization perpetuated negative stereotypes, impeding the prospects of successful integration.

Another case study to scrutinize is the collaboration between the public and private sectors in fostering entrepreneurship opportunities for refugees. By leveraging resources and expertise from various industries, innovative programs were devised to empower refugee entrepreneurs and provide them with the necessary tools to establish sustainable businesses. Several success stories emerged from this endeavor, showcasing the resilience and ingenuity of refugee communities. However, despite these notable successes, disparities in access to financial capital and mentorship persisted, posing obstacles to the broader economic inclusion of refugees.

Moreover, the relocation and resettlement efforts within rural areas underscore a mixed record of achievements and setbacks. While some regions displayed exemplary inclusivity and cultural sensitivity, welcoming refugees with open arms, others encountered resistance and hostility from local inhabitants. The disparities in reception policies and the lack of standardized support mechanisms contributed to varying outcomes, delineating the need for comprehensive and uniform strategies across all territories.

Ultimately, these case studies emphasize the necessity of adopting a multi-faceted approach that combines effective policy implementations with community engagement and targeted resource allocation. Recognizing the complexities inherent in addressing the refugee crisis, it is imperative to draw upon these experiences to inform future strategies and rectify inadequacies, ultimately striving towards a more cohesive and equitable integration framework.

## *Policy Recommendations and Future Strategies*

As the refugee crisis continues to present multifaceted challenges, France must develop comprehensive policy recommendations and future strategies to address the evolving needs of refugees and effectively manage their integration into French society. One crucial recommendation is the enhancement of coordination and cooperation among government agencies, non-governmental organizations, and international partners to ensure a unified approach to refugee assistance and support. This entails establishing clear communication channels and facilitating information sharing to streamline services and optimize resource allocation. Moreover, there is a vital need to prioritize long-term solutions that focus on sustainable integration, education, and employment opportunities for refugees. Policy reforms should aim to provide accessible language and vocational training, as well as promote cultural exchange initiatives to foster social inclusion and facilitate economic self-sufficiency. Additionally, leveraging technology and innovative solutions, such as digital platforms for access to legal aid and community networks for social integration, can significantly enhance the efficiency and effectiveness of refugee support programs. Investing in mental health services and trauma-informed care is also critical to address the psychological well-being of refugees and mitigate potential barriers to successful integration. Furthermore, the development of proactive measures to combat discrimination and xenophobia through public awareness campaigns and intercultural dialogue is essential in promoting a more welcoming and inclusive environment for refugees. Looking to the future, France must adopt a forward-looking approach by continuously reassessing and adapting its refugee policies in response to emerging global trends and geopolitical shifts. By actively engaging in dialogue with other European Union member states and international bodies, France can advocate for equitable burden-sharing mechanisms and collective responsibility in addressing the refugee crisis. Embracing a multilateral approach will be instrumental in fostering solidarity and shared commitment toward upholding the rights and dignity of refugees while maintaining regional stability. Ultimately, by embracing these policy recommendations and future strategies, France can reaffirm its leadership in humanitarian efforts and exemplify a model of compassion, resilience, and inclusivity in addressing the challenges posed by the refugee crisis.

## Conclusion: Reflections and Prospects

The refugee crisis has presented France with multifaceted challenges and profound opportunities, prompting deep reflection on the essence of humanitarianism, international cooperation, and national identity. As the nation navigates through this complex landscape, it becomes imperative to reflect on the outcomes of its policies and chart a course for the future. In doing so, it is crucial to acknowledge the successes and setbacks, drawing valuable insights from the experiences of the past. The central theme that emerges within this reflection is the need for a comprehensive, compassionate, and pragmatic approach to addressing the refugee crisis.

Looking ahead, France stands at a critical juncture with immense potential to shape prospects for refugees and host communities. Through sustained collaboration with international partners and local stakeholders, the nation can develop innovative strategies to enhance refugee integration, promote social cohesion, and harness the diverse skills and talents that newcomers bring. Moreover, there exists an opportunity to recalibrate existing policies, ensuring they align with evolving global dynamics while upholding the principles of solidarity and justice.

In contemplating the future, it is essential to underscore the significance of long-term resilience and adaptation. By investing in education, vocational training, and language support for refugees, France can nurture a resilient and empowered refugee population capable of contributing positively to society and the economy. This forward-looking approach promotes self-sufficiency and fosters a sense of belonging and dignity among displaced individuals and families.

Furthermore, as the global community grapples with the reverberating effects of conflicts, displacement, and climate change, France can play a pivotal role in advocating for durable solutions and fostering inclusive societies. Through proactive diplomacy, advocacy, and resource mobilization, the nation can champion the rights of refugees, advocate for conflict resolution, and address the root causes of forced displacement. Embracing such leadership will not only elevate France's standing in the international arena but will also reaffirm its commitment to upholding humanitarian values and human rights.

Ultimately, as France embarks on the next phase of its engagement with the refugee crisis, it is paramount to cultivate a collective ethos of empathy, resilience, and solidarity. By leveraging lessons from the past, refining policies, and adopting a forward-looking mindset, France can aspire to create a future where refugees are not merely survivors of adversity but vital contributors to a more inclusive and compassionate society. The journey ahead is intricate yet brimming with promise, calling for unwavering dedication, creativity, and vision as France carves out a meaningful and enduring legacy in shaping the prospects of refugees and the world at large.

# IN A NUTSHELL

## 1. Historical Context and Origins of the Crises since the Post-World War II Era

France has a long history of dealing with refugee crises, beginning with the influx of refugees following World War II. The immediate post-war period saw significant numbers of displaced persons from Eastern Europe, including Poles, Czechs, and Hungarians, fleeing communist regimes. The Spanish Civil War also led to the *Retirada*, where nearly half a million Spanish Republicans sought refuge in France in 1939. The 1940 German invasion of France caused a massive internal displacement, with millions fleeing the advancing German forces. Over the decades, France has continued to receive refugees from various global conflicts, including those from Vietnam, Cambodia, Laos, and more recently, from the Middle East and Africa.

## 2. Policy Framework and Legislative Responses

France's policy framework for refugees is rooted in the 1951 Geneva Convention, which it signed, and subsequent national laws. The French Office for the Protection of Refugees and Stateless Persons (OFPRA) was established in 1952 to manage asylum applications. Recent legislative responses include the 2018 amendments to the Asylum and Immigration Law, which aimed to streamline the asylum process and reduce application times. However, the new immigration bill debated in 2023 has raised concerns about weakening procedural safeguards for asylum seekers and limiting their rights.

## 3. Humanitarian Efforts and Aid Distribution

France is a significant donor to international humanitarian efforts, contributing to the UNHCR and other international organizations. In 2022, France provided substantial funding for crises in Ukraine, Africa, and the Middle East. France's humanitarian strategy for 2018-2022 emphasized increasing financial contributions and focusing on long-term crises, with a commitment to tripling its annual humanitarian aid by 2022. France also provides emergency aid, such as the €15 million announced in 2023 for Armenian refugees from Nagorno-Karabakh.

## 4. Integration and Settlement Programs

Integration of refugees in France involves multiple stakeholders, including government agencies, NGOs, and local communities. Programs like "Garantie jeune" provide support for young refugees, while various pilot programs offer comprehensive support packages, including accommodation, language, and vocational training. Resettlement in small towns and rural areas has shown positive results, with local communities playing a crucial role in the integration process. However, challenges remain, particularly in providing adequate housing and employment opportunities.

## 5. Cooperation with EU and International Agencies

France collaborates closely with the EU and international agencies to manage refugee crises. The EU's response to the Syrian refugee crisis, for instance, involved significant financial aid and support for neighboring countries hosting refugees. France also participates in EU-wide initiatives like the Common European Asylum System (CEAS) and has been involved in the EU-Turkey Statement aimed at managing migration flows. Additionally, France's contributions to the UNHCR and its role as a co-convenor of the Global Refugee Forum highlight its commitment to international cooperation.

## 6. Challenges in Asylum Seeker Processing

Processing asylum applications in France faces several challenges, including long waiting periods, inadequate housing, and difficulties in accessing the labor market. The new immigration bill has been criticized for potentially undermining the rights of asylum seekers by reducing procedural safeguards and limiting appeal opportunities. The European Court of Human Rights has also condemned France for the inhumane living conditions of some asylum seekers.

## 7. Public Perception and Societal Impact

Public perception of refugees in France is mixed, influenced by factors such as economic conditions, security concerns, and cultural integration. High-profile terrorist attacks and growing Islamophobia have heightened tensions, particularly regarding Syrian refugees. However, there are also positive examples of community mobilization and support for refugees, as seen in cities like Lyon. The rise of far-right political movements has further complicated the societal impact, often framing refugees as a threat rather than an opportunity.

## 8. Case Studies: Successes and Failures
### Successes

**Lyon's Community Mobilization**: The city of Lyon has successfully integrated Syrian refugees through local NGOs and community support, providing essential services and fostering cultural understanding.

**Small Town Resettlement**: Resettlement programs in small towns and rural areas have shown that refugees can become well-integrated members of local communities, with strong support from residents.

### Failures

**Housing Crisis**: The chronic shortage of adequate housing for refugees remains a significant failure, with many refugees living in precarious conditions for extended periods.

**Legislative Controversies**: The new immigration bill has faced criticism for potentially eroding the rights of asylum seekers and migrants, highlighting the ongoing challenges in balancing security concerns with humanitarian obligations.

In conclusion, while France has made significant efforts in managing refugee crises through policy frameworks, humanitarian aid, and integration programs, it continues to face substantial challenges. Addressing these issues requires a balanced approach that upholds human rights while ensuring effective integration and societal cohesion.

# References For Further Reading

Migrant women in France. DGCS/BAEI/LV. DGCS/BAEI/LV May 2020. https://rm.coe.int/migrant-women-in-france-note-coe-eng-june-2020-1-/16809f1557

Ministère des Affaires étrangères. "French immigration policy", March 2007. https://au.ambafrance.org/IMG/pdf/immigration_policy.pdf

The Law Library of Congress, Global Legal Research Directorate France: Law of Refugees (1994). https://tile.loc.gov/storage-services/service/ll/llglrd/2021699946/2021699946.pdf

Shoshana FINE, "The integration of refugees in France". Policy Department for Economic, Scientific and Quality of Life Policies Directorate-General for Internal Policies. PE 638.397 - August 2019. (European Parliament). https://www.europarl.europa.eu/RegData/etudes/STUD/2019/638397/IPOL_STU%282019%29638397%28ANN01%29_EN.pdf

Amb. DE RIVIÈRE, NICOLAS . "We Have a Collective Duty to Protect Migrants." France ONU, September 28, 2023. https://onu.delegfrance.org/we-have-a-collective-duty-to-protect-migrants.

Balla, Evanthia. "The European Union's Response to the Syrian Refugee Crisis." E-International Relations, April 22, 2023. https://www.e-ir.info/2023/04/22/the-european-unions-response-to-the-syrian-refugee-crisis/.

digilab.libs.uga.edu. "France's Refugee Story · Refugees, Immigration, Displaced Persons after WWII · Exhibits." Accessed May 24, 2024. https://digilab.libs.uga.edu/exhibits/exhibits/show/refugees/france.

France Diplomacy - Ministry for Europe and Foreign Affairs. "Armenia / Refugees from Nagorno-Karabakh – France Announces €15 Million in Additional Aid (08.12.23)," December 8, 2023. https://www.diplomatie.gouv.fr/en/country-files/armenia/news/article/armenia-refugees-from-nagorno-karabakh-france-announces-eur15-million-in.

France Diplomacy - Ministry for Europe and Foreign Affairs. "France's Humanitarian Strategy (2018-2022)," n.d. https://www.diplomatie.gouv.fr/en/french-foreign-policy/emergency-humanitarian-action/france-s-humanitarian-strategy-2018-2022/.

Global Focus. "France," n.d. https://reporting.unhcr.org/donors/france.

Human Rights Watch. "France: Immigration Bill Threatens Rights | Human Rights Watch," November 6, 2023. https://www.hrw.org/news/2023/11/06/france-immigration-bill-threatens-rights.

Le Monde. "What's in France's Controversial Immigration Law?" Le Monde.fr, December 20, 2023. https://www.lemonde.fr/en/france/article/2023/12/20/what-s-in-france-s-controversial-immigration-law_6361995_7.html.

Lemire-Waite, Sharlie. "Inter-Governmental and Community-Based Services for Syrian Refugees Living in France." Community Mobilization in Crisis, January 28, 2019. https://cmic-mobilize.org/inter-governmental-and-community-based-services-for-syrian-refugees-living-in-france/.

Niemann, Arne, and Julia Blöser. "Migration and the Mediterranean: The EU's Response to the 'European Refugee Crisis.'" Transnational Security Cooperation in the Mediterranean, January 2021, 75–113. https://doi.org/10.1007/978-3-030-54444-7_5.

Palais de la Porte Dorée. "The Retirada or Post-War Spanish Republican Exile | Musée de l'Histoire de L'immigration." www.histoire-immigration.fr, n.d. https://www.histoire-immigration.fr/en/migration-characteristics-by-country-of-origin/the-retirada-or-post-war-spanish-republican-exile.

Ripoll Servent, Ariadna. "The EU's Refugee 'Crisis': Framing Policy Failure as an Opportunity for Success." Politique Européenne N°65, no. 3 (2019): 178. https://doi.org/10.3917/poeu.065.0178.

Tardis, Matthieu. "Another Story from the 'Refugee Crisis' Resettlement in

Small Towns and Rural Areas in France Études de l'Ifri Matthieu TArDis Center for Migration and Citizenship," July 2019. https://www.ifri.org/sites/default/files/atoms/files/tardis_refugees_small_towns_france_2019.pdf.

Trouillard, Stéphanie . "Exodus: Refugees Remember Fleeing 1940 German Invasion." FRANCE 24, May 7, 2020. https://webdoc.france24.com/exodus-france-german-invasion-war-1940/.

# XXIV

# Cybersecurity and Digital Diplomacy

## Introduction to Cybersecurity in Franco-Arab Relations

International diplomacy has evolved significantly with the advent of the digital age, ushering in new challenges and opportunities for nations to engage in collaborative governance and strategic partnerships. As Franco-Arab relations continue to flourish across various domains, the criticality of cybersecurity in safeguarding diplomatic communications, protecting critical infrastructure, and countering cyber threats cannot be overstated. In the contemporary geopolitical landscape, where digital platforms serve as conduits for bilateral engagements and information sharing, robust cybersecurity measures are indispensable for preserving the trust and integrity of diplomatic interactions between France and Arab states.

The historical context of digital diplomacy within Franco-Arab relations provides significant insights into the evolving nature of cybersecurity. Over the years, France and Arab states have recognized the imperative of fortifying their cyber defense mechanisms to shield against malicious cyber activities that threaten national security and economic stability. A framework for addressing cybersecurity concerns has been established through joint efforts and bilateral agreements, signaling a commitment to promoting a secure and resilient digital environment for sustained diplomatic collaboration.

The increasing reliance on technology and interconnected networks has necessitated a proactive approach to cybersecurity, particularly in Franco-Arab relations. Modern societies' interdependence on digital infrastructures underscores the urgency of fending off cyber threats that can disrupt essential services and compromise sensitive information. With the proliferation of sophisticated cyber threats, including state-sponsored cyber espionage, ransomware attacks, and disinformation campaigns, the need for comprehensive cybersecurity strategies encompassing threat intelligence, incident response, and risk mitigation has become paramount in shaping the dynamics of digital diplomacy between France and Arab states.

As technology continues to evolve, so does the nature of cyber threats, compelling both nations to adapt and innovate in their cybersecurity endeavors. The convergence of traditional diplomacy with digital platforms has propelled discussions on enhancing cyber resilience and fostering international cooperation to combat emerging cyber challenges. Consequently, the evolution of cybersecurity within Franco-Arab relations is a testament to the synergistic adaptation of diplomatic practices in an era characterized by rapid technological advancements and unconventional threats.

## Historical Context of Digital Diplomacy Between France and the Arab States

The historical roots of digital diplomacy between France and Arab states can be traced back to the early days of the Internet and the emergence of digital communication technologies. As the world transitioned into the digital age, diplomatic efforts between France and Arab states adapted to the new technological landscape. The use of digital platforms for diplomatic purposes has seen significant evolution over the years, with both France and Arab states recognizing the potential of digital diplomacy in fostering bilateral relations, promoting cultural exchange, and addressing global challenges.

In the 1990s, France began to explore the possibilities offered by digital communication channels to engage with Arab states. This era marked the initial phase of digital diplomacy, using emails, websites, and online forums as tools for bilateral and multilateral communication. With the proliferation of the Internet, French embassies in Arab countries established their online presence, providing information about bilateral relations, consular services, and cultural events. Similarly, Arab diplomatic missions in France leveraged digital platforms to engage with the French public, disseminate information, and foster people-to-people connections.

The 21st century witnessed a fundamental shift in digital diplomacy with the advent of social media platforms, virtual summits, and online public diplomacy campaigns. France and Arab states embraced these emerging digital tools to project soft power, engage in public diplomacy, and influence international discourse. Digital platforms became instrumental in shaping narratives, conveying policy positions, and reaching out to diverse audiences across geographical boundaries. Moreover, digital diplomacy facilitates direct communication between government officials, diplomats, civil society actors, and the general public, enhancing transparency and accessibility in diplomatic engagements.

Challenges and opportunities have emerged in digital diplomacy due to the increasing reliance on digital technologies. Cyberspace has become a contested domain for geopolitical influence, where disinformation, cyberattacks, and digital espionage threaten bilateral relations between France and Arab states. Consequently, both parties have intensified efforts to promote cybersecurity, build digital resilience, and mitigate the risks associated with online diplomacy.

Looking ahead, the historical evolution of digital diplomacy between France and Arab states sets the stage for a deeper exploration of the role of technology in shaping contemporary diplomatic engagements. As digital innovation continues to redefine the landscape of international relations, understanding the historical context of digital diplomacy is essential for adapting to the evolving dynamics of Franco-Arab relations.

## Key Cyber Threats and Vulnerabilities in the Region

The Franco-Arab region faces many cyber threats and vulnerabilities that significantly affect national security, economic stability, and diplomatic relations. One of the primary challenges is the persistent threat of state-sponsored cyber espionage and sabotage. Hostile actors within and outside the region use targeted attacks to infiltrate government networks, critical infrastructure, and private enterprises. These attacks seek to steal sensitive information, disrupt vital services, and undermine trust between nations. Another pressing vulnerability stems from the proliferation of sophisticated malware and ransomware, which can swiftly propagate across interconnected systems, causing widespread damage and extortion. The growing reliance on digital technology in various sectors, such as finance, healthcare, and energy, has amplified the potential impact of cyber threats, including financial fraud, data breaches, and operational disruptions. Furthermore, the region grapples with protecting its digital infrastructure from distributed denial-of-service (DDoS) attacks designed to overwhelm networks and render online services inaccessible. In addition to these technical threats, social engineering tactics, such as phishing and impersonation, continue to exploit human vulnerabilities, making individuals and organizations susceptible to identity theft, fraud, and unauthorized access. With the rise of hyper-connected smart cities and Internet of Things (IoT) devices, growing concerns exist about the vulnerabilities associated with the convergence of physical and digital systems. This interconnectedness amplifies the potential for cyber-physical attacks on critical facilities, transportation networks, and urban utilities. Moreover, the complex geopolitical landscape of the region gives rise to hybrid cyber threats that blur the line between traditional espionage, information warfare, and influence operations. State and non-state actors leverage propaganda, disinformation, and social media manipulation to shape narratives and sow discord to pursue their strategic interests. Addressing these multifaceted cyber threats and vulnerabilities demands a comprehensive and collaborative approach involving robust cybersecurity measures, intelligence sharing, capacity building, and international cooperation. The effective management of cyber risks is instrumental in safeguarding the digital ecosystem, fostering trust among stakeholders, and promoting the resilience of Franco-Arab relations in an increasingly interconnected world.

## *France's Cyber Defense Strategies and Initiatives*

France has developed robust cyber defense strategies and initiatives to safeguard its national security interests and capacity-building efforts within the Franco-Arab context. Recognizing the evolving nature of cyber threats, France has adopted a comprehensive approach to cybersecurity that integrates defensive measures, proactive intelligence gathering, and international collaboration. One of the cornerstones of France's cyber defense framework is the coordination between the government, private sector, and academia to mitigate cyber risks and protect critical infrastructure. The French government has established specialized agencies and task forces dedicated to cybersecurity, working with law enforcement agencies to address cybercrime and enhance digital resilience. Furthermore, France has consistently invested in research and development to innovate cyber defense technologies, including advanced encryption methods, threat intelligence platforms, and incident response capabilities. The country also strongly emphasizes promoting cyber hygiene and awareness among its citizens, businesses, and government entities through education and training programs. In international cooperation, France actively participates in collaborative cybersecurity frameworks with Arab states and other global partners. This involves information sharing, joint exercises, and capacity-building initiatives aimed at bolstering the cyber defenses of all involved parties. By fostering alliances and knowledge exchange, France seeks to create a network of cyber allies that can collectively respond to emerging threats and malicious activities in the digital domain. Moreover, France advocates for establishing international norms and regulations to govern cyberspace, emphasizing the importance of responsible behavior and adherence to ethical principles in state-sponsored cyber operations. As part of its broader digital diplomacy agenda, France engages in cyber dialogues with Arab states to promote trust, transparency, and cooperation in mitigating cyber threats. Through these dialogues, France aims to build consensus on shared rules of engagement in cyberspace, paving the way for more resilient Franco-Arab cyber relations. Moving forward, France remains committed to enhancing its cyber defense capabilities and contributing to a secure and stable global cyberspace, recognizing the interconnected nature of digital threats and the imperative of collective action.

## *Collaborative Cybersecurity Frameworks*

In Franco-Arab cybersecurity cooperation, establishing collaborative frameworks plays a pivotal role in addressing the evolving cyber threats and safeguarding the digital infrastructure of both regions. Collaborative cybersecurity frameworks provide a structured approach to information sharing, joint threat analysis, and coordinated response mechanisms, reinforcing the resilience of interconnected networks and systems across France and Arab states. These frameworks entail multilateral agreements, information exchange protocols, and the establishment of joint task forces to counteract cyber threats that transcend national borders. Moreover, they facilitate harmonizing cybersecurity standards, best practices, and capacity-building efforts to enhance the overall cyber defense posture. At the core of collaborative frameworks is promoting trust and transparency among participating entities, fostering an environment conducive to effective cyber risk management and incident response. Such frameworks must encompass public-private partnerships, enabling collaboration between government bodies, regulatory agencies, private industries, and academic institutions. The synergy among diverse stakeholders amplifies the collective intelligence and resources to combat cyber threats while promoting innovation and knowledge transfer across domains. Furthermore, these collaborative frameworks serve as a conduit for diplomatic engagement, fostering mutual understanding and cooperation on shared cybersecurity concerns. By anchoring cybersecurity within diplomacy, such frameworks build enduring relationships and promote stability in the digital domain. As technology continues to evolve, collaborative frameworks must adapt to address emerging challenges, including the proliferation of Internet of Things (IoT) devices, artificial intelligence (AI)-driven threats, and the impact of geopolitical tensions on cybersecurity. Robust collaborative frameworks will underpin the resilience of critical infrastructure, financial systems, and strategic assets against advanced persistent threats and sophisticated cyber-attacks. Through sustained commitment and investment in collaborative cybersecurity initiatives, France and Arab states can fortify their digital ecosystems, laying the foundation for a secure and prosperous future in cyberspace.

## *Cyber Espionage and Information Warfare: Case Studies*

In international relations, cyber espionage and information warfare have become formidable tools for state actors to advance their strategic interests and exert influence on the global stage. This is particularly relevant in Franco-Arab relations, where the interconnected nature of digital communication networks has paved the way for sophisticated cyber threats and covert intelligence operations. The convergence of technological innovation and geopolitical rivalries has created a new battleground in cyberspace, where stealthy intrusions and disinformation campaigns can significantly impact diplomatic relations between nations. To illustrate the significance of these challenges, it is imperative to delve into real-world case studies that exemplify the complexities and implications of cyber espionage and information warfare in the Franco-Arab context. One such case involves the targeted cyber attacks on critical infrastructure and government networks in France and Arab countries, orchestrated by state-sponsored threat actors aiming to steal sensitive data and disrupt essential services. These incidences underscore the pressing need for robust cybersecurity measures and international cooperation to mitigate the region's ever-evolving cyber threats. Furthermore, using social media platforms to spread misinformation and propaganda has influenced public opinion and sowed discord within and between nations. Exploiting digital channels for disinformation campaigns has heightened tensions and strained diplomatic ties, posing significant challenges to fostering trust and cooperation in Franco-Arab relations. These case studies show that cyber espionage and information warfare are not confined to virtual realms but have tangible implications on geopolitics, national security, and international diplomacy. As such, policymakers and diplomats must remain vigilant and proactive in addressing these threats through collaborative efforts, information sharing, and developing resilient cybersecurity frameworks. Only through concerted action can the risks associated with cyber espionage and information warfare be effectively mitigated, thereby promoting stability, transparency, and mutual trust among nations in the digital age.

## *Digital Diplomacy: Tools and Practices*

In modern diplomacy, digital tools and practices have revolutionized how nations communicate, build relationships, and conduct international affairs. As France continues to engage with Arab states in the digital arena, it has employed various digital diplomacy tools and practices to strengthen diplomatic ties and promote mutual understanding. One key aspect of digital diplomacy is using social media platforms such as Twitter, Facebook, and Instagram as channels for official communication and public diplomacy. Through strategic content dissemination and engagement efforts, diplomats and government officials can directly connect with Arab audiences, convey key messages, and foster dialogue on important issues. Furthermore, digital platforms provide a space for cultural exchange programs, educational initiatives, and promotion of French heritage, fostering a deeper appreciation and understanding between France and Arab states. Additionally, virtual meetings, webinars, and online conferences have become integral components of digital diplomacy, allowing for efficient and scalable interactions between officials, experts, and stakeholders across borders. These platforms facilitate dialogue on various topics, including economic cooperation, security challenges, and environmental sustainability, enhancing collaboration and problem-solving. Moreover, digital tools enable consular services, visa applications, and citizen assistance to be streamlined and accessible, contributing to smoother bilateral relations and public satisfaction. In crisis management, digital channels serve as vital communication lifelines during conflict or emergencies, ensuring effective dissemination of critical information and support to distressed citizens. Embracing innovative technological solutions, France leverages digital resources to advance its diplomatic objectives and promote its national interests in the Arab world. However, France and Arab states must adapt to rapidly evolving cyber landscapes, address digital divides, and collectively navigate digital diplomacy's ethical and security implications. As digital diplomacy evolves, a harmonious balance between traditional diplomatic practices and cutting-edge digital tools will maintain trust and credibility in Franco-Arab relations.

## Impact of Cybersecurity on Bilateral Trade and Investment

The increasing interconnectedness of global economies has placed cybersecurity at the forefront of bilateral trade and investment considerations between France and Arab states. In an era where digital transactions and communications form the backbone of international commerce, the assurance of secure cyber infrastructure is paramount to fostering economic partnerships and maintaining trust between nations.

Cybersecurity directly impacts the facilitation of cross-border trade by safeguarding critical information and communication channels. Without adequate protection, data breaches or cyber-attacks can disrupt supply chains, compromise sensitive business negotiations, and erode confidence in financial transactions. For example, phishing attacks targeting trade-related emails or ransomware incidents affecting systems of multinational corporations can lead to significant financial losses and hinder the smooth flow of goods and services across borders.

Furthermore, a country's digital infrastructure's resilience is pivotal in attracting foreign direct investment (FDI). Potential investors assess a nation's cybersecurity readiness before committing capital, seeking assurances that their investments will be protected against cyber threats. A robust cybersecurity framework signals stability and reliability, encouraging investors to engage confidently in long-term economic partnerships.

Effective cybersecurity measures bolster trade and investment and foster innovation and digital cooperation in Franco-Arab relations. By mitigating the risks associated with cyber threats, such as intellectual property theft and industrial espionage, France and Arab states can create a conducive environment for technological collaboration and knowledge exchange. This, in turn, nurtures a more robust and mutually beneficial economic ecosystem.

Moreover, as digital transformations revolutionize industries, the assurance of cybersecurity becomes intertwined with the promotion of emerging sectors and innovative technologies. Protecting digital assets and intellectual property rights through cybersecurity mechanisms enables sustained growth in areas such as e-commerce, fintech, and renewable energy, thereby enriching the landscape of bilateral trade and investment opportunities.

As both France and Arab states emphasize expanding their economic footprints and engaging in cross-border ventures, the imperative of fortifying cybersecurity resilience cannot be overstated. By recognizing the profound influence of cybersecurity on bilateral trade and investment, these nations can collaboratively enhance digital trust, strengthen economic ties, and navigate the dynamic realm of international commerce with heightened security and confidence.

## *Educational and Cultural Exchanges in Cyberspace*

As diplomacy continues to evolve in the digital age, educational and cultural exchanges have found a new platform in cyberspace. This innovative approach has revolutionized cross-border interactions, enhancing connectivity and collaboration between France and Arab states. Through virtual exchange programs, educational institutions and cultural organizations break geographical barriers, foster mutual understanding, and promote intercultural dialogue.

Cyberspace has become a bridge that transcends traditional boundaries, enabling students and educators to engage in immersive virtual experiences. Collaborative online platforms facilitate language exchanges, art exhibitions, and interactive lectures, creating cross-cultural learning and appreciation opportunities. Virtual classrooms allow students to interact with peers from diverse backgrounds, challenging stereotypes and building empathy.

Furthermore, digital diplomacy has enabled the preservation and dissemination of cultural heritage. Museums, libraries, and historical sites can now offer virtual tours and digitized collections, allowing individuals to explore the richness of French and Arab cultures from anywhere in the world. This enhances cultural appreciation and stimulates interest in historical and artistic traditions, strengthening nation bonds.

In higher education, online learning initiatives have become instrumental in fostering academic partnerships and research collaborations. Virtual seminars, joint academic projects, and e-library access have facilitated knowledge exchange and scholarly discourse. This has contributed to the internationalization of curricula, enriching educational experiences, and nurturing a global mindset among students and faculty members.

Moreover, cyberspace serves as a medium for promoting multilingualism and understanding. Language learning platforms and online linguistic resources have empowered individuals to master foreign languages and appreciate diverse linguistic nuances. This linguistic competence not only aids in effective communication but also serves as a gateway to cross-cultural dialogue and international cooperation.

In conclusion, educational and cultural exchanges in cyberspace represent a dynamic avenue for enhancing Franco-Arab relations. The digital sphere offers boundless prospects for fostering mutual respect, academic collaboration, and cultural appreciation. Embracing these opportunities is crucial for nurturing a generation of globally engaged citizens and reinforcing the enduring ties between France and Arab states.

## *Future Challenges and Opportunities for Strengthening Cyber Alliance*

As the world becomes increasingly interconnected through digital technologies, the future of the Franco-Arab cyber alliance presents challenges and opportunities. One key challenge is the ever-evolving nature of cyber threats, which continue to pose significant risks to both nations. These threats range from sophisticated cyber-attacks to disinformation campaigns destabilizing diplomatic relations. The rapid technological advancements and the rise of new threat vectors such as quantum computing and artificial intelligence further complicate the cybersecurity landscape.

However, amid these challenges, numerous opportunities exist for strengthening the Franco-Arab cyber alliance. One of the foremost opportunities lies in the collaborative development and implementation of robust cybersecurity frameworks. By sharing best practices, intelligence, and expertise, France and Arab states can enhance their collective resilience against cyber threats. Moreover, fostering greater cooperation in areas such as joint cyber exercises, capacity building, and information sharing can pave the way for a more secure cyber environment.

Another area of opportunity is leveraging digital diplomacy to build trust and foster dialogue between the two parties. Digital platforms for diplomatic engagement can facilitate direct communication, cultural exchanges, and the promotion of mutual understanding. Platforms for virtual conferences, webinars, and e-diplomacy initiatives can serve as valuable tools for enhancing cooperation and collaboration in cyberspace.

Furthermore, the future presents prospects for innovative public-private partnerships in cybersecurity. Collaborations between government entities, private sector companies, and academic institutions can drive technological innovation, research, and talent development in cybersecurity. Leveraging the expertise of industry leaders and academia can result in cutting-edge solutions that address emerging cyber threats and contribute to the overall security of digital infrastructure.

In addition, both France and Arab states need to prioritize cybersecurity education and awareness programs. Investing in cybersecurity training and skills development for the next generation of cyber professionals can bolster the capabilities of both nations in combating cyber threats. Moreover, raising public awareness about cybersecurity risks and promoting responsible digital citizenship are crucial steps towards building a cyber-resilient society.

Ultimately, the future of the Franco-Arab cyber alliance hinges on proactive adaptation to emerging cyber challenges and seizing opportunities for constructive collaboration. By embracing technological innovation, fostering cooperation, and prioritizing cybersecurity, France and Arab states can forge a formidable cyber alliance that safeguards the interests and security of both parties in the digital age.

# IN A NUTSHELL

## 1. Introduction to Cybersecurity in Franco-Arab Relations

Cybersecurity has become a critical component of Franco-Arab relations, driven by the increasing digitization of economies and the rising threat of cyberattacks. Both France and Arab states recognize the importance of securing their digital infrastructures to protect national security, economic interests, and societal stability. The collaboration between these regions aims to address common cyber threats and enhance mutual cybersecurity capabilities.

## 2. Historical Context of Digital Diplomacy Between France and the Arab States

Digital diplomacy between France and Arab states has evolved significantly over the past few decades. France has been proactive in establishing cybersecurity strategies and frameworks, such as the 2015 National Strategy for Digital Security and the 2018 Strategic Review of Cyber Defense. Arab states, particularly the UAE and Saudi Arabia, have also developed robust digital diplomacy initiatives, leveraging digital tools to enhance their foreign relations and cybersecurity capabilities. The Abraham Accords have further facilitated cyber cooperation between Israel and Gulf states, highlighting the strategic importance of digital diplomacy in the region.

## 3. Key Cyber Threats and Vulnerabilities in the Region

The Middle East faces a diverse range of cyber threats, including state-sponsored attacks, ransomware, hacktivism, and attacks on critical infrastructure. Key vulnerabilities include outdated systems, insufficient cybersecurity measures, and the rapid digitization of key sectors like energy and finance. Social engineering, phishing, and malware distribution are prevalent attack vectors, with government and industrial organizations being prime targets.

## 4. France's Cyber Defense Strategies and Initiatives

France has implemented comprehensive cyber defense strategies to protect its digital infrastructure. The National Agency for the Security of Information Systems (ANSSI) plays a pivotal role in preventing and responding to cyber incidents. France's strategy includes developing sovereign cybersecurity solutions, enhancing public-private partnerships, and promoting cybersecurity awareness. The "France 2030" initiative aims to triple the cybersecurity sector's revenue and double employment by 2025.

## 5. Collaborative Cybersecurity Frameworks

France and Arab states have engaged in various collaborative cybersecurity frameworks to enhance their defenses. These include bilateral agreements, such as the memoranda of understanding (MoUs) signed by Saudi Arabia with Qatar, Romania, Spain, and Kuwait. International forums like the Global Cybersecurity Forum and the French-American Foundation's Cyber Security Conference also facilitate cooperation and knowledge sharing.

## 6. Cyber Espionage and Information Warfare: Case Studies

Cyber espionage and information warfare are significant concerns in Franco-Arab relations. Notable cases include the Lazarus Group's cyber espionage activities in the UAE and the sophisticated campaigns by Iranian APT groups targeting Israeli and Gulf state infrastructures. These incidents highlight the geopolitical dimensions of cyber threats and the need for robust defensive measures.

## 7. Digital Diplomacy: Tools and Practices

Digital diplomacy tools and practices are essential for managing cyber relations between France and Arab states. These include the use of social media for public diplomacy, cybersecurity education programs, and the establishment of cyber councils and agencies to coordinate efforts. France's international strategy for digital security emphasizes governance, economic security, and international cooperation.

## 8. Impact of Cybersecurity on Bilateral Trade and Investment

Cybersecurity significantly impacts bilateral trade and investment between France and Arab states. Secure digital environments are crucial for attracting foreign investment and ensuring the smooth operation of cross-border trade. Initiatives like Saudi Arabia's Vision 2030 and the UAE's economic visions underscore the importance of cybersecurity in achieving economic goals. Cyber threats, however, pose risks to these ambitions, necessitating continuous investment in cybersecurity measures.

## 9. Educational and Cultural Exchanges in Cyberspace

Educational and cultural exchanges in cyberspace are vital for building cybersecurity expertise and fostering mutual understanding. France and Arab states have launched various programs to enhance cybersecurity education, such as Israel's high school cybersecurity courses and France's cybersecurity training initiatives. These exchanges help develop a skilled workforce capable of addressing emerging cyber threats.

## 10. Future Challenges and Opportunities for Strengthening Cyber Alliance

Future challenges in strengthening the Franco-Arab cyber alliance include addressing the evolving nature of cyber threats, ensuring regulatory compliance, and fostering greater international cooperation. Opportunities lie in expanding collaborative frameworks, investing in advanced cybersecurity technologies, and enhancing public awareness and education. By leveraging these opportunities, France and Arab states can build a resilient cyber alliance capable of navigating the complexities of the digital age. In conclusion, the cybersecurity landscape in Franco-Arab relations is multifaceted, involving historical ties, strategic initiatives, and collaborative efforts to address common threats. By continuing to strengthen their cyber alliance, France and Arab states can enhance their security, economic prosperity, and diplomatic relations in the digital era.

# References For Further Reading

Antwi-Boateng, Osman, Khadija Ali, Mohammed Al, Antwi-Boateng Osman, Ali Khadija, A Mohammed, Mazrouei, Mohammed Al Mazrouei, and Khadija Al-. "The Challenges of Digital Diplomacy in the Era of Globalization: The Case of the United Arab Emirates." International Journal of Communication 15, no. 15 (2021): 4577–95. https://ijoc.org/index.php/ijoc/article/download/16150/3583.

Asharq Al Awsat. "Saudi Arabia, Four Countries Sign Cybersecurity MoUs." english.aawsat.com, November 3, 2023. https://english.aawsat.com/business/4645086-saudi-arabia-four-countries-sign-cybersecurity-mous.

CybelAngel. "An International Cybersecurity Collaboration," December 7, 2022. https://cybelangel.com/an-international-cybersecurity-collaboration/.

cyber.gouv.fr. "La Stratégie de La France En Matière de Cyberdéfense et Cybersécurité | ANSSI," April 16, 2013. https://cyber.gouv.fr/publications/la-strategie-de-la-france-en-matiere-de-cyberdefense-et-cybersecurite.

cyber.gouv.fr. "The French Approach to Cyber | ANSSI," October 3, 2023. https://cyber.gouv.fr/en/french-approach-cyber-0.

DataPatrol. "Cybersecurity Landscape in the Middle East 2024," March 4, 2024. https://datapatrol.com/cybersecurity-landscape-in-the-middle-east-2024/.

Editorial, MITSloan ME. "Cybersecurity Threats Just Got Worse in the UAE. Here's What You Can Do." MIT Sloan Management Review Middle East, March 12, 2024. https://www.mitsloanme.com/article/cybersecurity-threats-just-got-worse-in-the-uae-heres-what-you-can-do/.

France Diplomatie - Ministère de l'Europe et des Affaires étrangères. "La France et La Cybersécurité," January 2022. https://www.diplomatie.gouv.fr/fr/politique-etrangere-de-la-france/securite-desarmement-et-non-proliferation/lutter-contre-la-criminalite-organisee/la-france-et-la-cybersecurite/.

"GCI Scope and Framework Background," n.d. https://www.itu.int/en/ITU-D/Cybersecurity/Documents/GCIv4/New_Reference_Model_GCIv4_V2_.pdf.

Handler, Simon. "The 5×5—the State of Cybersecurity in the Middle East." Atlantic Council, June 15, 2021. https://www.atlanticcouncil.org/commentary/the-5x5-the-state-of-cybersecurity-in-the-middle-east/.

Help AG: Next-Gen Cybersecurity Services in the Middle East. "Top Middle East Cyber Threats – March 6, 2024," March 6, 2024. https://www.helpag.com/top-middle-east-cyber-threats-march-6-2024/.

Leyden, John . "Ransomware-As-a-Service Spawns Wave of Cyberattacks in Middle East." www.darkreading.com, February 29, 2024. https://www.darkreading.com/cyberattacks-data-breaches/ransomware-as-a-service-spawns-widespread-cyberattacks-in-mea.

McAteer, Patrick. "Rising Cyber Threats in the Middle East – a Virtual Battleground." SecurityHQ, November 29, 2023. https://www.securityhq.com/blog/rising-cyber-threats-in-the-middle-east-a-virtual-battleground/.

Ministère des technologies de la communication. "Arab Cybersecurity Strategy 2023-2027 White Paper," December 6, 2022. https://www.mtc.gov.tn/index.php?L=144&cHash=b3e38bd66cca618a6fa88cd65e6ef822&id=119&tx_ttnews%5Btt_news%5D=4479.

Mire, Maxime Juestz de. "France 2030 : Lancement Du Dispositif d'Accompagnement 'Cyber PME' Dans Le Cadre de La Stratégie Cybersécurité." Presse - Ministère des Finances, December 6, 2023. https://presse.economie.gouv.fr/france-2030-lancement-du-dispositif-daccompagnement-cyber-pme-dans-le-cadre-de-la-strategie-cybersecurite/.

Positive Technologies. "Cybersecurity Threatscape in the Middle East: 2022-2023." ptsecurity.com. Positive Technologies, July 17, 2023. https://www.ptsecurity.com/ww-en/analytics/middle-east-cybersecurity-threatscape-2022-2023/.

"State of the UAE - Cybersecurity Report 2024," 2024. https://www.cpx.net/media/hocl331j/state-of-the-uae-cybersecurity-report.pdf.

United Nations. "Without Adequate Guardrails, Artificial Intelligence Threatens Global Security in Evolution from Algorithms to Armaments, Speaker Tells First Committee | UN Press." press.un.org, October 24, 2023. https://press.un.org/en/2023/gadis3725.doc.htm.

www.entreprises.gouv.fr. "Stratégie d'Accélération Cybersécurité | Entreprises.gouv.fr," December 6, 2022. https://www.entreprises.gouv.fr/fr/strategies-d-acceleration/strategie-d-acceleration-cybersecurite.

www.fticonsulting.com. "Navigating Cybersecurity Threat Landscape Middle East | FTI," November 20, 2023. https://www.fticonsulting.com/insights/articles/navigating-cybersecurity-threat-landscape-middle-east.

# XXV

# Future of Franco-Arab Relations

### Future Trends

As we stand on the cusp of a new era, exploring how emerging technology, politics, and cultural trends will shape future Franco-Arab relations is imperative. The fast-paced technological advancements, particularly in fields like artificial intelligence, biotechnology, and renewable energy, are expected to revolutionize various sectors and industries. These technological advancements will foster economic growth and present opportunities for collaborative ventures between France and Arab states, leading to deeper integration and mutual benefit. Moreover, the proliferation of digital communication platforms and the internet will further facilitate cross-cultural exchanges and understanding, forging stronger ties between the two regions. In the political domain, the evolving global geopolitical landscape and shifting powers will significantly affect Franco-Arab relations. The emergence of new regional power centers and changing alliances will necessitate strategic recalibrations and diplomatic engagements to navigate these dynamic shifts effectively. Additionally, addressing pressing global challenges such as climate change, migration, and terrorism will demand close cooperation and concerted efforts from France and Arab countries. Culturally, the cross-pollination of ideas and values will continue to enrich the fabric of Franco-Arab interactions. With the proliferation of art, literature, and education programs, there will be an increased mingling of diverse cultural expressions, fostering mutual understanding and appreciation. Furthermore, initiatives promoting multiculturalism and diversity will play a pivotal role in fostering inclusivity and unity within the Franco-Arab context. In this section, we will delve into the multifaceted aspects of these emerging trends and their potential impact on shaping the future landscape of Franco-Arab relations. By critically examining these trends and their ramifications, we envision a roadmap that underscores the importance of proactive collaboration and dialogue between France and Arab states in navigating future complexities.

## *Technological Advancements and Their Impacts*

The future of Franco-Arab relations will undoubtedly be shaped by technological advancements rapidly transforming the global landscape. In this context, the convergence of digital technologies, artificial intelligence, and big data analytics presents opportunities and challenges for fostering closer ties between France and the Arab world. Industries such as renewable energy, smart infrastructure, healthcare, and transportation are poised to benefit from collaborative research and innovation. The proliferation of digital platforms and e-commerce creates new avenues for economic integration and cross-border investments. Moreover, technological advances facilitate greater cultural exchange and cross-cultural dialogue, further cementing the bonds between the two regions. However, the widespread adoption of disruptive technologies raises concerns regarding data privacy, cybersecurity, and ethical considerations. As Franco-Arab cooperation deepens in the technological sphere, it becomes imperative to address these issues through robust legal frameworks and bilateral agreements. Furthermore, the impacts of automation and job displacement must be carefully navigated to ensure inclusive growth and sustainable development. Embracing the Fourth Industrial Revolution will require concerted efforts to upskill the workforce, promote digital literacy, and foster entrepreneurship. From a geopolitical standpoint, technological advancements have strategic implications for defense collaboration, intelligence sharing, and cybersecurity initiatives. The intersection of technology and security necessitates close coordination in countering emerging threats and safeguarding critical infrastructure. Beyond traditional diplomatic exchanges, digital diplomacy has emerged as a crucial dimension in shaping public opinion and influencing narratives. Leveraging social media, digital storytelling, and virtual exchanges can foster greater understanding and empathy between the people of France and the Arab world. Therefore, policymakers, business leaders, and civil society must grasp the multifaceted nature of technological advancements and their far-reaching impacts on the future trajectory of Franco-Arab relations.

## *Economic Prospects and Collaborations*

The economic prospects of France and the Arab world present immense opportunities for collaboration and growth. As globalization continues to shape international trade, both the Franco-Arab economies stand to benefit from strategic partnerships and mutual investments. With a shared interest in energy, infrastructure, and technology sectors, the future promises increased economic integration. Moreover, the diversification of investment portfolios and the promotion of entrepreneurship are key factors that can further strengthen the economic ties between these two regions.

In recent years, bilateral trade agreements and joint ventures have surged in popularity to foster long-term economic prosperity. Developing strategic economic corridors, focusing on transport, logistics, and innovation, presents a transformative pathway toward sustainable economic development. Additionally, initiatives promoting knowledge exchange, research collaboration, and skill enhancement are instrumental in cultivating a conducive economic cooperation and growth environment.

Furthermore, leveraging the untapped potential of emerging markets within the Arab world is a compelling avenue for sustained economic collaboration. By identifying and capitalizing on shared interests and comparative advantages, both regions can harness their respective strengths to drive economic progress. Cross-border investments, technological innovation, and the facilitation of trade channels are pivotal components in realizing the full potential of economic prospects and collaboration.

As the global economy evolves, embracing a forward-looking approach toward economic integration is crucial for navigating the complexities of today's interconnected world. Embracing digital transformation, promoting sustainable practices, and spearheading inclusive economic policies lay the groundwork for a prosperous future built on mutual trust and shared prosperity. Both regions must engage in open dialogues, tackle economic challenges collectively, and explore innovative avenues for sustainable economic growth.

Ultimately, the convergence of economic prospects and collaborations between France and the Arab world signifies a powerful catalyst for transformative change. By aligning economic strategies, fostering an environment conducive to investment, and nurturing talent and innovation, the prospects of economic collaborations are poised to shape the socio-economic landscape with enduring impact.

## *Political Dynamics and Strategic Alignments*

The political landscape of Franco-Arab relations is a complex tapestry woven with historical, cultural, and geopolitical threads. Understanding the intricate web of alliances, disputes, and realignments is essential for mapping the future trajectory of these relations. At the heart of this dynamic are the shifting power dynamics within the Arab world and France's evolving role as both a European and Mediterranean power. In recent years, new power players have emerged in the Arab region, challenging traditional power structures and influence. The rise of non-state actors, ideological movements, and regional hegemons has added complexity to the political dynamics. Moreover, the strategic landscape has been shaped by the ongoing shifts in global power dynamics, including the evolving roles of the United States, China, Russia, and the European Union in the Arab world. These factors have heightened the need for strategic alignments as France and Arab states seek to navigate the complexities of contemporary geopolitics. Furthermore, the ever-changing nature of international relations, coupled with the impact of technological advancements, has influenced diplomatic approaches and strategic calculations. Digital diplomacy, cyber warfare, and information warfare have redefined traditional notions of political influence and strategic alignments. Speaking of alignments, one cannot overlook the impact of regional conflicts on the political dynamics of Franco-Arab relations. The proxy wars, sectarian tensions, and geopolitical rivalries in the Middle East have not only shaped the political landscape but also tested the resilience of diplomatic ties between France and Arab states. Navigating these challenges requires a nuanced understanding of each party's interests, aspirations, and red lines. The quest for strategic alignment necessitates a delicate balance between national interests, multilateral commitments, and diplomatic maneuvering. As such, the future of Franco-Arab relations hinges on the ability of both parties to adapt to the fluidity of the global order while maintaining a principled stance on issues of mutual concern. Building strategic solid alignments will require pursuing mutually beneficial partnerships, a commitment to dialogue, and a willingness to confront shared challenges. Embracing a forward-looking approach based on cooperation, trust-building, and conflict resolution will be the foundations for a resilient and proactive Franco-Arab relationship.

## Cultural Exchanges and Mutual Understanding

In Franco-Arab relations, cultural exchanges are pivotal in fostering mutual understanding and strengthening bilateral ties. These exchanges encompass many activities, including but not limited to art exhibitions, film festivals, literary events, music collaborations, and educational programs. Each of these initiatives serves as a platform for showcasing the rich cultural heritage of France and the Arab world, facilitating dialogue, and promoting cross-cultural engagement.

At the heart of cultural exchanges is the celebration and appreciation of diversity. By sharing language, traditions, and artistic expressions, Franco-Arab cultural exchanges bridge geographical distances and build bridges of empathy and solidarity. Through such cultural interactions, individuals gain insights into each other's histories, values, and belief systems, nurturing respect and openness towards one another.

Moreover, cultural exchanges contribute to the promotion of tolerance and inclusion. By embracing the differences and similarities between French and Arab cultures, societies on both sides are encouraged to embrace multiculturalism and combat biases and prejudices. This exchange of ideas and perspectives fosters an environment where diversity is celebrated, laying the groundwork for greater societal harmony and cohesion.

Importantly, these exchanges also significantly impact knowledge dissemination and learning. They provide opportunities for individuals to engage with new concepts, viewpoints, and cultural practices, enriching their intellectual and emotional experiences. Additionally, such engagements facilitate academic and intellectual collaborations, encouraging scholars, artists, and thought leaders to engage in mutual learning and cooperative research endeavors.

Furthermore, the cultural sector is an economic catalyst, driving creative industries and tourism. Promoting cultural tourism and heritage preservation generates economic benefits and enhances people-to-people connections, fostering long-lasting friendships and partnerships.

As we move towards the future of Franco-Arab relations, it is imperative to recognize the significance of cultural exchanges and mutual understanding. These initiatives are cornerstones for building enduring relationships, fostering respect, and creating a shared sense of global citizenship. Embracing the richness of diverse cultures paves the way for a more interconnected and harmonious world where collaboration and cooperation thrive for the collective benefit of all.

## *Environmental Initiatives and Joint Ventures*

Amid the complexity of Franco-Arab relations, environmental concerns have emerged as a crucial focus area for sustainable collaboration. The intertwining challenges of climate change, resource depletion, and ecological degradation necessitate concerted efforts from France and Arab states to devise innovative solutions and implement meaningful environmental initiatives. Various joint ventures have been initiated to address these pressing issues in recent years, reflecting an evolving paradigm of cooperation and shared responsibility. One prominent aspect of this collaboration revolves around renewable energy projects, wherein France and Arab countries are leveraging their respective expertise in solar, wind, and hydroelectric technologies to drive the transition toward cleaner energy sources. Collaborative research endeavors and technological exchanges foster advancements in renewable energy infrastructure and economic growth while mitigating the adverse impacts of fossil fuel dependency. Moreover, environmental sustainability extends beyond energy production, encompassing conservation efforts, biodiversity preservation, and sustainable natural resource management. Franco-Arab partnerships are actively engaged in initiatives to preserve delicate ecosystems, protect endangered species, and promote sustainable agricultural practices. These endeavors uphold environmental integrity, foster socio-economic development, and enhance resilience against ecological disruptions. Furthermore, waste management and pollution control constitute critical areas where joint initiatives are making tangible strides. Through knowledge sharing, technical assistance, and policy harmonization, France and Arab states work collaboratively to mitigate pollution levels, improve waste management systems, and promote circular economies. This convergence of efforts is instrumental in addressing transboundary environmental challenges and ensuring a healthier future for the planet. Additionally, water resource management and sustainable urban development are receiving heightened attention within the framework of Franco-Arab environmental cooperation. Given the increasing pressures on water resources and rapid urbanization trends, joint ventures are endeavoring to optimize water usage efficiency, implement integrated urban planning strategies, and enhance resilience against environmental risks. These initiatives contribute to environmental sustainability and facilitate equitable socio-economic development and prosperity for present and future generations. The collaborative architecture of environmental initiatives and joint ventures between France and Arab states epitomizes a commitment to shared stewardship, collective action, and long-term sustainability. As both parties navigate the evolving environmental landscape, the synergistic approach augurs well for addressing multifaceted environmental challenges and realizing a more resilient, inclusive, and environmentally conscious future.

## *Security Challenges and Defense Cooperation*

In Franco-Arab relations, security challenges and defense cooperation play pivotal roles in shaping the future landscape of the partnership between the two entities. The evolving geopolitical dynamics and the rise of non-traditional security threats have underscored the critical importance of fostering collaborative efforts in these domains.

The security challenges facing the Franco-Arab partnership are multifaceted and complex. From transnational terrorism and extremism to cyber threats and regional conflicts, the security landscape demands a comprehensive approach encompassing preventive measures and responsive strategies. Countering these challenges requires a high degree of coordination and intelligence sharing between France and Arab countries and a concerted effort to address the root causes of instability and turmoil in the region.

Defense cooperation emerges as a cornerstone of strengthening mutual trust and bolstering the collective capability to mitigate security risks. This entails exchanging military expertise, technology, and joint military exercises and training programs to enhance interoperability and crisis response capabilities. Moreover, collaborative initiatives in defense industry development and arms trade regulation are instrumental in promoting transparency and building consensus on arms control measures.

The significance of defense cooperation extends beyond addressing immediate security threats; it also serves as a means to foster diplomatic ties and fortify strategic alliances. By engaging in joint peacekeeping missions, border security operations, and counter-piracy efforts, France and Arab states can demonstrate their commitment to upholding regional stability and maintaining maritime and territorial integrity. Moreover, shared endeavors in arms limitation agreements and confidence-building measures cultivate confidence and predictability.

Furthermore, the emergence of hybrid warfare and the proliferation of asymmetric threats necessitate adaptive and forward-looking defense strategies. Collaboration in cybersecurity, intelligence-sharing, and counter-radicalization efforts is indispensable to preempting emerging threats and safeguarding critical infrastructure. Embracing technological advancements while abiding by ethical principles and international legal frameworks is key to harnessing the potential of defense innovation while mitigating the risks associated with misuse or proliferation.

In conclusion, the path forward for Franco-Arab security cooperation entails a comprehensive and nuanced approach to address diverse security challenges while fostering a resilient defense architecture. By prioritizing mutual interests, shared values, and a commitment to international peace and security, France and Arab countries can forge a robust framework for defense cooperation that safeguards their interests and contributes to global stability and prosperity.

## *Educational Partnerships and Scholarly Exchanges*

In Franco-Arab relations, educational partnerships and scholarly exchanges are pivotal in fostering mutual understanding, academic collaboration, and knowledge sharing between France and the Arab world. These partnerships serve as a cornerstone for building cultural bridges and facilitating intellectual dialogues that transcend geographical boundaries and contribute to enriching both societies' educational landscapes.

Educational collaboration between France and Arab countries encompasses a broad spectrum of activities, including student exchange programs, joint research initiatives, collaborative academic conferences, and establishing French educational institutions in the Arab world. These endeavors are instrumental in promoting cross-cultural competence, language proficiency, and academic excellence, thereby developing a globally oriented and culturally sensitive scholarly community.

Moreover, the exchange of scholars, researchers, and educators fosters an environment of intellectual synergy whereby diverse perspectives converge to address common challenges and pursue innovative solutions. By harnessing the collective expertise and academic resources of France and Arab states, educational partnerships facilitate interdisciplinary studies, stimulate intellectual discourse, and nurture a culture of innovation and progress within science, technology, humanities, and social sciences.

Furthermore, these collaborations lay the groundwork for nurturing future leaders and professionals equipped with a nuanced understanding of cultural diversity, international cooperation, and global challenges. This contributes to developing a well-rounded and cosmopolitan workforce and cultivates a cadre of individuals committed to advancing mutual respect, tolerance, and intercultural dialogue on regional and global scales.

Promoting linguistic diversity and preserving cultural heritage is at the heart of educational partnerships and scholarly exchanges. French language education in the Arab world facilitates access to a rich literary and intellectual tradition. It is a conduit for promoting intercultural communication, academic mobility, and exchanging ideas across linguistic frontiers.

In conclusion, educational partnerships and scholarly exchanges between France and Arab states testify to the enduring commitment to fostering intellectual collaboration, knowledge dissemination, and cultural interconnectedness. These initiatives enrich the academic landscape and imbue future generations with a profound appreciation for diversity, cultural heritage, and the pursuit of academic excellence within the context of Franco-Arab relations.

## *Human Rights and Governance Issues*

In the intricate web of Franco-Arab relations, the fundamental aspects of human rights and governance play a crucial role. As both France and Arab countries continue to navigate challenges in this arena, examining the evolving landscape and potential pathways for collaboration is imperative. Human rights encompass a broad spectrum of civil, political, economic, social, and cultural rights that form the cornerstone of democratic societies. Ensuring the protection and promotion of these rights is essential for fostering trust and stability between France and Arab states. Governance issues, including transparency, accountability, and the rule of law, are integral components that underpin effective cooperation and sustainable development. Identifying common ground and addressing disparities in human rights and governance frameworks is pivotal for advancing mutual respect and understanding. Applying international human rights law and best practices in governance catalyzes constructive dialogue and policy harmonization. Embracing diversity and inclusive decision-making processes contributes to shaping an environment that upholds universal human rights standards. Moreover, addressing governance challenges such as corruption and institutional reforms fosters an enabling environment for equitable socio-economic progress. Both France and Arab countries have a collective responsibility to uphold and advance human rights principles, recognizing the interdependence of peace, security, and human dignity. Through collaborative efforts, leveraging platforms such as multilateral organizations and diplomatic engagements, opportunities arise to address shared challenges and enhance respect for human rights and good governance. Engaging in open, respectful dialogue and knowledge exchanges regarding human rights mechanisms and governance practices ultimately reinforces the fabric of Franco-Arab relations. A proactive approach involving capacity-building initiatives, technical assistance, and public awareness campaigns is vital to sustain meaningful progress. Acknowledging historical contexts and addressing contemporary realities with a forward-looking perspective cultivates a climate of mutual trust and cooperation on human rights and governance. Looking ahead, embracing a culture of continuous improvement and adaptation to evolving global norms augurs well for nurturing a values-based partnership between France and Arab states. The future trajectory of Franco-Arab relations rests on upholding human rights and strengthening governance frameworks, a testament to their commitment to fostering a just and prosperous world.

## *Predictive Analysis and Future Scenarios*

The future of Franco-Arab relations is a subject of considerable interest and speculation, particularly in the context of evolving global dynamics. Predictive analysis allows exploring potential scenarios based on current trends and developments in the diplomatic, economic, cultural, and security domains. Several key factors must be considered when considering the future of Franco-Arab relations. One critical aspect is the impact of technological advancements on communication, trade, and collaboration. As digital transformation continues to reshape societies and economies, both France and Arab states are likely to leverage technology for enhanced connectivity and innovation. This could lead to closer partnerships in digital infrastructure, cybersecurity, and smart city development. Another pivotal consideration is the evolving geopolitical landscape and its implications for Franco-Arab relations. The strategic alignments and regional dynamics will significantly influence the cooperative and competitive aspects of the relationship. Furthermore, given the increasing interconnectedness of global economies, the future scenarios of economic prospects and collaborations between France and Arab states are subject to various variables. These include trade agreements, investment flows, energy cooperation, and the development of sustainable business strategies. Cultural exchanges and mutual understanding are also anticipated to play a fundamental role in shaping the future of Franco-Arab relations. With an emphasis on preserving cultural heritage, promoting diversity, and fostering intercultural dialogue, both parties can cultivate a more profound appreciation for each other's traditions and values. Environmental initiatives and joint ventures represent another area where future scenarios may unfold. Shared concerns about climate change, ecological sustainability, and environmental conservation present opportunities for collaborative efforts in renewable energy, conservation projects, and climate resilience strategies. Furthermore, addressing security challenges and enhancing defense cooperation is paramount for shaping future scenarios of Franco-Arab relations. As both regions confront evolving threats and transnational risks, the potential for collaborative security frameworks, intelligence sharing, and joint military exercises becomes increasingly significant. Educational partnerships and scholarly exchanges are expected to contribute to building bridges between France and Arab countries. The educational sector can be pivotal for nurturing mutual understanding and knowledge sharing by fostering academic cooperation, research collaboration, and student mobility programs. Throughout the predictive analysis, it is imperative to consider potential future scenarios regarding human rights and governance issues within Franco-Arab relations. By examining potential advancements in democratic governance, civil liberties, and social progress, stakeholders can anticipate the evolution of human rights frameworks and institutional reforms. In conclusion, the future scenarios of Franco-Arab relations are shaped by many complex factors, requiring careful consideration and strategic foresight. Predictive analysis enables us to explore these potential scenarios, but it is essential to acknowledge that continual adjustments, negotiations, and unforeseen events will influence the actual trajectory.

# IN A NUTSHELL

## 1. *Technological Advancements and Their Impacts*

Technological advancements are poised to significantly impact Franco-Arab relations. France and Arab states are increasingly collaborating on digital transformation and cybersecurity. For instance, France's National Strategy for Digital Security and the UAE's initiatives in artificial intelligence and smart cities highlight the mutual interest in leveraging technology for economic and security benefits. The establishment of joint research centers and technology parks, such as the collaboration between French and Emirati institutions, underscores the importance of technology in shaping future relations.

## 2. *Economic Prospects and Collaborations*

Economic collaboration between France and Arab states is robust and multifaceted. The UAE and France have established a

Comprehensive Strategic Energy Partnership, focusing on energy security and the transition to renewable energy. Additionally, the Maghreb region's integration with the EU, facilitated by France, presents significant economic opportunities, particularly in sectors like automotive manufacturing and renewable energy. The strategic dialogues and high-level business councils further enhance economic ties, promoting trade and investment across various sectors.

### 3. Political Dynamics and Strategic Alignments

The political dynamics between France and Arab states are influenced by historical ties and contemporary geopolitical shifts. France's strategic posture in the Middle East, including its partnerships with the UAE, Egypt, and Jordan, reflects a commitment to regional stability and security. The Abraham Accords and France's engagement in multilateral forums like the Baghdad Conference for Cooperation and Partnership highlight the evolving strategic alignments aimed at fostering peace and prosperity in the region.

### 4. Cultural Exchanges and Mutual Understanding

Cultural exchanges play a pivotal role in strengthening Franco-Arab relations. Initiatives like the Louvre Abu Dhabi and the presence of French educational institutions in the UAE, such as Paris-Sorbonne University, exemplify the deep cultural ties between the regions. These exchanges promote mutual understanding and tolerance, fostering long-term relationships between people and institutions. The teaching of French in UAE schools and the promotion of Arabic in France further enhance cultural connectivity.

## 5. Environmental Initiatives and Joint Ventures

Environmental cooperation is a growing area of focus in Franco-Arab relations. France and the UAE are collaborating on various environmental initiatives, including the Comprehensive Strategic Energy Partnership, which aims to address energy security and climate change. Joint ventures in renewable energy, such as solar and hydrogen projects in the Maghreb, highlight the potential for sustainable development and green technology collaboration. These initiatives align with global efforts to combat climate change and promote environmental sustainability.

## 6. Security Challenges and Defense Cooperation

Security challenges and defense cooperation are central to Franco-Arab relations. France's involvement in regional security, including its military presence and counter-terrorism efforts, underscores its commitment to regional stability. Collaborative defense agreements and joint military exercises with Arab states, particularly in the Gulf, enhance mutual security capabilities and address common threats such as terrorism and cyberattacks. The strategic dialogues and defense partnerships further solidify these security ties.

## 7. Educational Partnerships and Scholarly Exchanges

Educational partnerships and scholarly exchanges are vital for fostering long-term cooperation between France and Arab states. The presence of French universities in the UAE and the establishment of new educational programs, such as the international gaming and animation school Rubika in Abu Dhabi, highlight the commitment to academic collaboration. These partnerships facilitate knowledge exchange, research collaboration, and the development of a skilled workforce, contributing to the socio-economic development of both regions.

## 8. Human Rights and Governance Issues

Human rights and governance issues remain a complex aspect of Franco-Arab relations. While France advocates for human rights and democratic governance, its partnerships with authoritarian regimes in the Arab world often involve a delicate balance between promoting these values and maintaining strategic interests. The political dynamics in the region, characterized by authoritarian resilience and technocratic governance, present challenges for advancing human rights and democratic reforms. France's approach involves diplomatic engagement and support for civil society initiatives to promote governance reforms.

## 9. Predictive Analysis and Future Scenarios

Predictive analysis of Franco-Arab relations suggests several future scenarios. The continued emphasis on technological collaboration, economic integration, and cultural exchanges is likely to strengthen bilateral ties. However, geopolitical shifts, security challenges, and governance issues will require adaptive strategies and robust diplomatic engagement. The evolving multipolar world, with increasing influence from emerging powers, will also shape the future dynamics of Franco-Arab relations. By leveraging their historical ties and strategic partnerships, France and Arab states can navigate these complexities and build a resilient and mutually beneficial relationship.

In conclusion, the future of Franco-Arab relations is multifaceted, involving technological advancements, economic collaborations, political dynamics, cultural exchanges, environmental initiatives, security challenges, educational partnerships, human rights issues, and predictive analysis. By addressing these key areas, France and Arab states can enhance their cooperation and contribute to regional and global stability and prosperity.

# References For Further Reading

Yolanda Smits, Clémentine Daubeuf, Philippe Kern. "EUROPEAN CULTURAL INSTITUTES ABROAD". European Parliament. https://www.europarl.europa.eu/RegData/etudes/STUD/2016/563418/IPOL_STU%282016%29563418_EN.pdf

"Multipolarity: The New Global Economy". The World Bank. 2011. https://documents1.worldbank.org/curated/en/597691468150580088/pdf/626980PUB0Mult000public00BOX361489B.pdf

Michaël Tanchum. "Turkey's Maghreb–West Africa Economic Architecture: Challenges and Opportunities for the European Union". CENTRE FOR APPLIED TURKEY STUDIES (CATS) | WP NR. 03, JUNE 2021. https://www.swp-berlin.org/publications/products/arbeitspapiere/

CATS_Working_Paper_Nr_3_Michael_Tanchum_Turkeys_Maghreb_West_Africa_Economic_Architecture.pdf

"25th Anniversary of the Indo-French Strategic Partnership: Towards a Century of French-Indian Relations." Presidence de la republique. https://www.elysee.fr/admin/upload/default/0001/15/13ca1dc3c8938ae4ce52f5c53e149ddd251099cb.pdf

Larbi Sadiki, "On Tents, Fast Trains and the Greater Mediterranean: Franco-Maghrebi Relations". March 5, 2008. Carnegie. https://carnegieendowment.org/research/2008/03/on-tents-fast-trains-and-the-greater-mediterranean-franco-maghrebi-relations?lang=en

Al Otaiba, Hend . "Culture Fuels the UAE-France Relationship." The National,

September 26, 2021. https://www.thenationalnews.com/opinion/comment/2021/09/26/culture-is-at-the-heart-of-uae-france-relations/.

Anita Say Chan. "Data Journalism, Digital Universalism and Innovation in the Periphery." DataJournalism.com. Accessed May 24, 2024. https://datajournalism.com/read/handbook/two/training-data-journalists/data-journalism-digital-universalism-and-innovation-in-the-periphery.

"Choosing Europe's Future an INTER-INSTITUTIONAL EU PROJECT," 2024. https://www.espas.eu/files/espas_files/about/ESPAS-Global-Trends-to-2040-Choosing-Europes-Future.pdf.

El Karoui, Hakim. "A New Strategy for France in a New Arab World." Institut Montaigne, August 2017. https://www.institutmontaigne.org/en/publications/new-strategy-france-new-arab-world.

Fayet, Héloïse. "What Strategic Posture Should France Adopt in the Middle East?," November 2022. https://www.ifri.org/sites/default/files/atoms/files/fayet_focus112_pmo_us_2023.pdf.

France Diplomacy - Ministry for Europe and Foreign Affairs. "15th Session of the UAE-France Strategic Dialogue Discusses Growing Cooperation between UAE & France (19.06.23)." France Diplomacy, 2019. https://www.diplomatie.gouv.fr/en/country-files/united-arab-emirates/events/article/15th-session-of-the-uae-france-strategic-dialogue-discusses-growing-cooperation.

France Diplomacy - Ministry for Europe and Foreign Affairs. "France and Algeria," August 2022. https://www.diplomatie.gouv.fr/en/country-files/algeria/france-and-algeria-64943/.

France in the UK. "France and UAE Extend Their Strategic Partnership," July 21, 2022. https://uk.ambafrance.org/France-and-UAE-extend-their-strategic-partnership.

Geranmayeh, Ellie. "Profile: Ellie Geranmayeh." ECFR, September 29, 2023. https://ecfr.eu/profile/ellie_geranmayeh/.

Hadfield, Amelia, and Christian Turner. "Entente Cordiale Redux: The Impact of Brexit on British and French Foreign and Security Policy." Contemporary British History 37, no. 4 (August 2, 2023): 633–55. https://doi.org/10.1080/13619462.2023.2237315.

National Intelligence Council. "2025 Global Trends Final Report," 2025. https://www.dni.gov/files/documents/Newsroom/Reports%20and%20Pubs/2025_Global_Trends_Final_Report.pdf.

Storm, Lise. "Political Dynamics in the Arab World and the Future of Ideologies." www.iemed.org. Accessed May 24, 2024. https://www.iemed.org/publication/political-dynamics-in-the-arab-world-and-the-future-of-ideologies/?lang=fr.

www.frstrategie.org. "Notes de La FRS :: Foundation for Strategic Research :: FRS." Accessed May 24, 2024. https://www.frstrategie.org/en/publications/notes.

www.gmfus.org. "Alliances in a Shifting Global Order: Rethinking Transatlantic Engagement with Global Swing States | Strengthening Transatlantic Cooperation," May 2, 2023. https://www.gmfus.org/news/alliances-shifting-global-order-rethinking-transatlantic-engagement-global-swing-states.

Yakoubi, Myriam. "The French, the British and Their Middle Eastern Mandates (1918-1939): Two Political Strategies." Revue Française de Civilisation Britannique. French Journal of British Studies XXVII, no. 1 (January 4, 2022). https://journals.openedition.org/rfcb/8787.

# XXVI

# *Conclusion*

## SUMMARY OF KEY FINDINGS

Throughout the book, the evaluation of Franco-Arab relations is a comprehensive and illuminating journey, deeply anchored in historical context while shedding light on modern-day implications. The colonial legacy and early diplomacy set the stage for a complex yet influential relationship that has evolved. De Gaulle's vision reshaped the dynamics, marking a pivotal turning point in Franco-Arab relations. Navigating the Cold War era brought unique challenges and opportunities, shaping the bilateral engagement between France and Arab countries. The process of decolonization and independence showcased the fruition of nationalistic aspirations and its impact on diplomatic ties. Economic partnerships and energy interests underscored the mutual benefits and interdependence, laying the foundation for sustained collaboration. Cultural diplomacy and exchange programs fostered mutual understanding and empathy, strengthening bilateral bonds. France's engagement with the Gulf States has been diplomatically significant and strategically crucial in the broader geopolitical landscape. Cooperation in education and research has been instrumental in knowledge exchange and human capital development, reinforcing the bilateral relationship. Addressing the challenges of terrorism and security cooperation has led to the evolution of counterterrorism strategies and bilateral security frameworks aimed at safeguarding common interests. Human rights and democracy promotion have been an intrinsic part of France's foreign policy, influencing the discourse and direction of Franco-Arab relations. Peacekeeping and conflict resolution efforts have exemplified France's commitment to regional stability and peace, playing a constructive role in mitigating conflicts. Environmental cooperation and sustainable development initiatives have reflected a shared commitment to addressing global challenges and pursuing sustainable pathways. The Arab Spring revolutions represented a watershed moment, shaping the dynamics of Franco-Arab relations and the French response to regional developments. Macron's presidency ushered in a new chapter, emphasizing the recalibration of priorities and a rejuvenation of bilateral engagement. Economic reforms and investment opportunities have unlocked new avenues for economic collaboration and prosperity, projecting promising trajectories for future economic synergies. Immigration policies and integration challenges underscore the complexities and imperatives of inclusive societal integration, presenting challenges and opportunities. France's role in Middle East conflicts has exemplified the complexities of diplomatic maneuvering and the persistent pursuit of peaceful resolution. Security threats and regional stability have necessitated concerted efforts toward safeguarding shared interests and bolstering stability. France's influence in North Africa extends beyond geographical proximity, encompassing cultural, economic, and strategic dimensions of collaboration and engagement. Soft power and public diplomacy have underpinned the fabric of Franco-Arab relations, shaping narratives and cultivating goodwill. Gender equality and women's rights have emerged as essential components of the bilateral agenda, underscoring the commitment to societal progress and equity. France's proactive stance in addressing the refugee crisis has demonstrated solidarity and compassion, reflecting a principled approach to humanitarian challenges. Cybersecurity and digital diplomacy have emerged as critical facets of contemporary engagement, signaling the imperative shift toward technological cooperation and resilience. Finally, envisioning the future of Franco-Arab relations entails embracing progressive paradigms rooted in trust, reciprocity, innovation, and inclusive growth, aiming to forge enduring partnerships built on shared values and collective aspirations.

## EVALUATING FRANCO-ARAB RELATIONS: HISTORICAL CONTEXT TO MODERN DAY

The evaluation of Franco-Arab relations demands a comprehensive analysis, tracing the historical trajectories and modern developments that have shaped this dynamic relationship. The connection between France and the Arab world is deeply rooted in a complex interplay of historical legacies, geopolitical shifts, and sociocultural ties. Since colonial times, France has maintained a significant presence in various Arab countries, influencing policies, trade, and cultural exchanges. The Algiers Accord of 1962 marked a crucial juncture, signaling the end of the Algerian War and laying the groundwork for rediscovering France's relations with the Arab states. This historical turning point initiated a series of diplomatic overtures and realignments, forging new paths for cooperation and engagement. The oil crisis of the 1970s further underscored the strategic importance of Arab countries, compelling France to recalibrate its economic and political policies. In recent decades, efforts to address shared challenges such as terrorism, migration, and regional stability have necessitated deeper collaboration and dialogue. The evolving geopolitical landscape, marked by the Arab Spring uprisings and the complexities of conflict in the Middle East, has tested the resilience and adaptability of Franco-Arab relations. Moreover, new global powers and technological advancements have introduced novel dimensions to this partnership, creating opportunities for synergy and competition. The shift towards renewable energy, digital innovation, and sustainable development has added fresh impetus to bilateral discussions and joint initiatives. It is essential to critically evaluate the multifaceted narrative of Franco-Arab relations, navigating through historical imprints, contemporary engagements, and future aspirations.

This examination serves as a foundation for charting a pragmatic and forward-looking roadmap that reflects the evolving realities of the international landscape.

## MAJOR CHALLENGES FACED AND OVERCOME

The journey of Franco-Arab relations has been marked by numerous challenges that have tested the resilience and strength of the partnership. From historical conflicts to contemporary geopolitical upheavals, France and the Arab world have encountered formidable obstacles in their quest for cooperation and understanding. One of the significant challenges faced was the lingering impact of colonial history, which created deep-seated distrust and resentment among Arab countries. The legacy of colonialism had cast a shadow over diplomatic endeavors, making it challenging to forge mutually beneficial relationships. Additionally, the rise of extremist ideologies and terrorist threats posed a persistent challenge to regional stability, requiring coordinated efforts to address security concerns and counter-radicalization. Moreover, economic disparities and developmental imbalances within the Arab region presented hurdles in establishing sustainable and equitable partnerships. These challenges demanded innovative approaches and steadfast commitment to overcome historical prejudices and nurture constructive engagement. Overcoming these obstacles required bold leadership, empathetic diplomacy, and a genuine willingness to bridge longstanding divides. France and Arab countries gradually navigated through complex historical grievances and ideological differences, striving to build a foundation of trust and collaboration. Through dialogue, mutual respect, and concerted efforts, the parties involved undertook the arduous task of addressing contentious issues and finding common ground. Over time, significant milestones were achieved in fostering cultural exchanges, promoting economic ties, and enhancing people-to-people connections, paving the way for a more inclusive and interconnected relationship. Furthermore, proactive measures were taken to confront security challenges, with joint initiatives aimed at combatting terrorism, reinforcing stability, and promoting peacebuilding efforts in conflict-affected areas. The journey of overcoming challenges underscored the resilience and determination of France and Arab countries to surmount obstacles and build a future of shared prosperity and cooperation.

## OPPORTUNITIES FOR ENHANCED COOPERATION

In assessing the future of Franco-Arab relations, it is essential to recognize the myriad opportunities for enhanced cooperation in the contemporary geopolitical landscape. One avenue for bolstering collaboration lies in trade and economic partnerships. The economic potential between France and the Arab world remains vast, with increased investment, technological exchange, and infrastructural development opportunities. Both regions can benefit from enhanced economic growth and sustainable development by leveraging these prospects. Furthermore, cultural diplomacy represents an influential platform for fostering mutual understanding and appreciation between societies. Through cultural exchanges, artistic collaborations, and educational initiatives, France and the Arab countries can enrich their longstanding cultural ties while promoting intercultural dialogue and empathy. This strengthens people-to-people connections and lays the groundwork for greater collaboration in various domains. Moreover, amid the evolving digital landscape, immense potential exists for innovation and knowledge-sharing. France's expertise in technology and the Arab world's burgeoning tech sector offer fertile ground for collaborative ventures in digital infrastructure, cybersecurity, and information technology. Strategic cooperation could yield substantial progress in e-governance, education, and healthcare. Another notable opportunity lies in the sphere of renewable energy and sustainable development. As the global community increasingly grapples with environmental challenges, France and the Arab states are well-positioned to form alliances centered on green technologies, climate action, and ecological conservation. By aligning efforts toward sustainability, both parties can spearhead meaningful change and set new standards for environmental stewardship on a global scale. Additionally, enhancing cooperation in education and research promises to nurture intellectual exchange and academic synergy. Collaborative initiatives in higher education, scientific discovery, and innovation could pave the way for breakthroughs in diverse sectors, cultivating a thriving ecosystem of shared knowledge and expertise. Ultimately, these opportunities for enhanced cooperation underscore the potential for deeper, more comprehensive engagement between France and the Arab world. The two entities can forge a resilient partnership rooted in mutual prosperity, innovation, and enduring friendship by capitalizing on these avenues.

## IMPACT OF CHANGED GLOBAL DYNAMICS

The landscape of international relations has undergone significant transformations in recent decades, exerting profound effects on Franco-Arab cooperation. The end of the Cold War and the emergence of new global powers have expanded the range of diplomatic opportunities and challenges for France and the Arab world. The rise of non-state actors, transnational threats, and the increasing interconnectedness of economic, social, and political systems have reshaped the dynamics of international diplomacy. The proliferation of information and communication technologies has facilitated excellent connectivity and introduced vulnerabilities that demand innovative responses. Furthermore, the shifting tides of geopolitical influence, particularly in the Middle East and North Africa, necessitate a nuanced approach to policy-making and engagement. Amidst this backdrop, the need for adaptability and foresight in Franco-Arab relations has never been more pressing.

One of the primary consequences of changed global dynamics is the reconfiguration of power structures and alliances, influencing the strategic calculus of France and Arab states. The evolving nature of security threats, including terrorism, cyber-attacks, and regional conflicts, underscores the imperative for collaborative efforts in maintaining peace and stability. Moreover, economic interdependence and geopolitical rivalries directly affect trade, investment, and energy cooperation. Recognizing the multi-faceted impact of globalization and regional dynamics, it is paramount for policymakers from both sides to comprehend the intricate linkages and interdependencies that underpin contemporary international affairs.

Simultaneously, the changing global landscape has engendered new avenues for cooperation, innovation, and mutual enrichment. Enhanced people-to-people connections, cultural exchanges, and educational initiatives have fostered an environment of greater understanding and appreciation between France and the Arab world. Technological advancements have opened vistas for collaborative endeavors in renewable energy, digital infrastructure, and sustainable development. The convergence of interests in combating climate change, promoting inclusive growth, and harnessing the potential of emerging markets presents an opportunity to align diplomatic priorities and forge enduring partnerships.

Furthermore, the recalibration of global dynamics demands a proactive approach to addressing transnational challenges, including migration, pandemics, and environmental degradation. France and Arab countries' ability to navigate these complexities will depend on their capacity to adapt, innovate, and engage constructively with diverse stakeholders. Embracing the possibilities brought forth by changed global dynamics while effectively mitigating the associated risks requires astute leadership, robust institutions, and a shared commitment to upholding the principles of international norms and cooperation.

As such, comprehending the impact of changed global dynamics on Franco-Arab relations is pivotal in charting a course for the future characterized by resilience, reciprocity, and relevance. By recognizing the evolving complexities and seizing the opportunities embedded within, both entities can secure a position of influence and mutual benefit amidst the myriad challenges of the twenty-first-century global order.

## RECOMMENDATIONS FOR FUTURE POLICIES

As we conclude our exploration of the intricate tapestry of Franco-Arab relations, it becomes imperative to deliberate on the recommendations for future policies that could strengthen this relationship in the coming years. The evolving global landscape demands a proactive and adaptive approach to diplomacy, and Franco-Arab relations are no exception to this paradigm. Firstly, it is essential for policymakers to prioritize robust dialogues and sustained engagement across diverse domains such as economic cooperation, cultural exchange, security collaboration, and environmental sustainability. This multifaceted approach can help foster mutual understanding and amplify the positive impact of bilateral relations. Additionally, nurturing an environment of trust and respect through transparent communication and adherence to international norms will solidify the foundations of enduring cooperation between France and the Arab world. Emphasizing the importance of people-to-people connections and educational exchanges can cultivate greater empathy and intercultural appreciation, laying the groundwork for long-term harmony. Furthermore, aligning policies with the United Nations Sustainable Development Goals can guide joint initiatives to address socio-economic challenges and promote inclusive growth. In the context of changing global dynamics, it is pivotal for France and Arab countries to adapt their policies to harness the benefits of technological advancements and digital transformations, thereby leveraging innovation as a catalyst for progress. Moreover, enhancing collaboration in cybersecurity, healthcare, renewable energy, and space exploration can pave the way for mutually beneficial partnerships in emerging sectors. It is incumbent upon both parties to actively address shared threats and challenges, including extremism, terrorism, and regional instability, by collaborating closely on security frameworks and counterterrorism efforts. Implementing forward-looking immigration policies that promote integration, diversity, and social cohesion will contribute to sustainable communities and facilitate the positive integration of immigrant populations. Finally, embracing a holistic approach to gender equality and women's empowerment across various spheres of society and governance can bestow far-reaching socio-economic benefits, promoting equity and sustainable development. These strategic recommendations are aimed at fortifying Franco-Arab relations in the face of contemporary challenges and unlocking new avenues for prosperous collaboration, thus charting a course toward a more resilient and harmonious future.

## PROSPECTIVE AREAS FOR DIPLOMATIC EXPANSION

As Franco-Arab relations evolve, several prospective areas emerge for diplomatic expansion, offering opportunities to bolster bilateral ties and address mutual challenges. One such area is enhancing political dialogue and cooperation on regional security issues, including stabilizing conflict zones and countering terrorism. Strengthening collaboration in peacekeeping and conflict resolution efforts can promote stability and foster trust between France and Arab countries. Moreover, economic diplomacy presents a promising avenue for deepening engagement, focusing on diversifying trade partnerships, encouraging investment, and fostering sustainable development initiatives. Embracing cultural diplomacy through exchange programs and educational partnerships can facilitate greater understanding and build enduring connections between societies. Furthermore, addressing environmental challenges and promoting sustainable practices could be a common platform for joint initiatives, emphasizing the shared commitment to preserving the planet. The digital realm offers another rich prospect for diplomatic expansion, with a growing emphasis on cybersecurity cooperation and harnessing technological advancements for mutual benefit. As the international landscape transforms, exploring new arenas, such as space exploration and innovation in scientific research, presents exciting prospects for collaborative endeavors that can shape the future. Additionally, investing in people-to-people exchanges and supporting civil society engagement can significantly enrich the fabric of Franco-Arab relations. These prospective areas not only offer avenues for diplomatic expansion but also hold the potential to cultivate enduring bonds, foster innovation, and address pressing global challenges, thereby contributing to a more interconnected and prosperous world.

## TECHNOLOGICAL ADVANCEMENTS AND FUTURE COLLABORATIONS

The advancement of technology has been a key driver in shaping the landscape of Franco-Arab relations. In recent years, France and Arab countries have recognized the immense potential for collaboration in the tech sector. The convergence of digital innovation, artificial intelligence, and renewable energy technologies presents a prime opportunity for mutual growth and development. As we stand on the brink of the Fourth Industrial Revolution, both parties must embrace a forward-looking approach toward technological advancements and foster collaborations that benefit their respective economies and advance global progress. One of the burgeoning areas of collaboration is in the field of renewable energy and sustainable infrastructure. With the pressing need to address climate change and transition towards clean energy sources, there is a vast scope for joint initiatives in developing green technologies, smart cities, and efficient energy management systems. Moreover, the rapid evolution of digitalization and e-governance paves the way for enhanced public service delivery and administrative efficiency. Through knowledge exchange and strategic partnerships, France and Arab countries can embark on a transformative journey towards building technologically resilient societies. Furthermore, cybersecurity and digital diplomacy underscore the criticality of securing digital assets and establishing robust cyber defenses. Given the rise of cyber threats globally, collaborative efforts in cybersecurity research, capacity-building, and information sharing can fortify the collective resilience against emerging cyber risks. Looking ahead, the advent of frontier technologies such as quantum computing, biotechnology, and space exploration unveils a new frontier for innovative collaborations. By leveraging each other's expertise and resources, France and Arab countries can position themselves at the forefront of technological breakthroughs, thereby solidifying their partnership on a global scale. It is paramount for both parties to forge strategic alliances that nurture a culture of innovation, knowledge transfer, and ethical, technological deployment. As we venture into an era defined by technological leaps, the roadmap for future collaborations between France and Arab countries must prioritize ethical, inclusive, and sustainable approaches that uphold the values of shared prosperity and societal well-being. By fostering a conducive environment for technological advancements and cultivating strong synergies across various domains, both entities can collectively propel the trajectory of human progress and lead the world toward a more interconnected and prosperous future.

## PROMOTING SUSTAINABLE AND INCLUSIVE GROWTH

As we conclude our analysis of Franco-Arab relations, it is essential to underscore the importance of promoting sustainable and inclusive growth. The economic, social, and environmental dynamics within which these two regions operate necessitate a concerted effort towards fostering long-term sustainability and inclusivity. This proposition rests on the foundational principle that sustained economic development can only be achieved if inclusive, leaving no community or region behind. In this vein, sustainable economic growth is inexorably linked with equity considerations, environmental conservation, and international cooperation. The key to this endeavor is aligning national and regional policies with the United Nations' Sustainable Development Goals (SDGs), which tie Franco-Arab relations to broader global strategies for sustainable development. Initiatives aiming at sustainable growth must focus on environmental conservation, renewable energy adoption, and efficient resource management to mitigate climate change impacts. Furthermore, inclusive growth can be advanced through targeted investments in education, healthcare, and infrastructure, ensuring that all segments of society can participate in and benefit from economic advancements. Cross-regional collaborations should prioritize knowledge exchange, technology transfer, and capacity building to support sustainable and inclusive economic initiatives. Recognizing the potential synergies between French expertise in areas such as renewable energy and Arab countries' abundant natural resources, joint ventures and research partnerships could significantly contribute to sustainable growth. Moreover, inclusive growth requires addressing disparities in income distribution, reducing poverty, and promoting gender equality to maximize human capital and entrepreneurship potential. Policies and partnerships must empower marginalized communities and promote diversity and inclusion in the economic landscape. Promoting sustainable and inclusive growth will enhance the prosperity and well-being of the Franco-Arab regions and contribute to more stability and resilience in the face of global challenges. By advocating for policies and practices prioritizing sustainable and inclusive growth, France and Arab countries can forge a resilient partnership founded on mutual prosperity and shared values.

## FINAL THOUGHTS: ENVISIONING A ROBUST PARTNERSHIP

As we conclude our exploration of Franco-Arab relations, it is imperative to envision a future characterized by a robust and dynamic partnership between France and the Arab world. Such a vision is grounded in a holistic approach that recognizes the historical ties, cultural affinities, and shared interests that form the foundation of this relationship. Looking ahead, both parties need to cultivate a contemporary framework built on mutual respect, understanding, and cooperation. The trajectory of this partnership should be guided by a commitment to addressing common challenges while harnessing the opportunities that lie ahead. One key aspect of envisioning a robust partnership involves fostering inclusive economic growth and sustainable development. This entails prioritizing initiatives that promote economic diversification, innovation, and equitable access to resources. Embracing modern technologies and digital platforms can also serve as catalysts for enhancing connectivity and driving socio-economic progress. Furthermore, it is crucial to recognize the significance of people-to-people exchanges and educational collaborations in nurturing a robust Franco-Arab partnership. Both regions can build bridges that transcend geographical boundaries by fostering cultural awareness, language proficiency, and academic synergies. Empowering women and youth through targeted programs and initiatives can create a more inclusive and vibrant partnership. Diplomatic expansion and strategic dialogue are integral components of envisaging a robust partnership. This involves leveraging diplomatic channels to address regional and global issues, foster peace and stability, and uphold shared values. Moreover, joint efforts to counter common security threats and promote regional integration can strengthen cooperation. The future of Franco-Arab relations also warrants a proactive approach toward tackling environmental challenges and advancing sustainable practices. Collaborative endeavors in renewable energy, climate resilience, and conservation efforts can reinforce the bonds of partnership. As we envision a robust partnership, it is essential to underscore the significance of embracing diversity, fostering intercultural dialogue, and upholding the principles of equality and respect. This collective vision should resonate with a forward-looking perspective that transcends short-term considerations and embraces a long-term commitment to mutual prosperity and shared progress. The potential for Franco-Arab relations to evolve into a resilient, multifaceted, and mutually beneficial partnership becomes evident within this aspirational framework. By harnessing the collective strengths, innovations, and capabilities of both France and the Arab world, the prospect of forging a robust partnership remains not only plausible but also imperative for navigating the complex global landscape.

www.ingramcontent.com/pod-product-compliance
Lightning Source LLC
Chambersburg PA
CBHW051522020426
42333CB00016B/1736